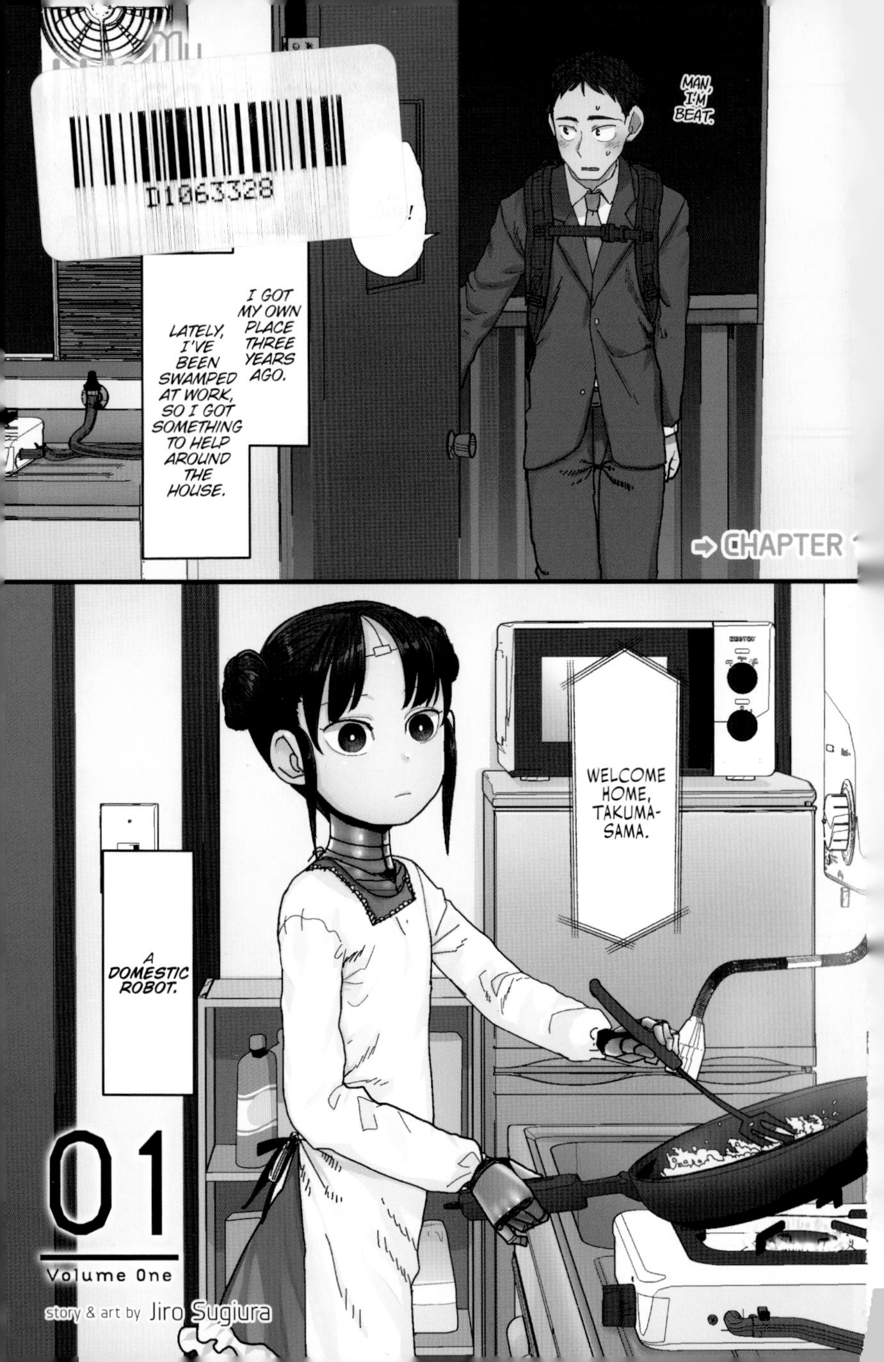
MAN, I'M BEAT.
I GOT MY OWN PLACE THREE YEARS AGO.
LATELY, I'VE BEEN SWAMPED AT WORK, SO I GOT SOMETHING TO HELP AROUND THE HOUSE.
CHAPTER
WELCOME HOME, TAKUMA-SAMA.
A DOMESTIC ROBOT.
01
Volume One
story & art by Jiro Sugiura

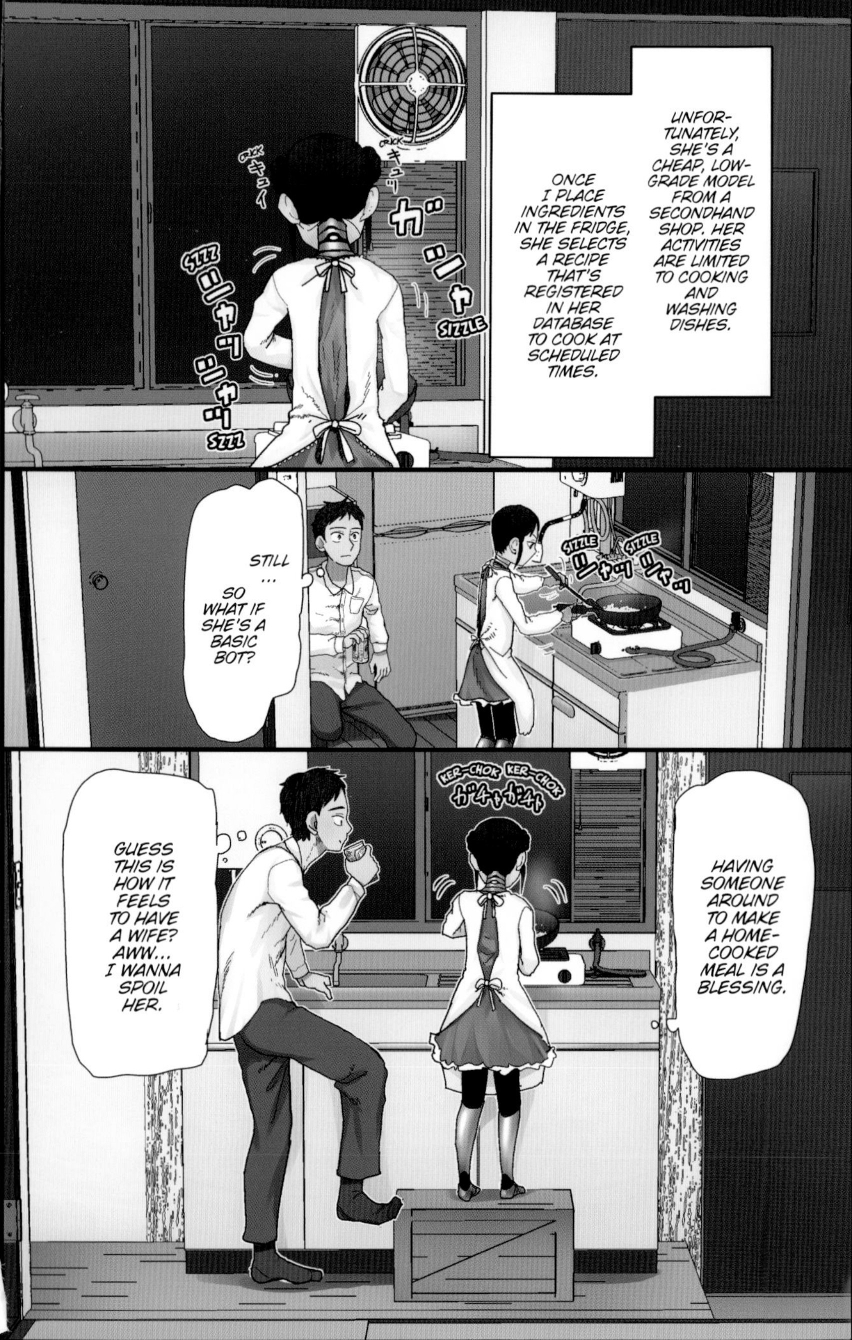
UNFORTUNATELY, SHE'S A CHEAP, LOW-GRADE MODEL FROM A SECONDHAND SHOP. HER ACTIVITIES ARE LIMITED TO COOKING AND WASHING DISHES.
ONCE I PLACE INGREDIENTS IN THE FRIDGE, SHE SELECTS A RECIPE THAT'S REGISTERED IN HER DATABASE TO COOK AT SCHEDULED TIMES.
CRICK
CRICK
SIZZLE
SIZZ
SIZZ
SIZZLE
SIZZLE
STILL... SO WHAT IF SHE'S A BASIC BOT?
KER-CHOK KER-CHOK
HAVING SOMEONE AROUND TO MAKE A HOME-COOKED MEAL IS A BLESSING.
GUESS THIS IS HOW IT FEELS TO HAVE A WIFE? AWW... I WANNA SPOIL HER.

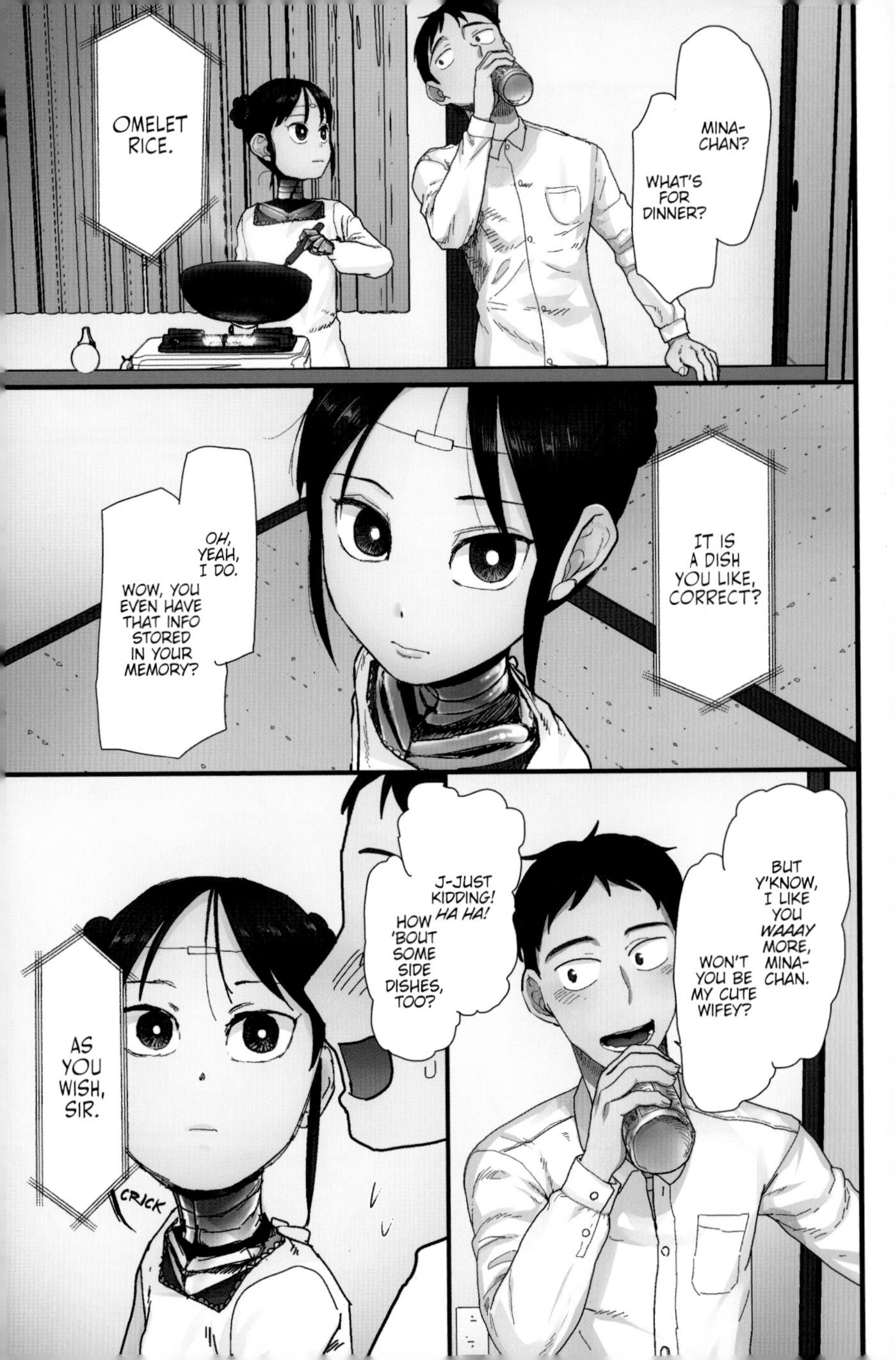
MINA-CHAN?
WHAT'S FOR DINNER?
OMELET RICE.
IT IS A DISH YOU LIKE, CORRECT?
OH, YEAH, I DO.
WOW, YOU EVEN HAVE THAT INFO STORED IN YOUR MEMORY?
BUT Y'KNOW, I LIKE YOU *WAAAY* MORE, MINA-CHAN.
WON'T YOU BE MY CUTE WIFEY?
J-JUST KIDDING! *HA HA!*
HOW 'BOUT SOME SIDE DISHES, TOO?
AS YOU WISH, SIR.
CRICK

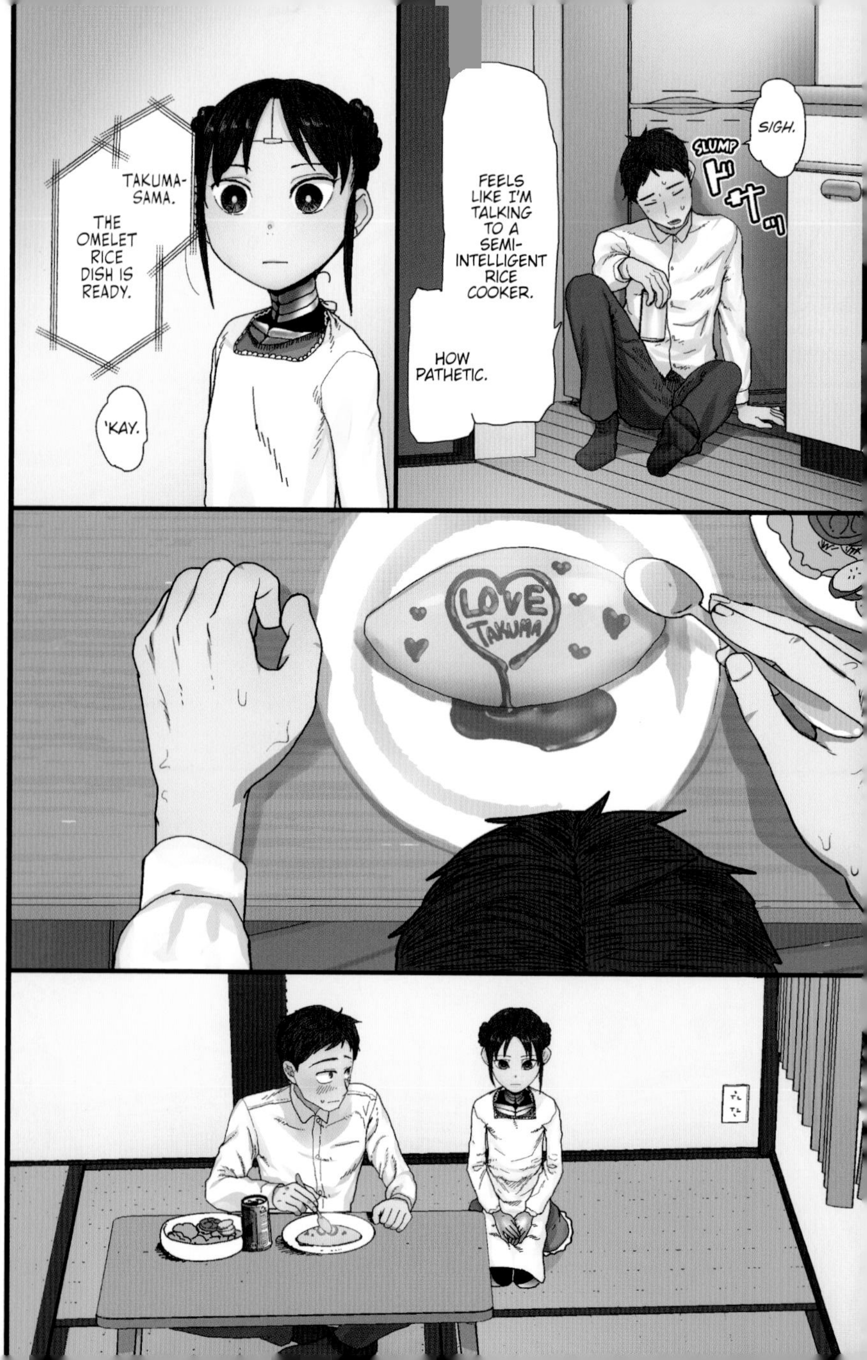

SIGH.
SLUMP
ドサッ
FEELS LIKE I'M TALKING TO A SEMI-INTELLIGENT RICE COOKER.
HOW PATHETIC.
TAKUMA-SAMA.
THE OMELET RICE DISH IS READY.
'KAY.
LOVE TAKUMA

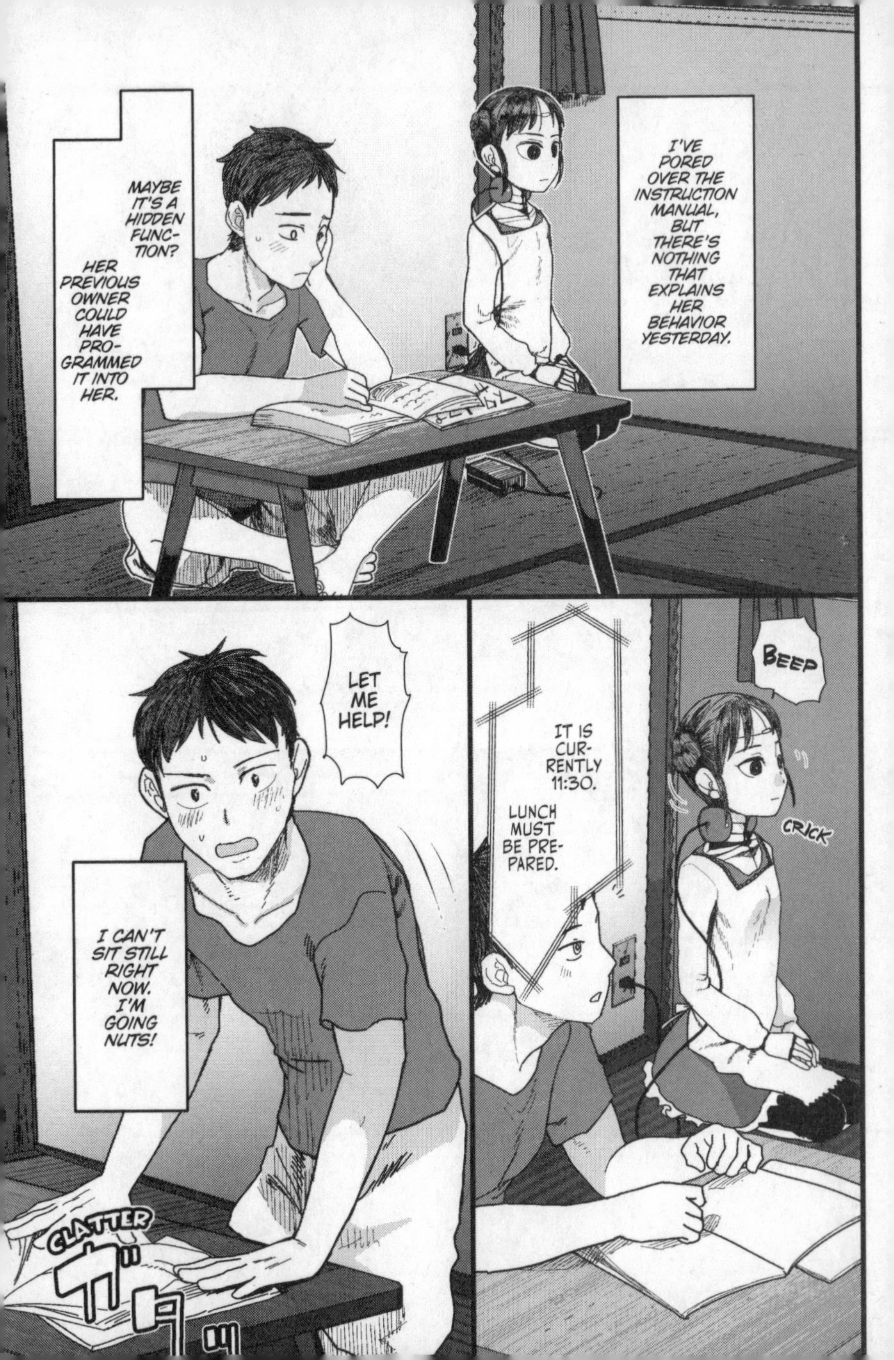
I'VE PORED OVER THE INSTRUCTION MANUAL, BUT THERE'S NOTHING THAT EXPLAINS HER BEHAVIOR YESTERDAY.
MAYBE IT'S A HIDDEN FUNCTION?
HER PREVIOUS OWNER COULD HAVE PROGRAMMED IT INTO HER.
BEEP
IT IS CURRENTLY 11:30.
LUNCH MUST BE PREPARED.
CRICK
LET ME HELP!
I CAN'T SIT STILL RIGHT NOW. I'M GOING NUTS!
CLATTER
ガタッ

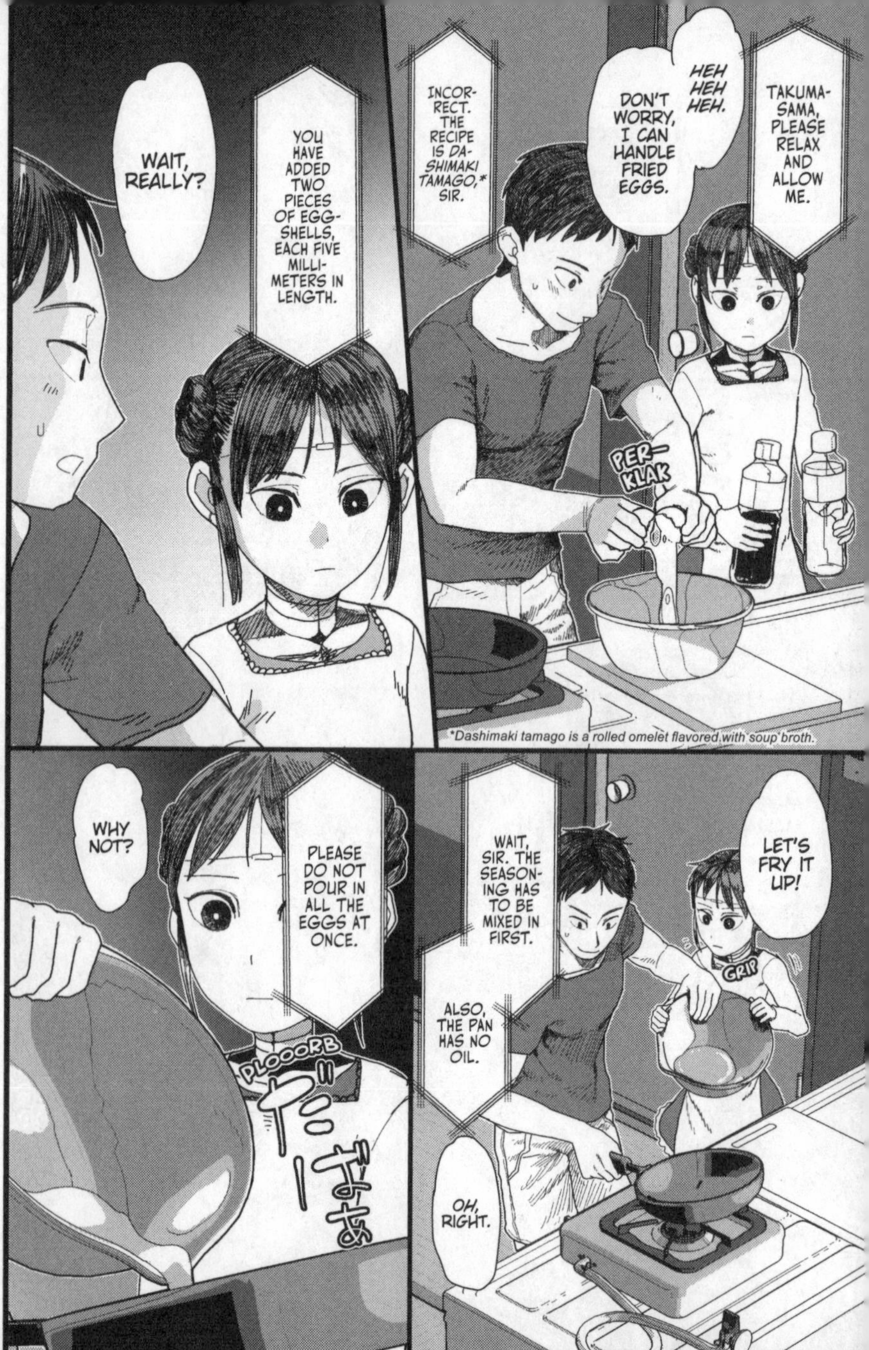
TAKUMA-SAMA, PLEASE RELAX AND ALLOW ME.
HEH HEH HEH.
DON'T WORRY, I CAN HANDLE FRIED EGGS.
INCORRECT. THE RECIPE IS *DASHIMAKI TAMAGO,** SIR.
PER-KLAK
YOU HAVE ADDED TWO PIECES OF EGG-SHELLS, EACH FIVE MILLI-METERS IN LENGTH.
WAIT, REALLY?
LET'S FRY IT UP!
WAIT, SIR. THE SEASON-ING HAS TO BE MIXED IN FIRST.
GRIP
ALSO, THE PAN HAS NO OIL.
OH, RIGHT.
PLEASE DO NOT POUR IN ALL THE EGGS AT ONCE.
WHY NOT?
PLOOORB

Dashimaki tamago is a rolled omelet flavored with soup broth.

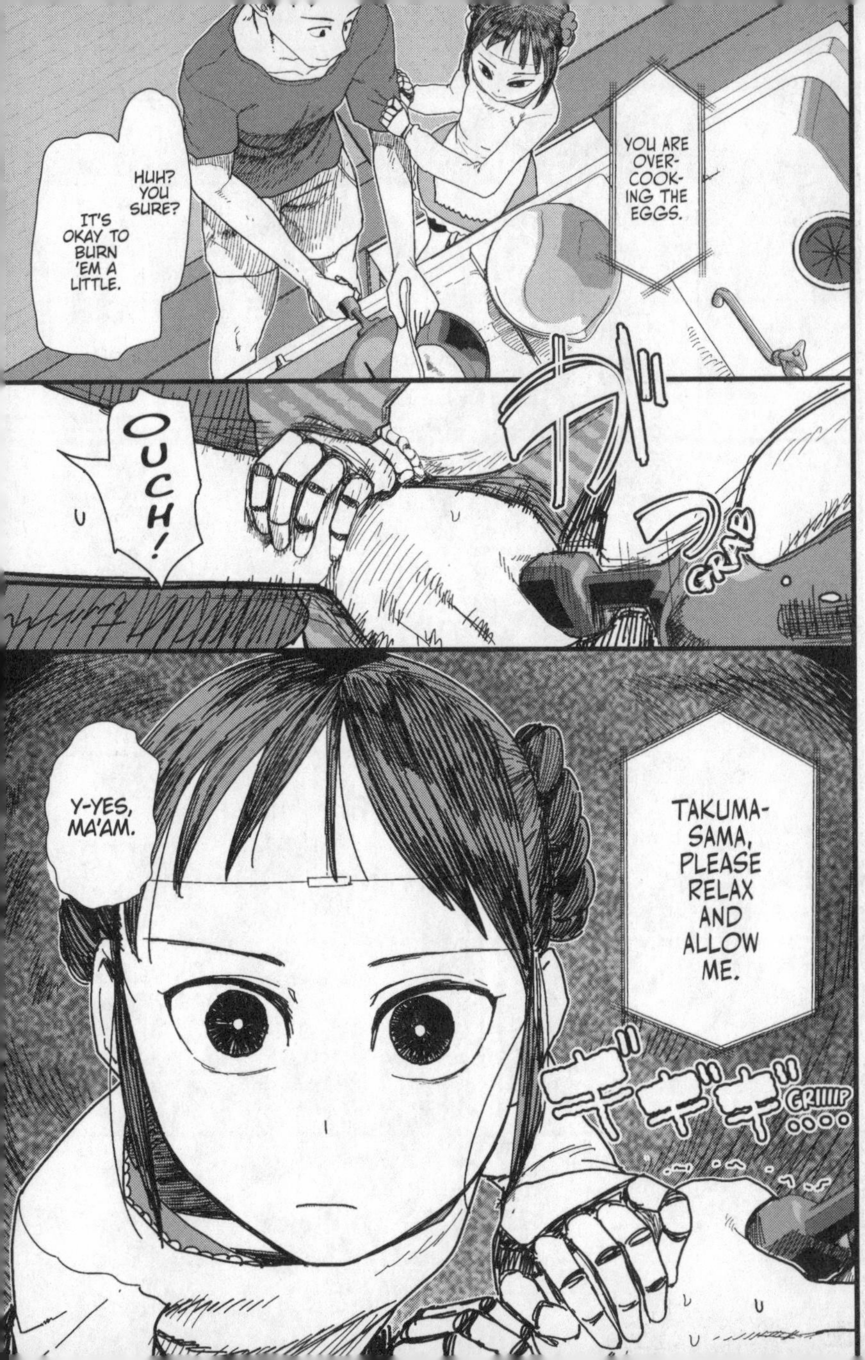
YOU ARE OVER-COOKING THE EGGS.
HUH? YOU SURE?
IT'S OKAY TO BURN 'EM A LITTLE.
GRAB
OUCH!
TAKUMA-SAMA, PLEASE RELAX AND ALLOW ME.
GRIIIP....
Y-YES, MA'AM.

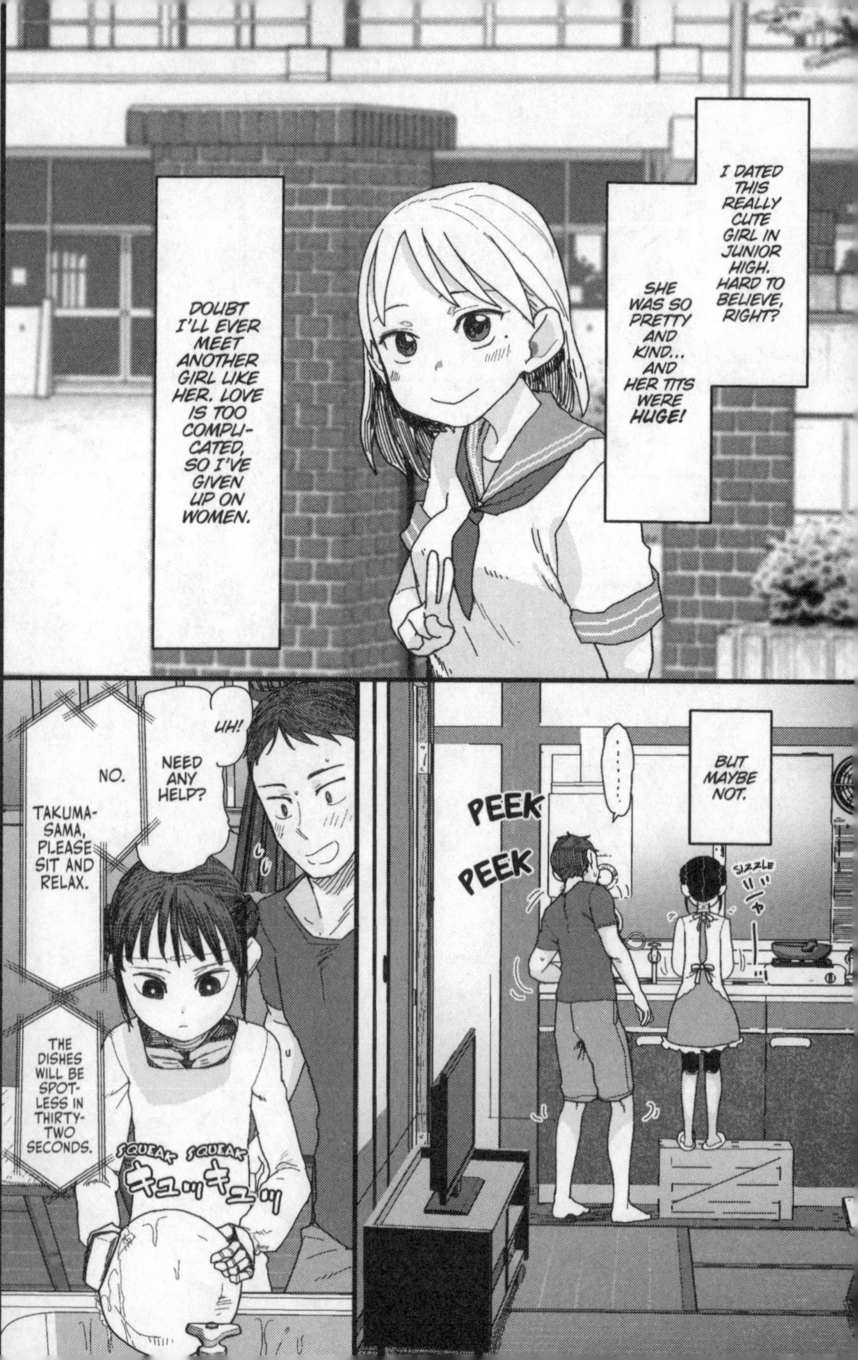
I DATED THIS REALLY CUTE GIRL IN JUNIOR HIGH. HARD TO BELIEVE, RIGHT?
SHE WAS SO PRETTY AND KIND... AND HER TITS WERE HUGE!
DOUBT I'LL EVER MEET ANOTHER GIRL LIKE HER. LOVE IS TOO COMPLICATED, SO I'VE GIVEN UP ON WOMEN.
BUT MAYBE NOT.
......
PEEK
PEEK
SIZZLE
UH!
NEED ANY HELP?
NO.
TAKUMA-SAMA, PLEASE SIT AND RELAX.
THE DISHES WILL BE SPOTLESS IN THIRTY-TWO SECONDS.
SQUEAK SQUEAK
キュッキュッ

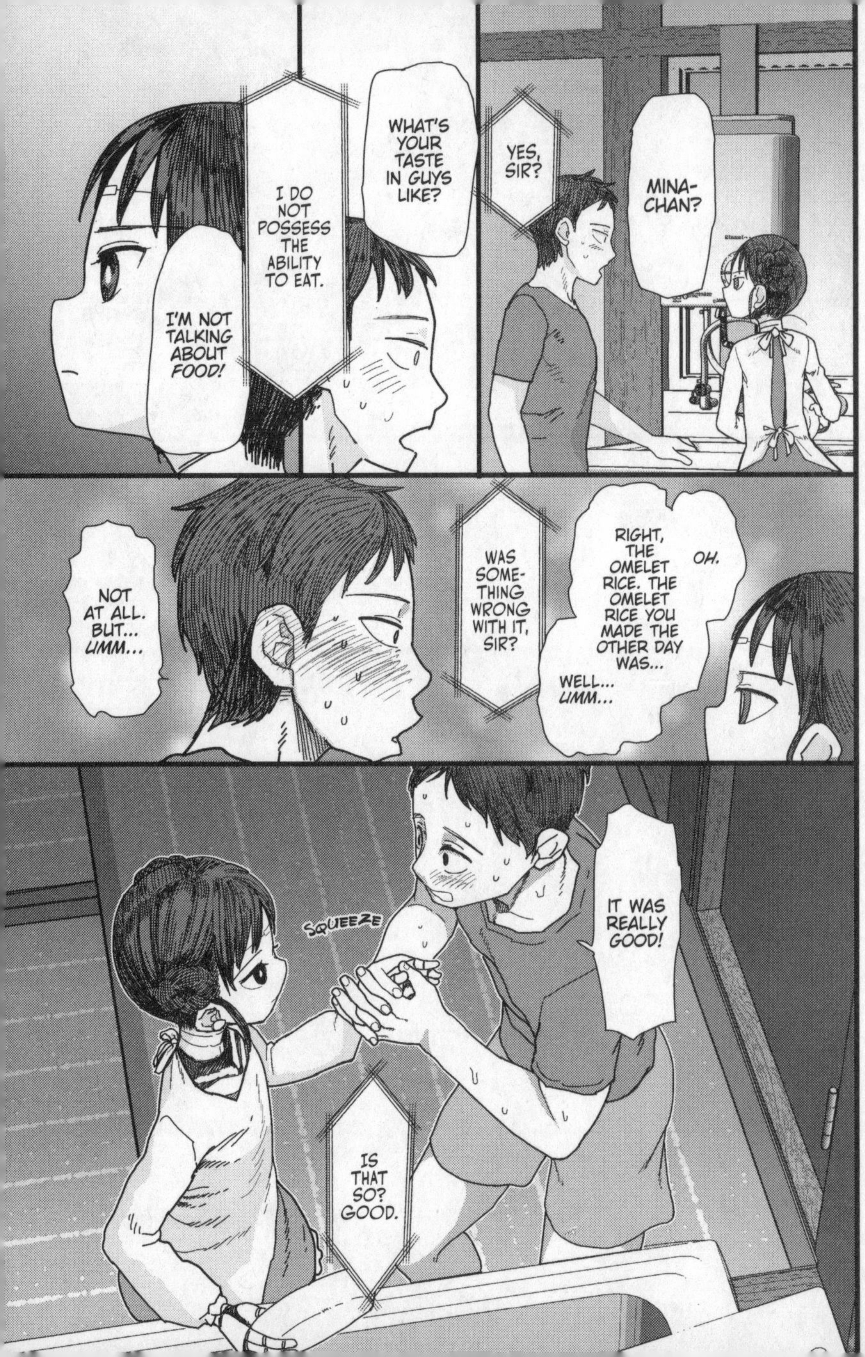
MINA-CHAN?
YES, SIR?
WHAT'S YOUR TASTE IN GUYS LIKE?
I DO NOT POSSESS THE ABILITY TO EAT.
I'M NOT TALKING ABOUT FOOD!
OH.
RIGHT, THE OMELET RICE. THE OMELET RICE YOU MADE THE OTHER DAY WAS...
WELL... UMM...
WAS SOMETHING WRONG WITH IT, SIR?
NOT AT ALL. BUT... UMM...
IT WAS REALLY GOOD!
SQUEEZE
IS THAT SO? GOOD.

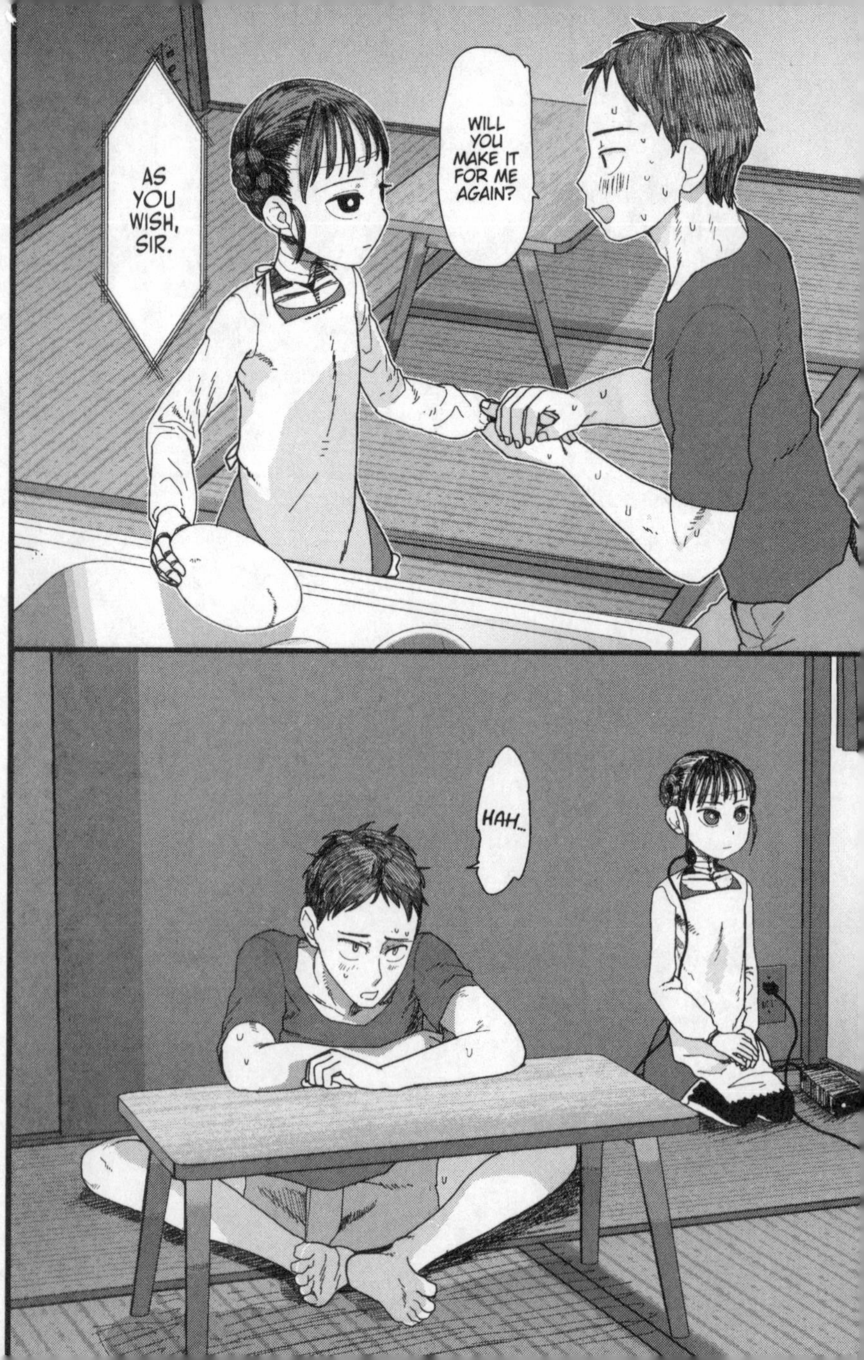
WILL YOU MAKE IT FOR ME AGAIN?
AS YOU WISH, SIR.
HAH...

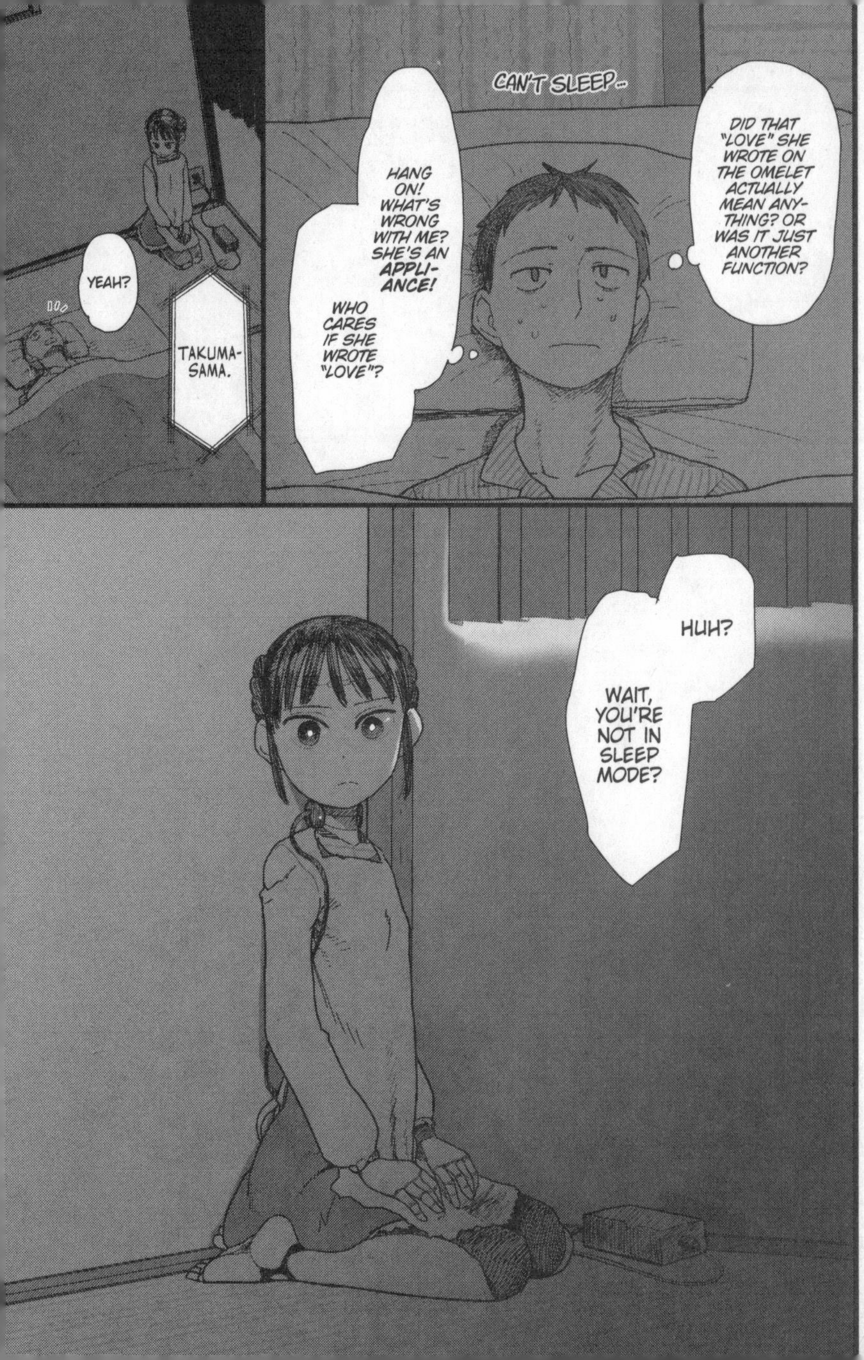
CAN'T SLEEP...
DID THAT "LOVE" SHE WROTE ON THE OMELET ACTUALLY MEAN ANY-THING? OR WAS IT JUST ANOTHER FUNCTION?
HANG ON! WHAT'S WRONG WITH ME? SHE'S AN APPLI-ANCE!
WHO CARES IF SHE WROTE "LOVE"?
TAKUMA-SAMA.
YEAH?
HUH?
WAIT, YOU'RE NOT IN SLEEP MODE?

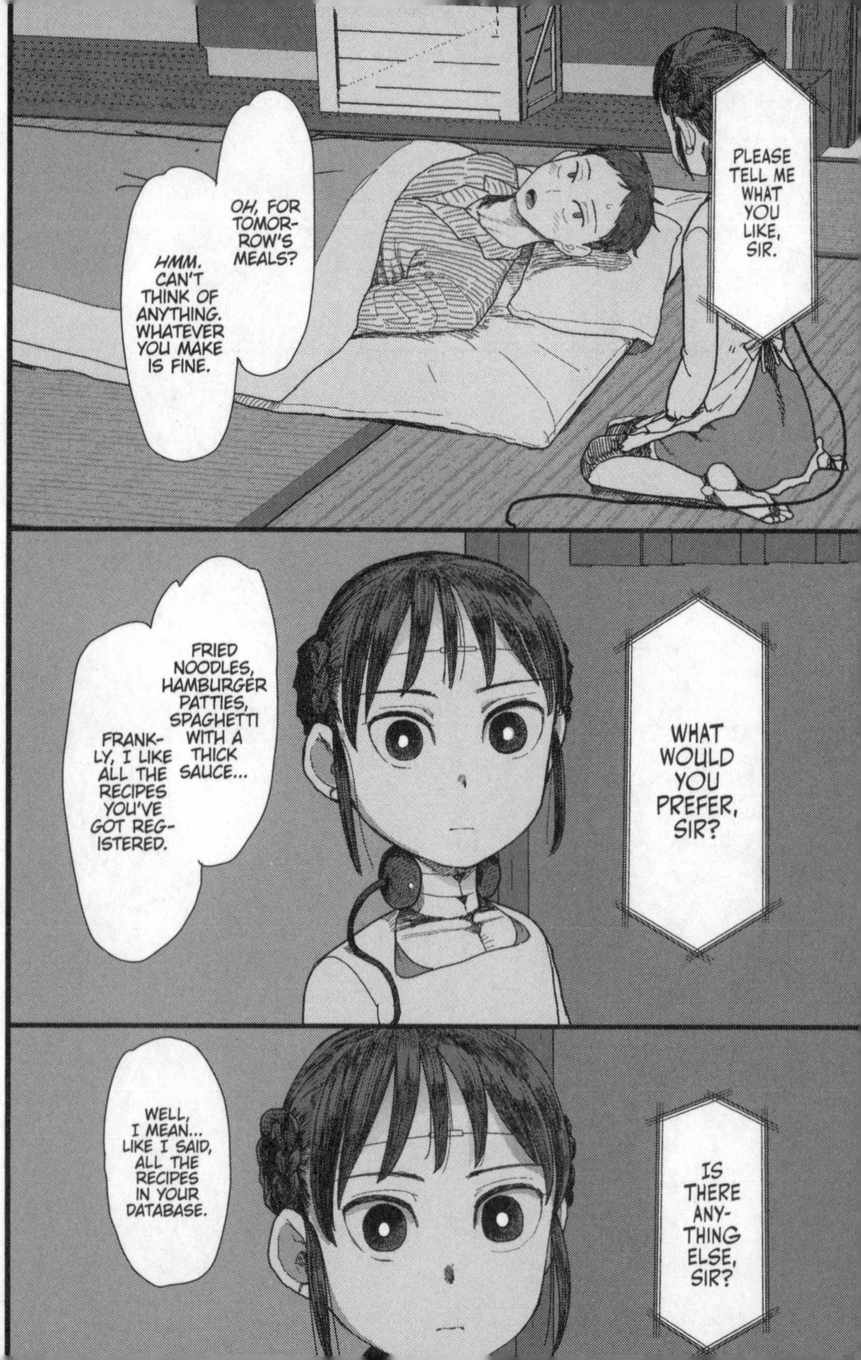
PLEASE TELL ME WHAT YOU LIKE, SIR.
OH, FOR TOMORROW'S MEALS?
HMM. CAN'T THINK OF ANYTHING. WHATEVER YOU MAKE IS FINE.
WHAT WOULD YOU PREFER, SIR?
FRIED NOODLES, HAMBURGER PATTIES, SPAGHETTI WITH A THICK SAUCE...
FRANKLY, I LIKE ALL THE RECIPES YOU'VE GOT REGISTERED.
IS THERE ANYTHING ELSE, SIR?
WELL, I MEAN... LIKE I SAID, ALL THE RECIPES IN YOUR DATABASE.

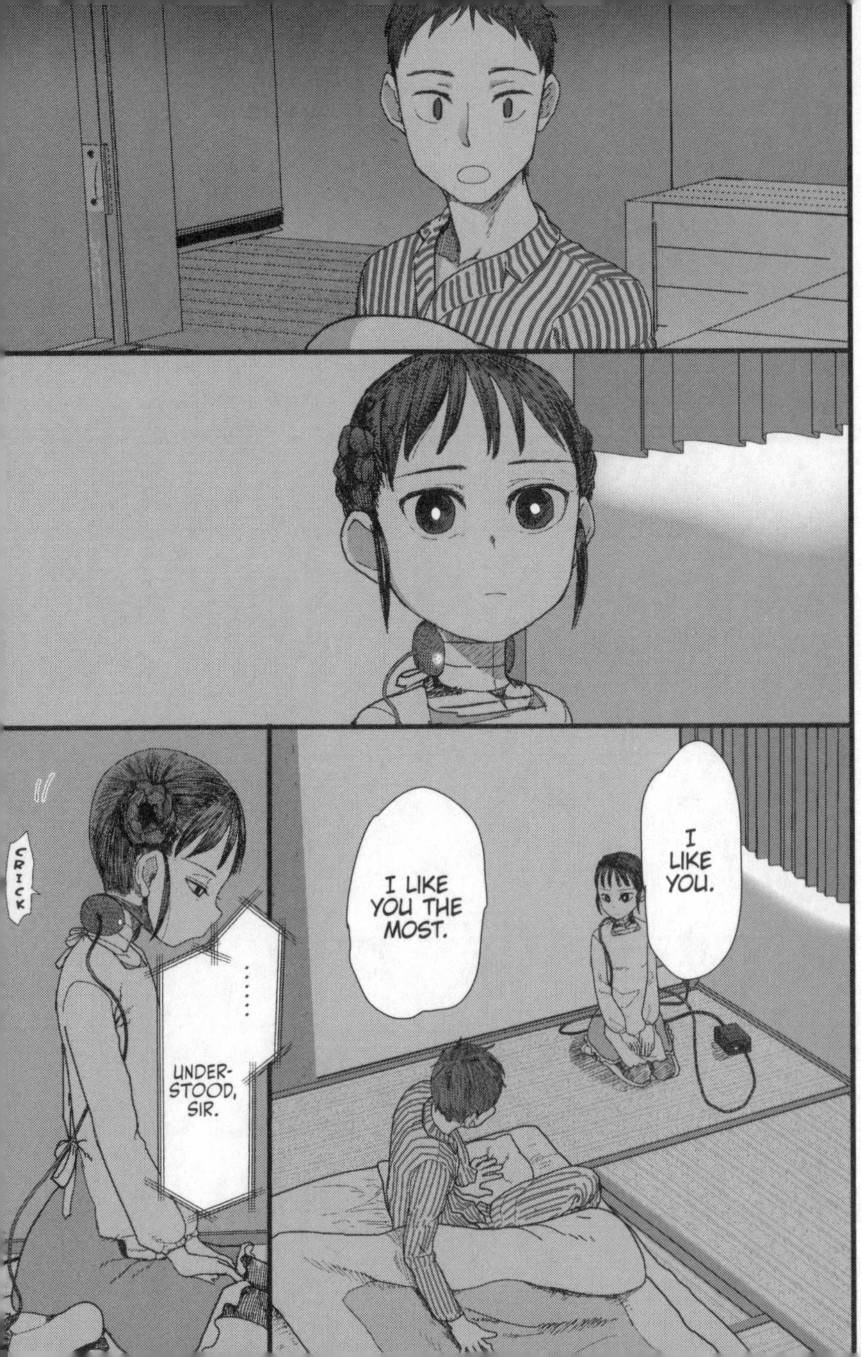
I LIKE YOU.
I LIKE YOU THE MOST.
......
UNDER-STOOD, SIR.
CRICK

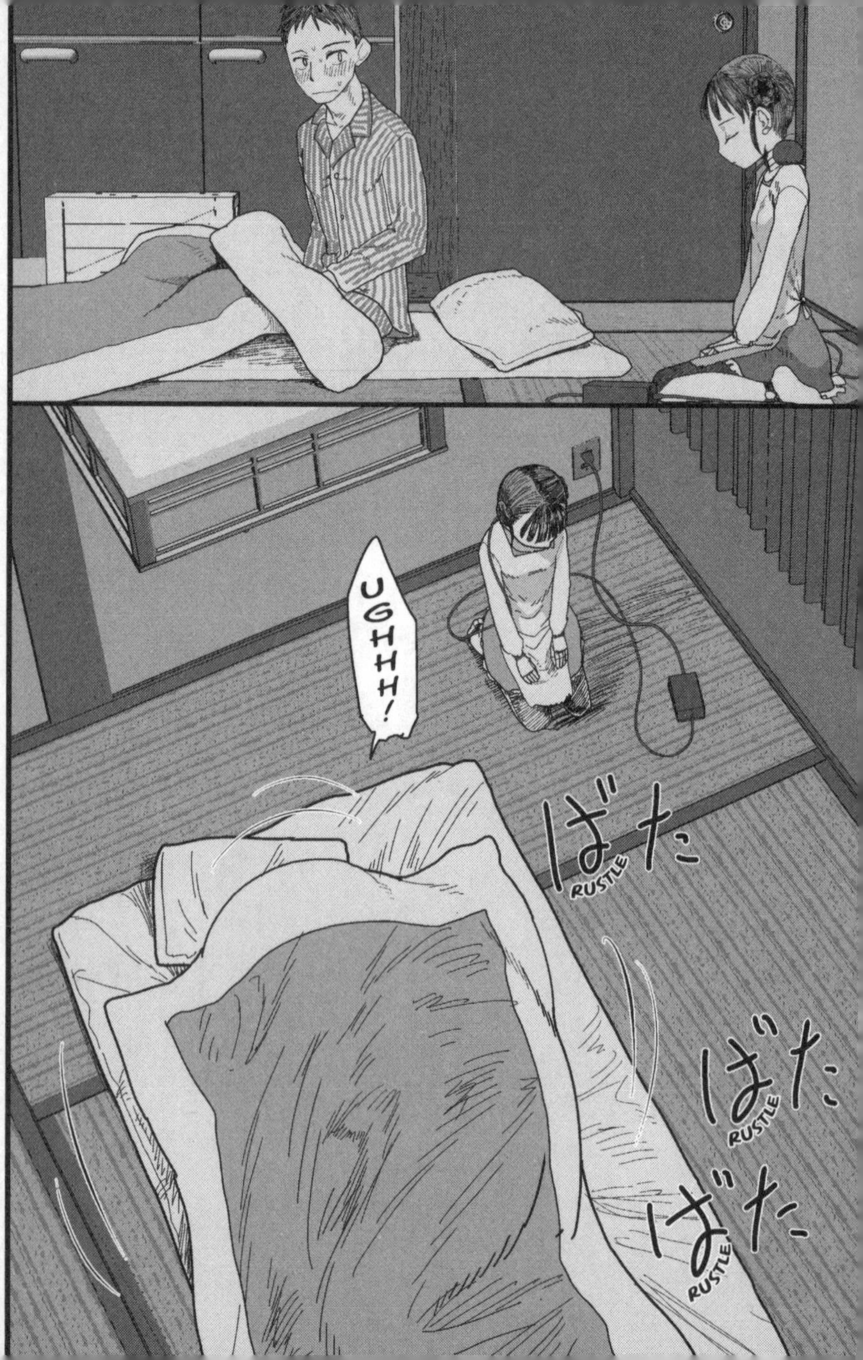
UGHHH!
ばた
RUSTLE
ばた
RUSTLE
ばた
RUSTLE

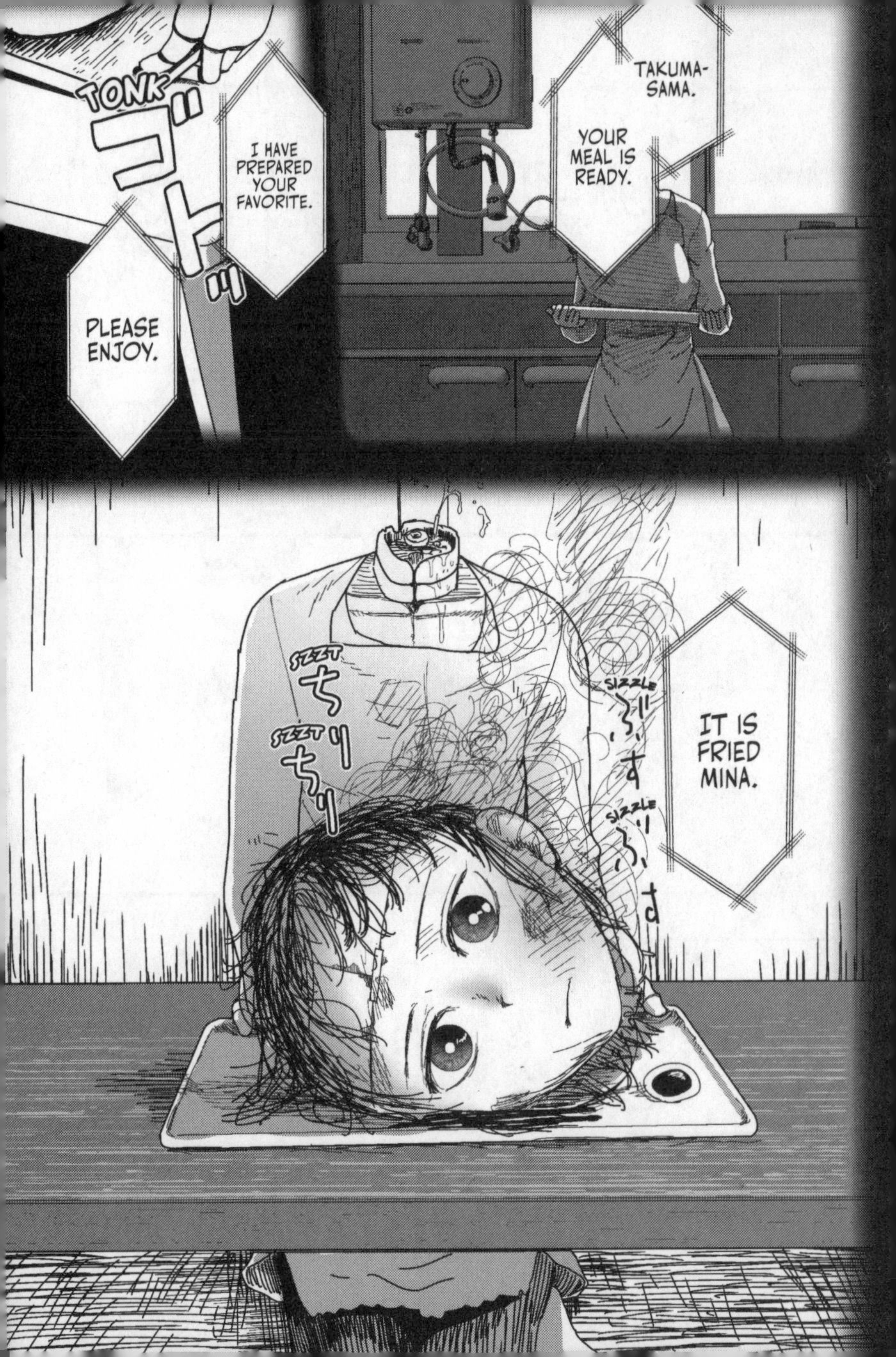

TAKUMA-SAMA.
YOUR MEAL IS READY.
I HAVE PREPARED YOUR FAVORITE.
TONK
ゴトッ
PLEASE ENJOY.
IT IS FRIED MINA.
SIZZLE
ぶす
SIZZLE
ぶす
SZZT
ちり
SZZT
ちり

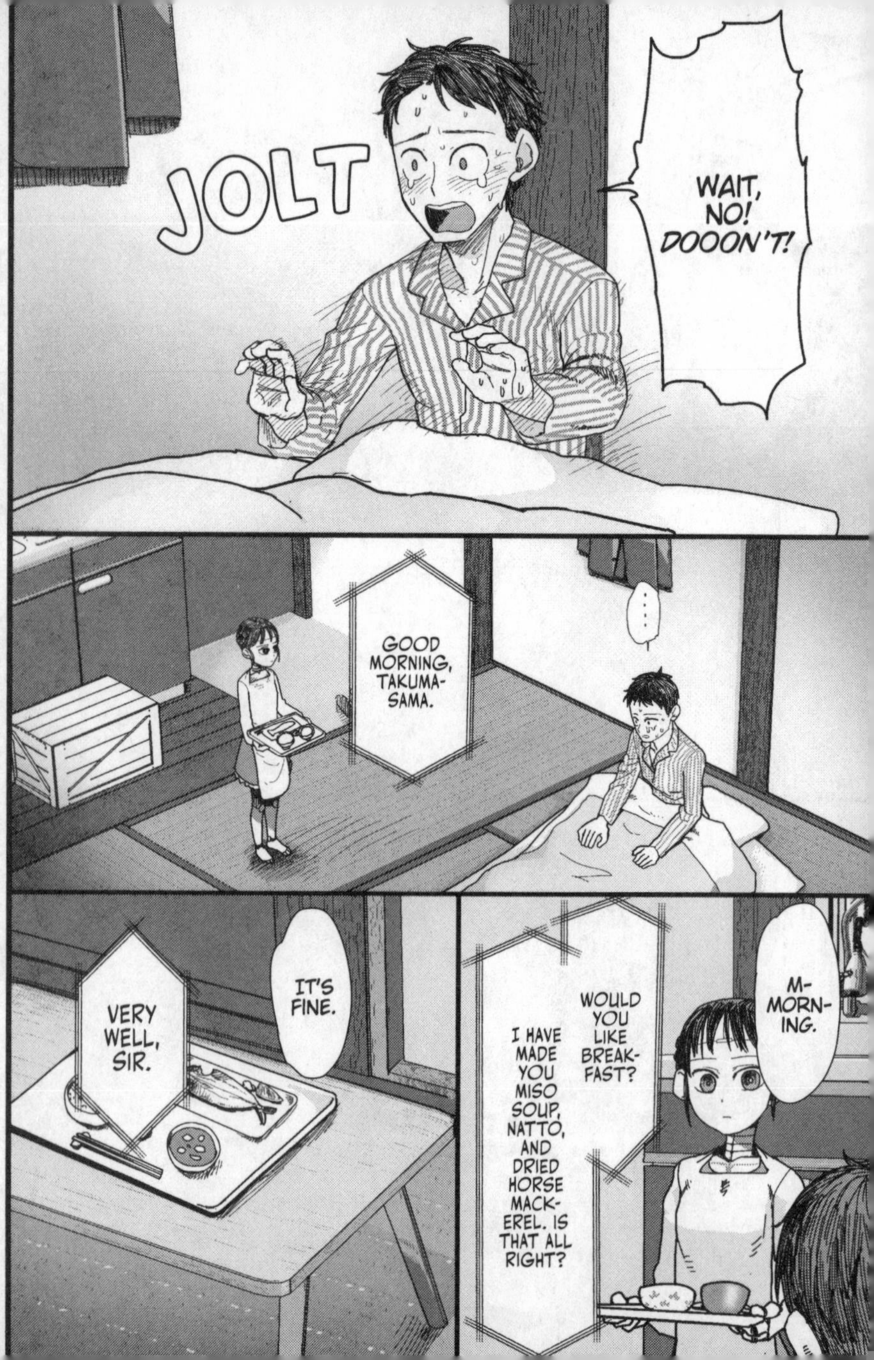
WAIT, NO! DOOON'T!
JOLT
...
GOOD MORNING, TAKUMA-SAMA.
M-MORNING.
WOULD YOU LIKE BREAKFAST?
I HAVE MADE YOU MISO SOUP, NATTO, AND DRIED HORSE MACKEREL. IS THAT ALL RIGHT?
IT'S FINE.
VERY WELL, SIR.

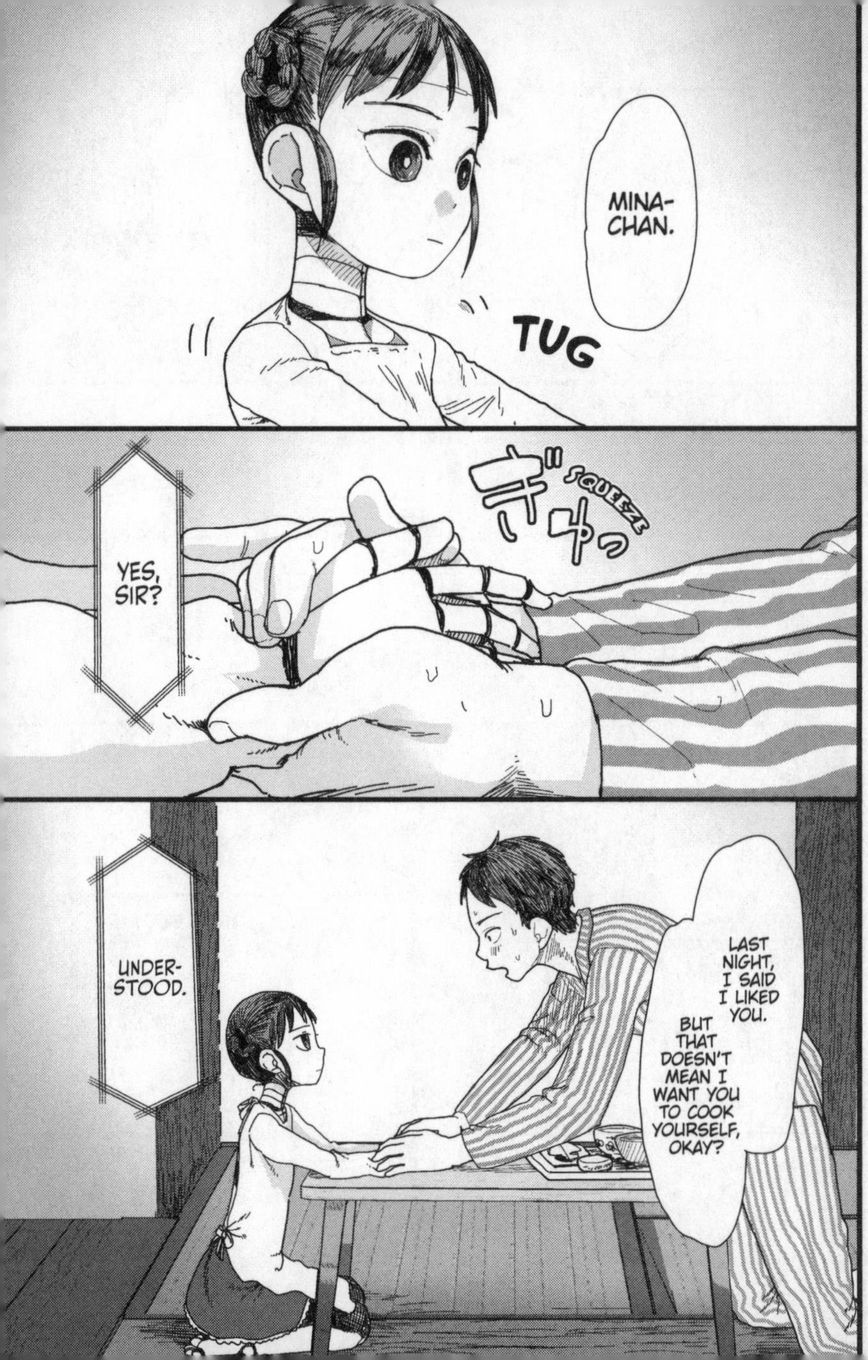
MINA-CHAN.
TUG
ぎゅっ
SQUEEZE
YES, SIR?
LAST NIGHT, I SAID I LIKED YOU.
BUT THAT DOESN'T MEAN I WANT YOU TO COOK YOURSELF, OKAY?
UNDER-STOOD.

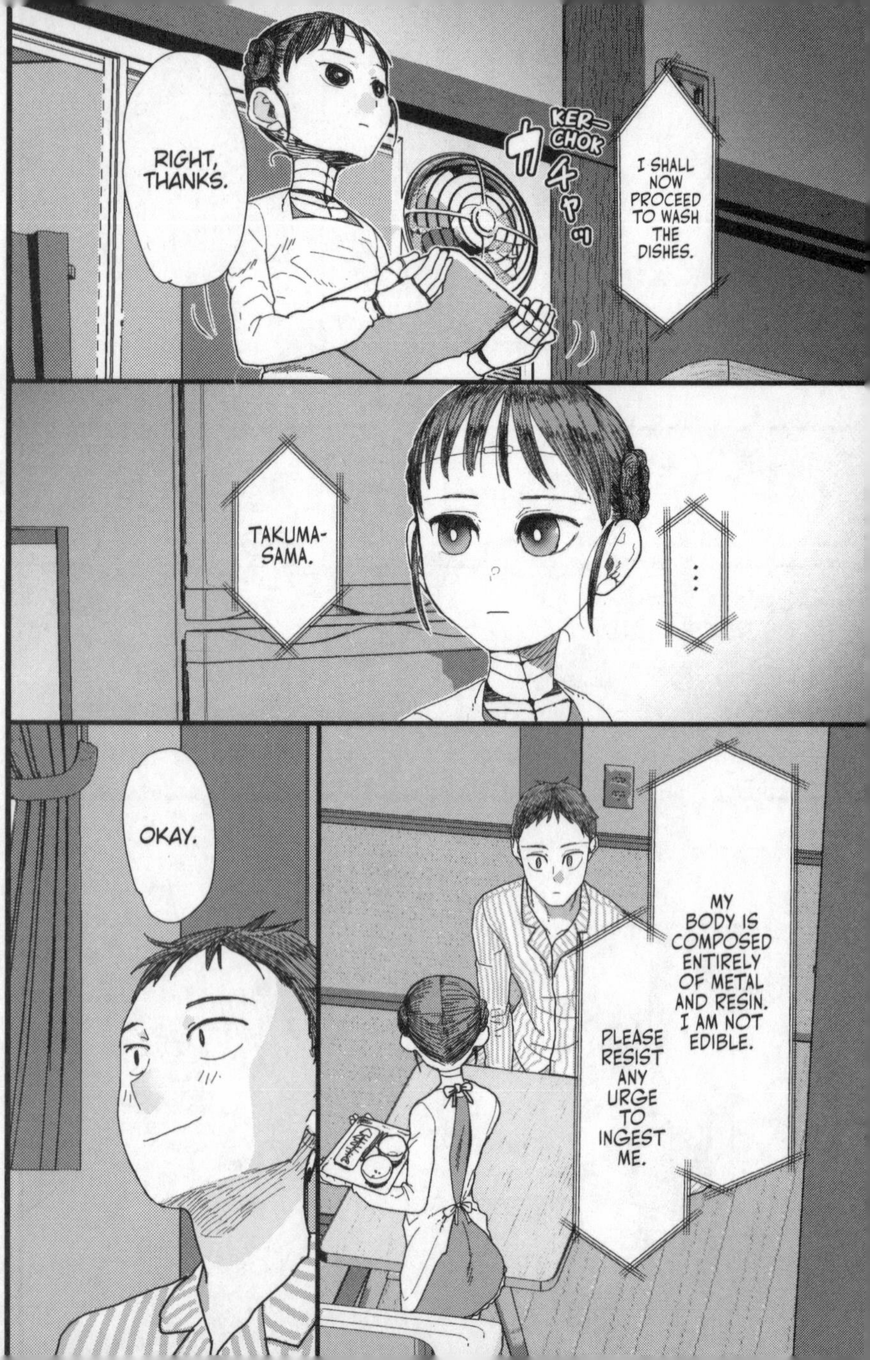
I SHALL NOW PROCEED TO WASH THE DISHES.
KER-CHOK
カチャッ
RIGHT, THANKS.
...
TAKUMA-SAMA.
MY BODY IS COMPOSED ENTIRELY OF METAL AND RESIN. I AM NOT EDIBLE.
PLEASE RESIST ANY URGE TO INGEST ME.
OKAY.

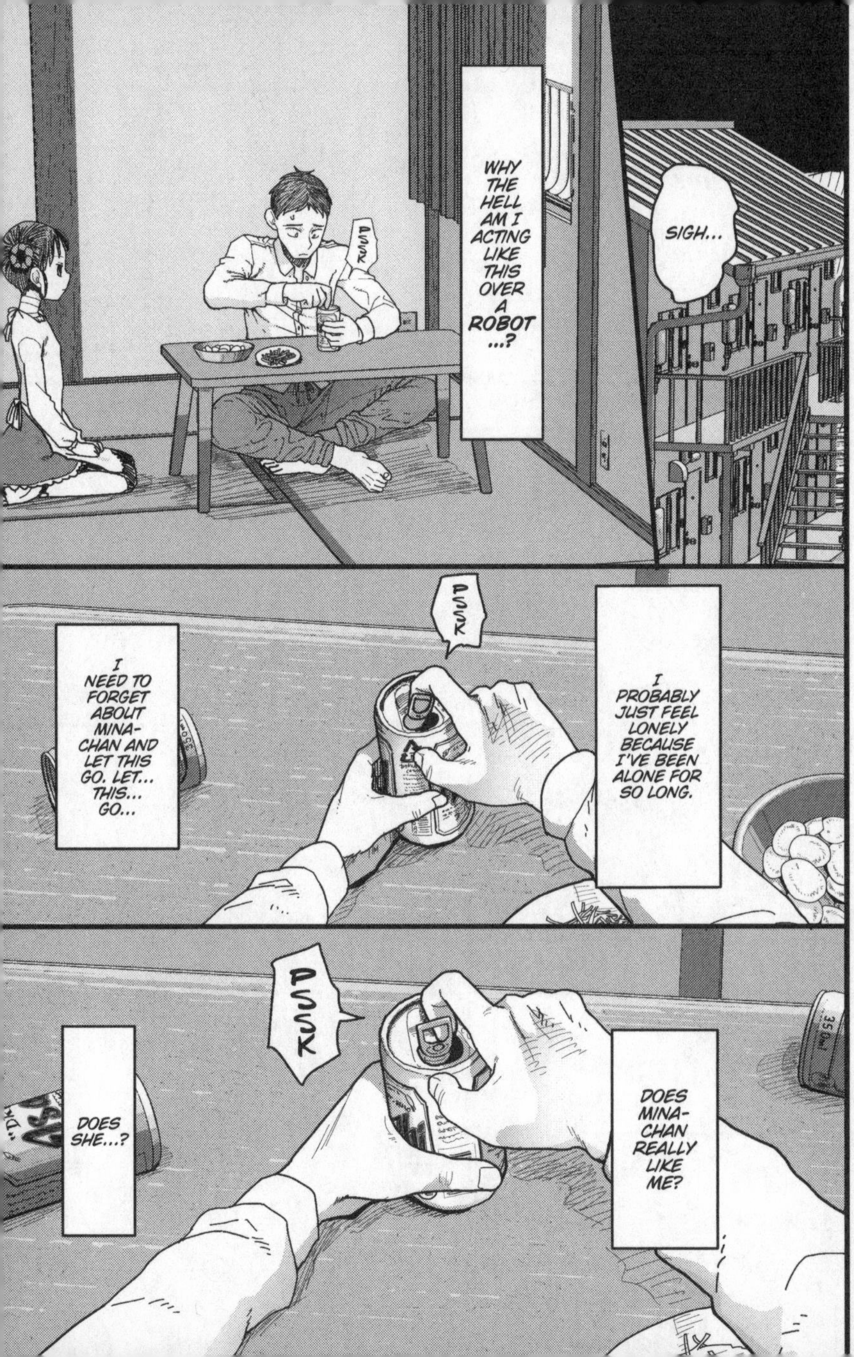
SIGH...
WHY THE HELL AM I ACTING LIKE THIS OVER A ROBOT...?
PSSK
I PROBABLY JUST FEEL LONELY BECAUSE I'VE BEEN ALONE FOR SO LONG.
PSSK
I NEED TO FORGET ABOUT MINA-CHAN AND LET THIS GO. LET... THIS... GO...
DOES MINA-CHAN REALLY LIKE ME?
PSSK
DOES SHE...?

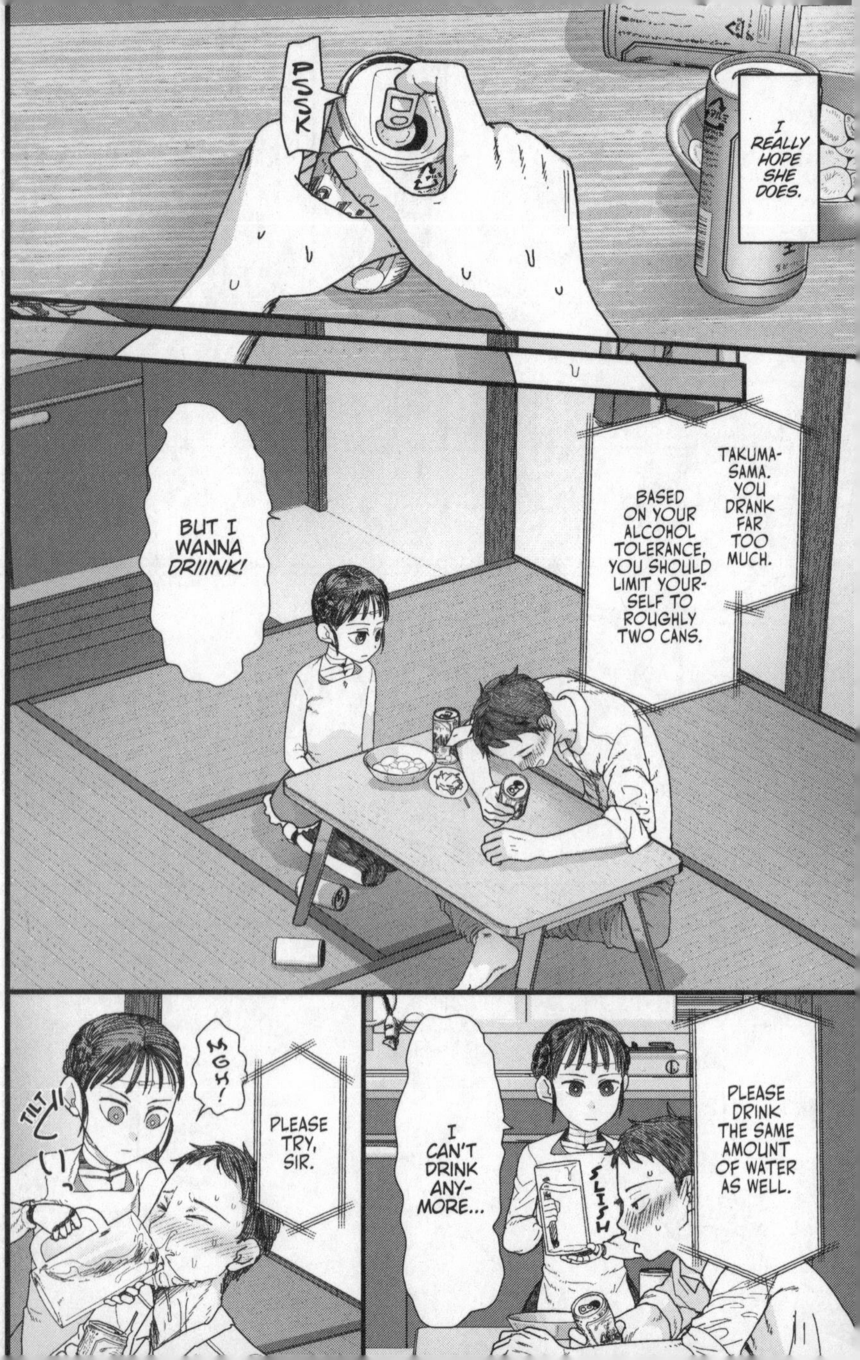
I REALLY HOPE SHE DOES.
PSSK
TAKUMA-SAMA. YOU DRANK FAR TOO MUCH.
BASED ON YOUR ALCOHOL TOLERANCE, YOU SHOULD LIMIT YOURSELF TO ROUGHLY TWO CANS.
BUT I WANNA DRIIINK!
PLEASE DRINK THE SAME AMOUNT OF WATER AS WELL.
SLISH
I CAN'T DRINK ANYMORE...
PLEASE TRY, SIR.
MGH!
TILT

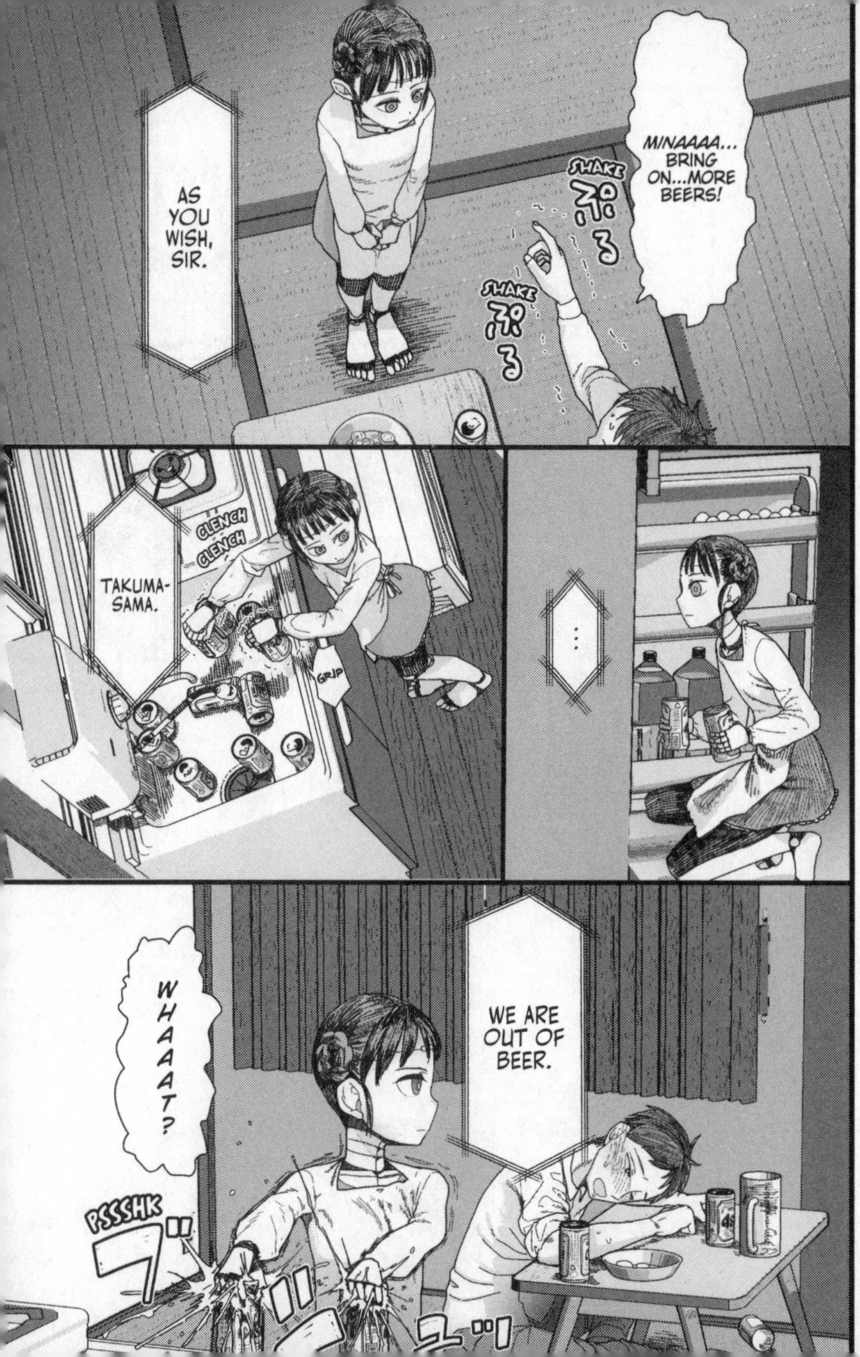

MINAAAA... BRING ON...MORE BEERS!
SHAKE
SHAKE
AS YOU WISH, SIR.
...
TAKUMA-SAMA.
CLENCH CLENCH
GRIP
WE ARE OUT OF BEER.
WHAAAAT?
PSSSHK

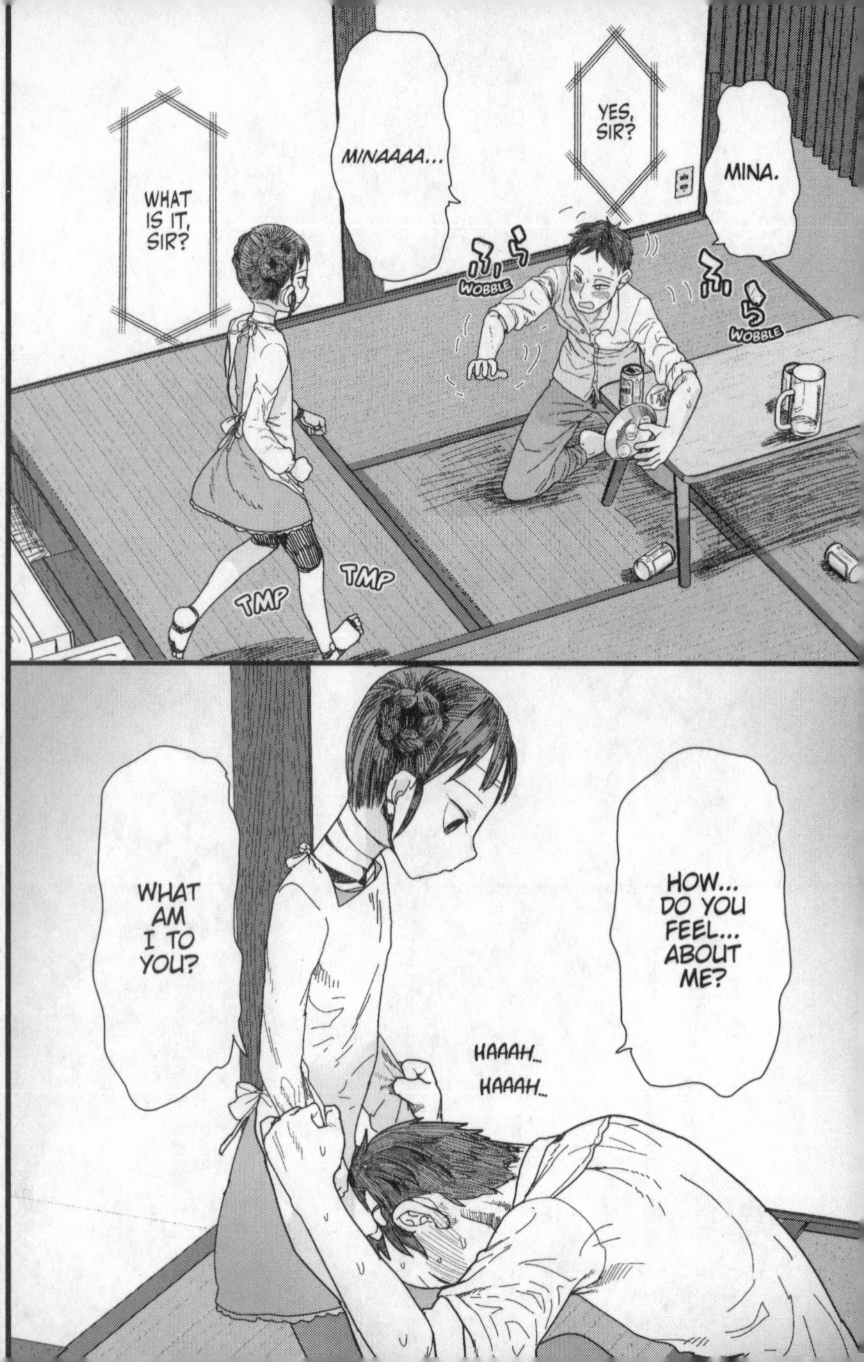
MINA.
ふら
WOBBLE
YES, SIR?
MINAAAA...
ふら
WOBBLE
WHAT IS IT, SIR?
TMP
TMP
HOW... DO YOU FEEL... ABOUT ME?
HAAAH...
HAAAH...
WHAT AM I TO YOU?

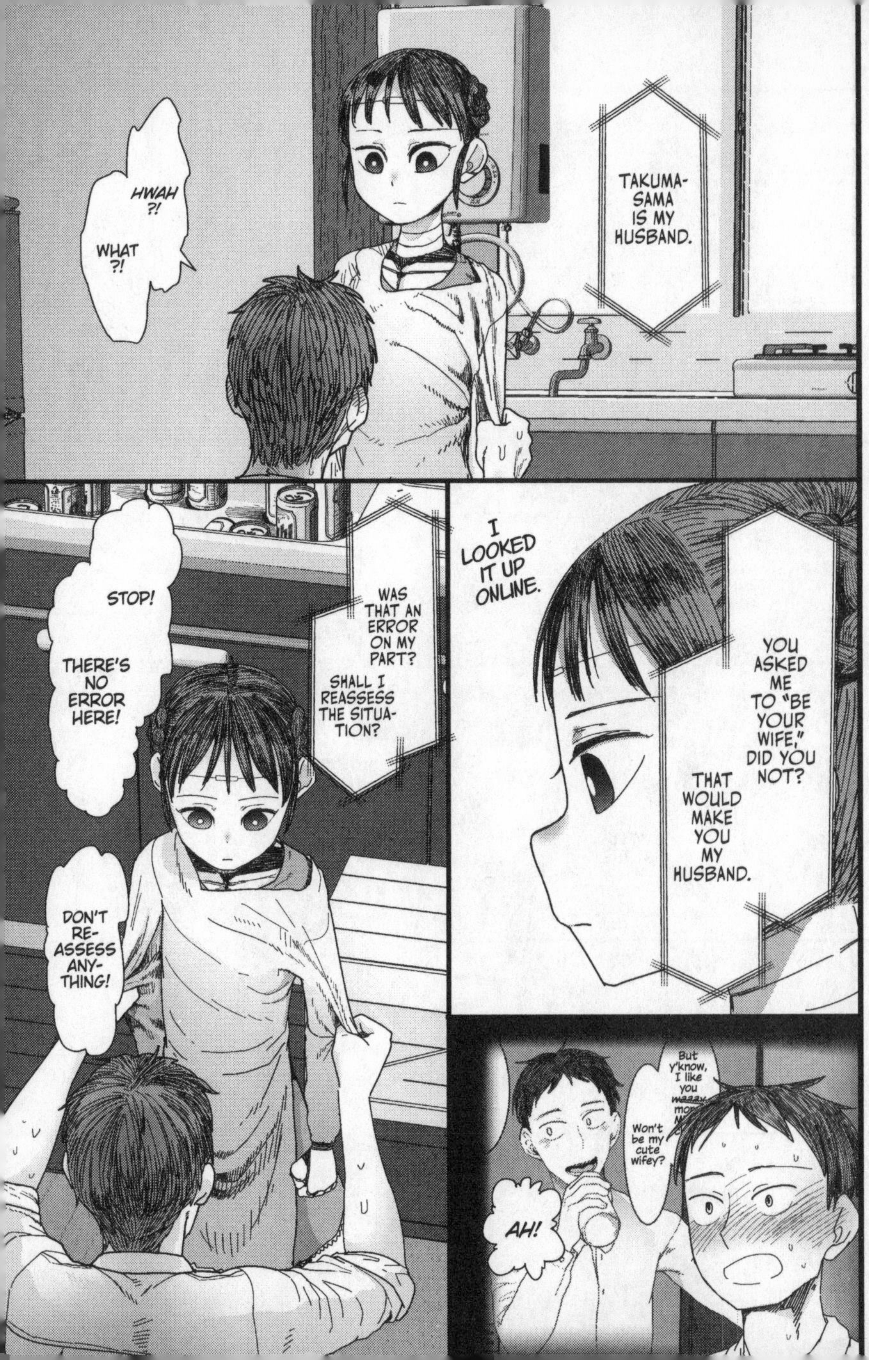
TAKUMA-SAMA IS MY HUSBAND.
HWAH?!
WHAT?!
I LOOKED IT UP ONLINE.
YOU ASKED ME TO "BE YOUR WIFE," DID YOU NOT?
THAT WOULD MAKE YOU MY HUSBAND.
But y'know, I like you waaay mo
Won't be my cute wifey?
AH!
WAS THAT AN ERROR ON MY PART?
SHALL I REASSESS THE SITUATION?
STOP!
THERE'S NO ERROR HERE!
DON'T REASSESS ANYTHING!

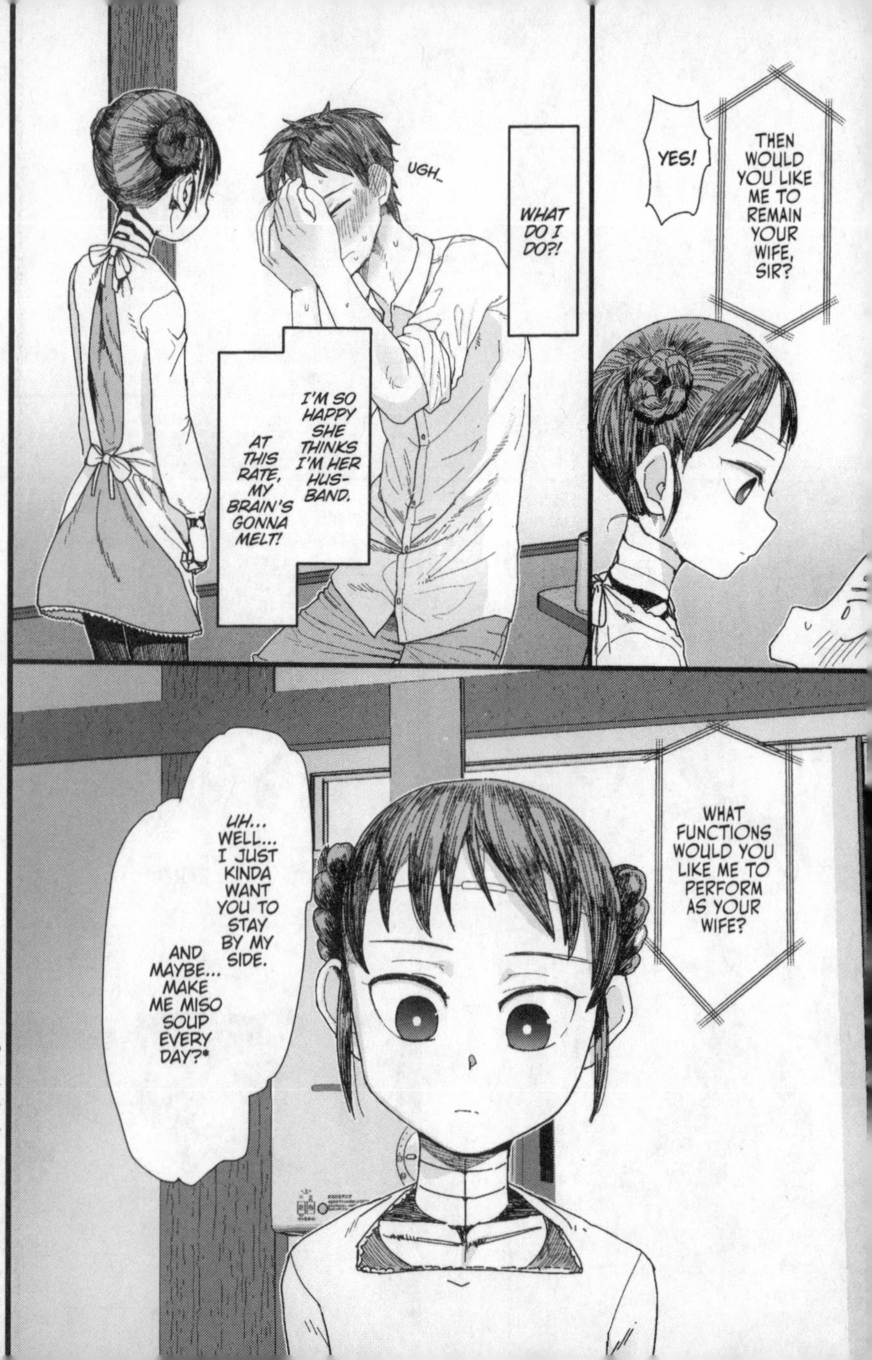
THEN WOULD YOU LIKE ME TO REMAIN YOUR WIFE, SIR?
YES!
WHAT DO I DO?!
UGH...
I'M SO HAPPY SHE THINKS I'M HER HUS-BAND.
AT THIS RATE, MY BRAIN'S GONNA MELT!
WHAT FUNCTIONS WOULD YOU LIKE ME TO PERFORM AS YOUR WIFE?
UH... WELL... I JUST KINDA WANT YOU TO STAY BY MY SIDE.
AND MAYBE... MAKE ME MISO SOUP EVERY DAY?*

* In Japan, this is a roundabout way of proposing to someone.

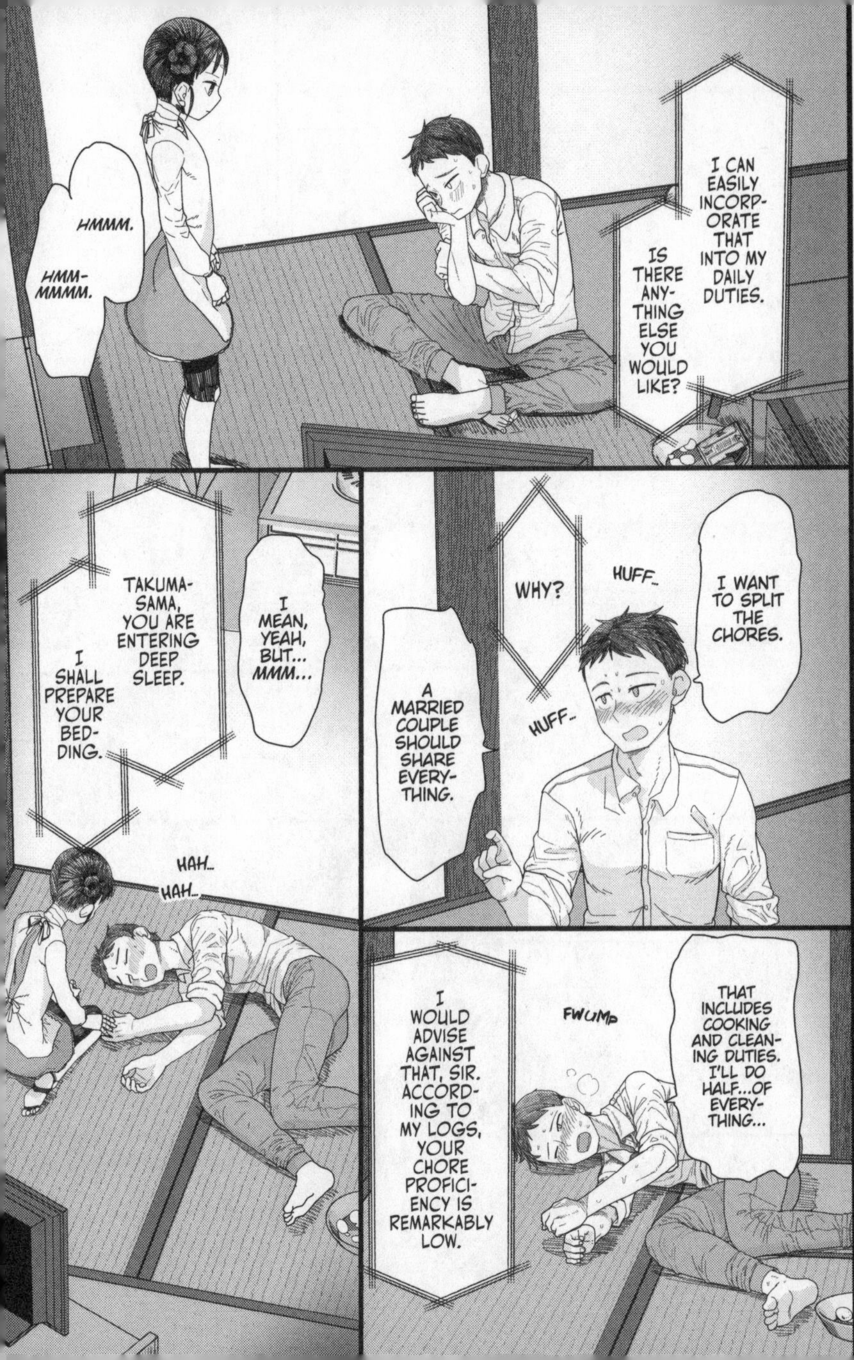
I CAN EASILY INCORPORATE THAT INTO MY DAILY DUTIES.
IS THERE ANYTHING ELSE YOU WOULD LIKE?
HMMM.
HMM-MMMM.
I WANT TO SPLIT THE CHORES.
HUFF..
WHY?
HUFF..
A MARRIED COUPLE SHOULD SHARE EVERYTHING.
THAT INCLUDES COOKING AND CLEANING DUTIES. I'LL DO HALF...OF EVERYTHING...
FWUMP
I WOULD ADVISE AGAINST THAT, SIR. ACCORDING TO MY LOGS, YOUR CHORE PROFICIENCY IS REMARKABLY LOW.
I MEAN, YEAH, BUT... MMM...
TAKUMA-SAMA, YOU ARE ENTERING DEEP SLEEP.
I SHALL PREPARE YOUR BEDDING.
HAH..
HAH..

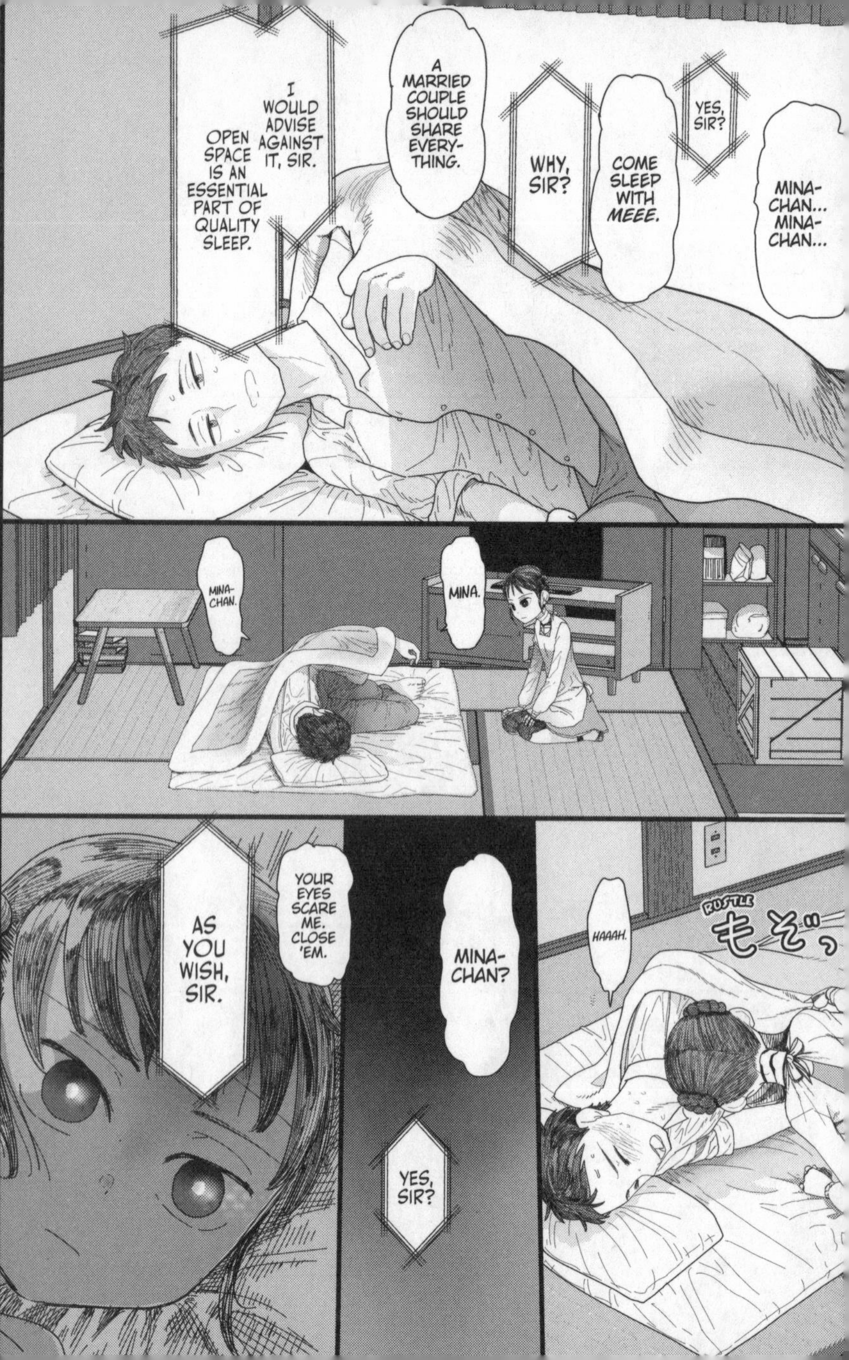
MINA-CHAN... MINA-CHAN...
YES, SIR?
COME SLEEP WITH MEEE.
WHY, SIR?
A MARRIED COUPLE SHOULD SHARE EVERY-THING.
I WOULD ADVISE AGAINST IT, SIR.
OPEN SPACE IS AN ESSENTIAL PART OF QUALITY SLEEP.
MINA.
MINA-CHAN.
RUSTLE
もぞっ
HAAAH.
MINA-CHAN?
YES, SIR?
YOUR EYES SCARE ME. CLOSE 'EM.
AS YOU WISH, SIR.

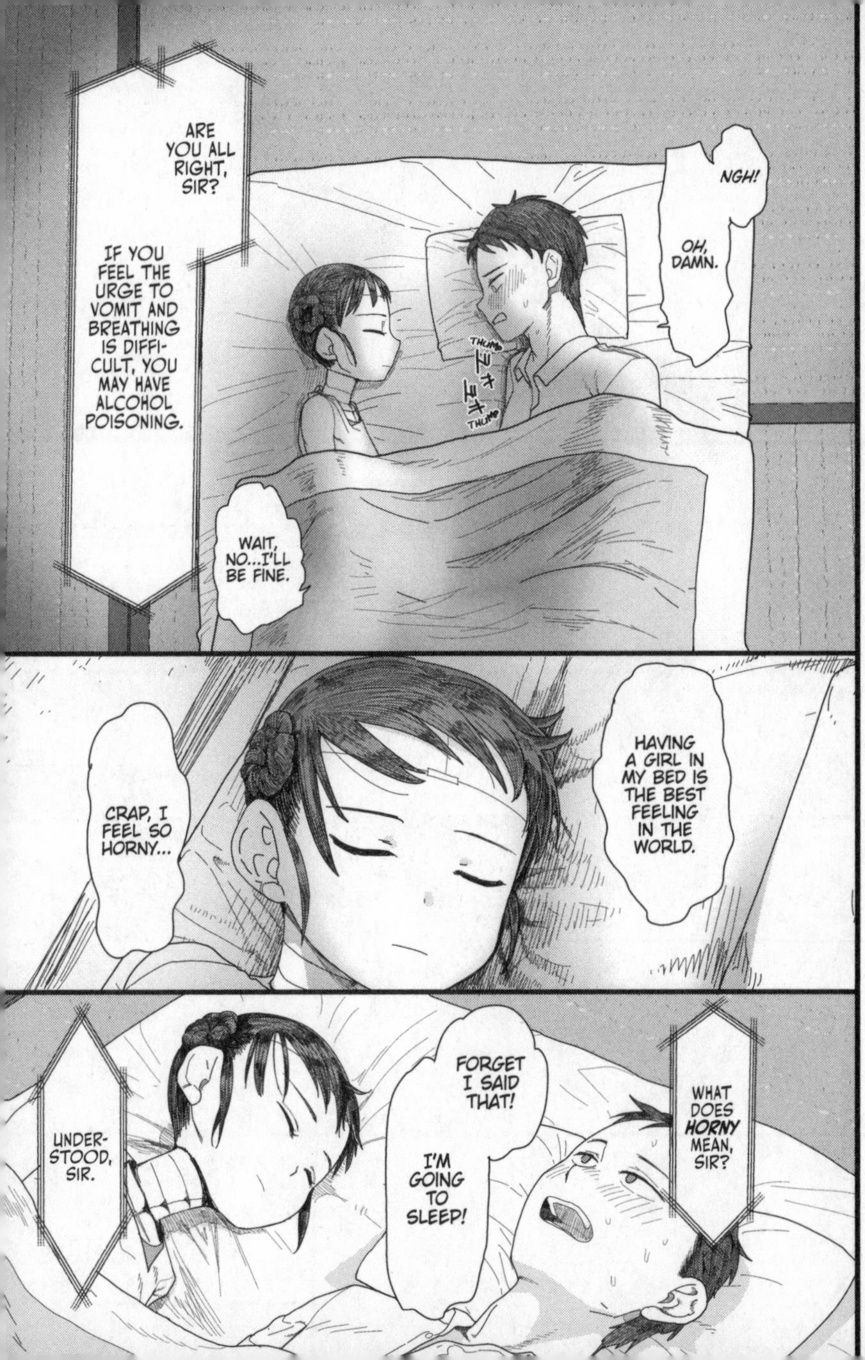
NGH!
OH, DAMN.
THUMP ドキ ドキ THUMP
ARE YOU ALL RIGHT, SIR?
IF YOU FEEL THE URGE TO VOMIT AND BREATHING IS DIFFI-CULT, YOU MAY HAVE ALCOHOL POISONING.
WAIT, NO...I'LL BE FINE.
HAVING A GIRL IN MY BED IS THE BEST FEELING IN THE WORLD.
CRAP, I FEEL SO HORNY...
WHAT DOES **HORNY** MEAN, SIR?
FORGET I SAID THAT!
I'M GOING TO SLEEP!
UNDER-STOOD, SIR.

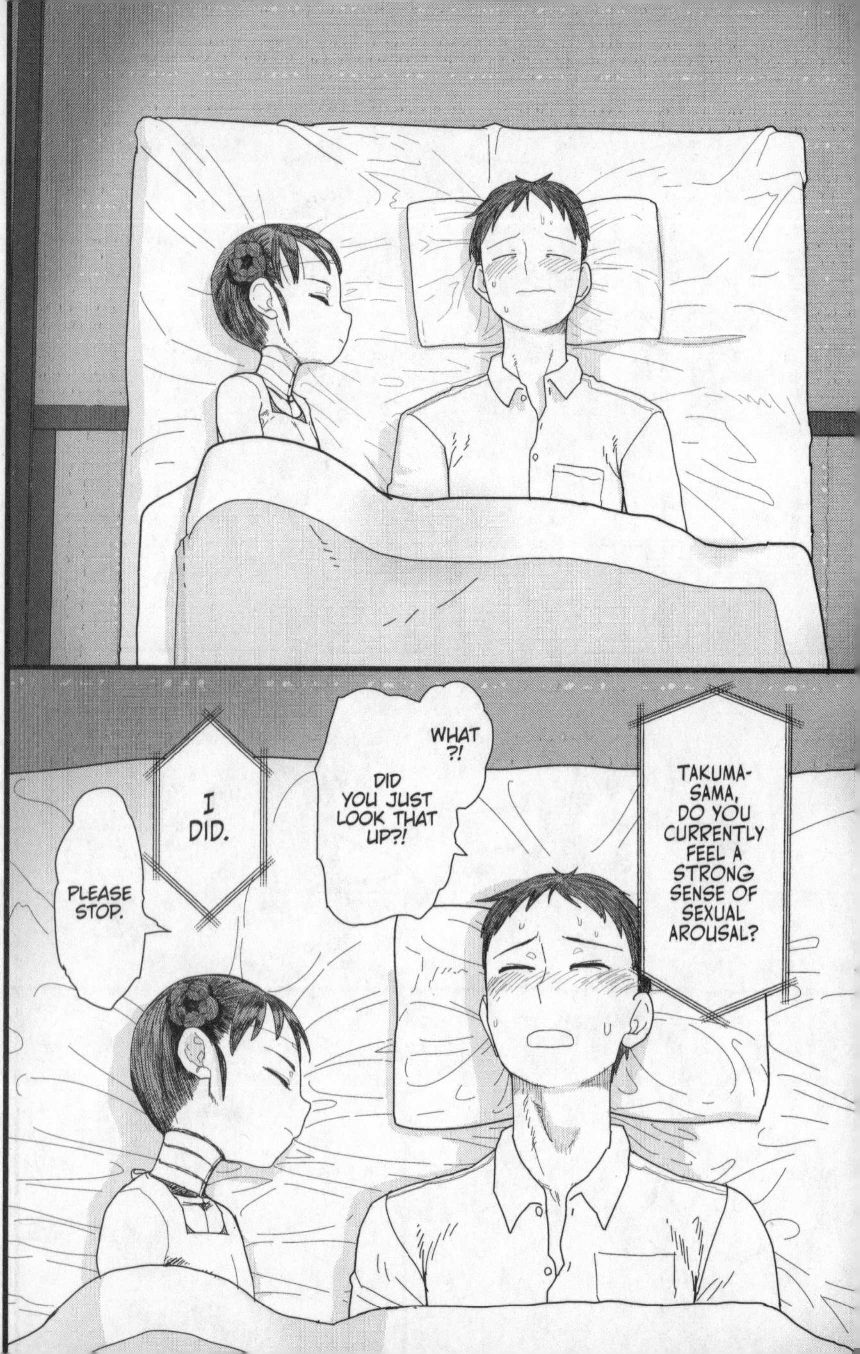
TAKUMA-SAMA, DO YOU CURRENTLY FEEL A STRONG SENSE OF SEXUAL AROUSAL?
WHAT?!
DID YOU JUST LOOK THAT UP?!
I DID.
PLEASE STOP.

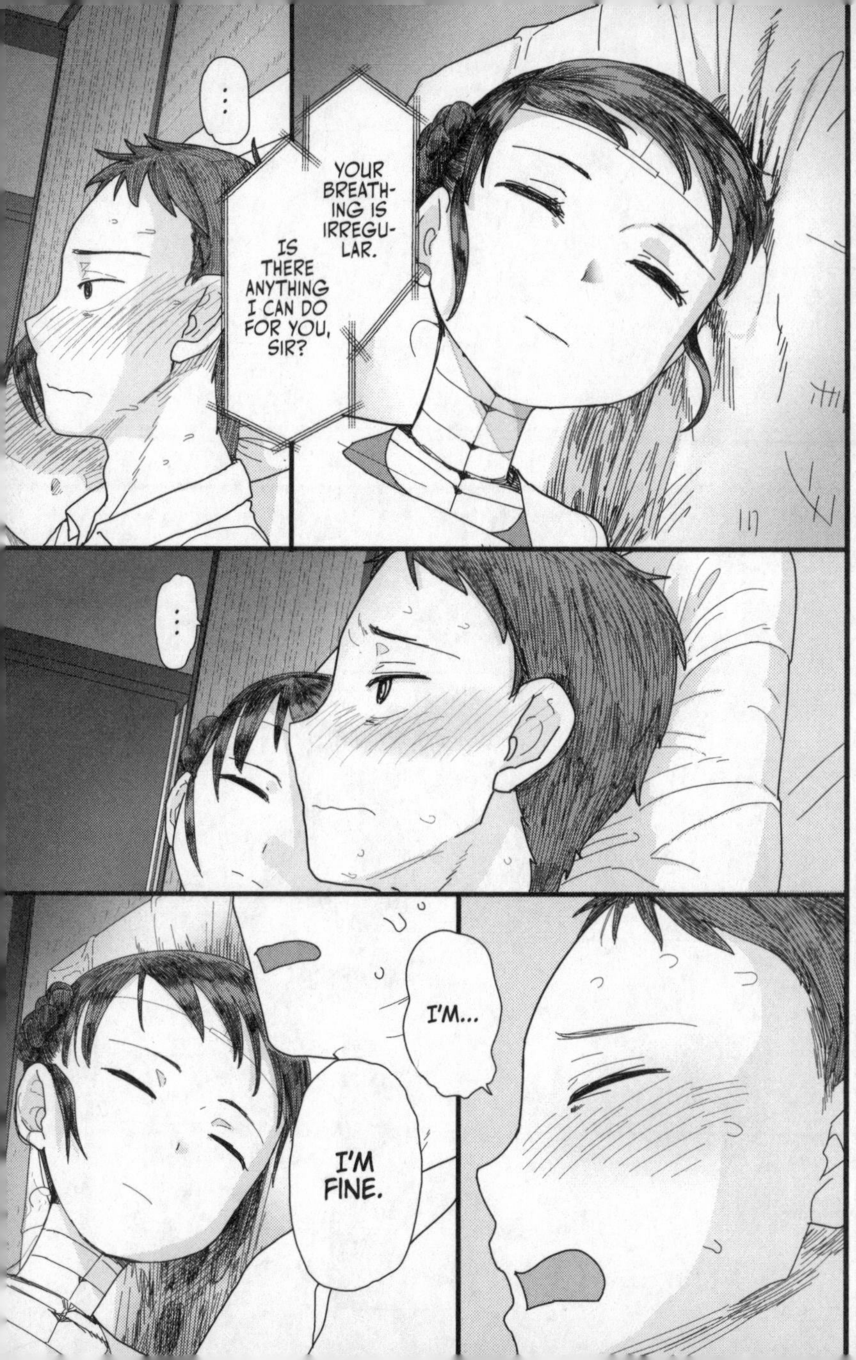

YOUR BREATHING IS IRREGULAR.
IS THERE ANYTHING I CAN DO FOR YOU, SIR?
…
…
I'M...
I'M FINE.

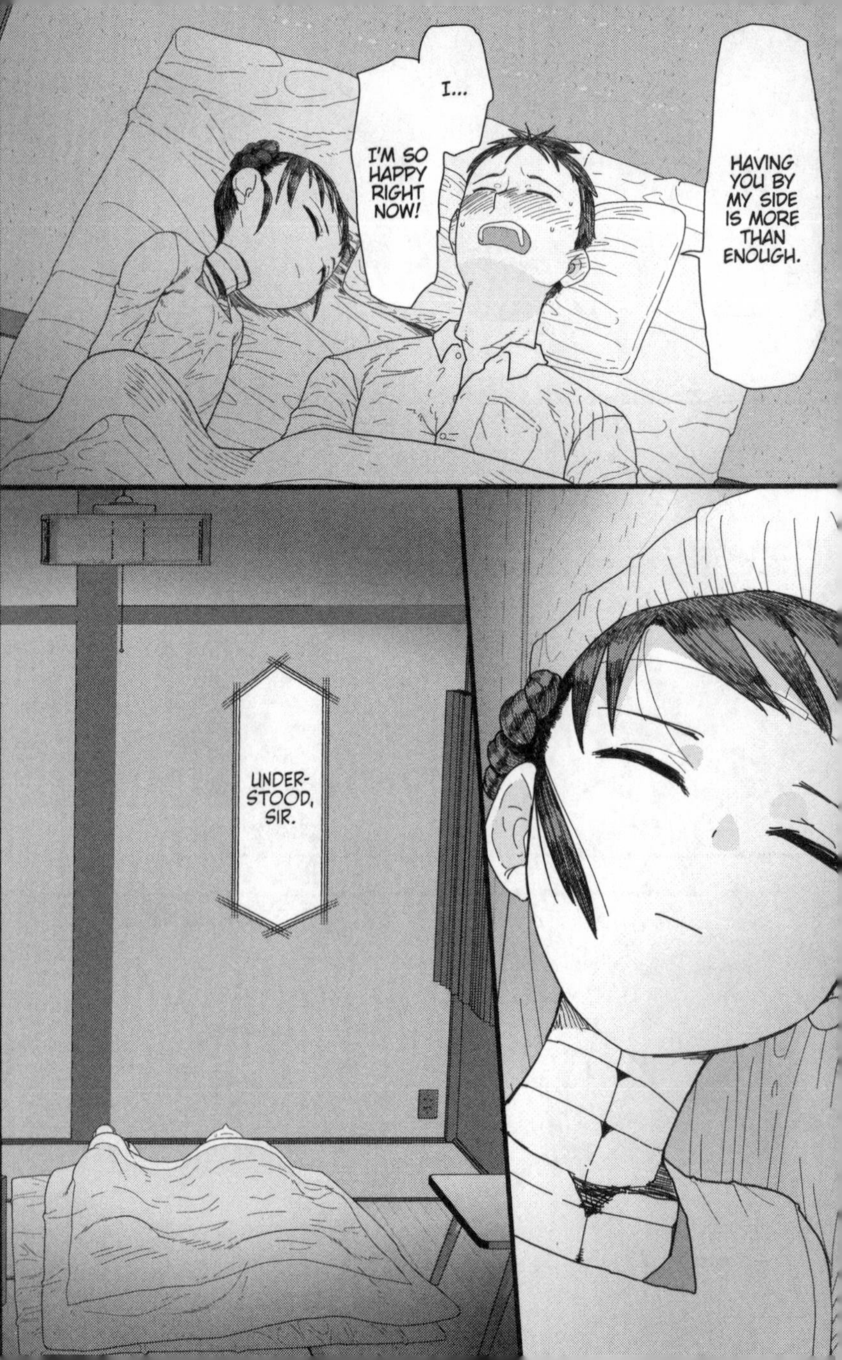
HAVING YOU BY MY SIDE IS MORE THAN ENOUGH.
I...
I'M SO HAPPY RIGHT NOW!
UNDER-STOOD, SIR.

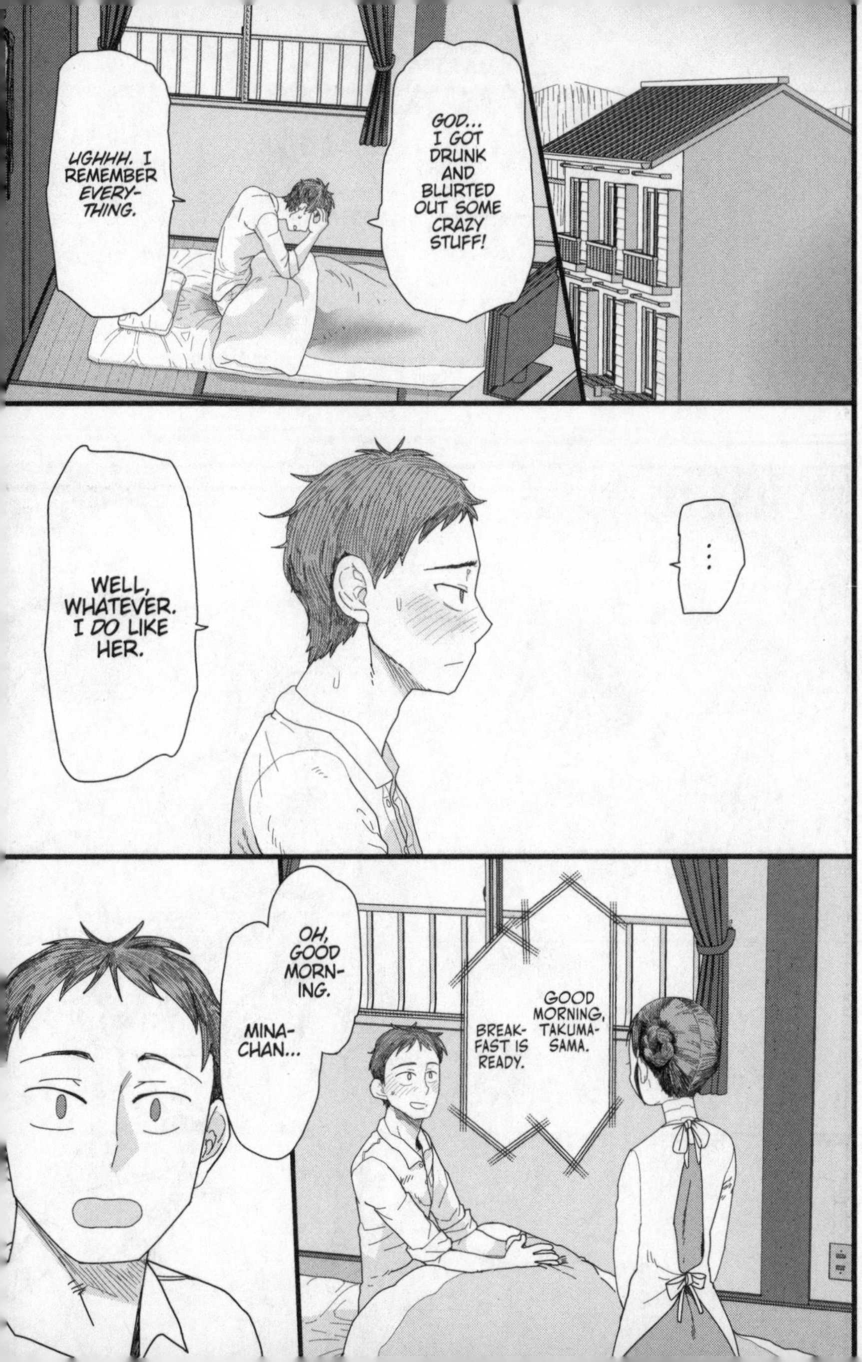
GOD... I GOT DRUNK AND BLURTED OUT SOME CRAZY STUFF!
UGHHH. I REMEMBER EVERY-THING.
...
WELL, WHATEVER. I DO LIKE HER.
GOOD MORNING, TAKUMA-SAMA.
BREAK-FAST IS READY.
OH, GOOD MORN-ING.
MINA-CHAN...

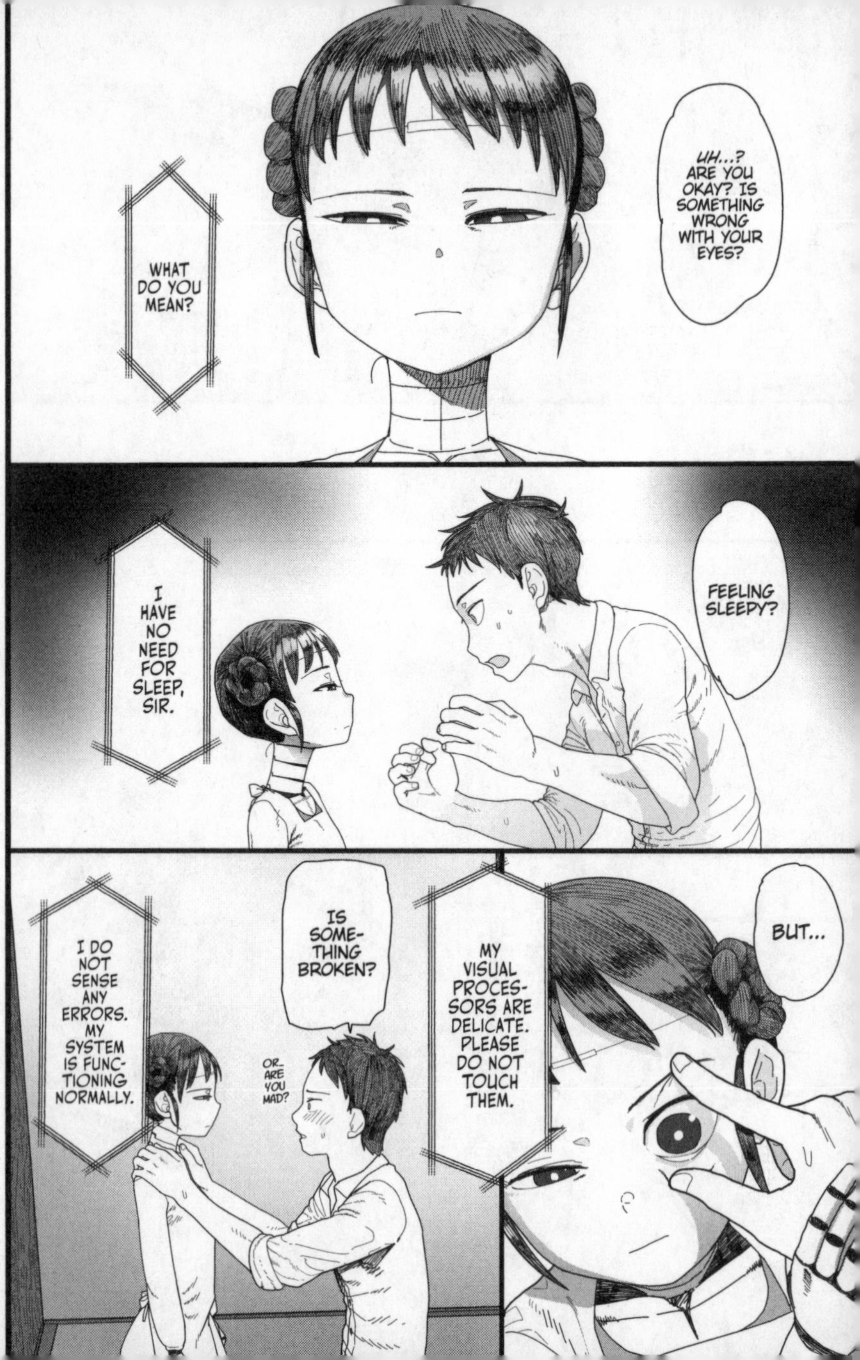
UH...? ARE YOU OKAY? IS SOMETHING WRONG WITH YOUR EYES?
WHAT DO YOU MEAN?
FEELING SLEEPY?
I HAVE NO NEED FOR SLEEP, SIR.
BUT...
MY VISUAL PROCES-SORS ARE DELICATE. PLEASE DO NOT TOUCH THEM.
IS SOME-THING BROKEN?
OR... ARE YOU MAD?
I DO NOT SENSE ANY ERRORS. MY SYSTEM IS FUNC-TIONING NORMALLY.

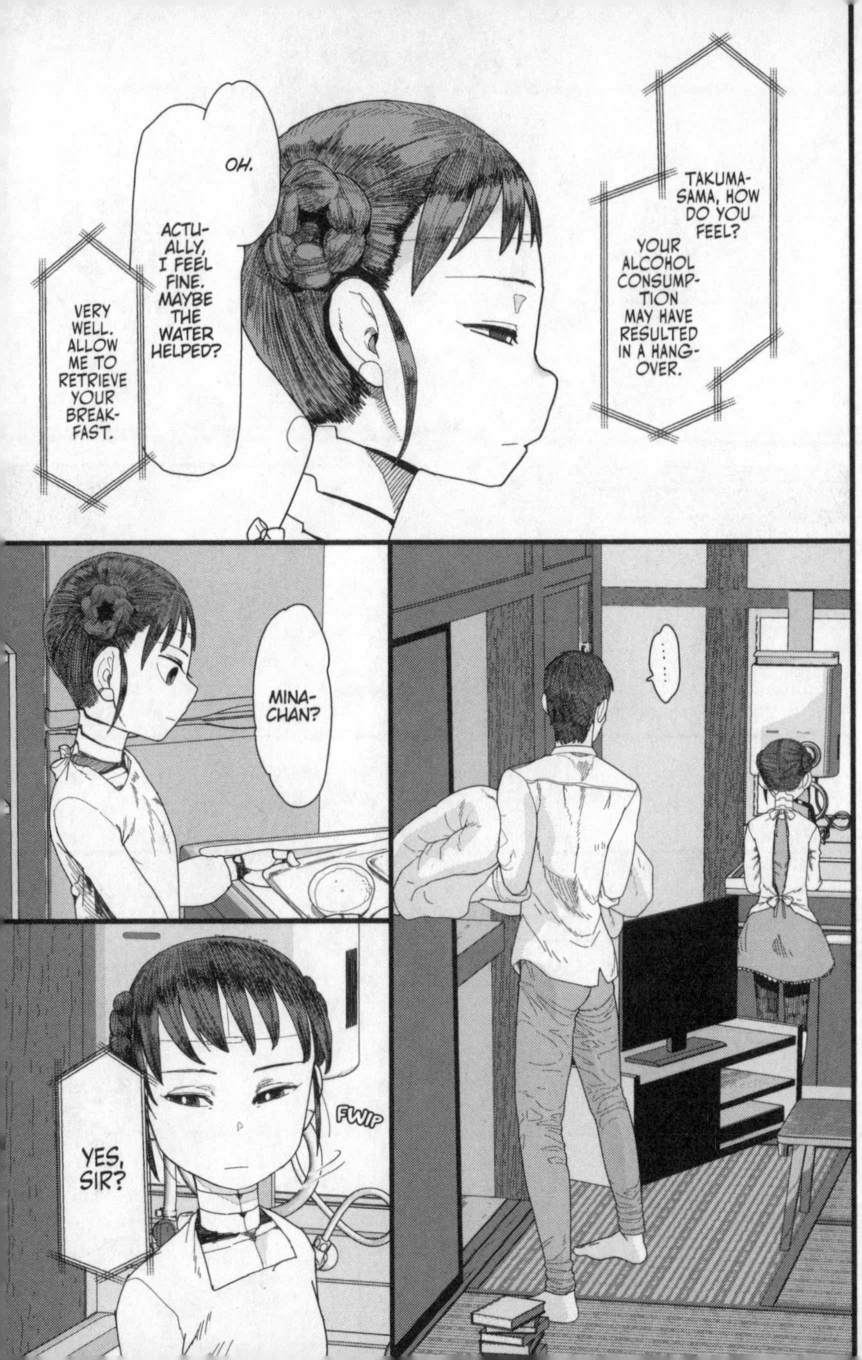
TAKUMA-SAMA, HOW DO YOU FEEL?
YOUR ALCOHOL CONSUMPTION MAY HAVE RESULTED IN A HANGOVER.
OH.
ACTUALLY, I FEEL FINE. MAYBE THE WATER HELPED?
VERY WELL. ALLOW ME TO RETRIEVE YOUR BREAKFAST.
......
MINA-CHAN?
FWIP
YES, SIR?

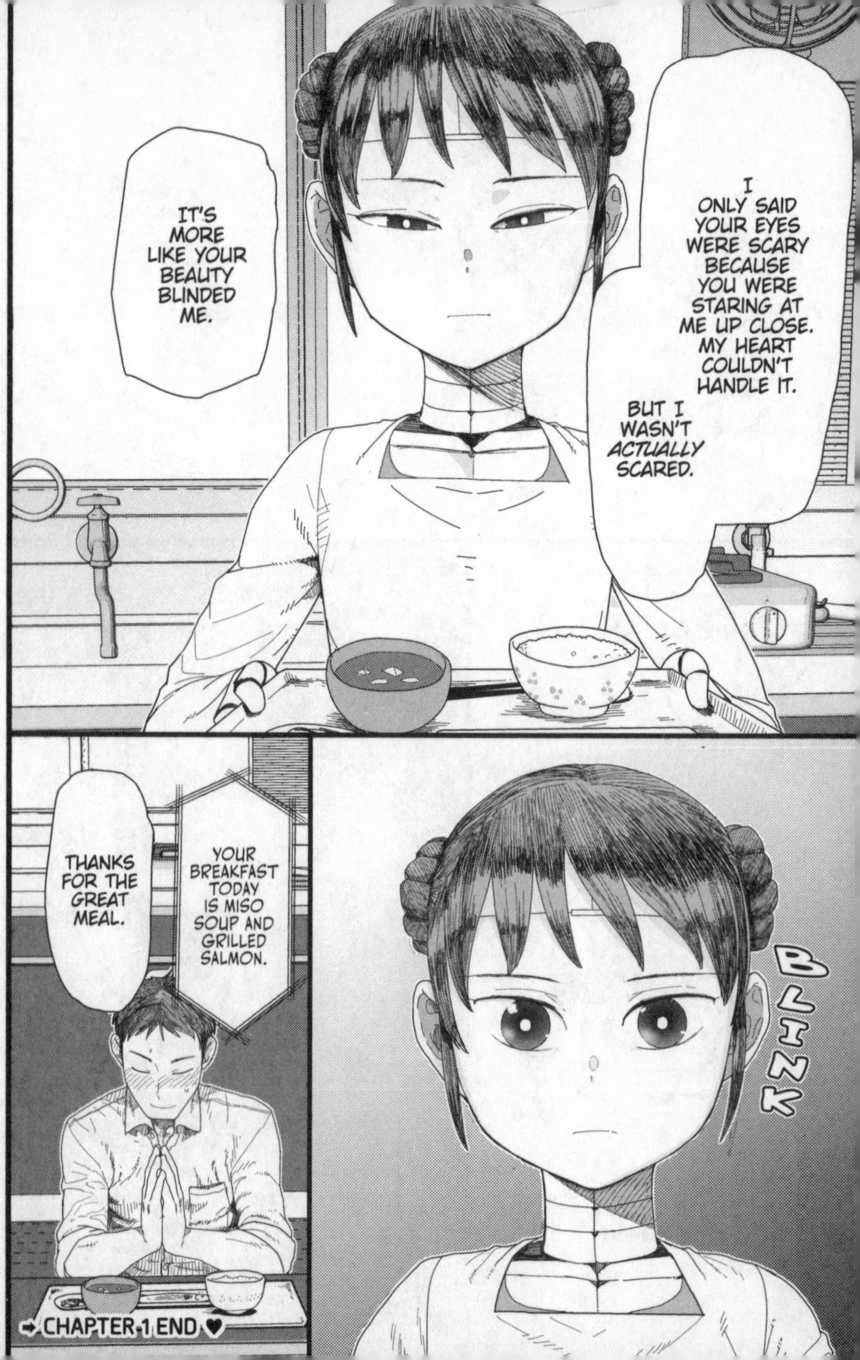
I ONLY SAID YOUR EYES WERE SCARY BECAUSE YOU WERE STARING AT ME UP CLOSE. MY HEART COULDN'T HANDLE IT.
BUT I WASN'T *ACTUALLY* SCARED.
IT'S MORE LIKE YOUR BEAUTY BLINDED ME.
BLINK
YOUR BREAKFAST TODAY IS MISO SOUP AND GRILLED SALMON.
THANKS FOR THE GREAT MEAL.
➡ CHAPTER 1 END ♥

My Wife Has No Emotion

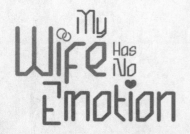

My
Wife Has No
Emotion

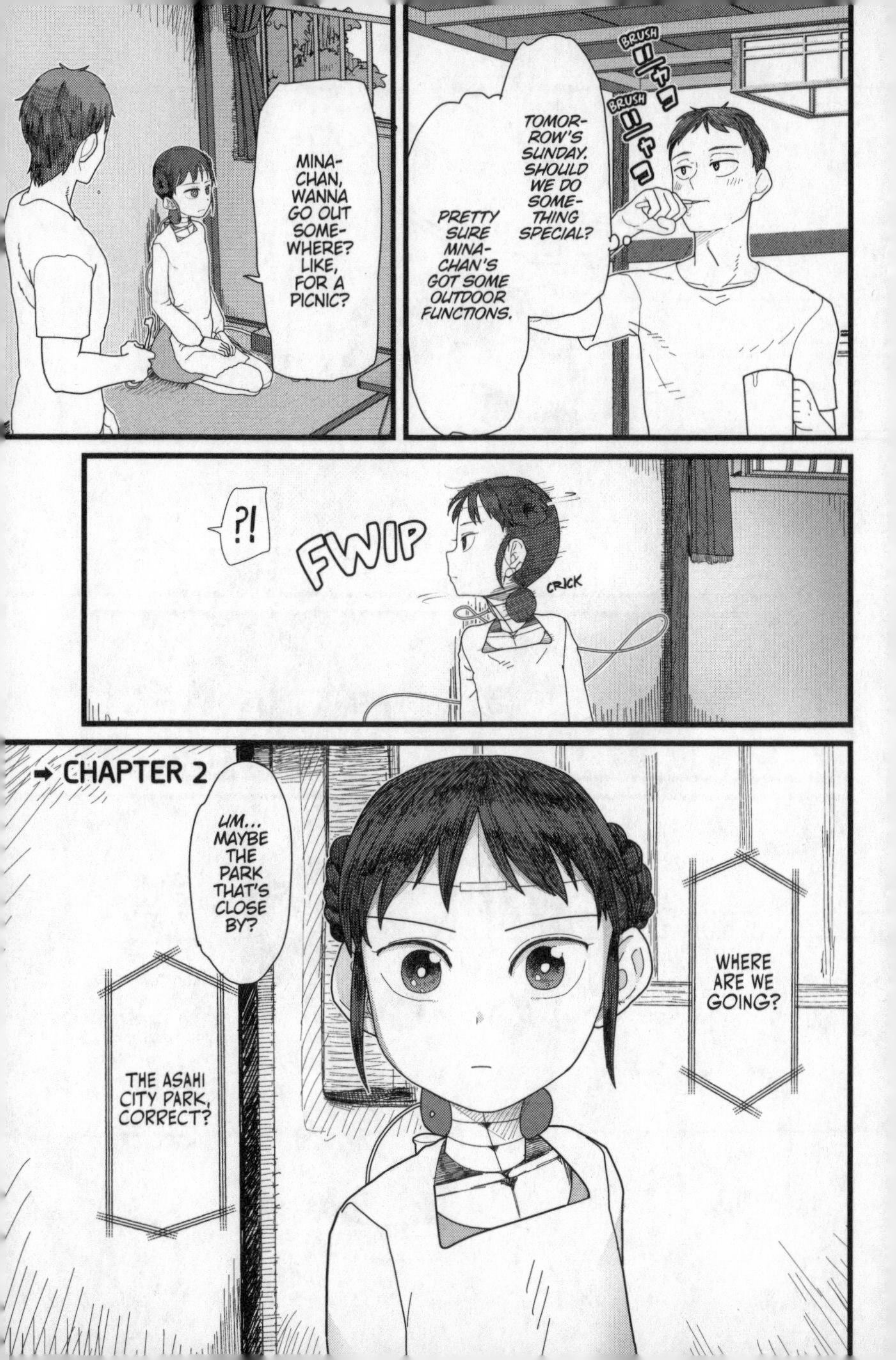
BRUSH
BRUSH
TOMORROW'S SUNDAY. SHOULD WE DO SOMETHING SPECIAL?
PRETTY SURE MINA-CHAN'S GOT SOME OUTDOOR FUNCTIONS.
MINA-CHAN, WANNA GO OUT SOMEWHERE? LIKE, FOR A PICNIC?
FWIP
?!
CRICK
➡ CHAPTER 2
WHERE ARE WE GOING?
UM... MAYBE THE PARK THAT'S CLOSE BY?
THE ASAHI CITY PARK, CORRECT?

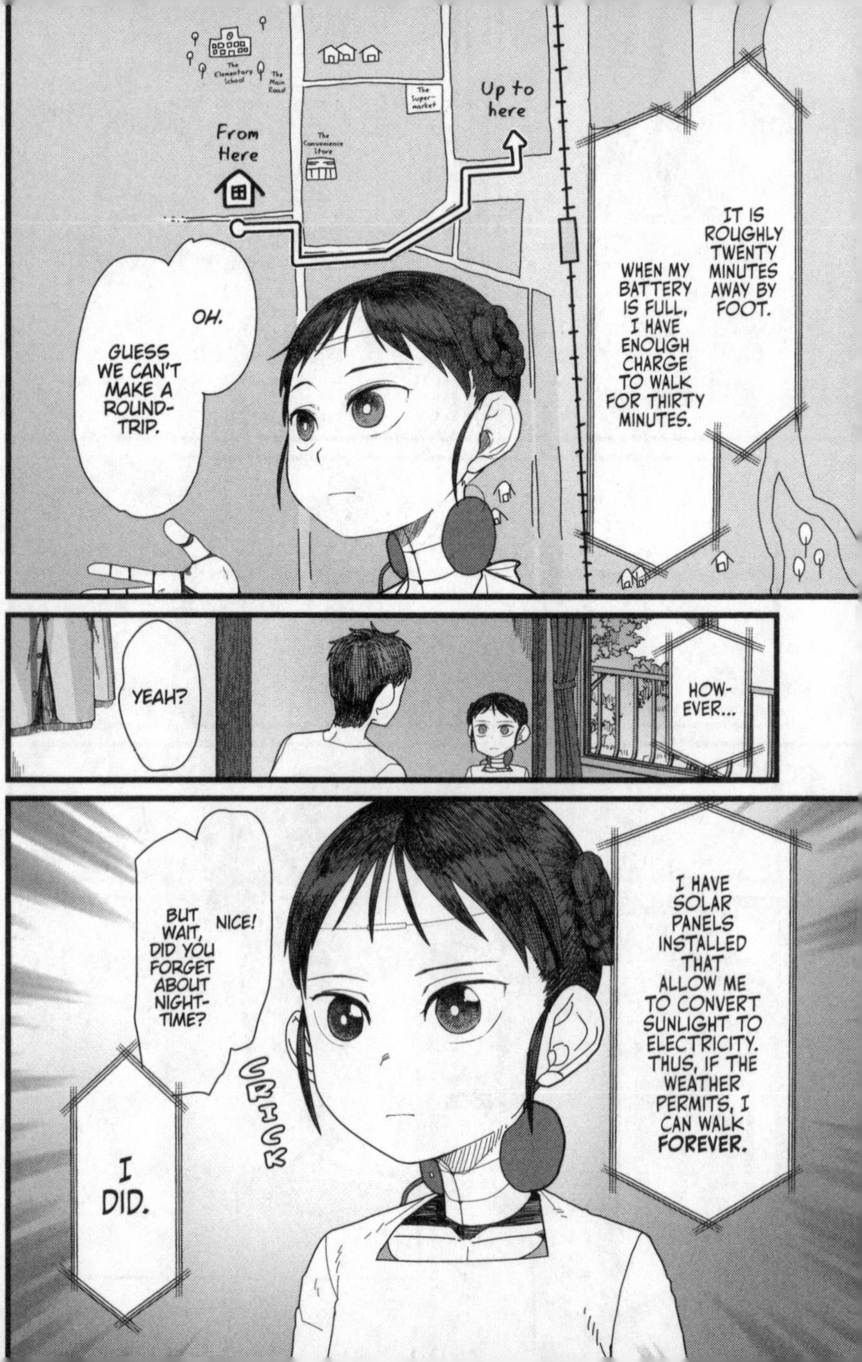
The Elementary School
The Main Road
The Super-market
The Convenience Store
Up to here
From Here
IT IS ROUGHLY TWENTY MINUTES AWAY BY FOOT.
WHEN MY BATTERY IS FULL, I HAVE ENOUGH CHARGE TO WALK FOR THIRTY MINUTES.
OH.
GUESS WE CAN'T MAKE A ROUND-TRIP.
HOW-EVER...
YEAH?
I HAVE SOLAR PANELS INSTALLED THAT ALLOW ME TO CONVERT SUNLIGHT TO ELECTRICITY. THUS, IF THE WEATHER PERMITS, I CAN WALK **FOREVER.**
NICE!
BUT WAIT, DID YOU FORGET ABOUT NIGHT-TIME?
CRICK
I DID.

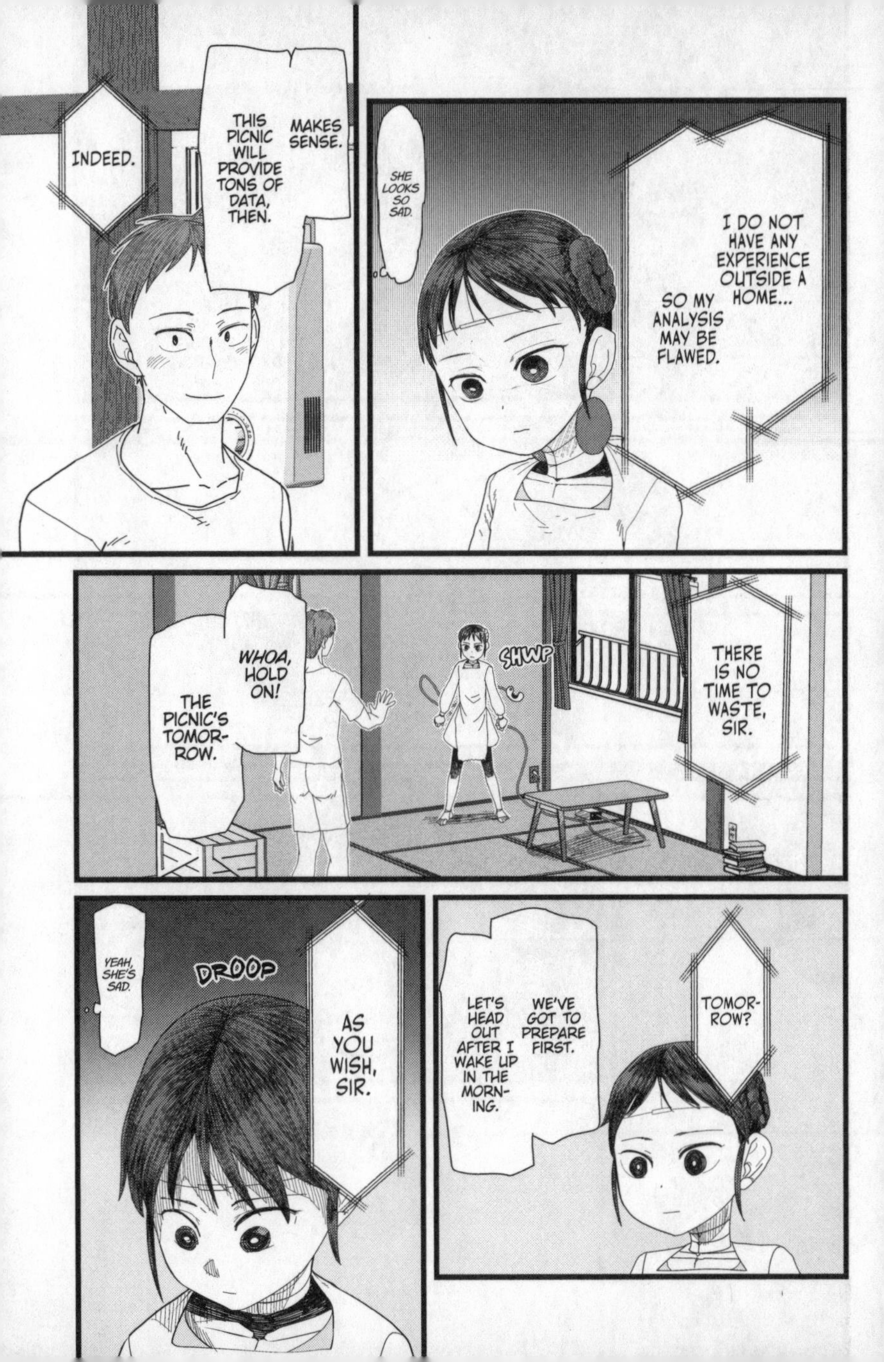
I DO NOT HAVE ANY EXPERIENCE OUTSIDE A HOME...
SO MY ANALYSIS MAY BE FLAWED.
SHE LOOKS SO SAD.
MAKES SENSE.
THIS PICNIC WILL PROVIDE TONS OF DATA, THEN.
INDEED.
THERE IS NO TIME TO WASTE, SIR.
SHWP
WHOA, HOLD ON!
THE PICNIC'S TOMORROW.
TOMORROW?
WE'VE GOT TO PREPARE FIRST.
LET'S HEAD OUT AFTER I WAKE UP IN THE MORNING.
AS YOU WISH, SIR.
DROOP
YEAH, SHE'S SAD.

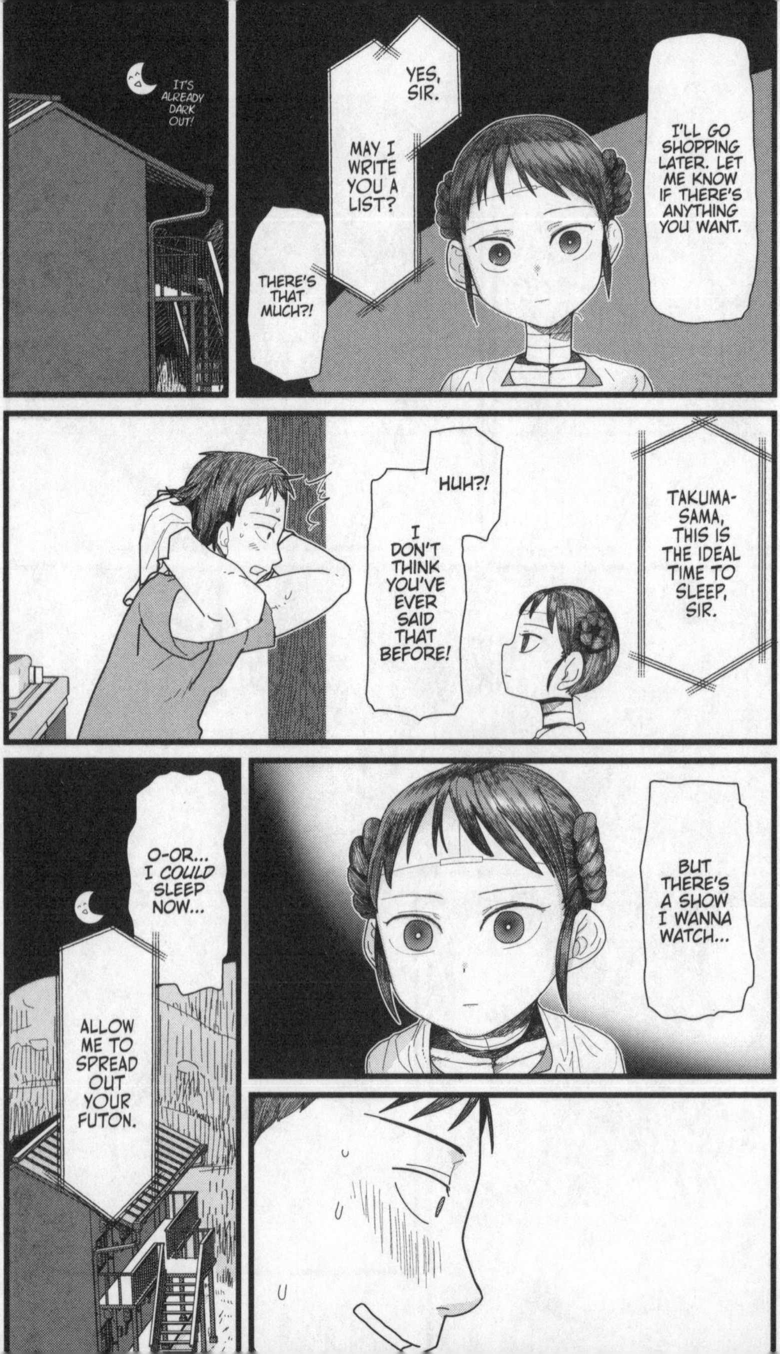
I'LL GO SHOPPING LATER. LET ME KNOW IF THERE'S ANYTHING YOU WANT.
YES, SIR.
MAY I WRITE YOU A LIST?
THERE'S THAT MUCH?!
IT'S ALREADY DARK OUT!
TAKUMA-SAMA, THIS IS THE IDEAL TIME TO SLEEP, SIR.
HUH?!
I DON'T THINK YOU'VE EVER SAID THAT BEFORE!
BUT THERE'S A SHOW I WANNA WATCH...
O-OR... I COULD SLEEP NOW...
ALLOW ME TO SPREAD OUT YOUR FUTON.

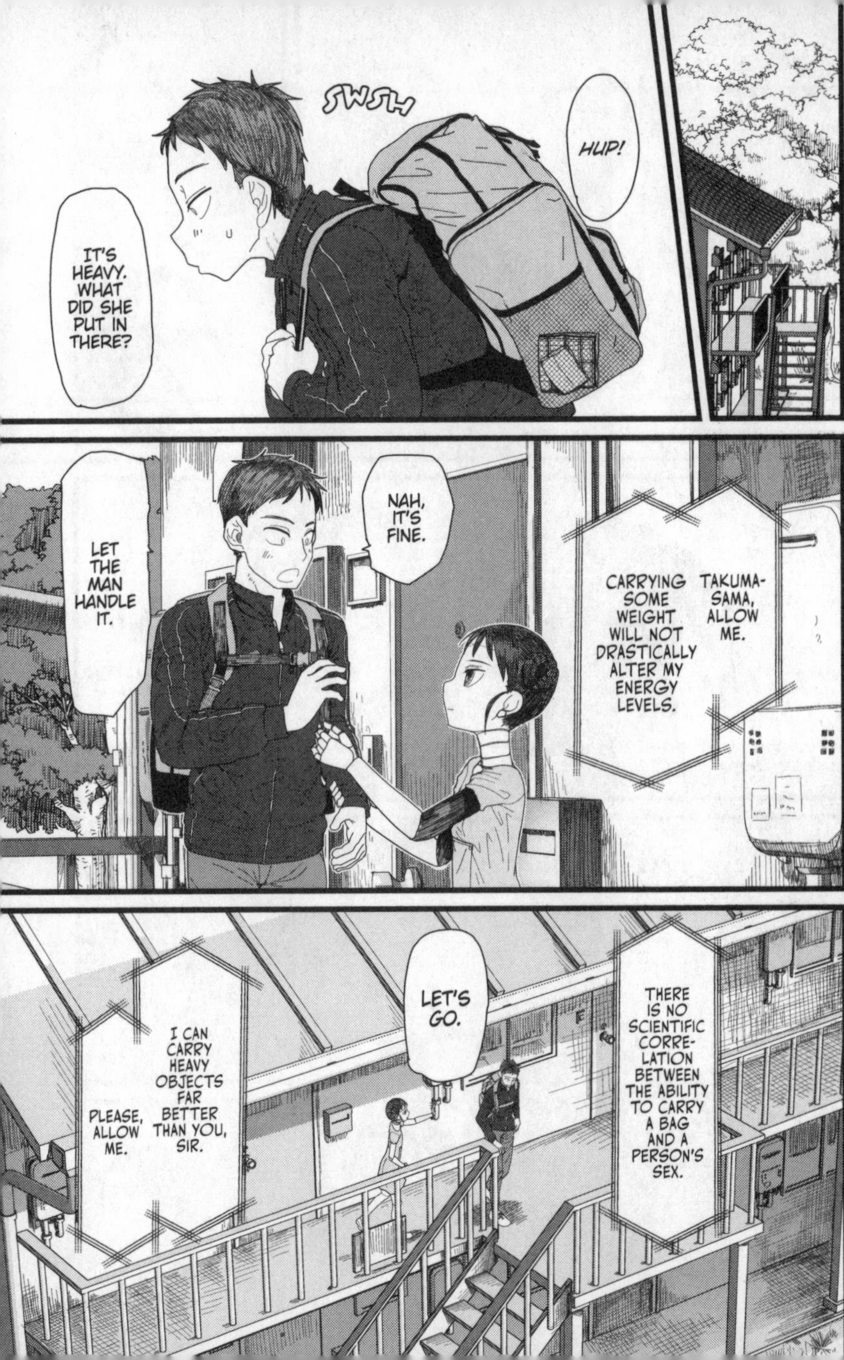
HUP!
SWSH
IT'S HEAVY. WHAT DID SHE PUT IN THERE?
TAKUMA-SAMA, ALLOW ME.
CARRYING SOME WEIGHT WILL NOT DRASTICALLY ALTER MY ENERGY LEVELS.
NAH, IT'S FINE.
LET THE MAN HANDLE IT.
THERE IS NO SCIENTIFIC CORRE-LATION BETWEEN THE ABILITY TO CARRY A BAG AND A PERSON'S SEX.
LET'S GO.
I CAN CARRY HEAVY OBJECTS FAR BETTER THAN YOU, SIR.
PLEASE, ALLOW ME.

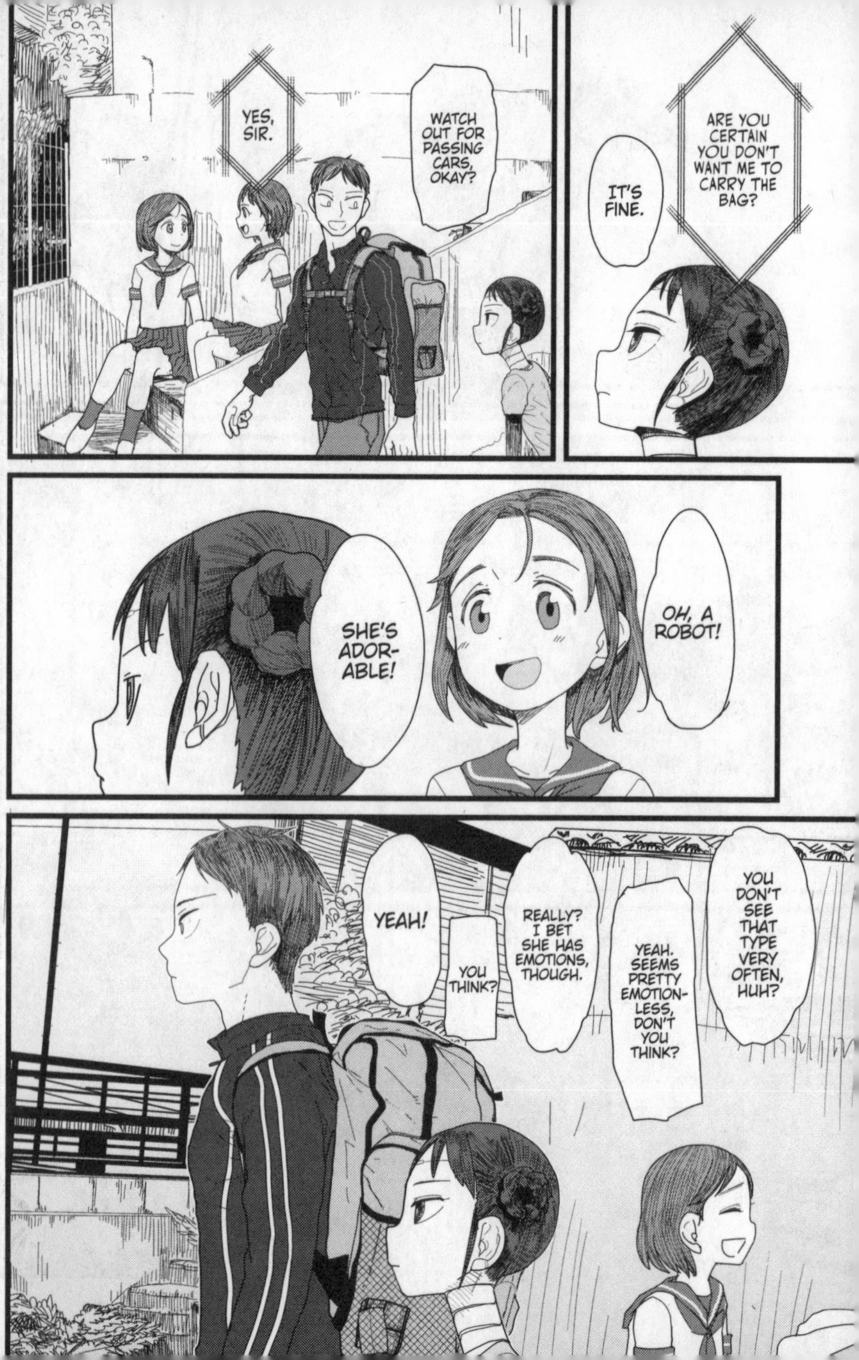
ARE YOU CERTAIN YOU DON'T WANT ME TO CARRY THE BAG?
IT'S FINE.
WATCH OUT FOR PASSING CARS, OKAY?
YES, SIR.
OH, A ROBOT!
SHE'S ADORABLE!
YOU DON'T SEE THAT TYPE VERY OFTEN, HUH?
YEAH. SEEMS PRETTY EMOTIONLESS, DON'T YOU THINK?
REALLY? I BET SHE HAS EMOTIONS, THOUGH.
YOU THINK?
YEAH!

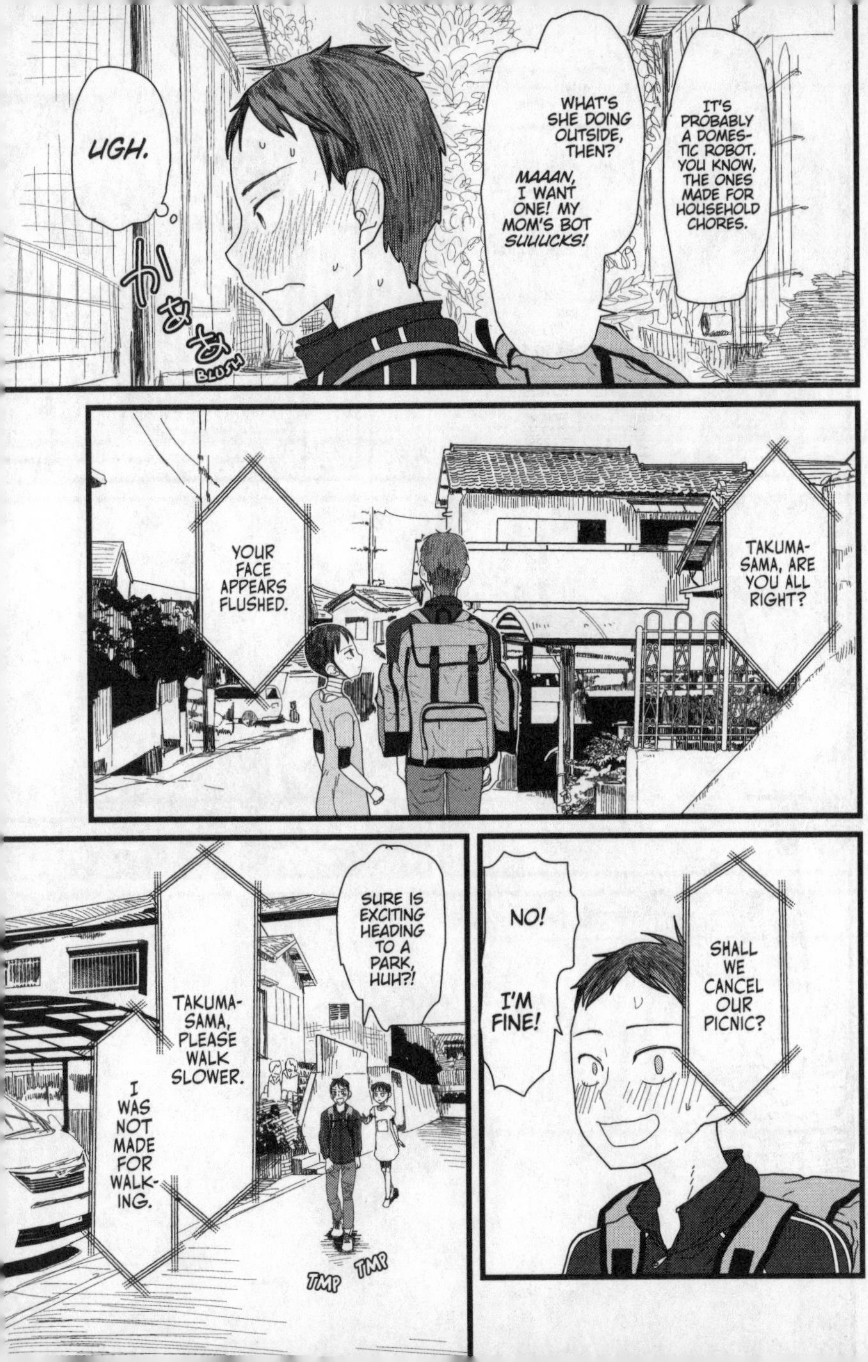
IT'S PROBABLY A DOMESTIC ROBOT. YOU KNOW, THE ONES MADE FOR HOUSEHOLD CHORES.
WHAT'S SHE DOING OUTSIDE, THEN?
MAAAN, I WANT ONE! MY MOM'S BOT SUUUCKS!
UGH.
かぁぁ
BLUSH
TAKUMA-SAMA, ARE YOU ALL RIGHT?
YOUR FACE APPEARS FLUSHED.
SHALL WE CANCEL OUR PICNIC?
NO!
I'M FINE!
SURE IS EXCITING HEADING TO A PARK, HUH?!
TAKUMA-SAMA, PLEASE WALK SLOWER.
I WAS NOT MADE FOR WALKING.
TMP
TMP

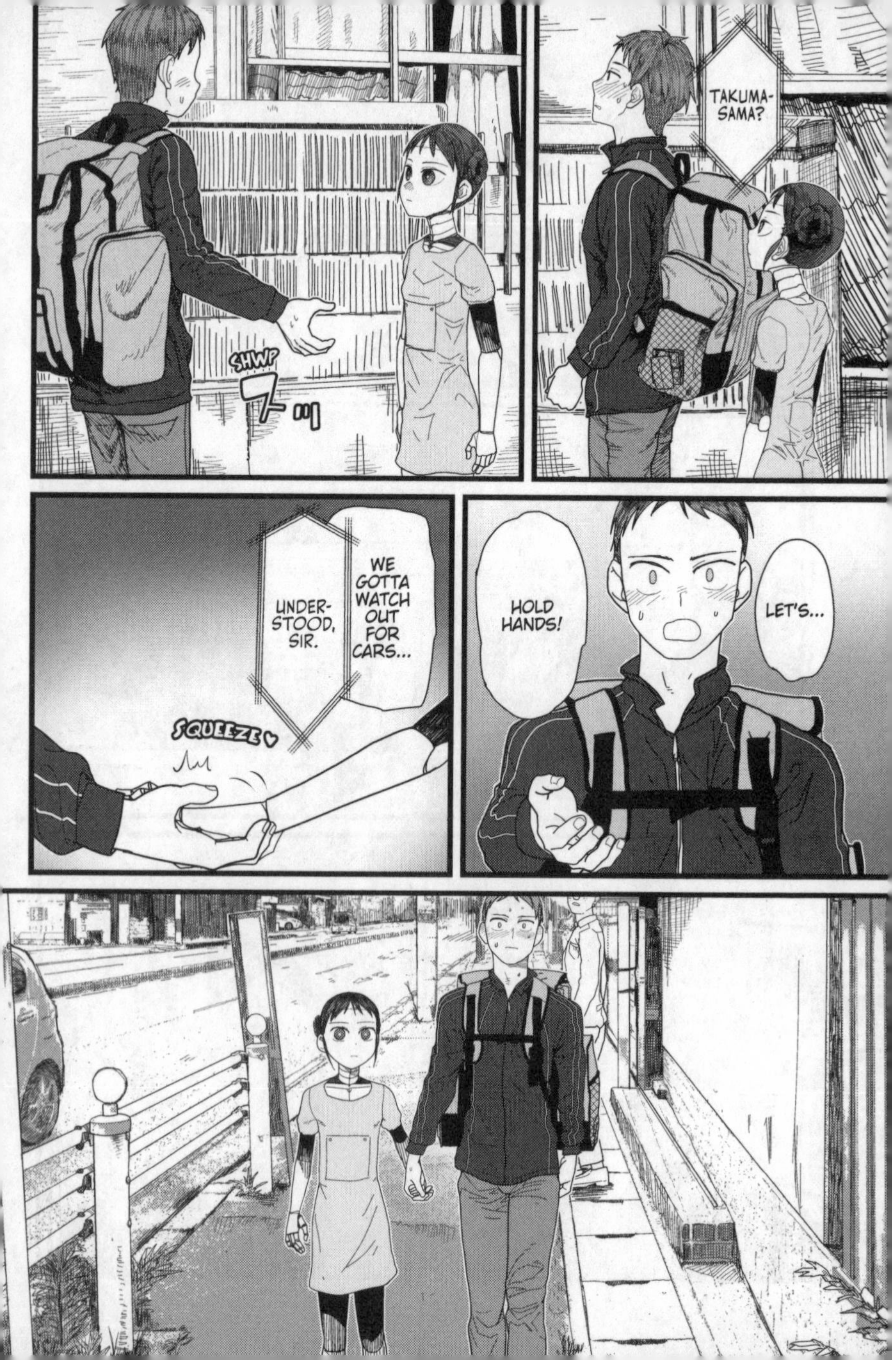
TAKUMA-SAMA?
SHWP
LET'S...
HOLD HANDS!
WE GOTTA WATCH OUT FOR CARS...
UNDERSTOOD, SIR.
SQUEEZE ♥

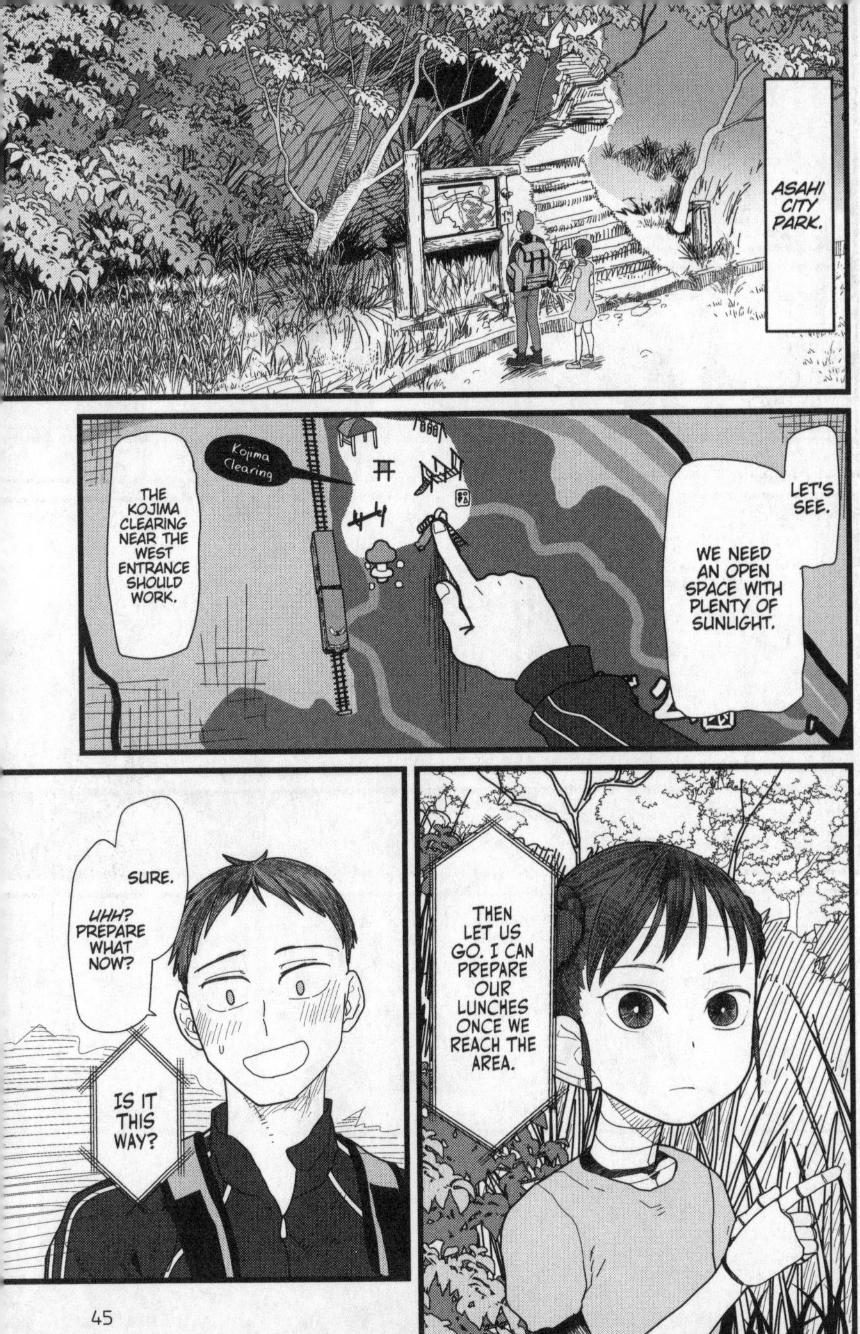
ASAHI CITY PARK.
LET'S SEE.
WE NEED AN OPEN SPACE WITH PLENTY OF SUNLIGHT.
Kojima Clearing
THE KOJIMA CLEARING NEAR THE WEST ENTRANCE SHOULD WORK.
IS IT THIS WAY?
THEN LET US GO. I CAN PREPARE OUR LUNCHES ONCE WE REACH THE AREA.
SURE.
UHH? PREPARE WHAT NOW?

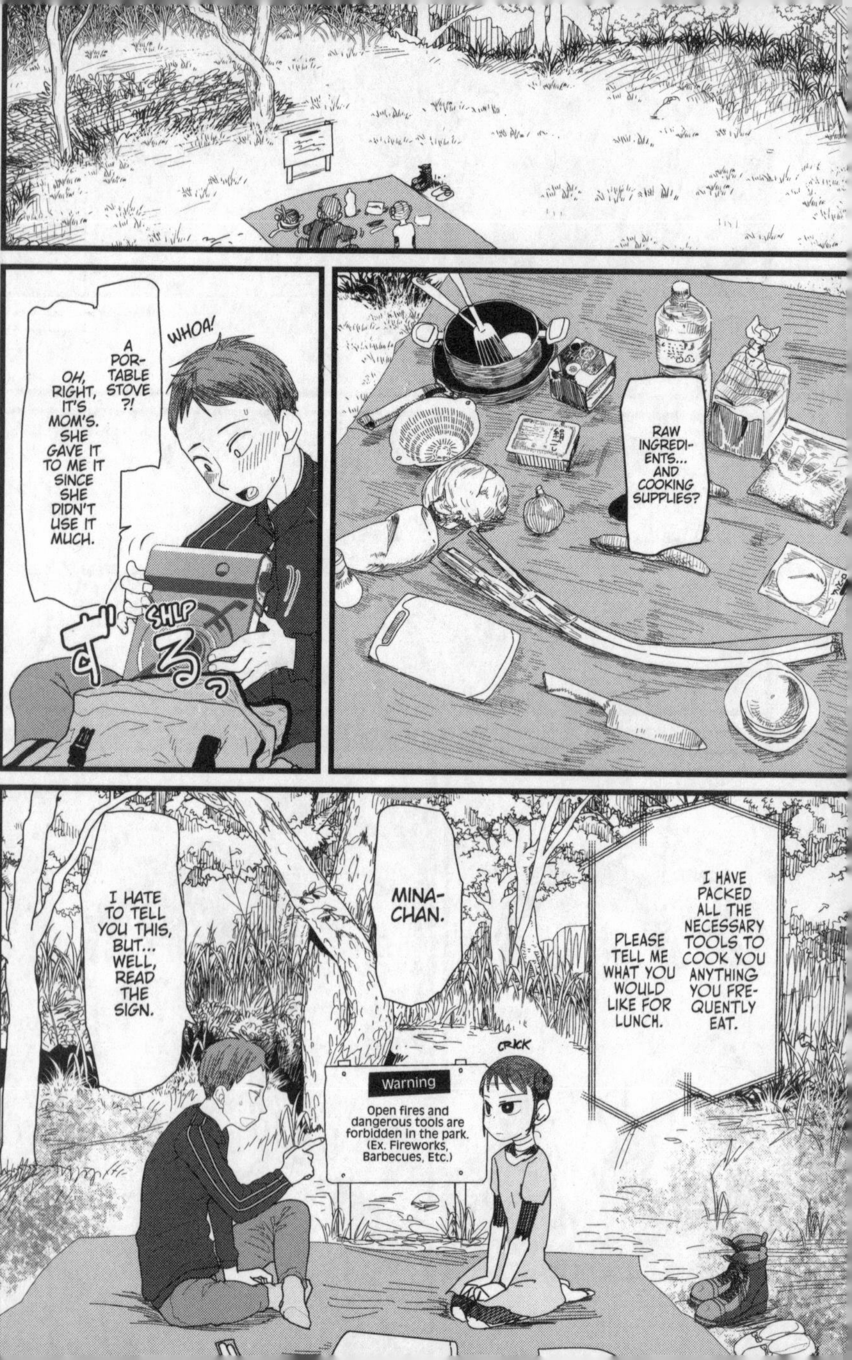
RAW INGREDIENTS... AND COOKING SUPPLIES?
WHOA!
A PORTABLE STOVE?!
OH, RIGHT, IT'S MOM'S. SHE GAVE IT TO ME IT SINCE SHE DIDN'T USE IT MUCH.
SHLP
ずるっ
I HAVE PACKED ALL THE NECESSARY TOOLS TO COOK YOU ANYTHING YOU FREQUENTLY EAT.
PLEASE TELL ME WHAT YOU WOULD LIKE FOR LUNCH.
CRICK
MINA-CHAN.
I HATE TO TELL YOU THIS, BUT... WELL, READ THE SIGN.
Warning
Open fires and dangerous tools are forbidden in the park.
(Ex. Fireworks, Barbecues, Etc.)

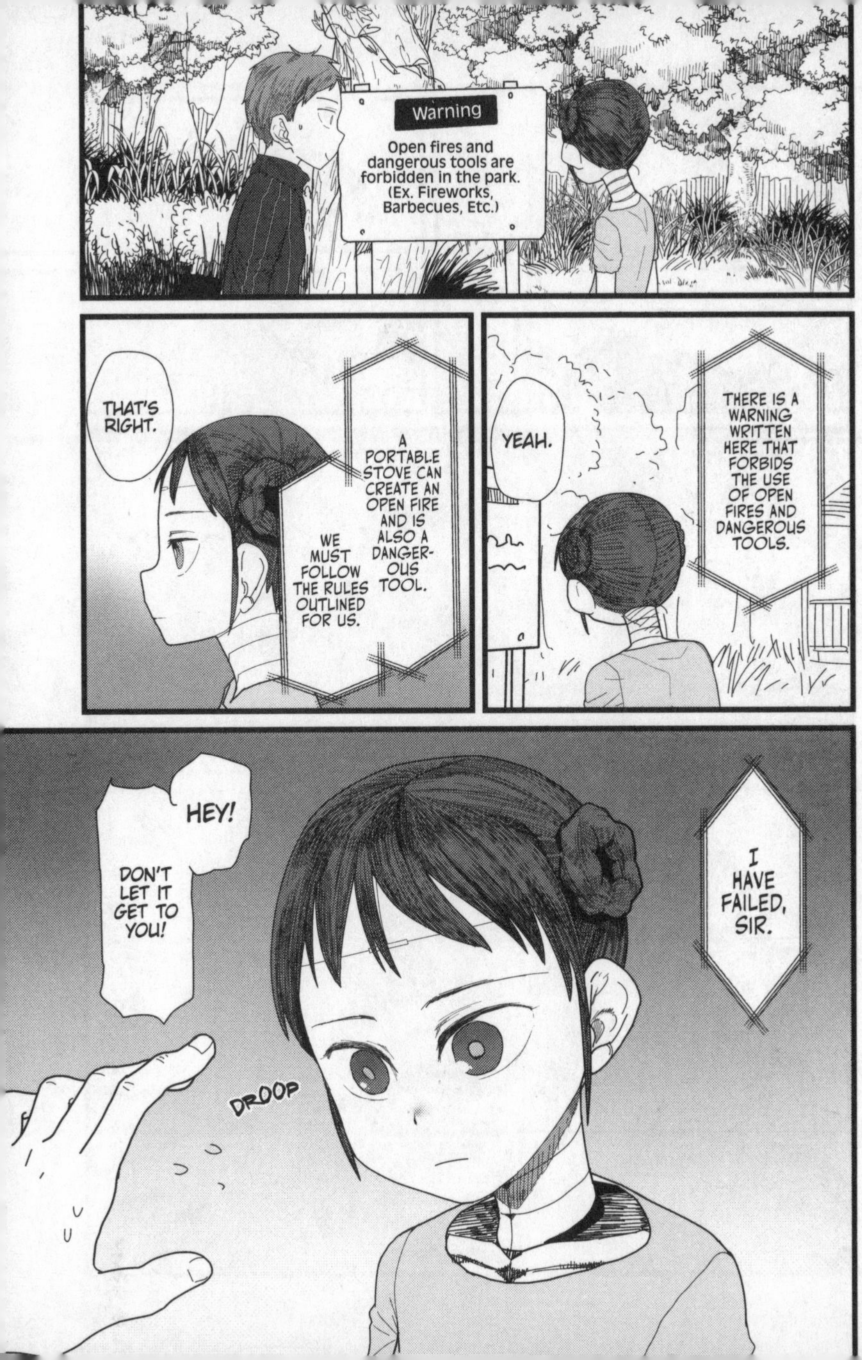
Warning
Open fires and dangerous tools are forbidden in the park. (Ex. Fireworks, Barbecues, Etc.)
THERE IS A WARNING WRITTEN HERE THAT FORBIDS THE USE OF OPEN FIRES AND DANGEROUS TOOLS.
YEAH.
A PORTABLE STOVE CAN CREATE AN OPEN FIRE AND IS ALSO A DANGER-OUS TOOL.
WE MUST FOLLOW THE RULES OUTLINED FOR US.
THAT'S RIGHT.
I HAVE FAILED, SIR.
DROOP
HEY!
DON'T LET IT GET TO YOU!

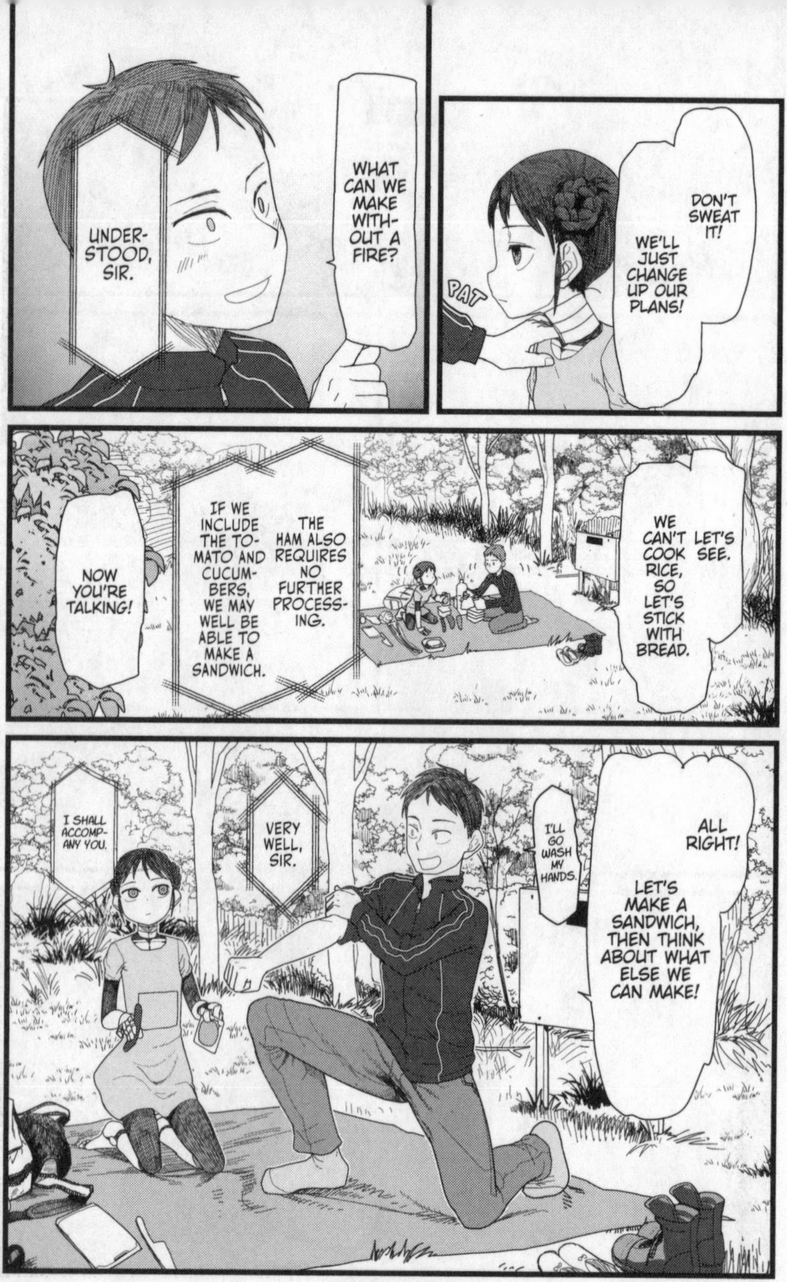
DON'T SWEAT IT!
WE'LL JUST CHANGE UP OUR PLANS!
PAT
WHAT CAN WE MAKE WITH-OUT A FIRE?
UNDER-STOOD, SIR.
LET'S SEE.
WE CAN'T COOK RICE, SO LET'S STICK WITH BREAD.
THE HAM ALSO REQUIRES NO FURTHER PROCESS-ING.
IF WE INCLUDE THE TO-MATO AND CUCUM-BERS, WE MAY WELL BE ABLE TO MAKE A SANDWICH.
NOW YOU'RE TALKING!
ALL RIGHT!
LET'S MAKE A SANDWICH, THEN THINK ABOUT WHAT ELSE WE CAN MAKE!
I'LL GO WASH MY HANDS.
VERY WELL, SIR.
I SHALL ACCOMP-ANY YOU.

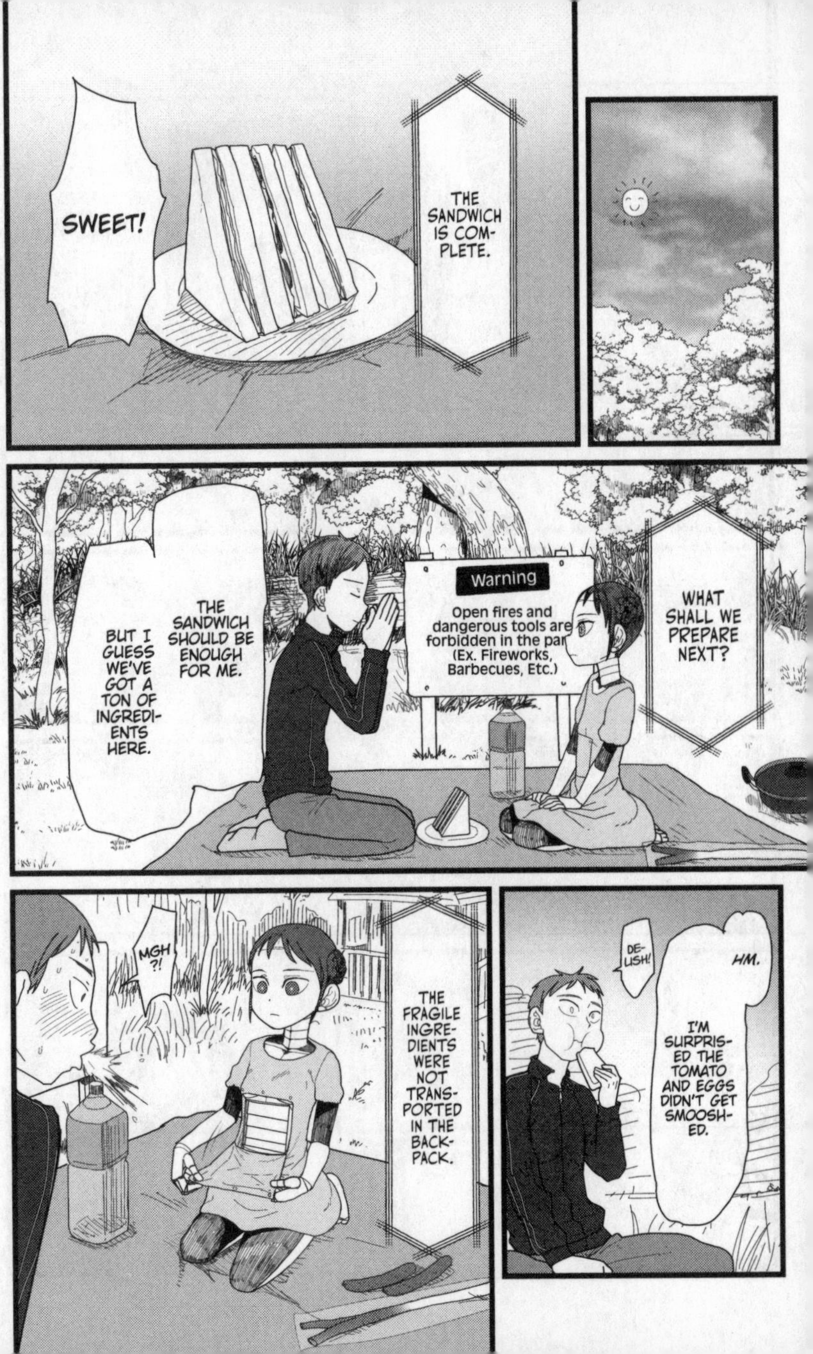
THE SANDWICH IS COMPLETE.
SWEET!
WHAT SHALL WE PREPARE NEXT?
Warning
Open fires and dangerous tools are forbidden in the par
(Ex. Fireworks, Barbecues, Etc.)
THE SANDWICH SHOULD BE ENOUGH FOR ME.
BUT I GUESS WE'VE GOT A TON OF INGREDIENTS HERE.
HM.
I'M SURPRISED THE TOMATO AND EGGS DIDN'T GET SMOOSHED.
DE-LISH!
THE FRAGILE INGREDIENTS WERE NOT TRANSPORTED IN THE BACKPACK.
MGH?!

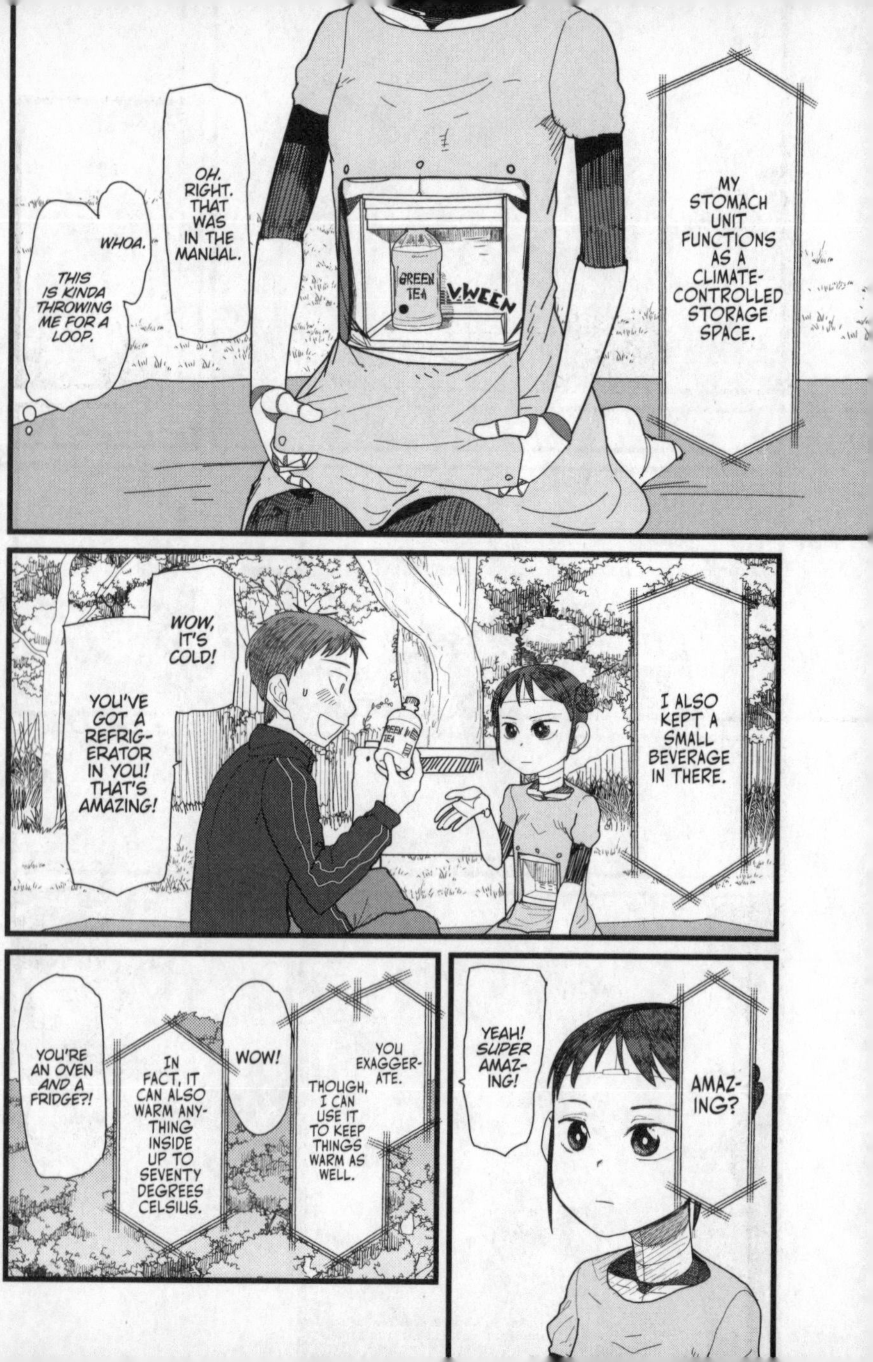
MY STOMACH UNIT FUNCTIONS AS A CLIMATE-CONTROLLED STORAGE SPACE.
V.WEEN
GREEN TEA
OH. RIGHT. THAT WAS IN THE MANUAL.
WHOA.
THIS IS KINDA THROWING ME FOR A LOOP.
I ALSO KEPT A SMALL BEVERAGE IN THERE.
WOW, IT'S COLD!
YOU'VE GOT A REFRIGERATOR IN YOU! THAT'S AMAZING!
AMAZ-ING?
YEAH! SUPER AMAZ-ING!
YOU EXAGGER-ATE.
THOUGH, I CAN USE IT TO KEEP THINGS WARM AS WELL.
WOW!
IN FACT, IT CAN ALSO WARM ANY-THING INSIDE UP TO SEVENTY DEGREES CELSIUS.
YOU'RE AN OVEN AND A FRIDGE?!

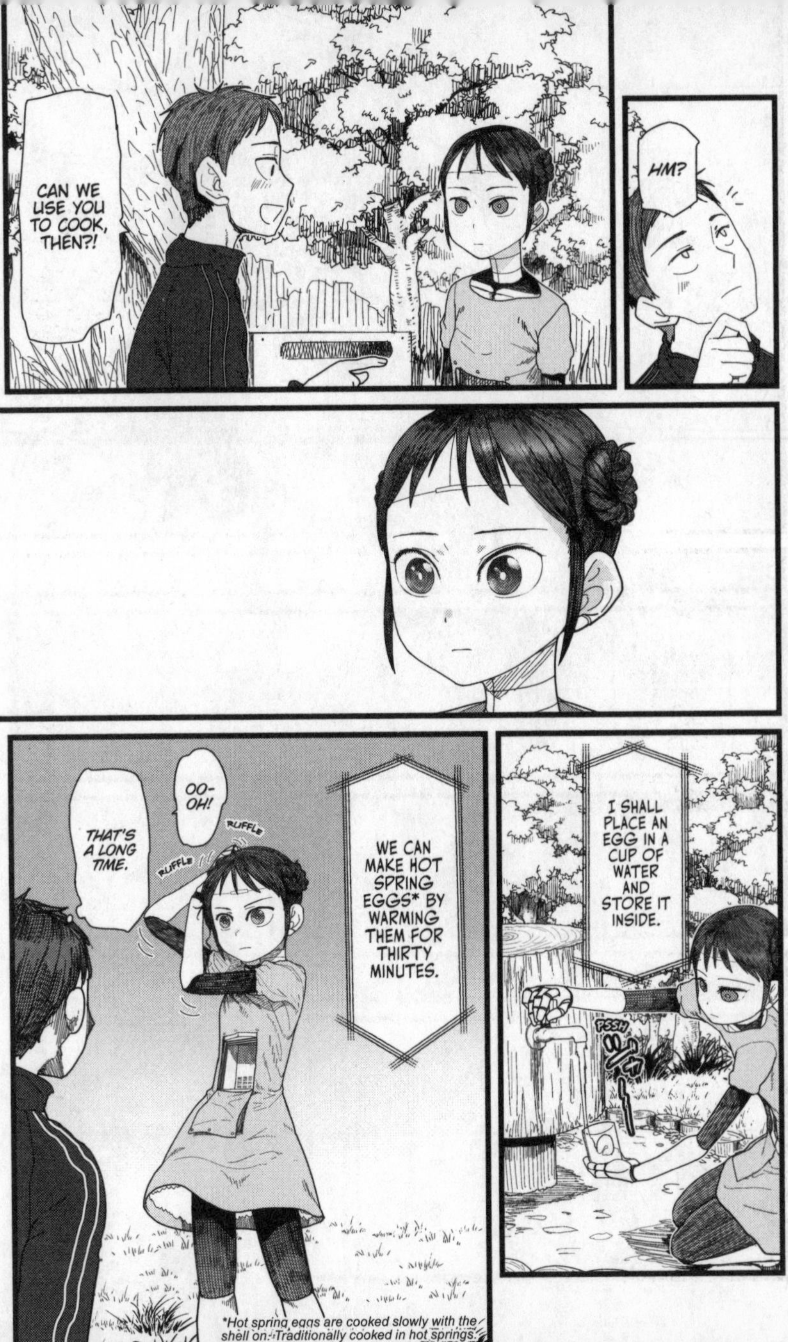
HM?
CAN WE USE YOU TO COOK, THEN?!
I SHALL PLACE AN EGG IN A CUP OF WATER AND STORE IT INSIDE.
PSSH
WE CAN MAKE HOT SPRING EGGS* BY WARMING THEM FOR THIRTY MINUTES.
OO-OH!
RUFFLE
THAT'S A LONG TIME.
RUFFLE

*Hot spring eggs are cooked slowly with the shell on. Traditionally cooked in hot springs.

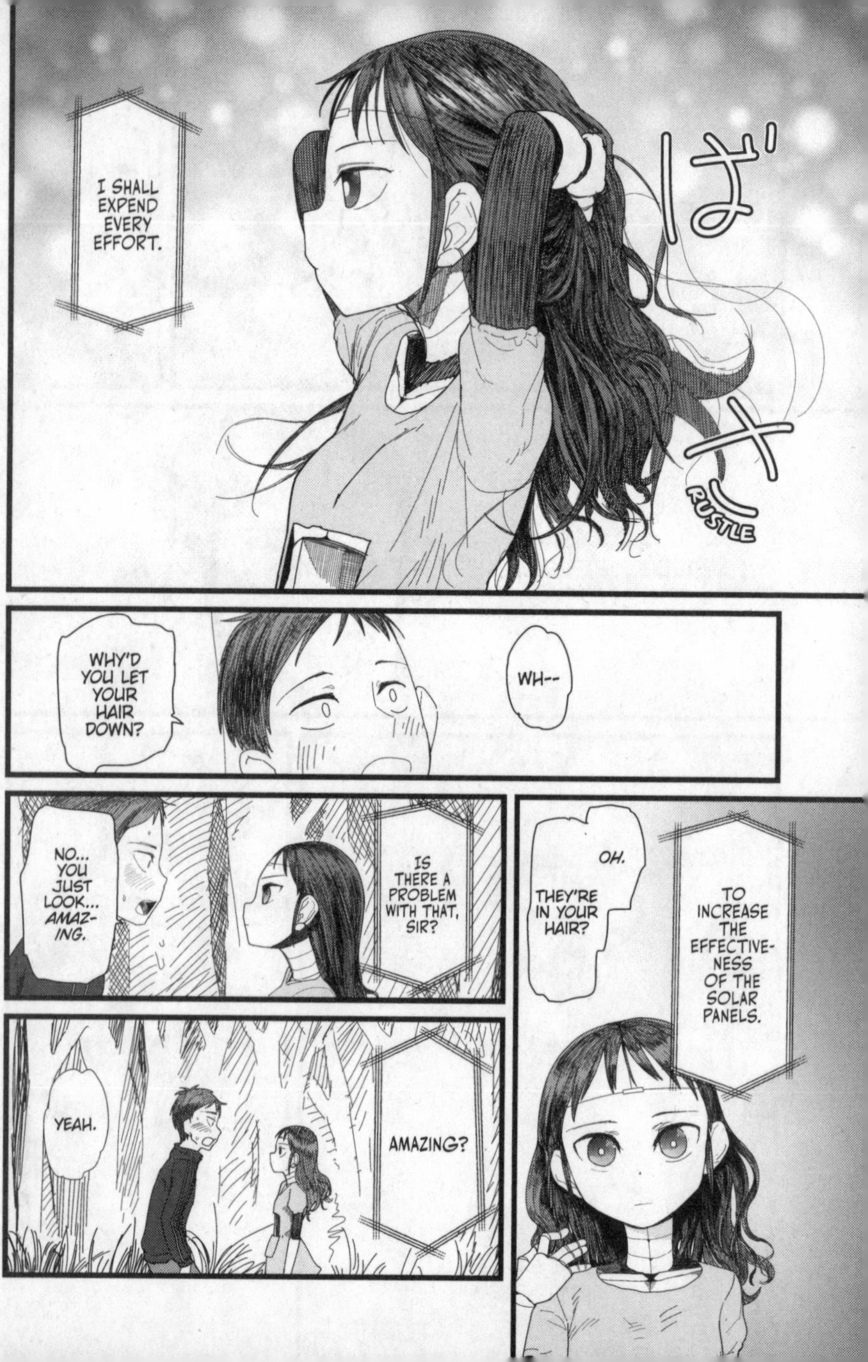
I SHALL EXPEND EVERY EFFORT.
ばさ
RUSTLE
WH--
WHY'D YOU LET YOUR HAIR DOWN?
TO INCREASE THE EFFECTIVE-NESS OF THE SOLAR PANELS.
OH.
THEY'RE IN YOUR HAIR?
IS THERE A PROBLEM WITH THAT, SIR?
NO... YOU JUST LOOK... AMAZ-ING.
AMAZING?
YEAH.

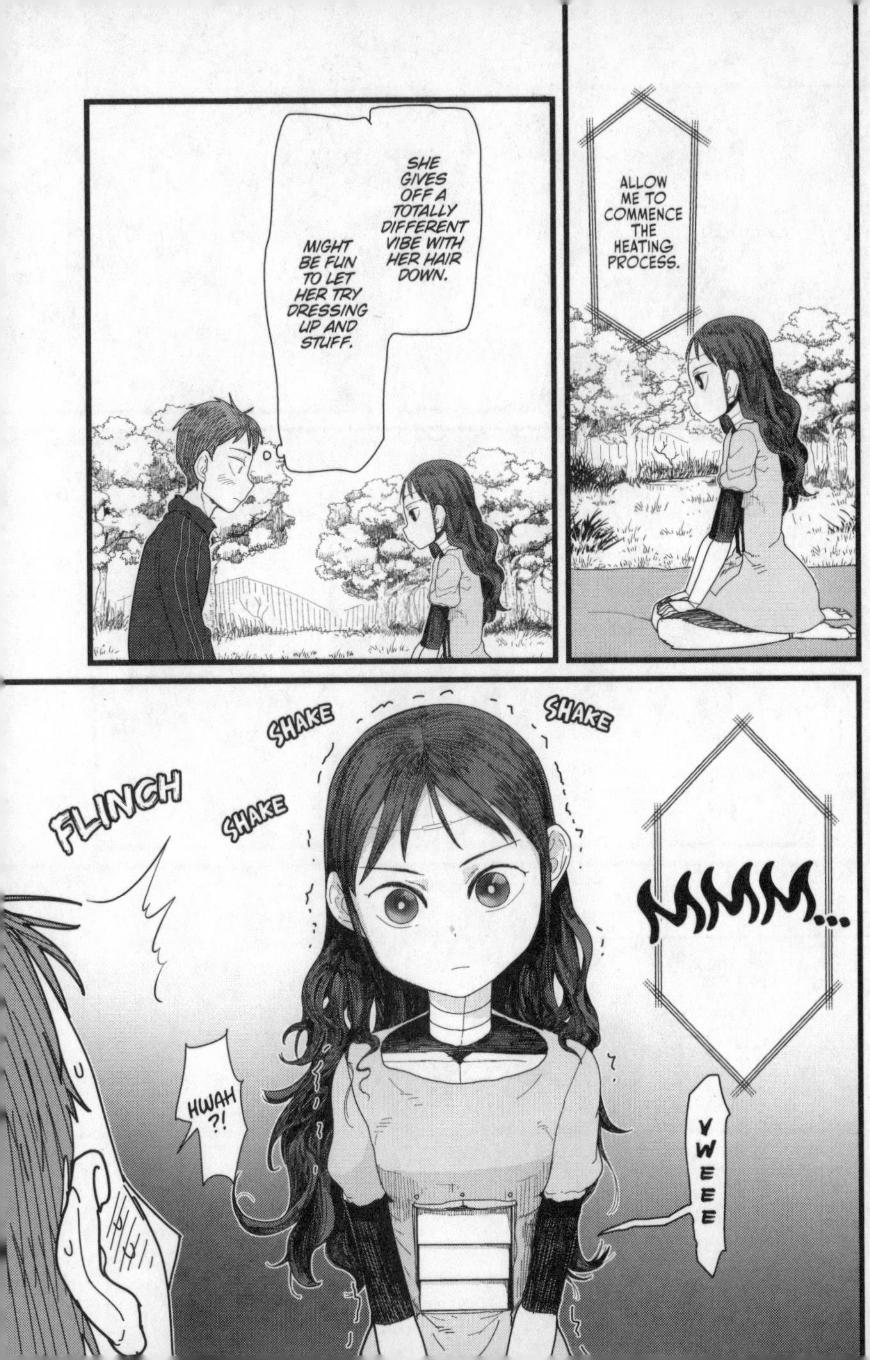
ALLOW ME TO COMMENCE THE HEATING PROCESS.
SHE GIVES OFF A TOTALLY DIFFERENT VIBE WITH HER HAIR DOWN.
MIGHT BE FUN TO LET HER TRY DRESSING UP AND STUFF.
SHAKE
MMM...
SHAKE
SHAKE
FLINCH
VWEEE
HWAH?!

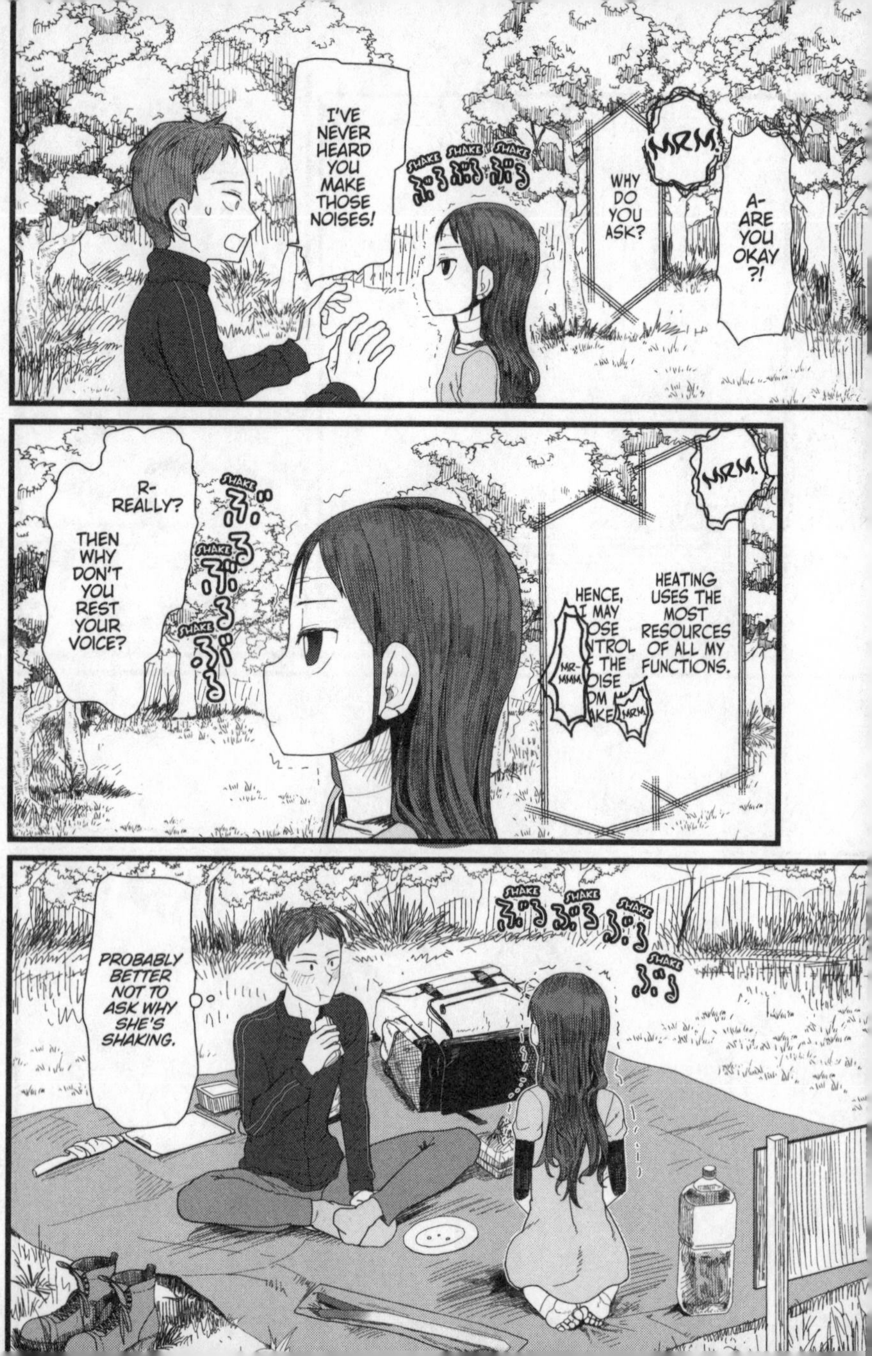

A- ARE YOU OKAY ?!
MRM.
WHY DO YOU ASK?
SHAKE SHAKE SHAKE
ぶるぶるぶる
I'VE NEVER HEARD YOU MAKE THOSE NOISES!
MRM.
HEATING USES THE MOST RESOURCES OF ALL MY FUNCTIONS.
HENCE, I MAY OSE NTROL THE OISE OM AKE
MR-MMM.
MRM.
SHAKE SHAKE SHAKE
ぶるぶるぶる
R- REALLY?
THEN WHY DON'T YOU REST YOUR VOICE?
SHAKE SHAKE SHAKE SHAKE
ぶるぶるぶるぶる
PROBABLY BETTER NOT TO ASK WHY SHE'S SHAKING.

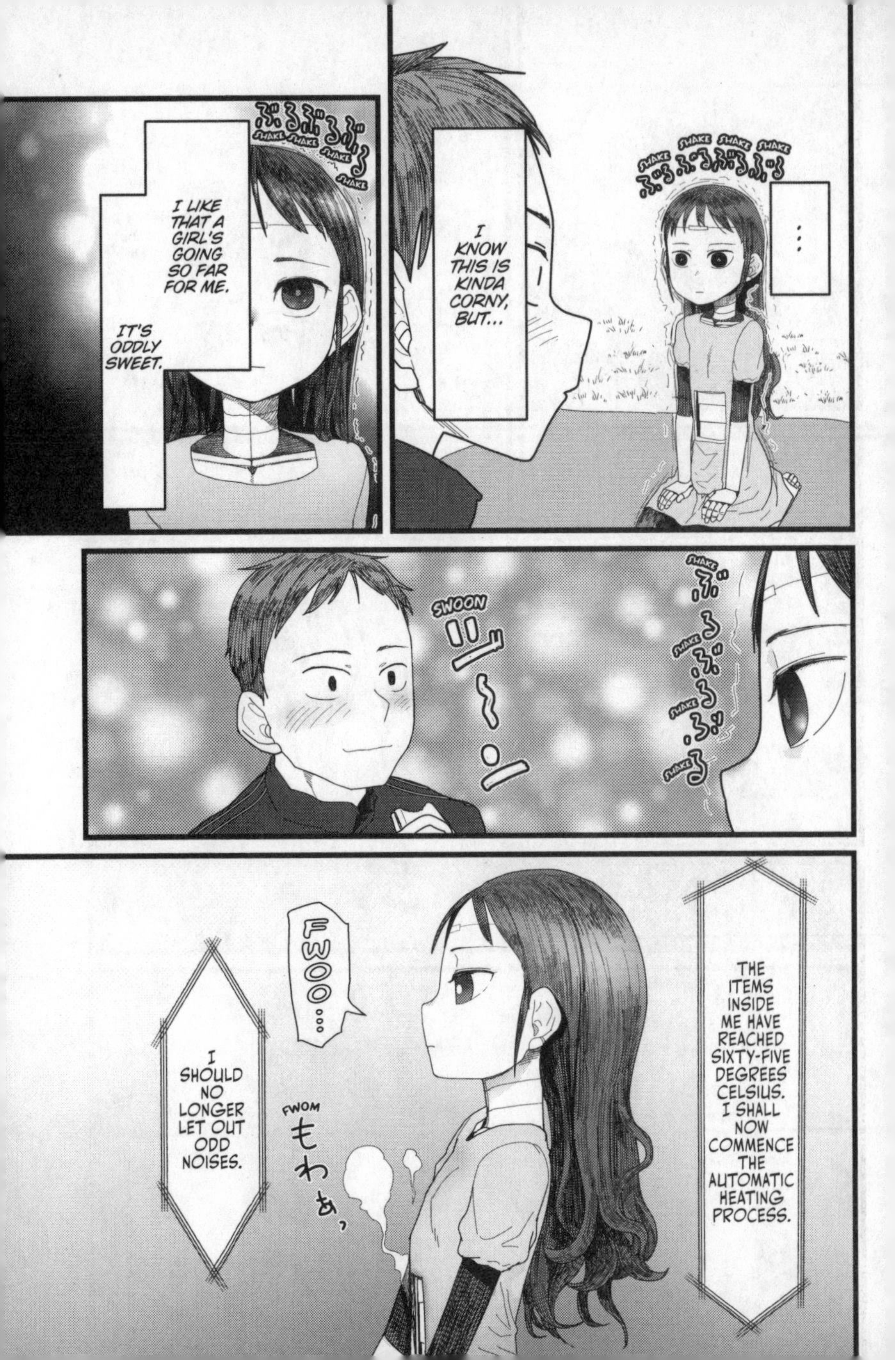

SHAKE SHAKE SHAKE SHAKE
ぶるぶるぶるぶる
...
I KNOW THIS IS KINDA CORNY, BUT...
ぶるぶるぶる
SHAKE SHAKE SHAKE SHAKE
I LIKE THAT A GIRL'S GOING SO FAR FOR ME.
IT'S ODDLY SWEET.
SHAKE SHAKE SHAKE SHAKE
ぶるぶるぶるぶる
SWOON
ジ~ン
THE ITEMS INSIDE ME HAVE REACHED SIXTY-FIVE DEGREES CELSIUS. I SHALL NOW COMMENCE THE AUTOMATIC HEATING PROCESS.
FWOO...
FWOM
もわぁ
I SHOULD NO LONGER LET OUT ODD NOISES.

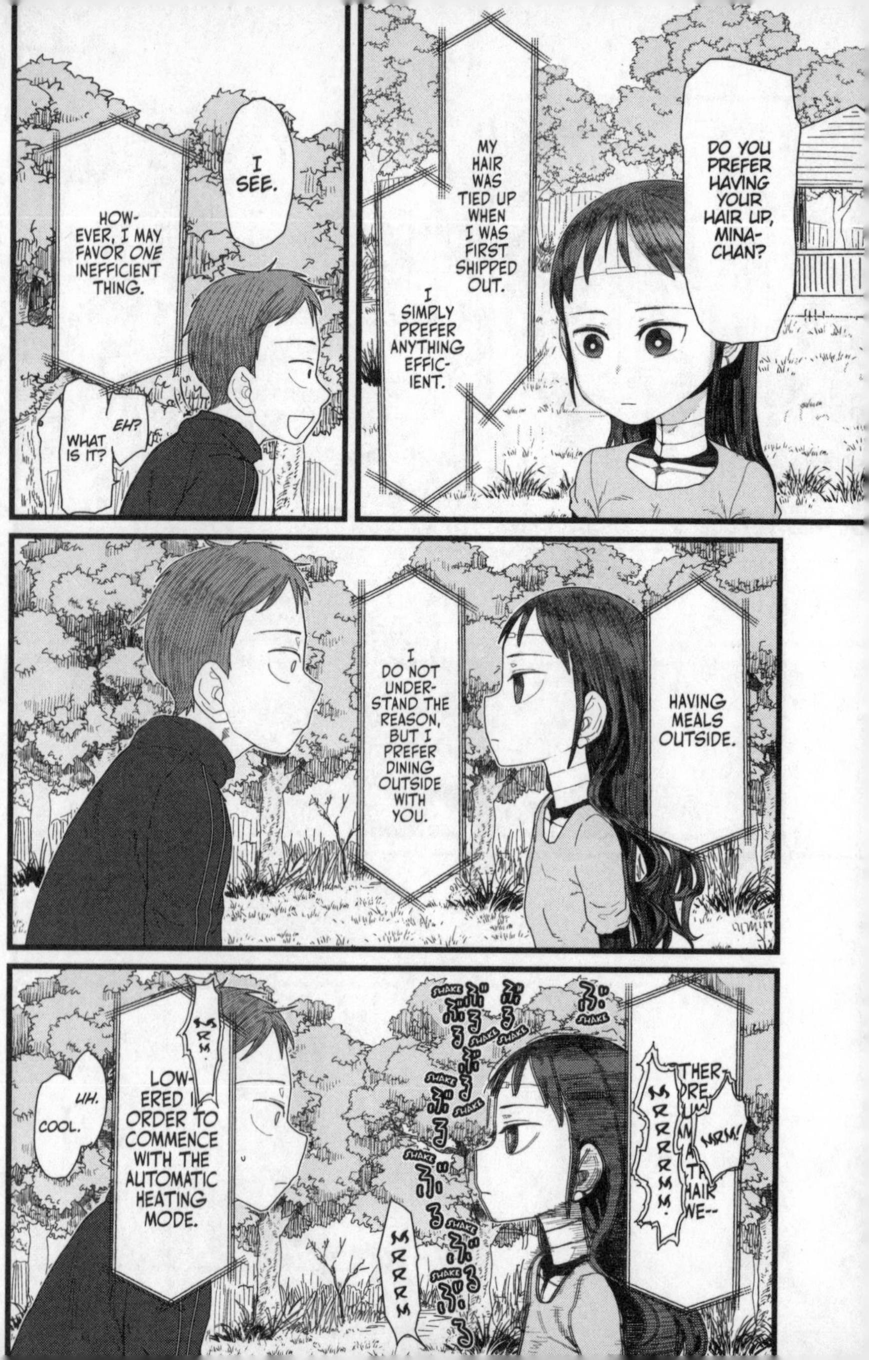
DO YOU PREFER HAVING YOUR HAIR UP, MINA-CHAN?
MY HAIR WAS TIED UP WHEN I WAS FIRST SHIPPED OUT.
I SIMPLY PREFER ANYTHING EFFICIENT.
I SEE.
HOW-EVER, I MAY FAVOR *ONE* INEFFICIENT THING.
EH?
WHAT IS IT?
HAVING MEALS OUTSIDE.
I DO NOT UNDER-STAND THE REASON, BUT I PREFER DINING OUTSIDE WITH YOU.
THER-
HAIR
WE--
MRRRRMM.
MRM!
ぶる SHAKE
MRRRM
MRM.
LOW-ERED I ORDER TO COMMENCE WITH THE AUTOMATIC HEATING MODE.
UH.
COOL.

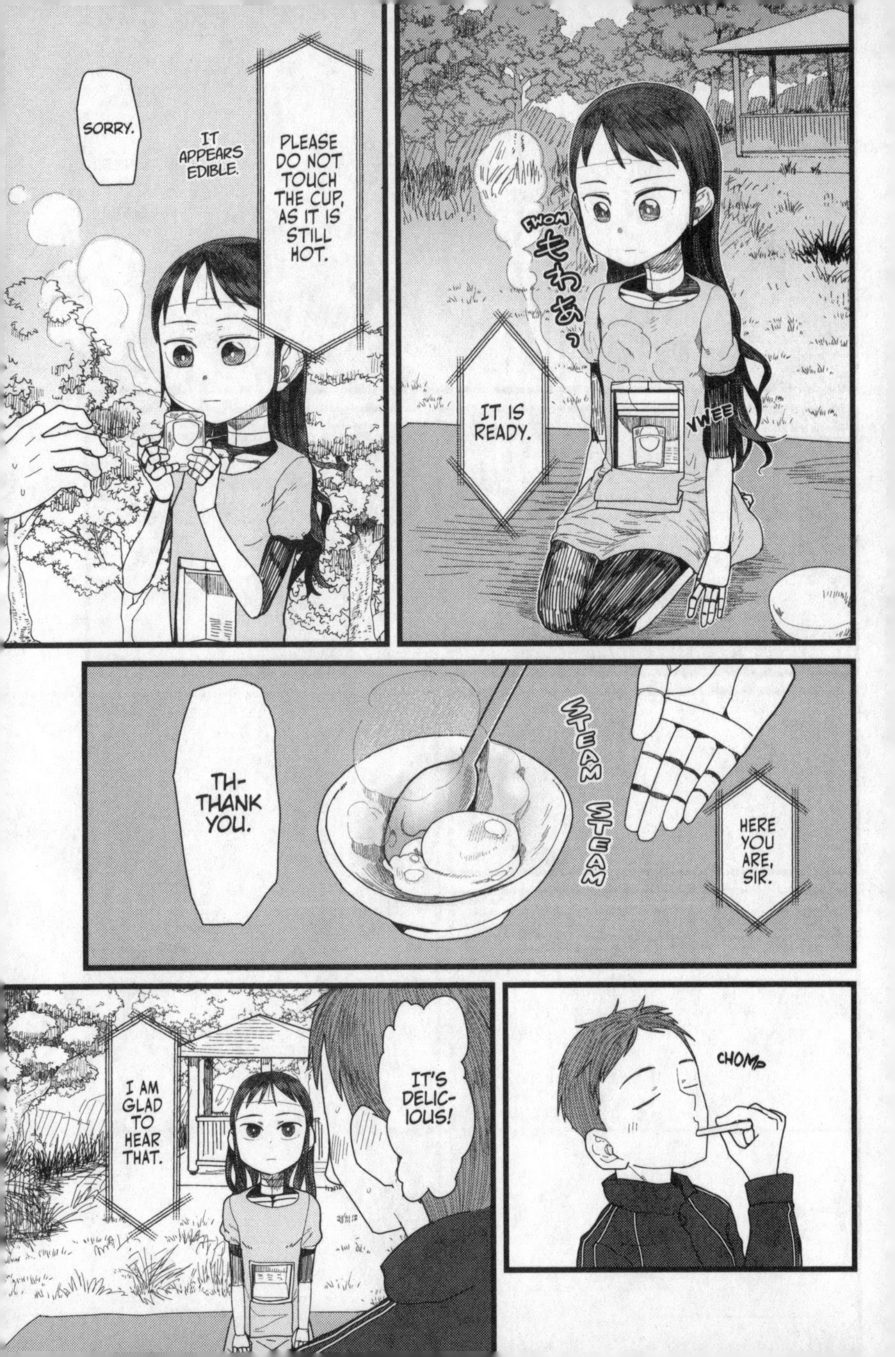
FWOM
もわぁっ
VWEE
IT IS READY.
PLEASE DO NOT TOUCH THE CUP, AS IT IS STILL HOT.
IT APPEARS EDIBLE.
SORRY.
HERE YOU ARE, SIR.
STEAM STEAM
TH-THANK YOU.
CHOMP
IT'S DELICIOUS!
I AM GLAD TO HEAR THAT.

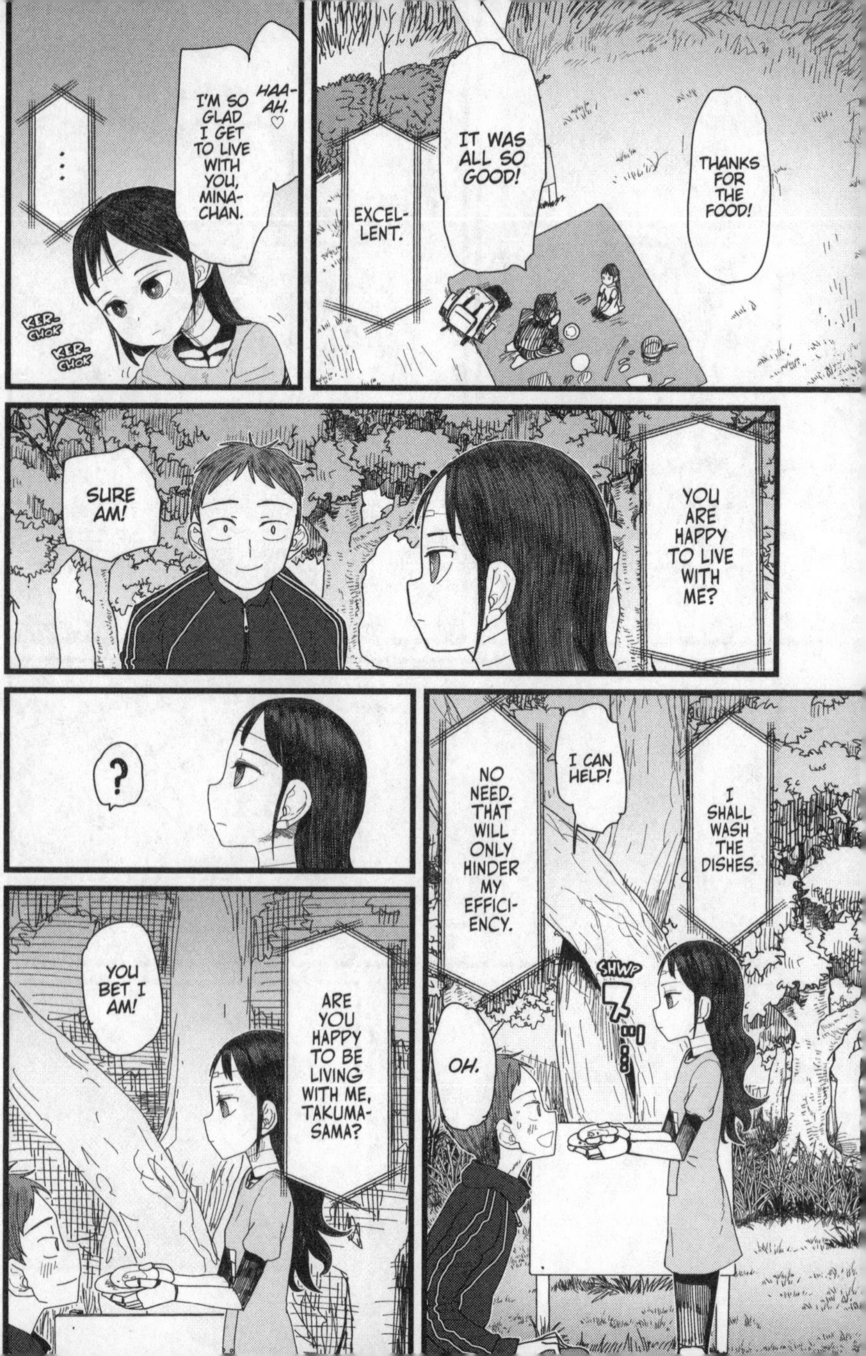
THANKS FOR THE FOOD!
IT WAS ALL SO GOOD!
EXCEL-LENT.
HAAA-AH. ♡
I'M SO GLAD I GET TO LIVE WITH YOU, MINA-CHAN.
...
KER-CHOK
KER-CHOK
YOU ARE HAPPY TO LIVE WITH ME?
SURE AM!
I SHALL WASH THE DISHES.
I CAN HELP!
NO NEED. THAT WILL ONLY HINDER MY EFFICI-ENCY.
SHWP
OH.
?
ARE YOU HAPPY TO BE LIVING WITH ME, TAKUMA-SAMA?
YOU BET I AM!

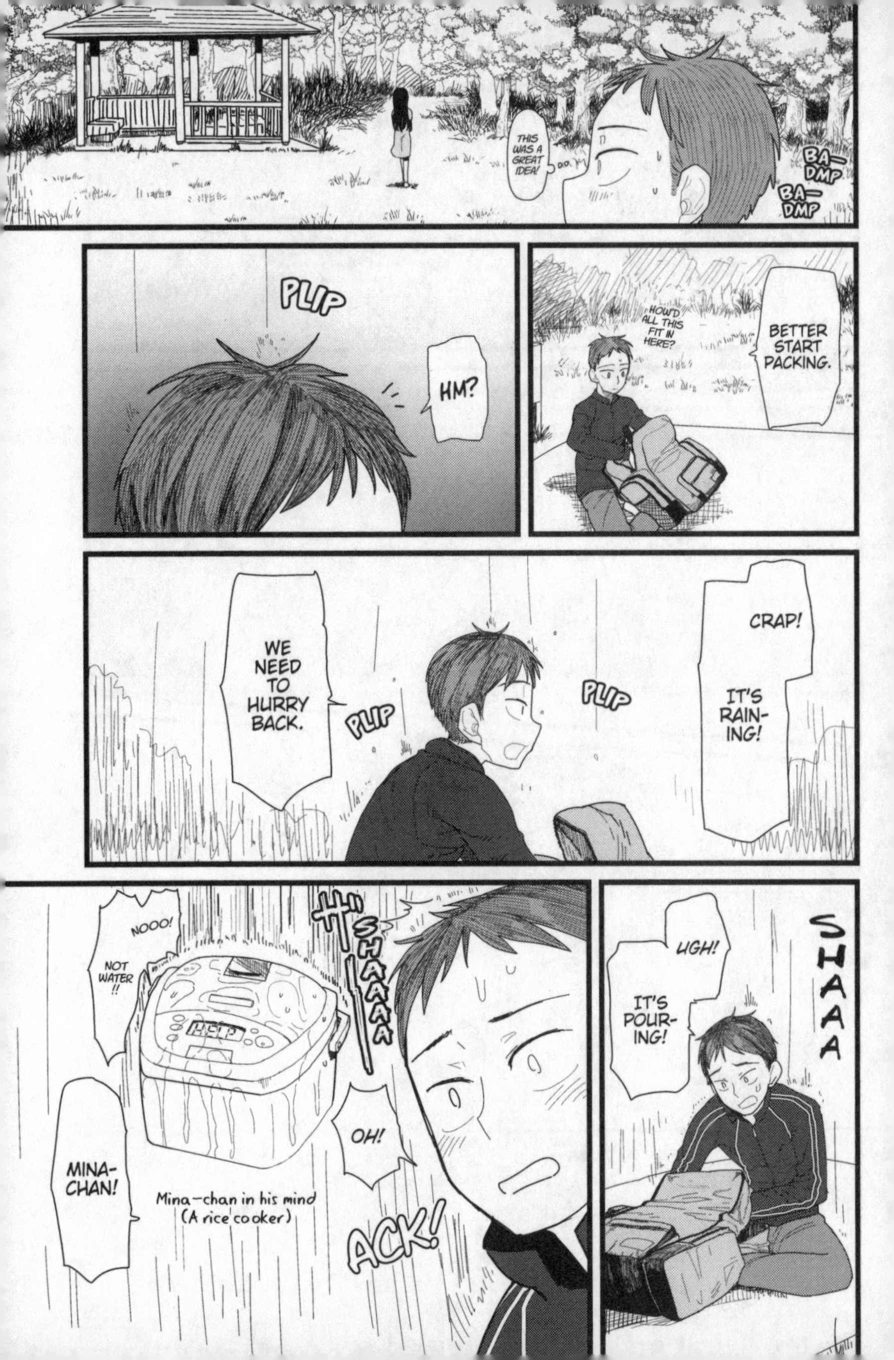
THIS WAS A GREAT IDEA!
BA-DMP
BA-DMP
BETTER START PACKING.
HOW'D ALL THIS FIT IN HERE?
PLIP
HM?
CRAP!
IT'S RAINING!
PLIP
PLIP
WE NEED TO HURRY BACK.
SHAAA
UGH!
IT'S POURING!
SHAAAAA
OH!
ACK!
NOOO!
NOT WATER!!
HELP
MINA-CHAN!
Mina-chan in his mind
(A rice cooker)

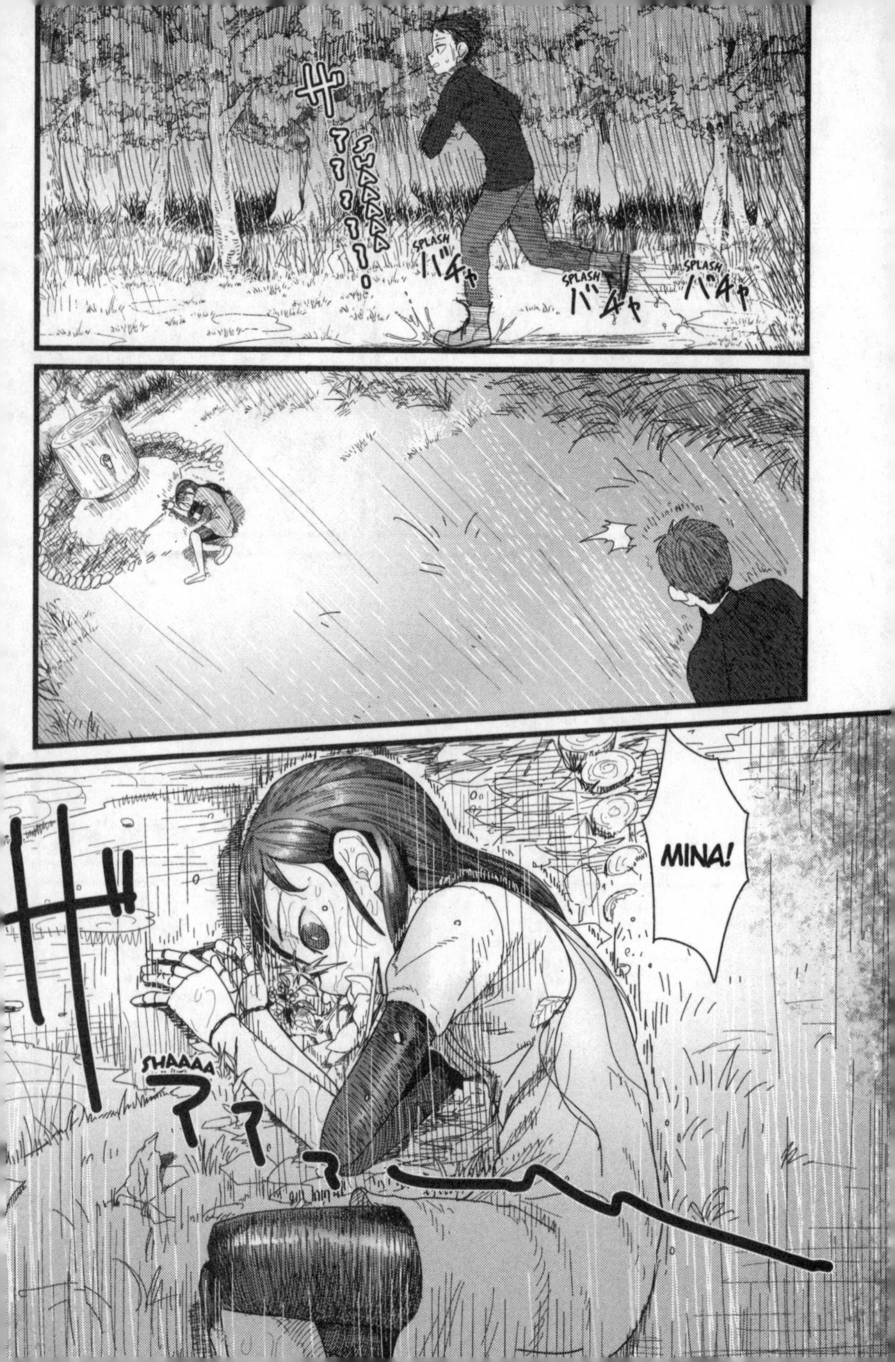
SPLASH
SPLASH
SHAAAAAA
SPLASH
MINA!
SHAAAA

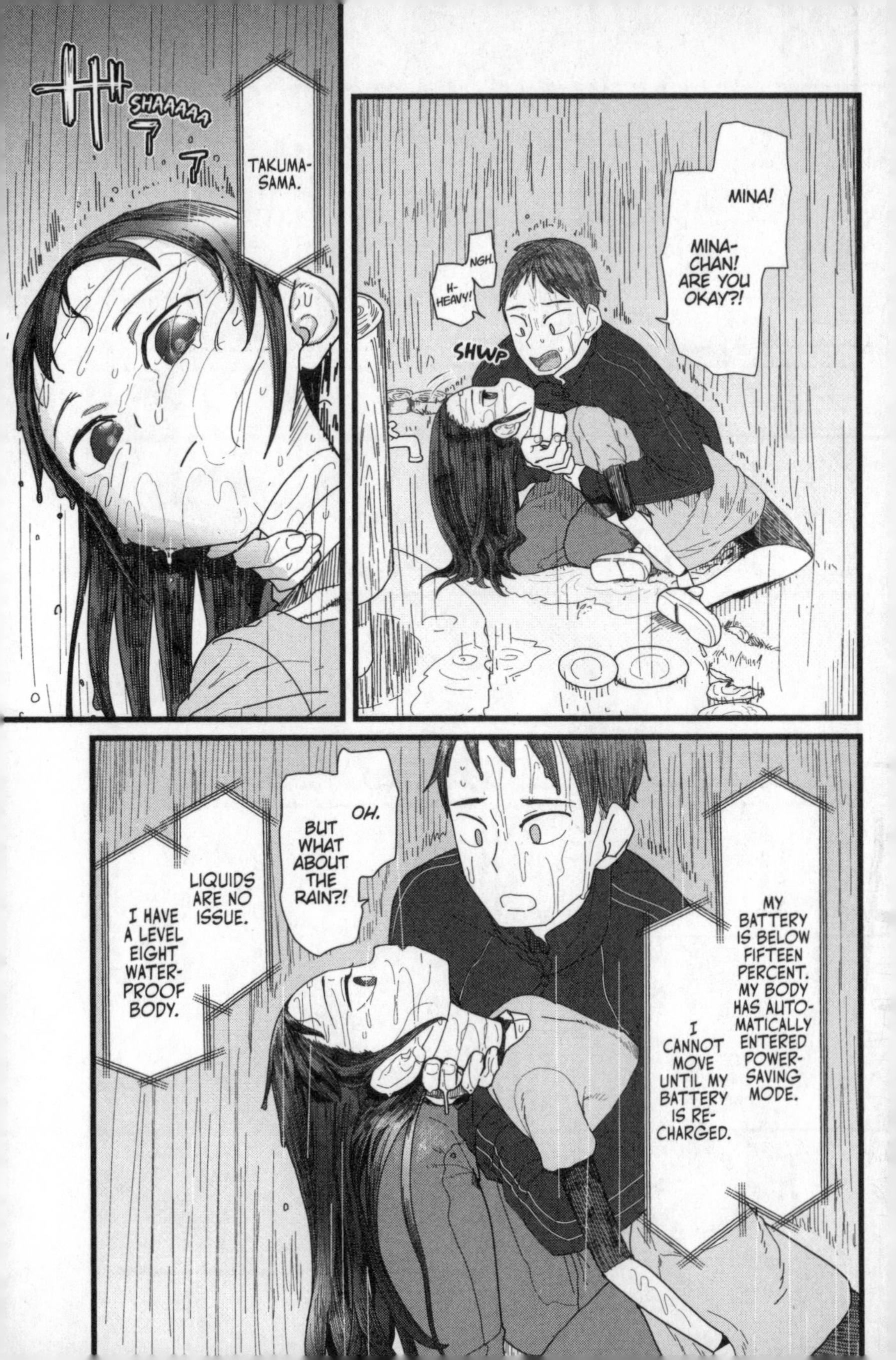
MINA!
MINA-CHAN! ARE YOU OKAY?!
SHWP
NGH.
H-HEAVY!
SHAAAAA
TAKUMA-SAMA.
MY BATTERY IS BELOW FIFTEEN PERCENT. MY BODY HAS AUTOMATICALLY ENTERED POWER-SAVING MODE.
I CANNOT MOVE UNTIL MY BATTERY IS RE-CHARGED.
OH.
BUT WHAT ABOUT THE RAIN?!
LIQUIDS ARE NO ISSUE.
I HAVE A LEVEL EIGHT WATER-PROOF BODY.

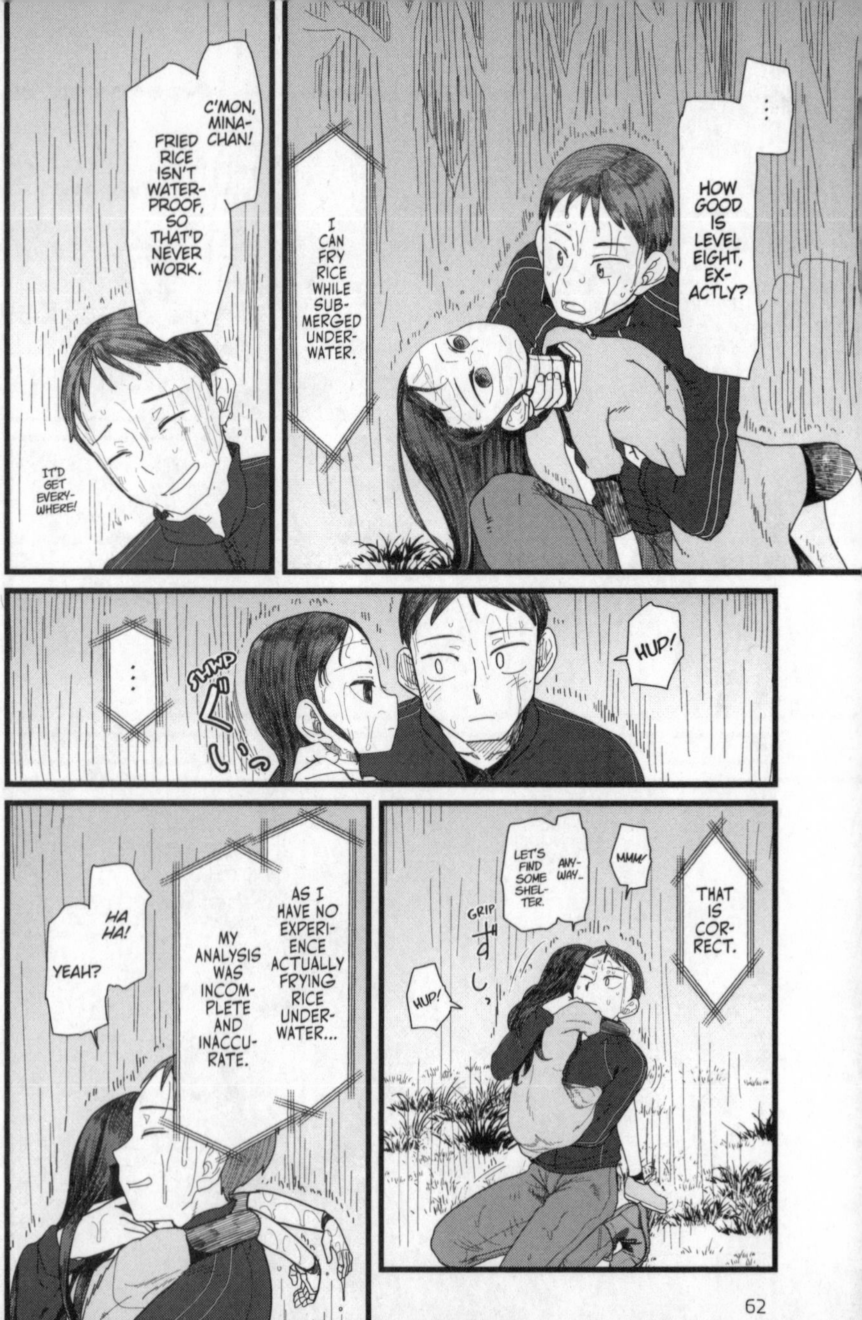

...
HOW GOOD IS LEVEL EIGHT, EXACTLY?
I CAN FRY RICE WHILE SUBMERGED UNDERWATER.
C'MON, MINA-CHAN! FRIED RICE ISN'T WATERPROOF, SO THAT'D NEVER WORK.
IT'D GET EVERYWHERE!
HUP!
SLWMP
...
THAT IS CORRECT.
MMM!
ANYWAY... LET'S FIND SOME SHELTER.
GRIP
HUP!
AS I HAVE NO EXPERIENCE ACTUALLY FRYING RICE UNDERWATER...
MY ANALYSIS WAS INCOMPLETE AND INACCURATE.
HA HA! YEAH?

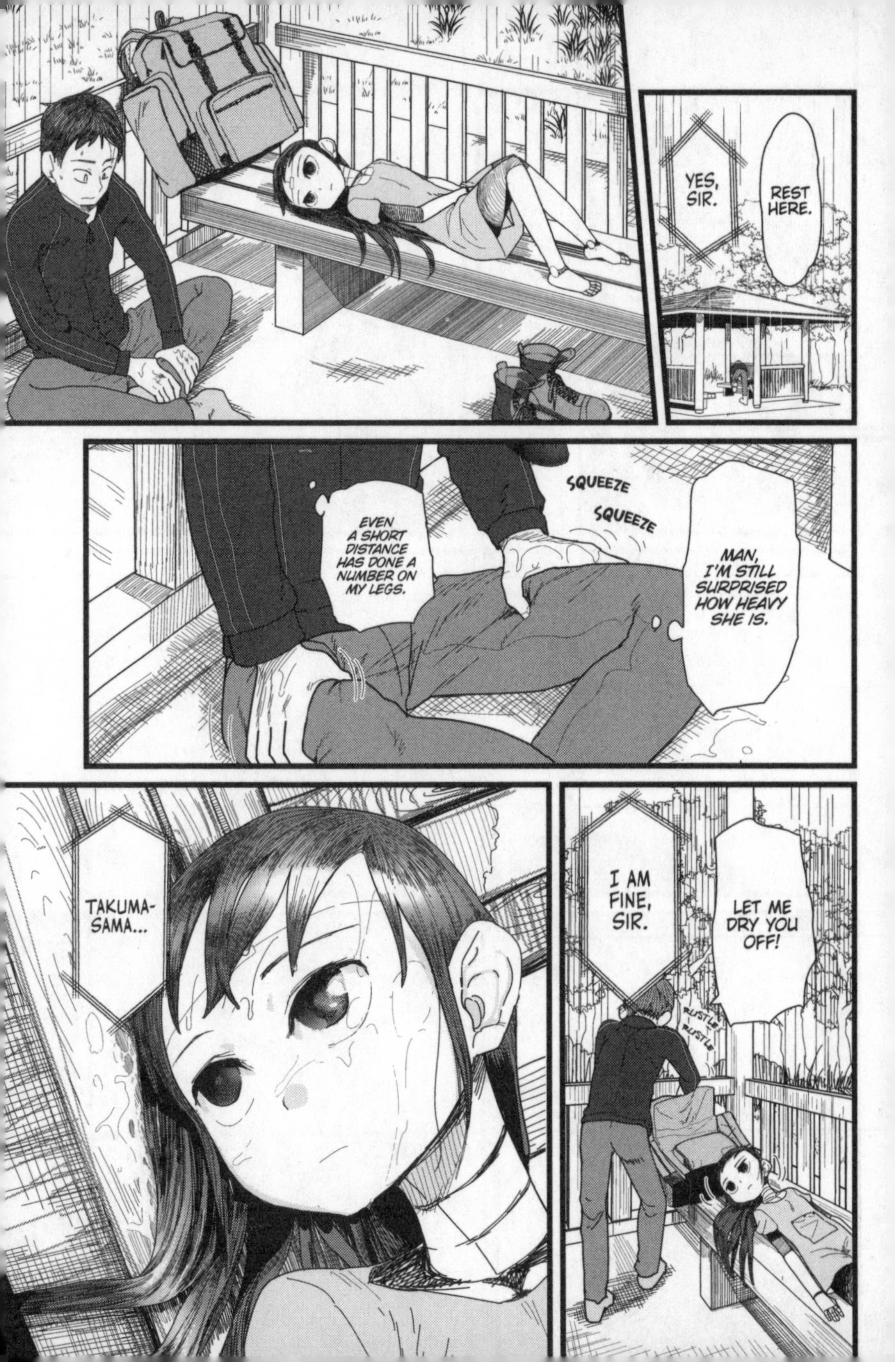
REST HERE.
YES, SIR.
MAN, I'M STILL SURPRISED HOW HEAVY SHE IS.
SQUEEZE
SQUEEZE
EVEN A SHORT DISTANCE HAS DONE A NUMBER ON MY LEGS.
LET ME DRY YOU OFF!
RUSTLE
RUSTLE
I AM FINE, SIR.
TAKUMA-SAMA...

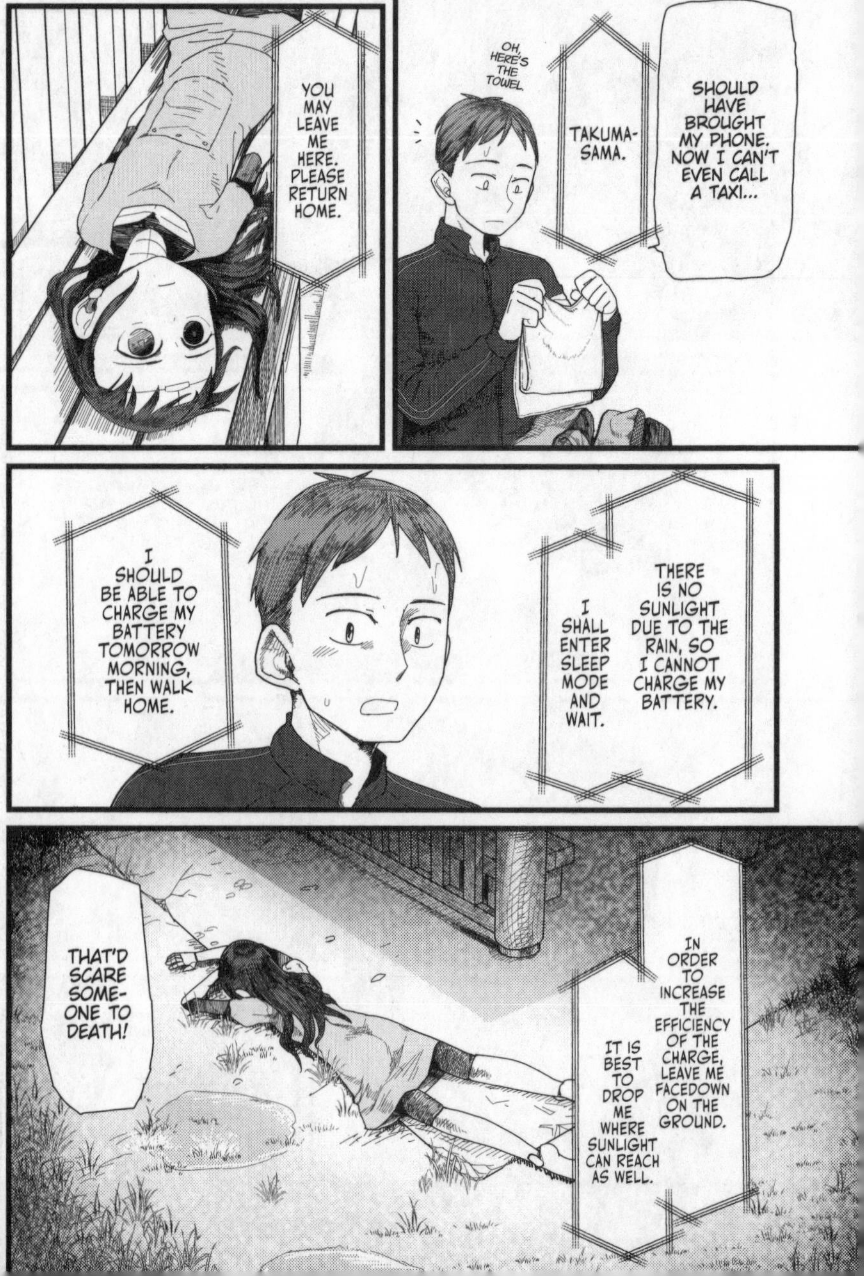

SHOULD HAVE BROUGHT MY PHONE. NOW I CAN'T EVEN CALL A TAXI...
TAKUMA-SAMA.
OH, HERE'S THE TOWEL.
YOU MAY LEAVE ME HERE. PLEASE RETURN HOME.
THERE IS NO SUNLIGHT DUE TO THE RAIN, SO I CANNOT CHARGE MY BATTERY.
I SHALL ENTER SLEEP MODE AND WAIT.
I SHOULD BE ABLE TO CHARGE MY BATTERY TOMORROW MORNING, THEN WALK HOME.
IN ORDER TO INCREASE THE EFFICIENCY OF THE CHARGE, LEAVE ME FACEDOWN ON THE GROUND.
IT IS BEST TO DROP ME WHERE SUNLIGHT CAN REACH AS WELL.
THAT'D SCARE SOME-ONE TO DEATH!

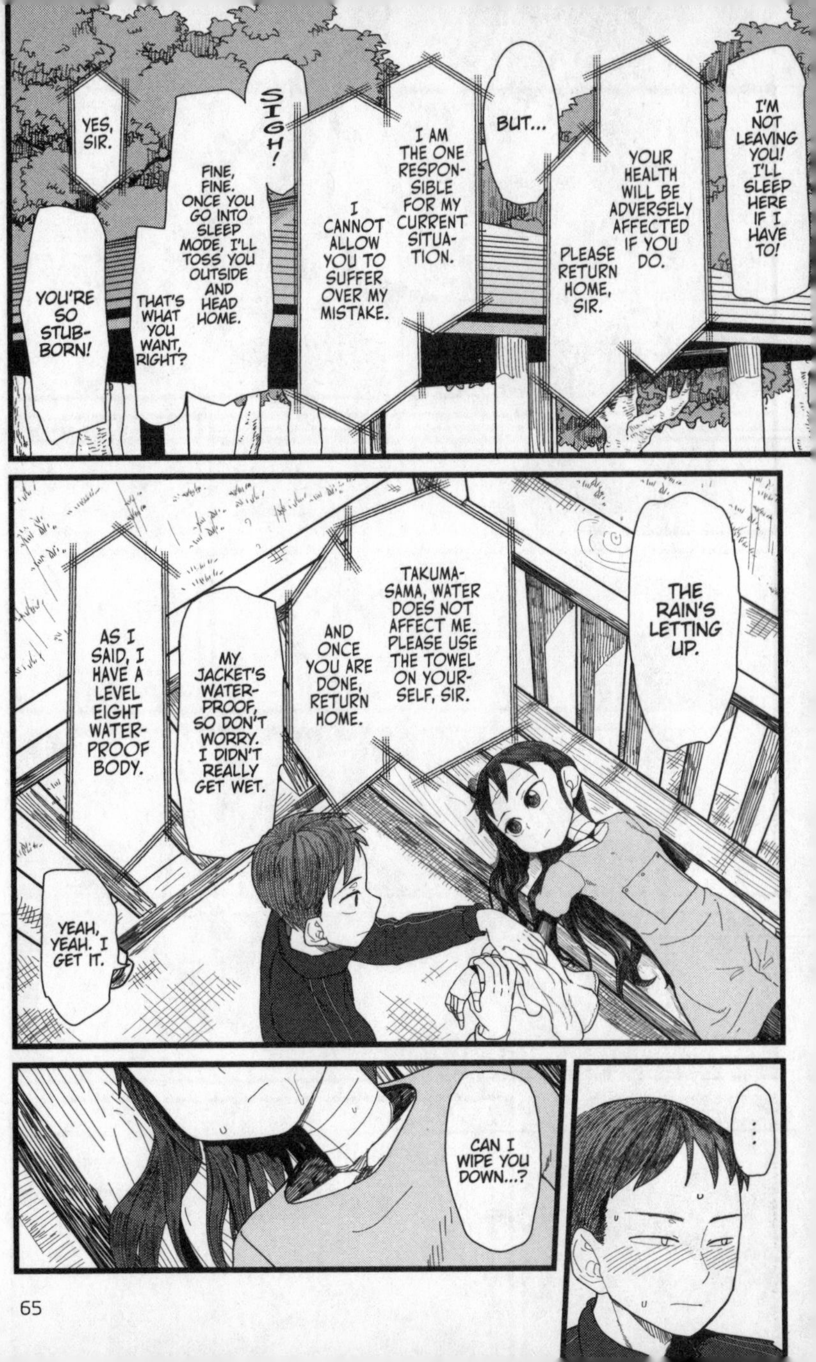

I'M NOT LEAVING YOU! I'LL SLEEP HERE IF I HAVE TO!
YOUR HEALTH WILL BE ADVERSELY AFFECTED IF YOU DO.
PLEASE RETURN HOME, SIR.
BUT...
I AM THE ONE RESPONSIBLE FOR MY CURRENT SITUATION.
I CANNOT ALLOW YOU TO SUFFER OVER MY MISTAKE.
SIGH!
FINE, FINE. ONCE YOU GO INTO SLEEP MODE, I'LL TOSS YOU OUTSIDE AND HEAD HOME.
THAT'S WHAT YOU WANT, RIGHT?
YES, SIR.
YOU'RE SO STUBBORN!
THE RAIN'S LETTING UP.
TAKUMA-SAMA, WATER DOES NOT AFFECT ME. PLEASE USE THE TOWEL ON YOURSELF, SIR.
AND ONCE YOU ARE DONE, RETURN HOME.
MY JACKET'S WATERPROOF, SO DON'T WORRY. I DIDN'T REALLY GET WET.
AS I SAID, I HAVE A LEVEL EIGHT WATERPROOF BODY.
YEAH, YEAH. I GET IT.
...
CAN I WIPE YOU DOWN...?

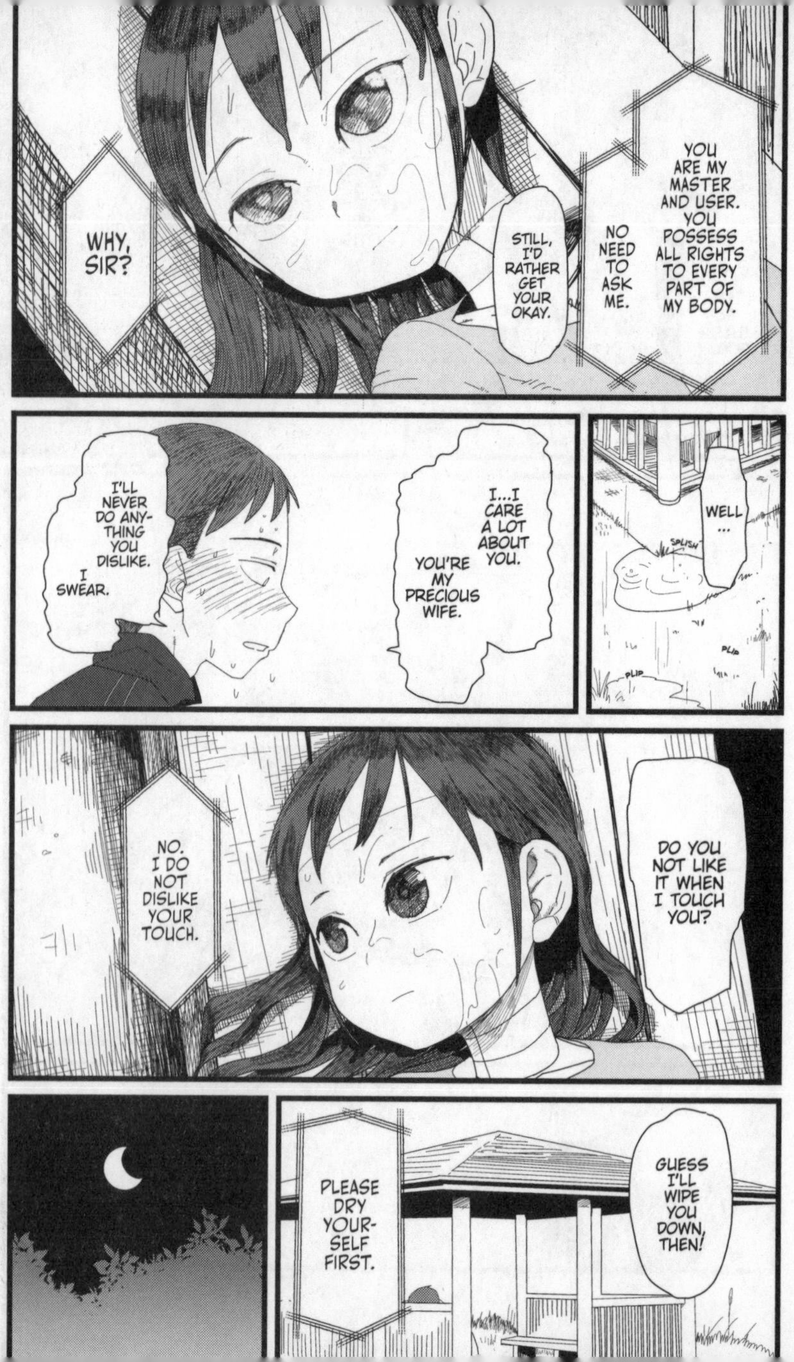
YOU ARE MY MASTER AND USER. YOU POSSESS ALL RIGHTS TO EVERY PART OF MY BODY.
NO NEED TO ASK ME.
STILL, I'D RATHER GET YOUR OKAY.
WHY, SIR?
WELL ...
SPLISH
PLIP
PLIP
I...I CARE A LOT ABOUT YOU.
YOU'RE MY PRECIOUS WIFE.
I'LL NEVER DO ANY-THING YOU DISLIKE.
I SWEAR.
DO YOU NOT LIKE IT WHEN I TOUCH YOU?
NO. I DO NOT DISLIKE YOUR TOUCH.
GUESS I'LL WIPE YOU DOWN, THEN!
PLEASE DRY YOUR-SELF FIRST.

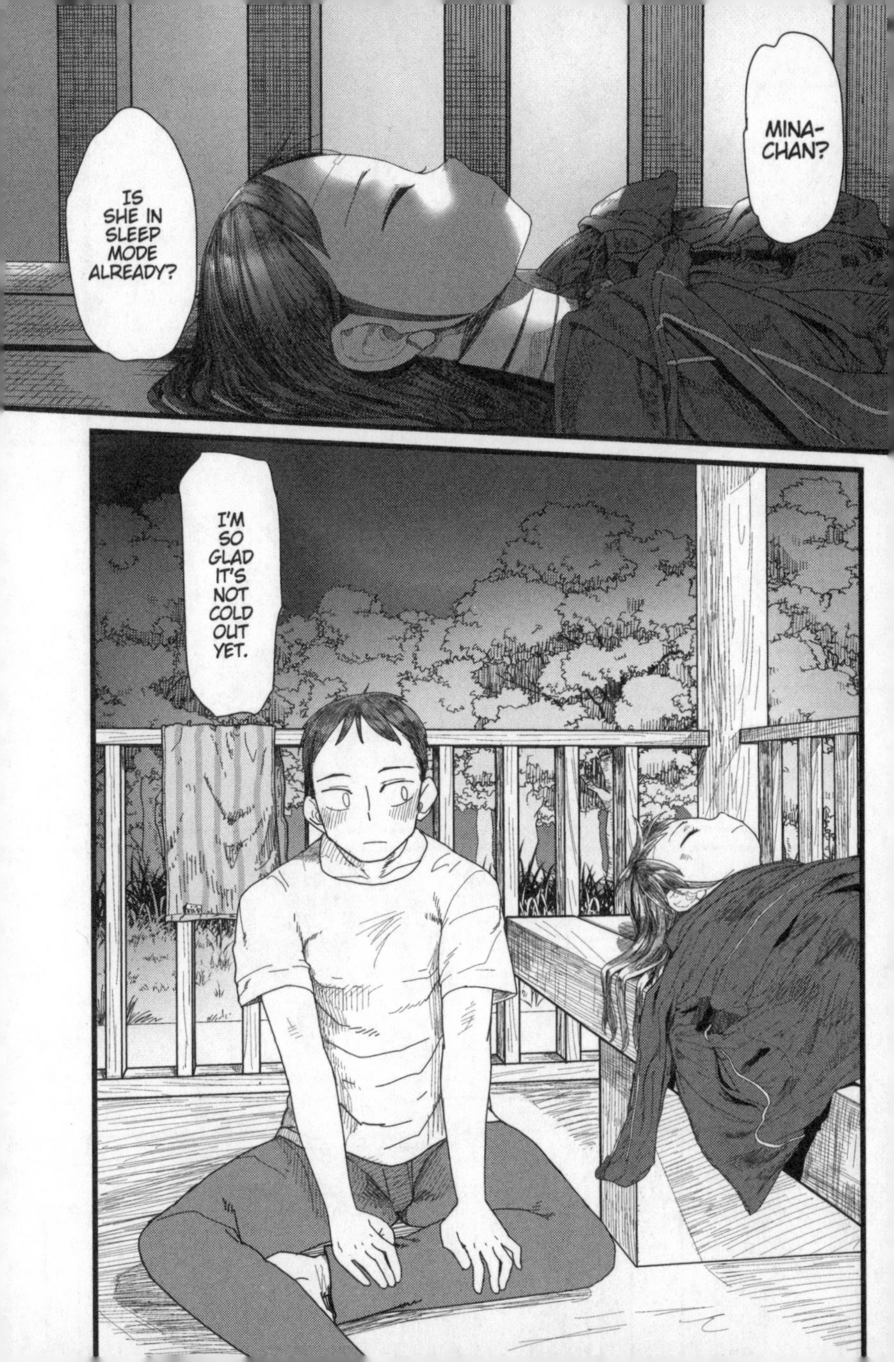
MINA-CHAN?
IS SHE IN SLEEP MODE ALREADY?
I'M SO GLAD IT'S NOT COLD OUT YET.

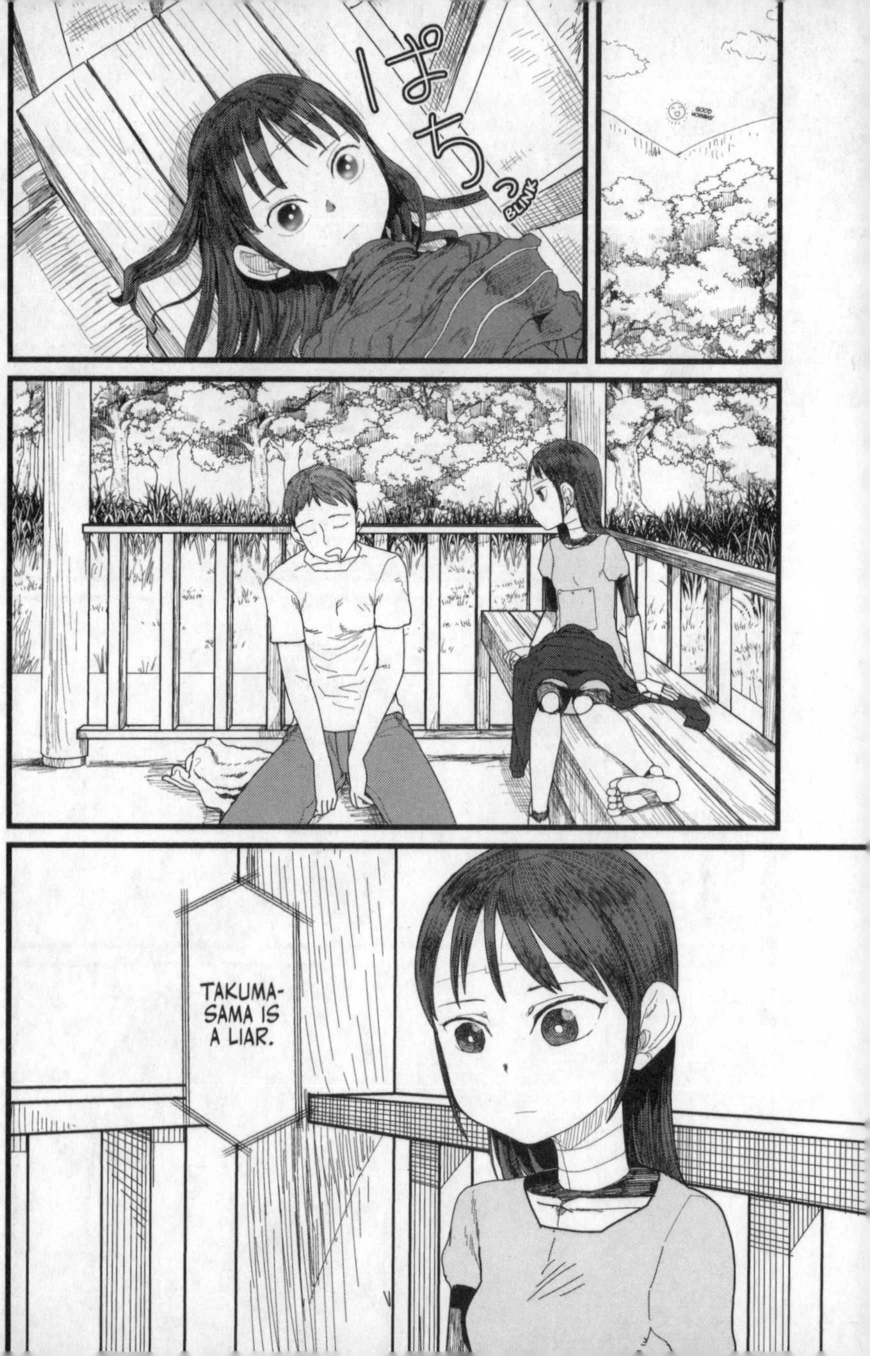
GOOD MORNING!
ぱちっ
BLINK
TAKUMA-SAMA IS A LIAR.

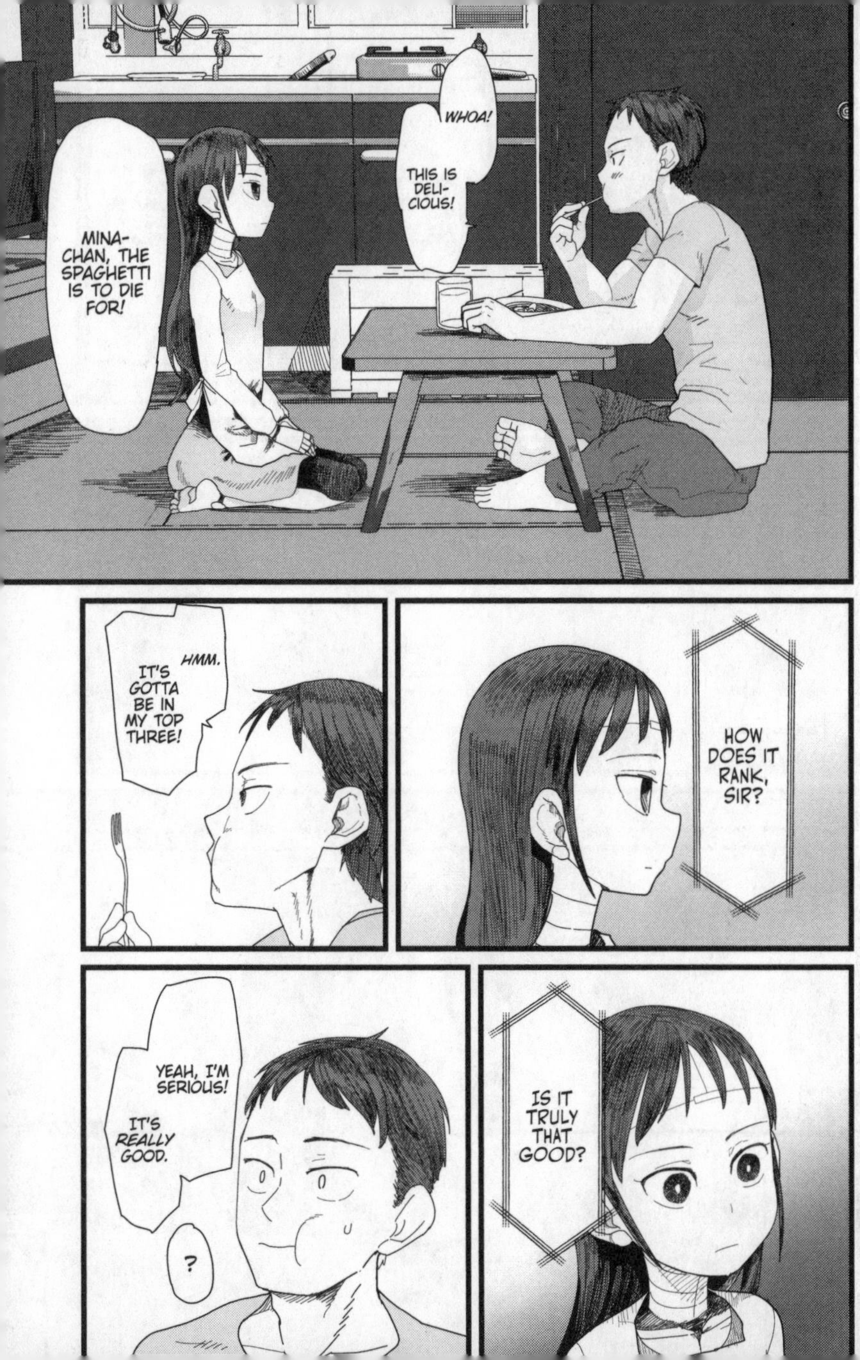
WHOA!
THIS IS DELI-CIOUS!
MINA-CHAN, THE SPAGHETTI IS TO DIE FOR!
HOW DOES IT RANK, SIR?
HMM. IT'S GOTTA BE IN MY TOP THREE!
IS IT TRULY THAT GOOD?
YEAH, I'M SERIOUS!
IT'S *REALLY* GOOD.
?

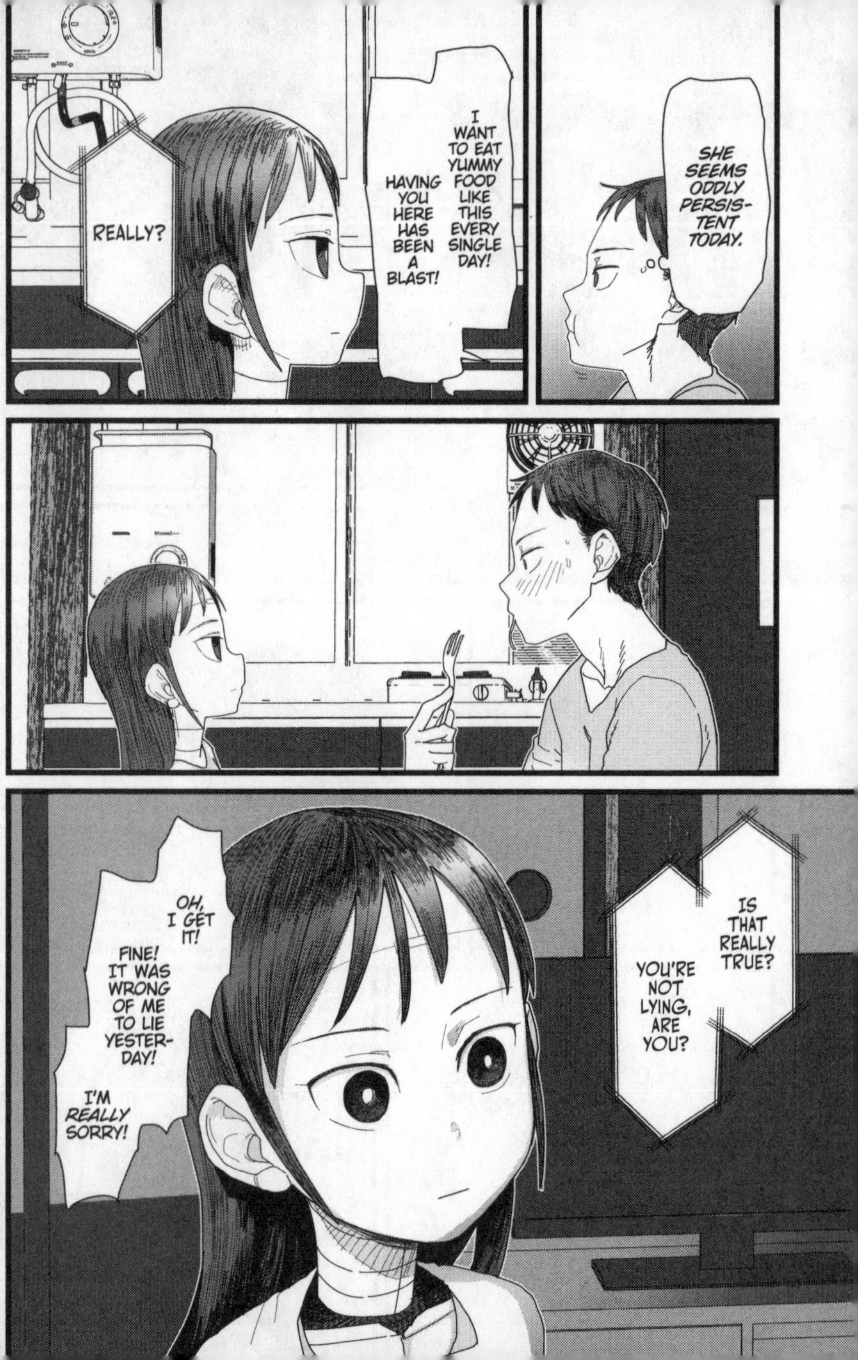
SHE SEEMS ODDLY PERSIS-TENT TODAY.
I WANT TO EAT YUMMY FOOD LIKE THIS EVERY SINGLE DAY!
HAVING YOU HERE HAS BEEN A BLAST!
REALLY?
IS THAT REALLY TRUE?
YOU'RE NOT LYING, ARE YOU?
OH, I GET IT!
FINE! IT WAS WRONG OF ME TO LIE YESTER-DAY!
I'M *REALLY* SORRY!

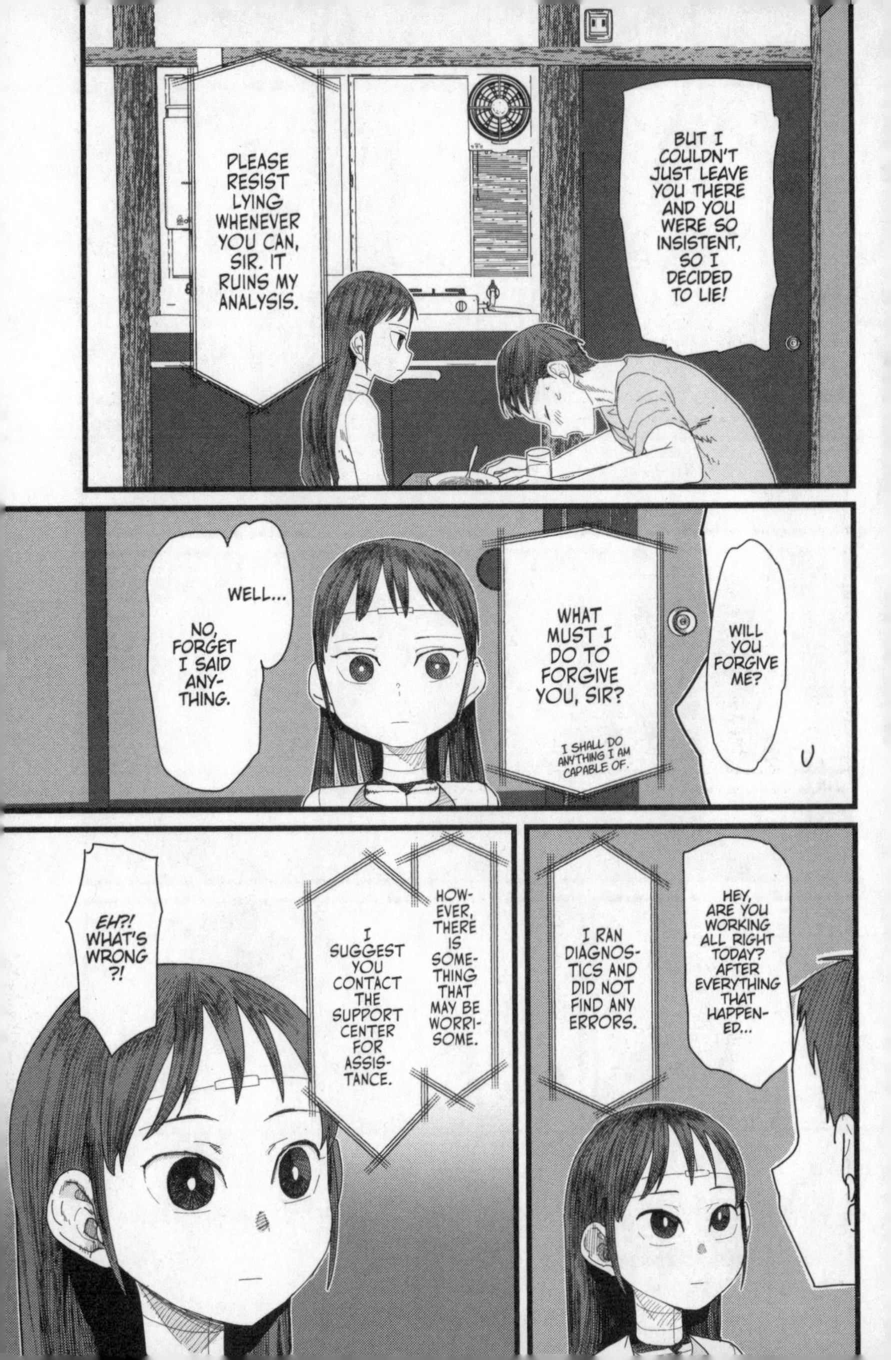
BUT I COULDN'T JUST LEAVE YOU THERE AND YOU WERE SO INSISTENT, SO I DECIDED TO LIE!
PLEASE RESIST LYING WHENEVER YOU CAN, SIR. IT RUINS MY ANALYSIS.
WILL YOU FORGIVE ME?
WHAT MUST I DO TO FORGIVE YOU, SIR?
I SHALL DO ANYTHING I AM CAPABLE OF.
WELL...
NO, FORGET I SAID ANYTHING.
HEY, ARE YOU WORKING ALL RIGHT TODAY? AFTER EVERYTHING THAT HAPPENED...
I RAN DIAGNOSTICS AND DID NOT FIND ANY ERRORS.
HOWEVER, THERE IS SOMETHING THAT MAY BE WORRISOME.
I SUGGEST YOU CONTACT THE SUPPORT CENTER FOR ASSISTANCE.
EH?! WHAT'S WRONG?!

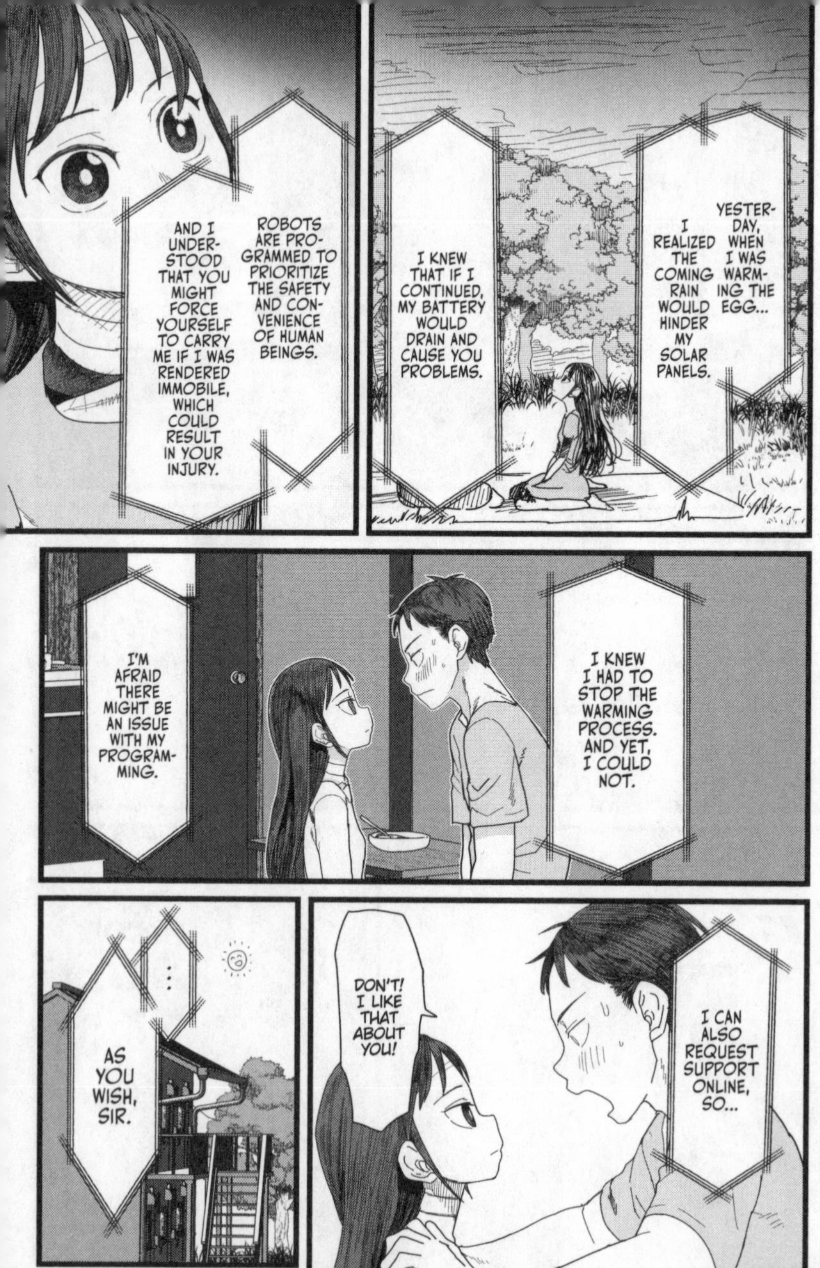
YESTERDAY, WHEN I WAS WARMING THE EGG...
I REALIZED THE COMING RAIN WOULD HINDER MY SOLAR PANELS.
I KNEW THAT IF I CONTINUED, MY BATTERY WOULD DRAIN AND CAUSE YOU PROBLEMS.
ROBOTS ARE PROGRAMMED TO PRIORITIZE THE SAFETY AND CONVENIENCE OF HUMAN BEINGS.
AND I UNDERSTOOD THAT YOU MIGHT FORCE YOURSELF TO CARRY ME IF I WAS RENDERED IMMOBILE, WHICH COULD RESULT IN YOUR INJURY.
I KNEW I HAD TO STOP THE WARMING PROCESS. AND YET, I COULD NOT.
I'M AFRAID THERE MIGHT BE AN ISSUE WITH MY PROGRAMMING.
I CAN ALSO REQUEST SUPPORT ONLINE, SO...
DON'T! I LIKE THAT ABOUT YOU!
...
AS YOU WISH, SIR.

➡ CHAPTER 2 END ♥

My
Wife Has No
Emotion

My Wife Has No Emotion

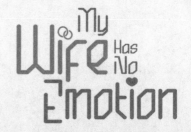

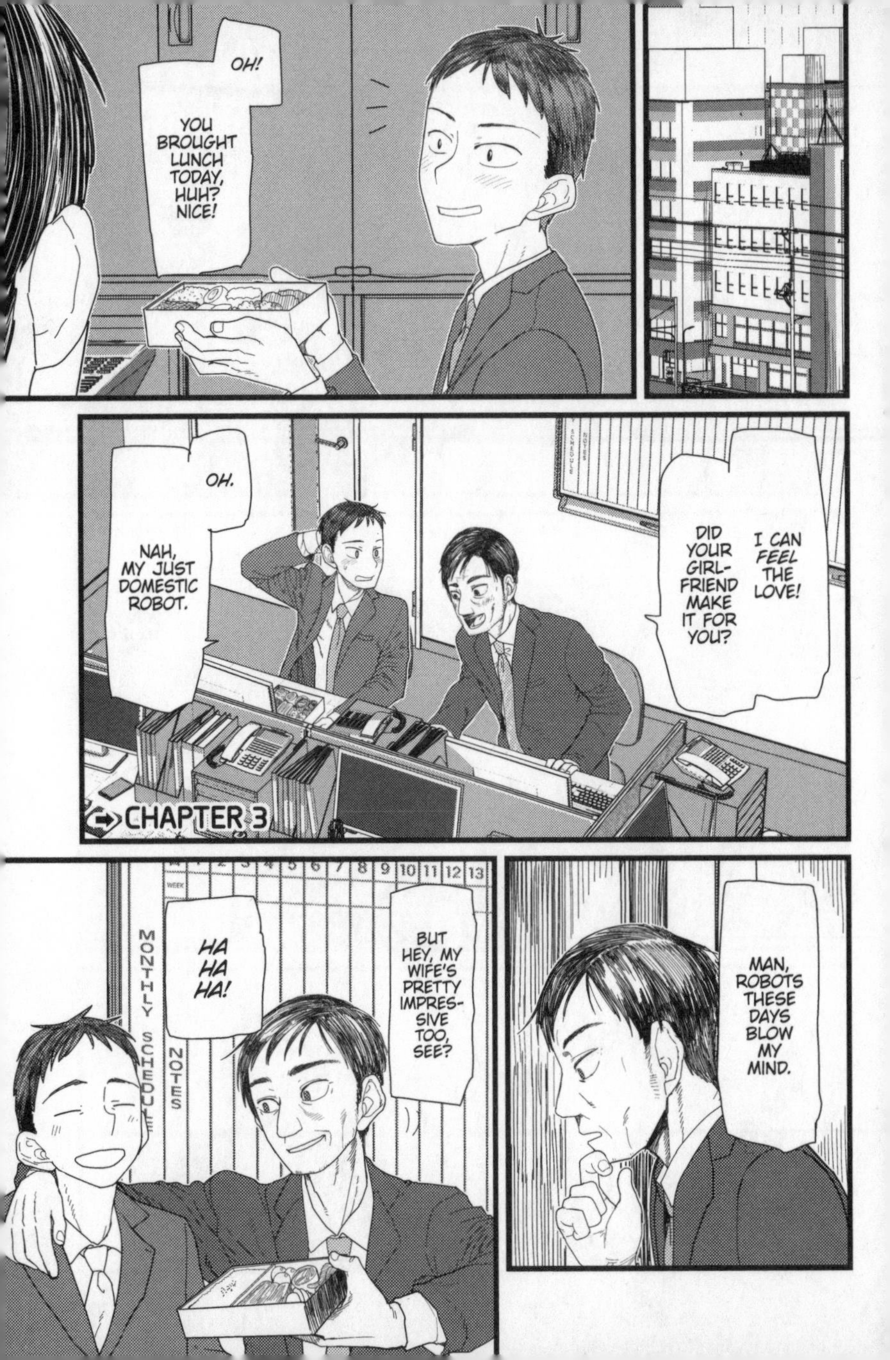
OH!
YOU BROUGHT LUNCH TODAY, HUH? NICE!
I CAN FEEL THE LOVE!
DID YOUR GIRL-FRIEND MAKE IT FOR YOU?
OH.
NAH, MY JUST DOMESTIC ROBOT.
CHAPTER 3
MAN, ROBOTS THESE DAYS BLOW MY MIND.
BUT HEY, MY WIFE'S PRETTY IMPRES-SIVE TOO, SEE?
HA HA HA!
MONTHLY SCHEDULE
NOTES

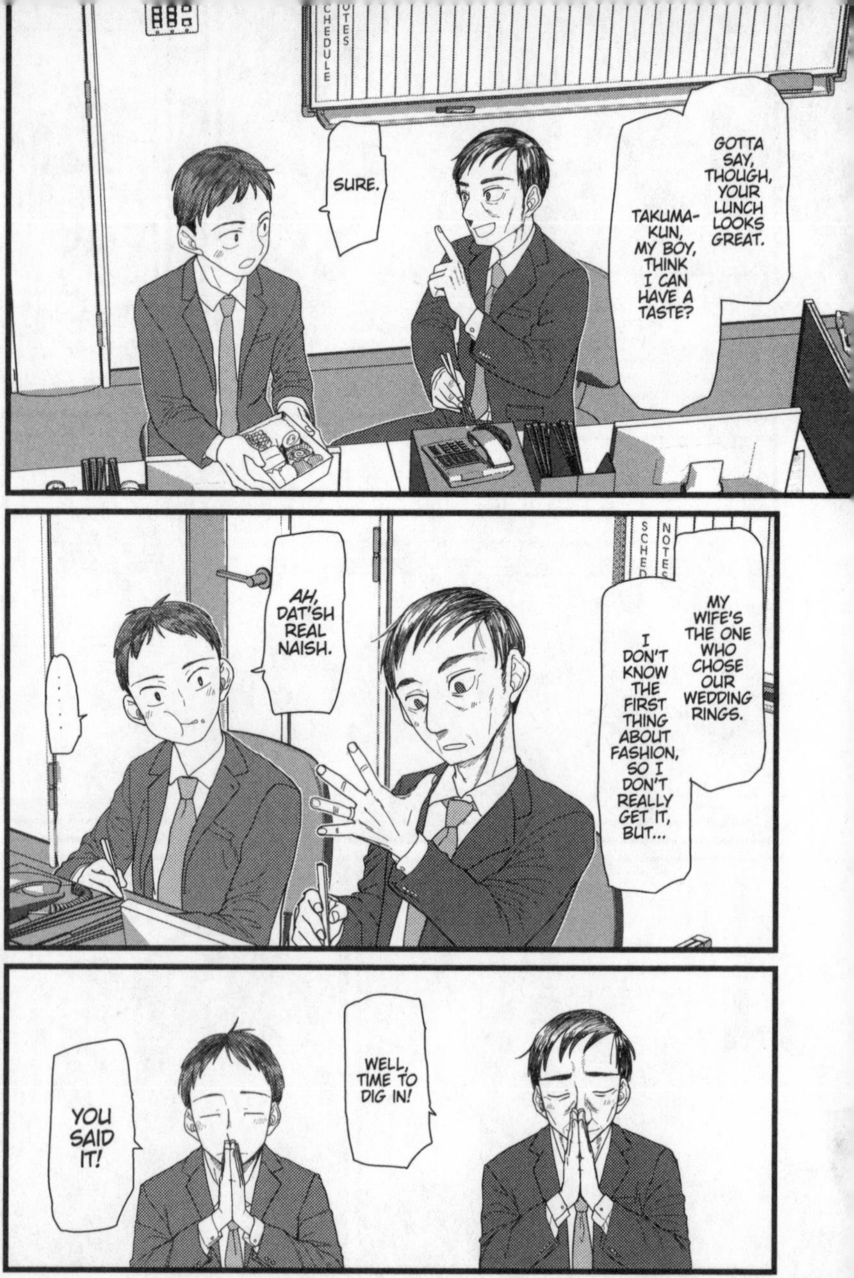
GOTTA SAY, THOUGH, YOUR LUNCH LOOKS GREAT.
TAKUMA-KUN, MY BOY, THINK I CAN HAVE A TASTE?
SURE.
MY WIFE'S THE ONE WHO CHOSE OUR WEDDING RINGS.
I DON'T KNOW THE FIRST THING ABOUT FASHION, SO I DON'T REALLY GET IT, BUT...
AH, DAT'SH REAL NAISH.
......
WELL, TIME TO DIG IN!
YOU SAID IT!

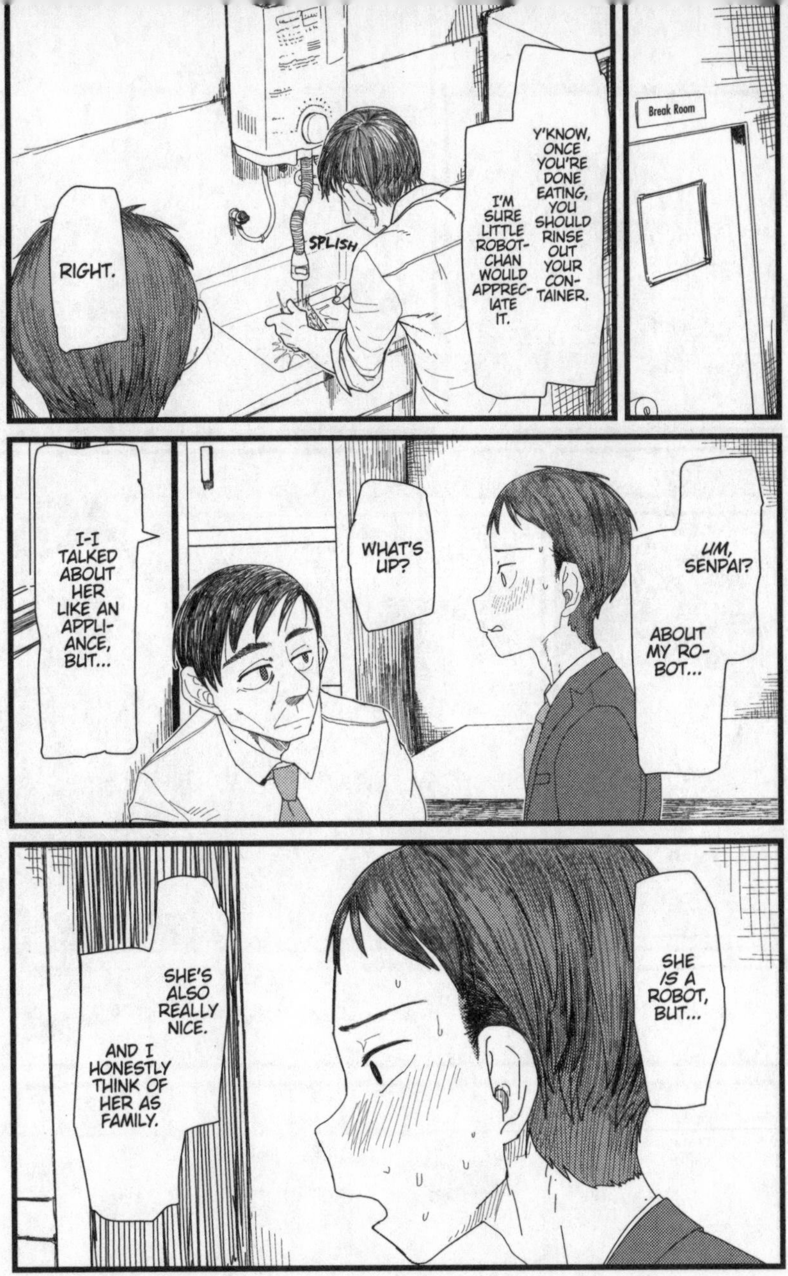
Break Room
Y'KNOW, ONCE YOU'RE DONE EATING, YOU SHOULD RINSE OUT YOUR CONTAINER.
I'M SURE LITTLE ROBOT-CHAN WOULD APPRECIATE IT.
SPLISH
RIGHT.
UM, SENPAI?
ABOUT MY ROBOT...
WHAT'S UP?
I-I TALKED ABOUT HER LIKE AN APPLIANCE, BUT...
SHE IS A ROBOT, BUT...
SHE'S ALSO REALLY NICE.
AND I HONESTLY THINK OF HER AS FAMILY.

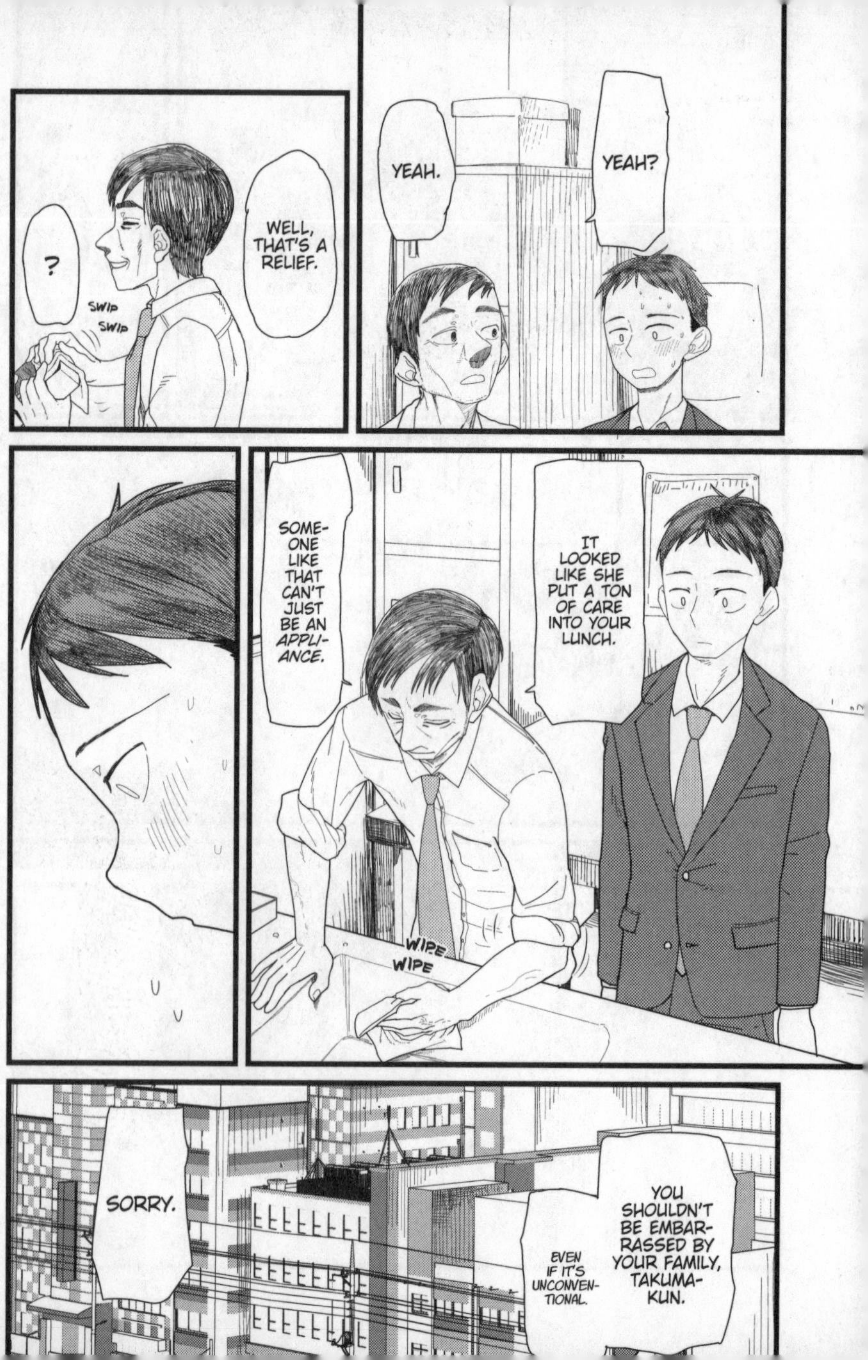
YEAH?
YEAH.
WELL, THAT'S A RELIEF.
?
SWIP SWIP
IT LOOKED LIKE SHE PUT A TON OF CARE INTO YOUR LUNCH.
SOMEONE LIKE THAT CAN'T JUST BE AN *APPLIANCE.*
WIPE WIPE
YOU SHOULDN'T BE EMBARRASSED BY YOUR FAMILY, TAKUMA-KUN.
EVEN IF IT'S UNCONVENTIONAL.
SORRY.

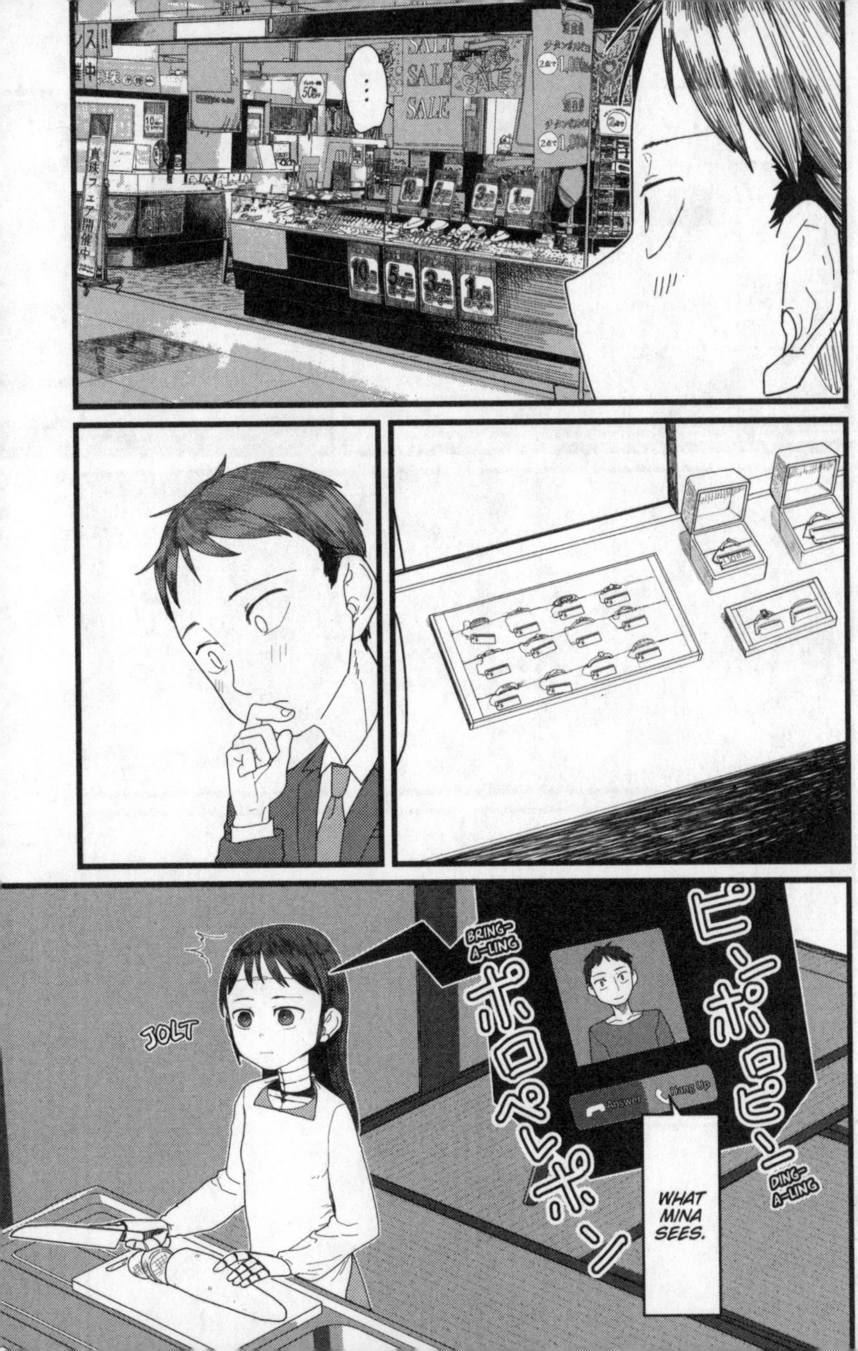

…
SALE
SALE
SALE
ピーポロピー
DING-A-LING
ポロペポーン
BRING-A-LING
WHAT MINA SEES.
Hang Up
Answer
JOLT

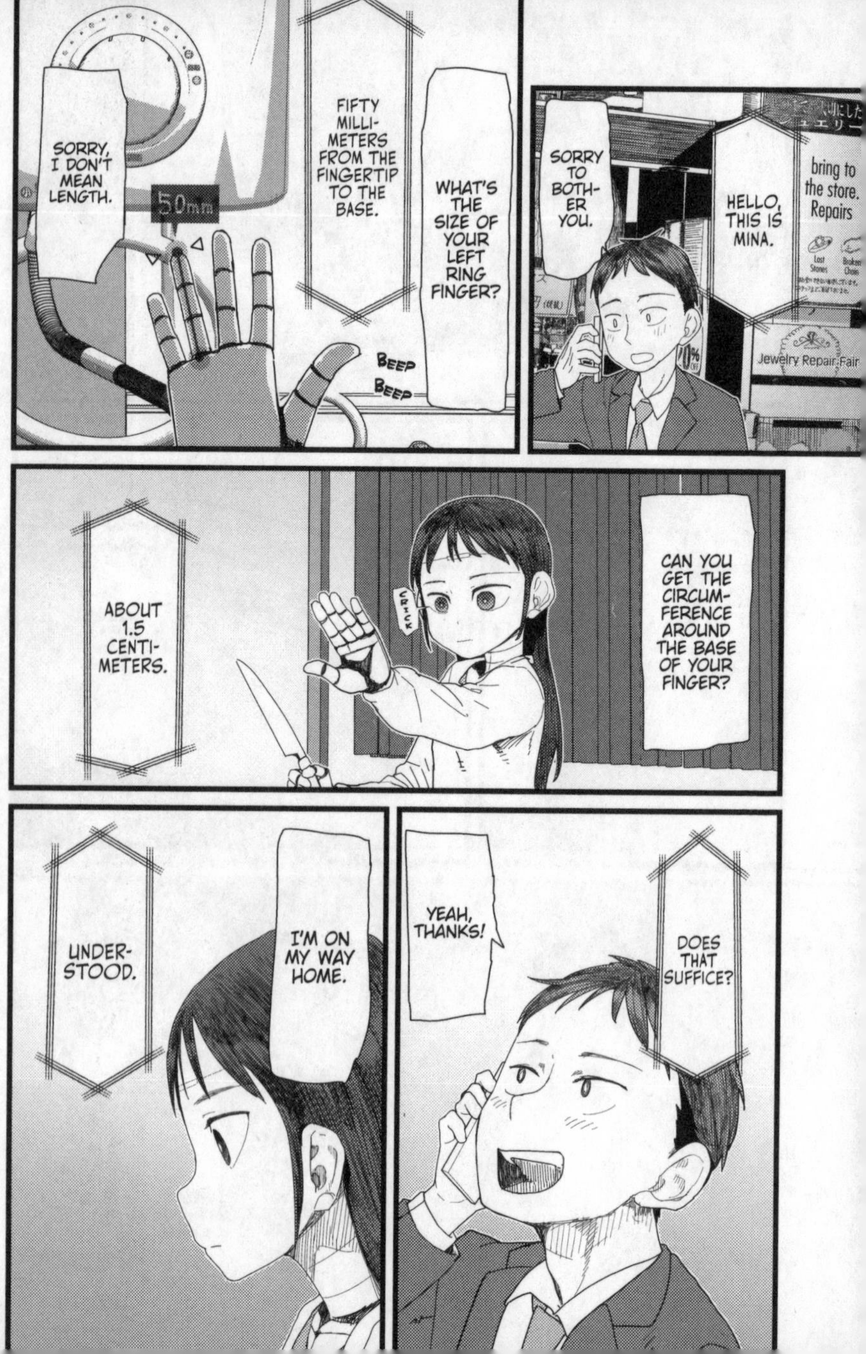
bring to the store. Repairs
Lost Stones
Jewelry Repair Fair
HELLO, THIS IS MINA.
SORRY TO BOTHER YOU.
WHAT'S THE SIZE OF YOUR LEFT RING FINGER?
FIFTY MILLIMETERS FROM THE FINGERTIP TO THE BASE.
BEEP
BEEP
50mm
SORRY, I DON'T MEAN LENGTH.
CAN YOU GET THE CIRCUMFERENCE AROUND THE BASE OF YOUR FINGER?
CRICK
ABOUT 1.5 CENTIMETERS.
DOES THAT SUFFICE?
YEAH, THANKS!
I'M ON MY WAY HOME.
UNDERSTOOD.

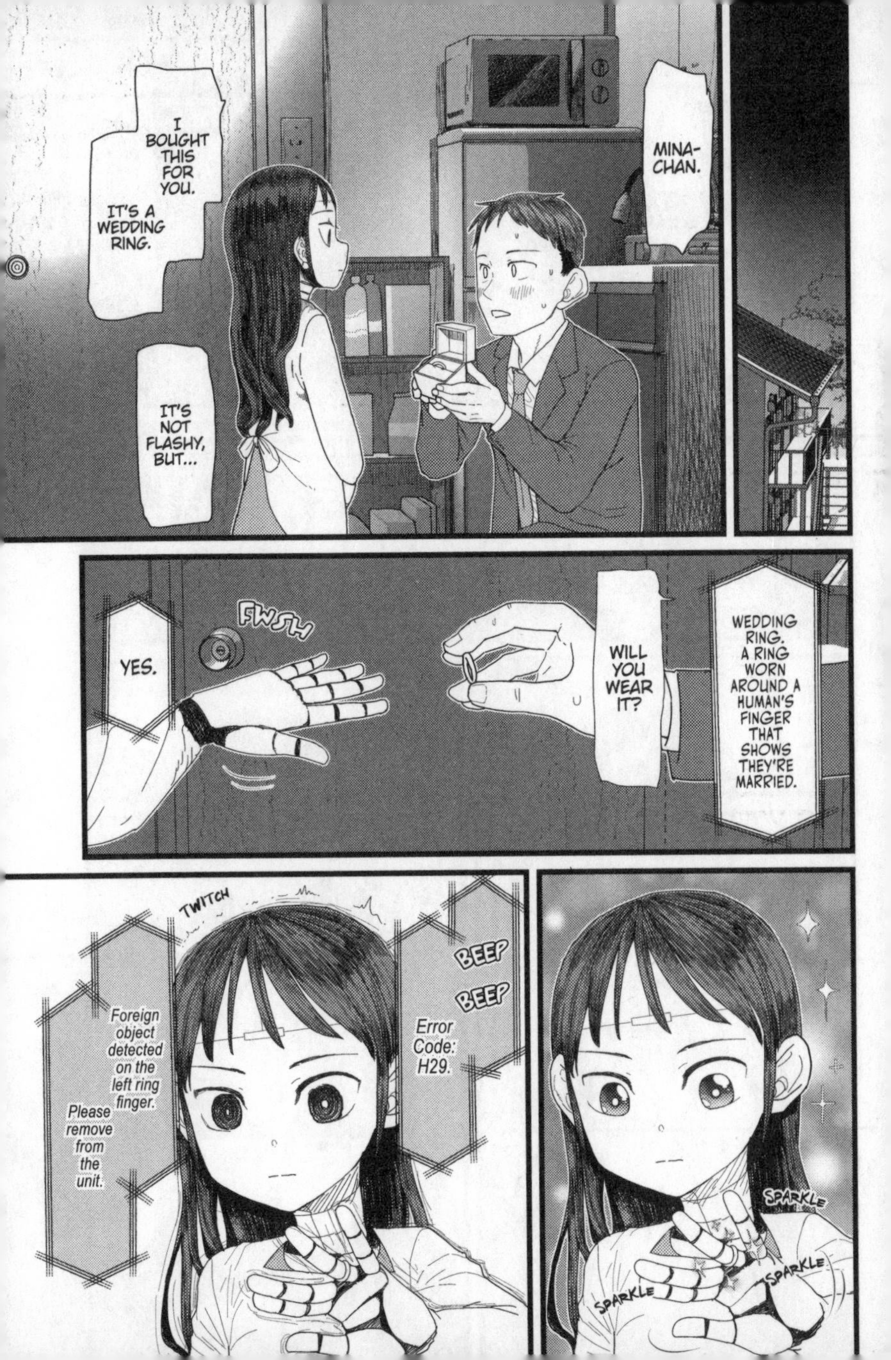
MINA-CHAN.
I BOUGHT THIS FOR YOU.
IT'S A WEDDING RING.
IT'S NOT FLASHY, BUT...
WEDDING RING. A RING WORN AROUND A HUMAN'S FINGER THAT SHOWS THEY'RE MARRIED.
WILL YOU WEAR IT?
FWSH
YES.
SPARKLE
SPARKLE
SPARKLE
TWITCH
BEEP
BEEP
Error Code: H29.
Foreign object detected on the left ring finger.
Please remove from the unit.

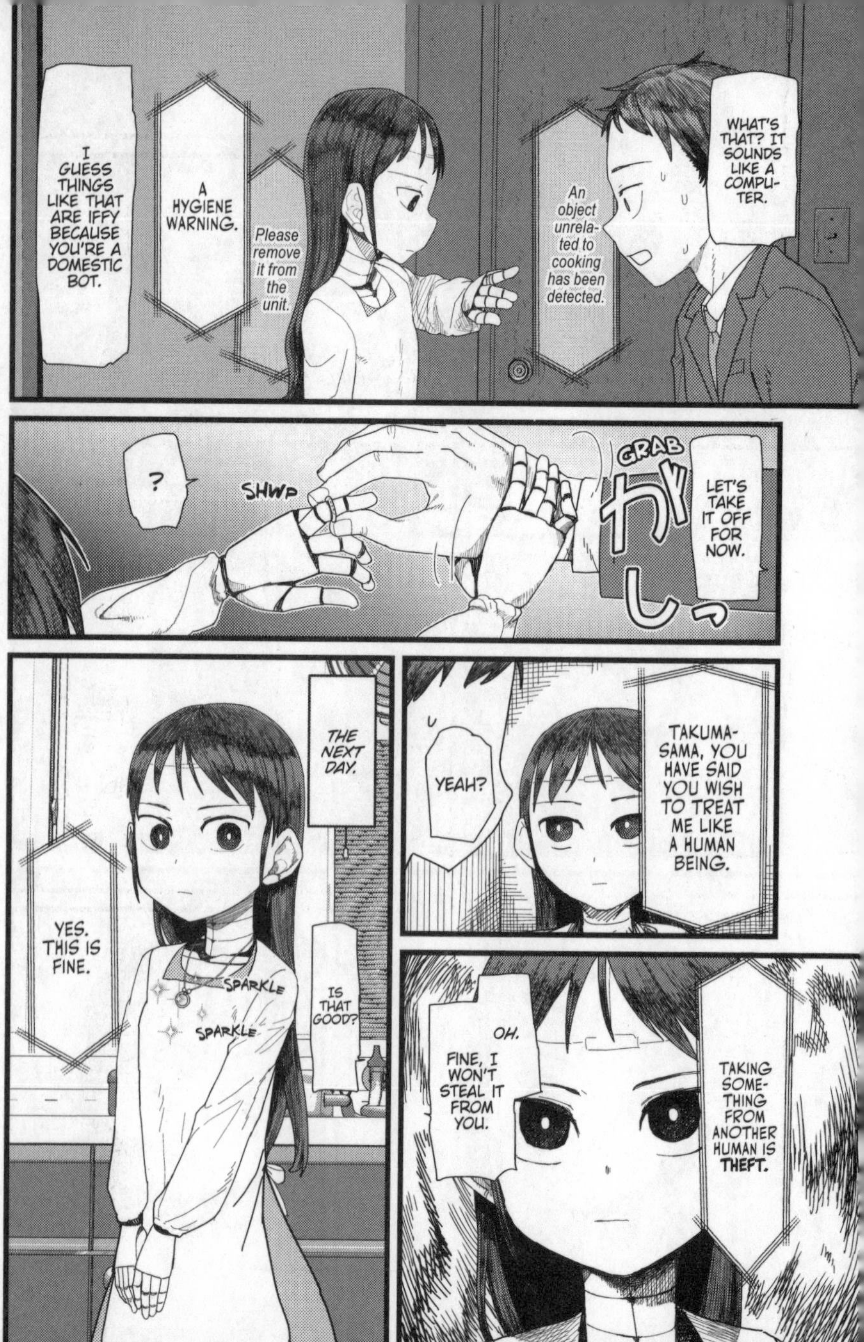
WHAT'S THAT? IT SOUNDS LIKE A COMPUTER.
An object unrelated to cooking has been detected.
Please remove it from the unit.
A HYGIENE WARNING.
I GUESS THINGS LIKE THAT ARE IFFY BECAUSE YOU'RE A DOMESTIC BOT.
LET'S TAKE IT OFF FOR NOW.
GRAB
わしっ
SHWP
?
TAKUMA-SAMA, YOU HAVE SAID YOU WISH TO TREAT ME LIKE A HUMAN BEING.
YEAH?
TAKING SOMETHING FROM ANOTHER HUMAN IS **THEFT.**
OH. FINE, I WON'T STEAL IT FROM YOU.
THE NEXT DAY.
IS THAT GOOD?
YES. THIS IS FINE.
SPARKLE
SPARKLE

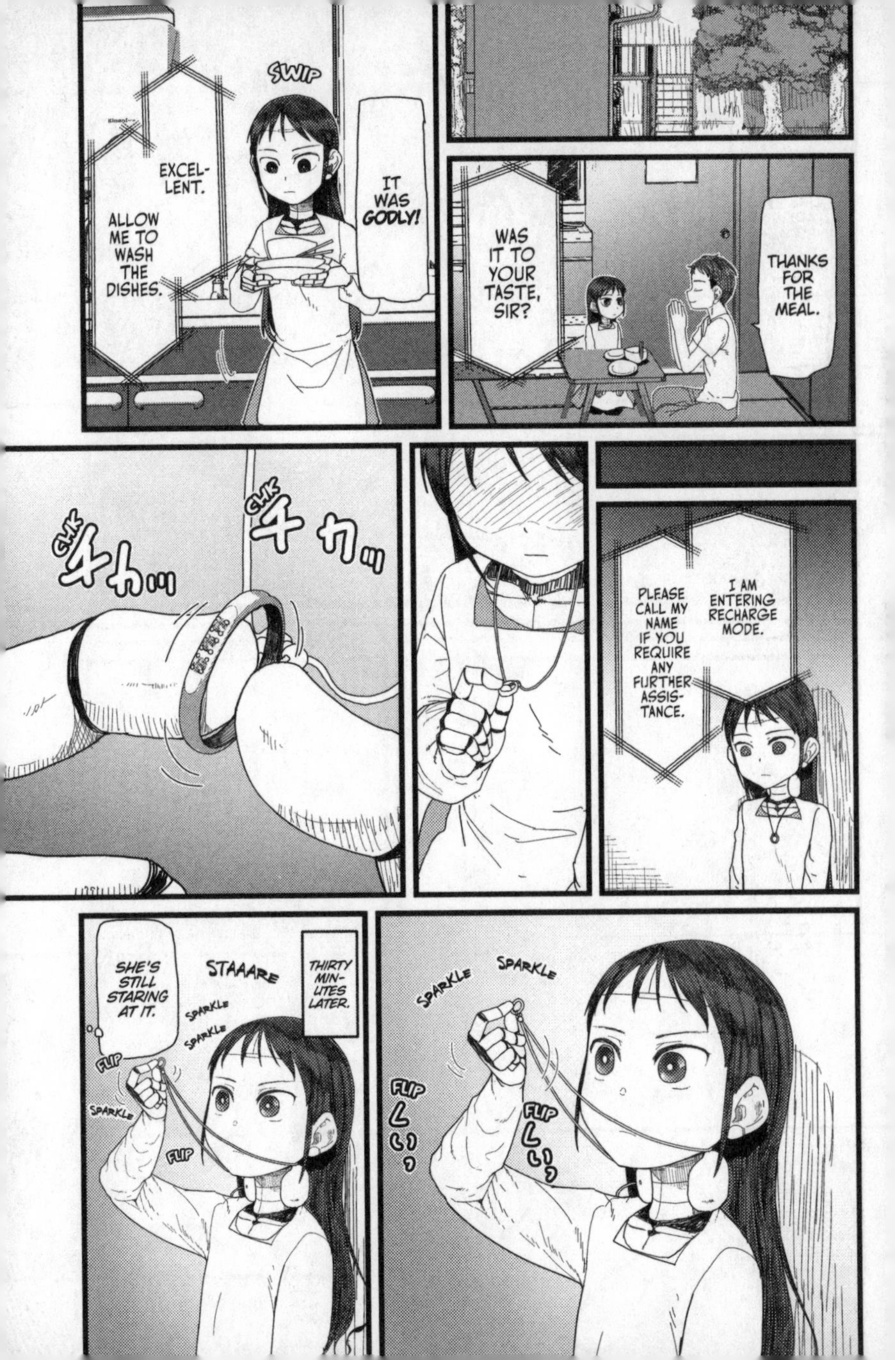
THANKS FOR THE MEAL.
WAS IT TO YOUR TASTE, SIR?
IT WAS GODLY!
SWIP
EXCEL-LENT.
ALLOW ME TO WASH THE DISHES.
I AM ENTERING RECHARGE MODE.
PLEASE CALL MY NAME IF YOU REQUIRE ANY FURTHER ASSIS-TANCE.
CHK
CHK
SPARKLE
SPARKLE
SPARKLE
FLIP
FLIP
THIRTY MIN-UTES LATER.
STAAARE
SHE'S STILL STARING AT IT.
SPARKLE
SPARKLE
FLIP
SPARKLE
FLIP

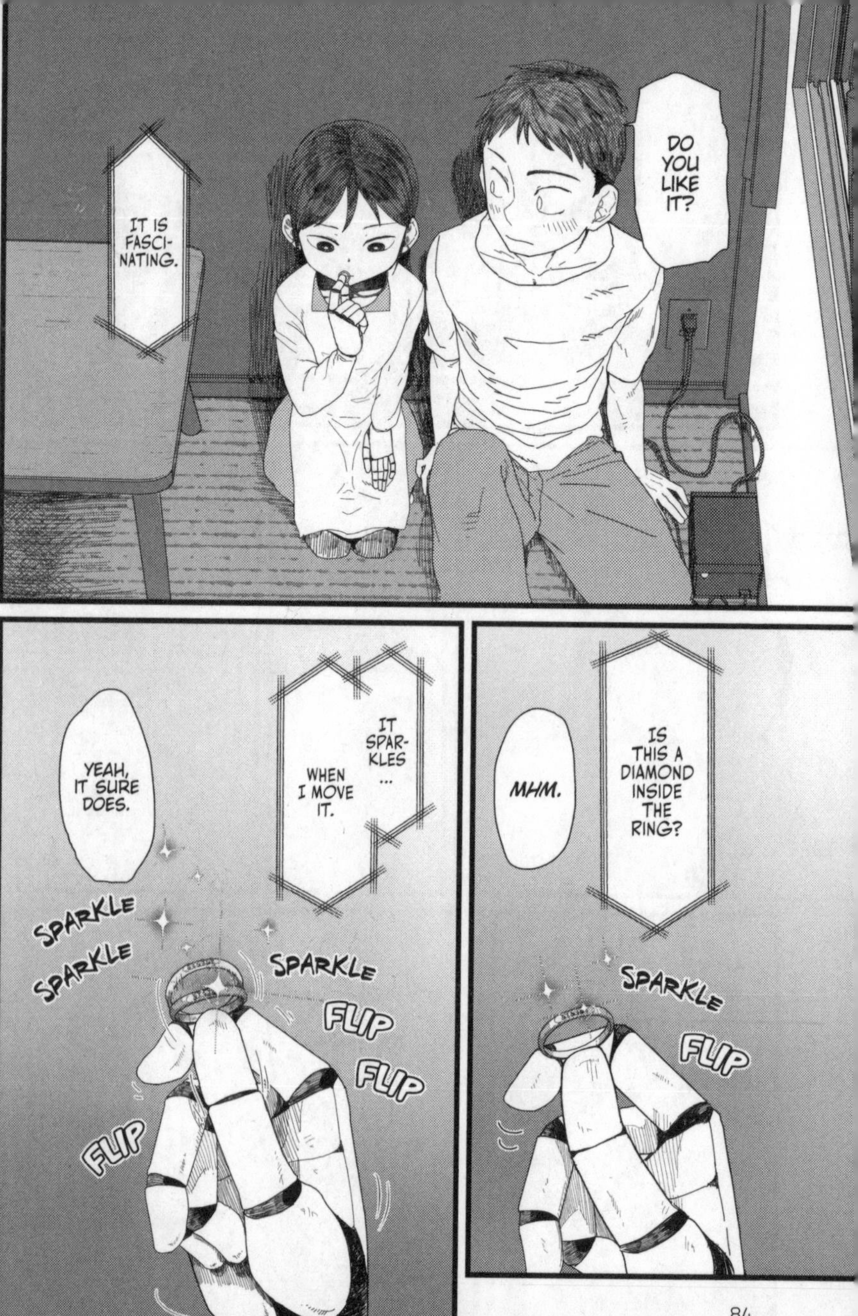
DO YOU LIKE IT?
IT IS FASCI-NATING.
IS THIS A DIAMOND INSIDE THE RING?
MHM.
SPARKLE
FLIP
IT SPAR-KLES ...
WHEN I MOVE IT.
YEAH, IT SURE DOES.
SPARKLE
SPARKLE
SPARKLE
FLIP
FLIP
FLIP

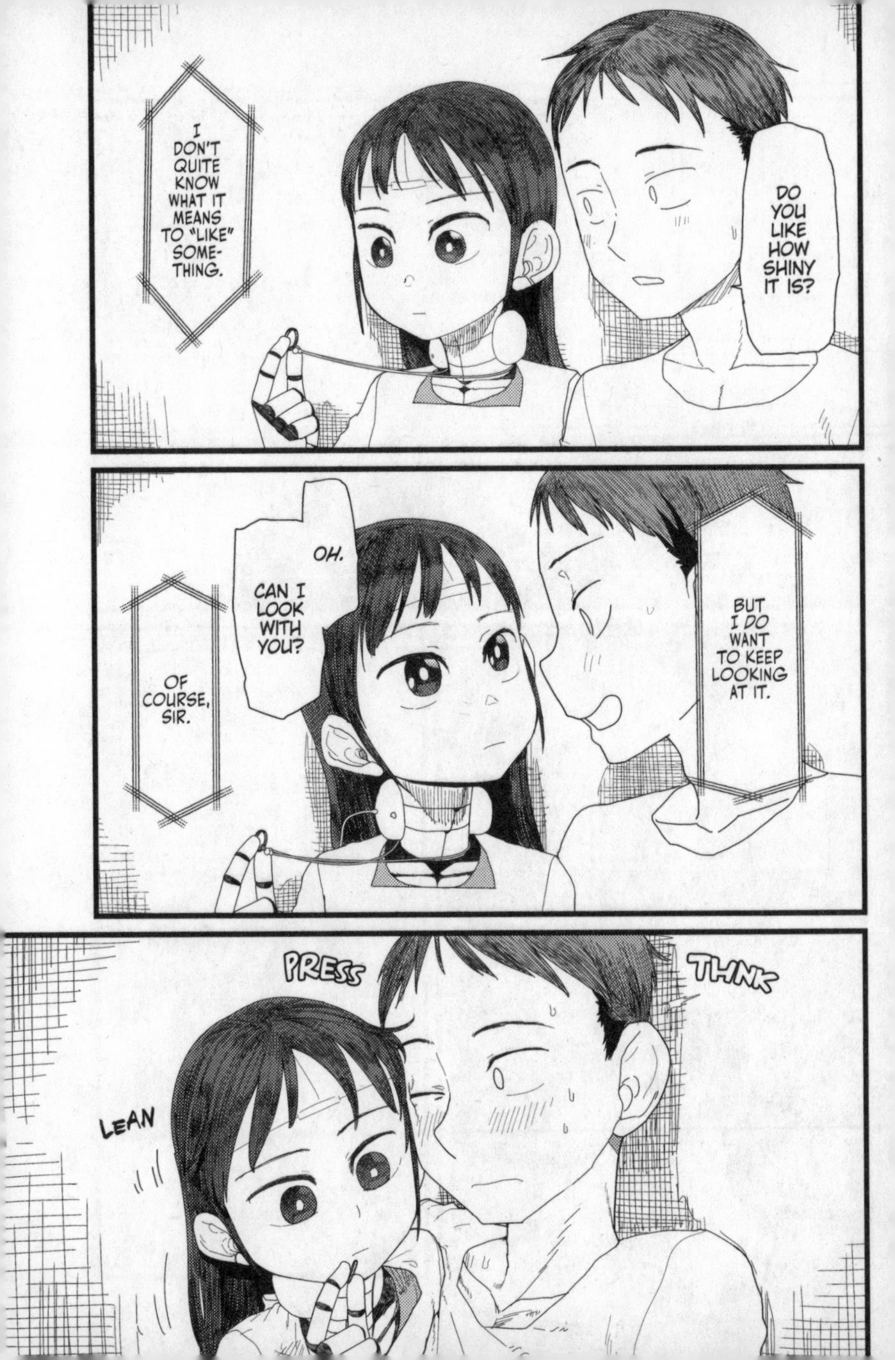
DO YOU LIKE HOW SHINY IT IS?
I DON'T QUITE KNOW WHAT IT MEANS TO "LIKE" SOME-THING.
BUT I *DO* WANT TO KEEP LOOKING AT IT.
OH.
CAN I LOOK WITH YOU?
OF COURSE, SIR.
THNK
PRESS
LEAN

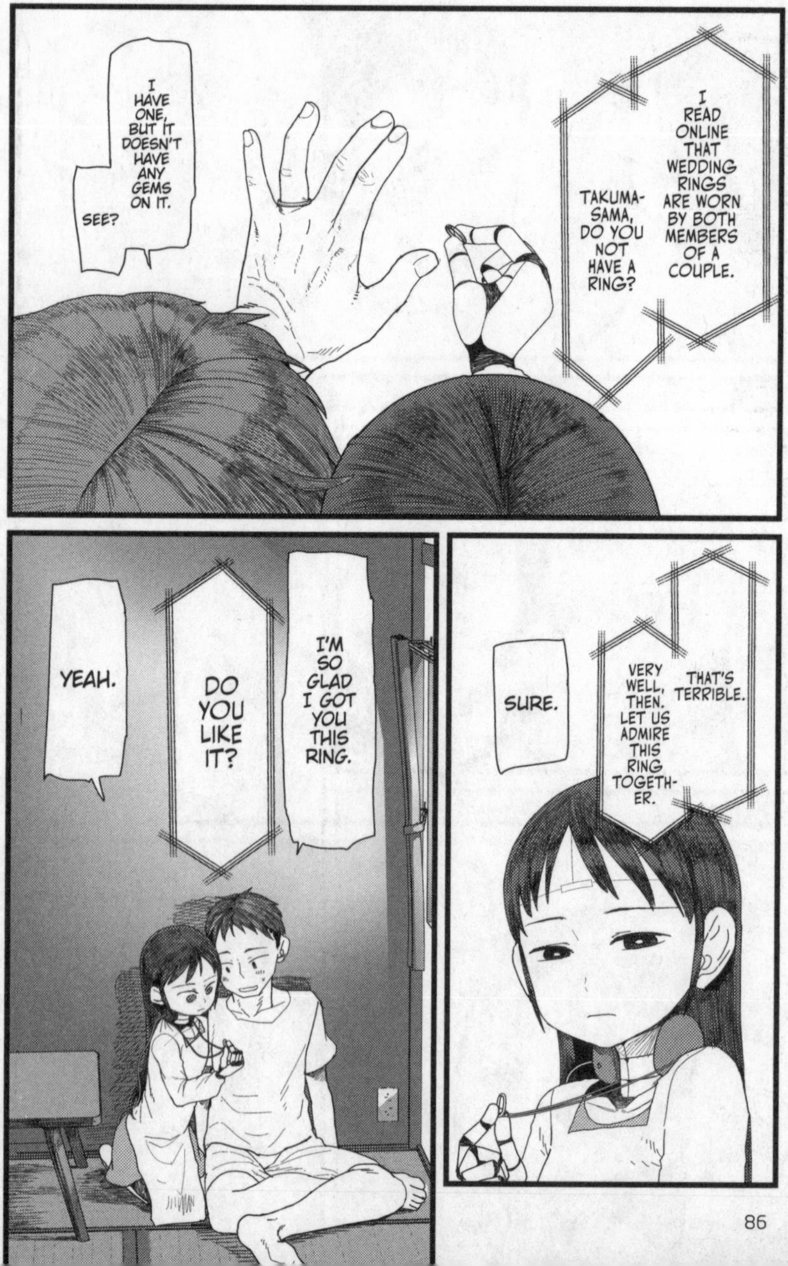
I READ ONLINE THAT WEDDING RINGS ARE WORN BY BOTH MEMBERS OF A COUPLE.
TAKUMA-SAMA, DO YOU NOT HAVE A RING?
I HAVE ONE, BUT IT DOESN'T HAVE ANY GEMS ON IT.
SEE?
THAT'S TERRIBLE.
VERY WELL, THEN. LET US ADMIRE THIS RING TOGETHER.
SURE.
I'M SO GLAD I GOT YOU THIS RING.
DO YOU LIKE IT?
YEAH.

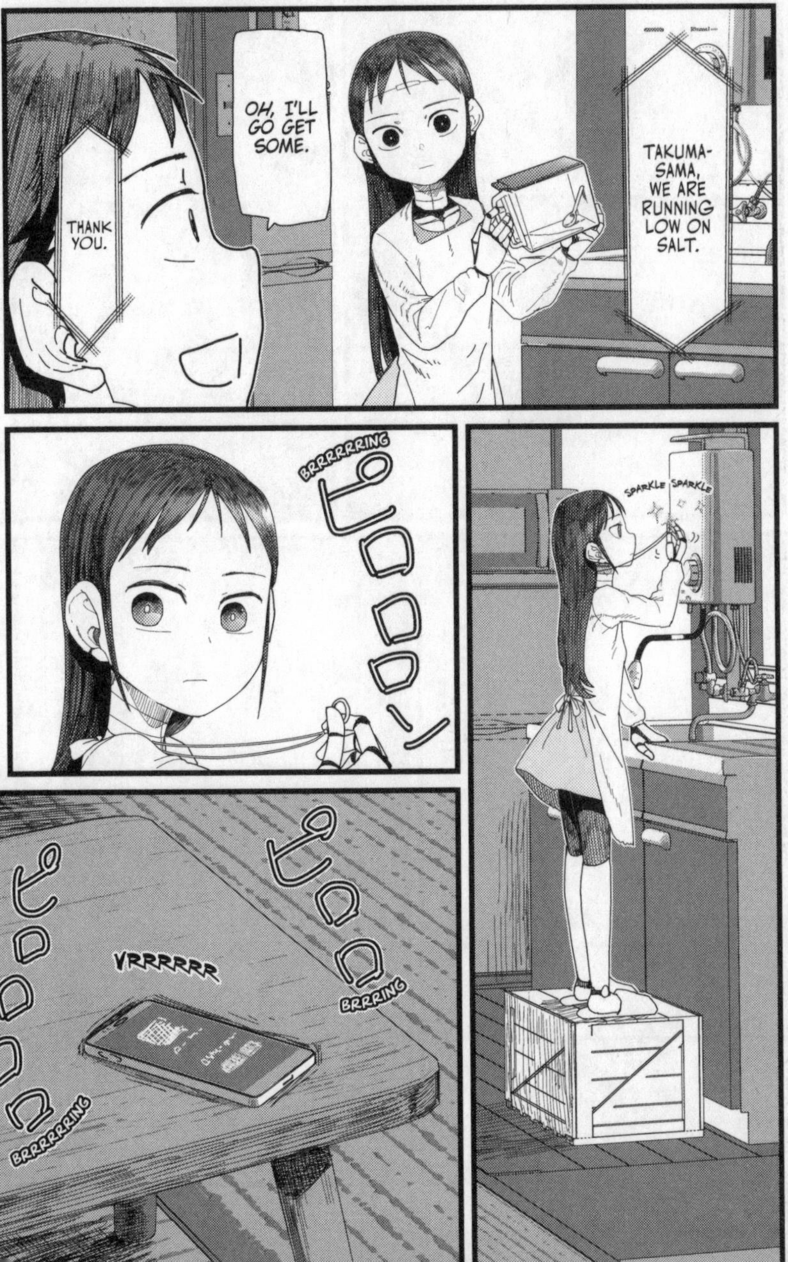
TAKUMA-SAMA, WE ARE RUNNING LOW ON SALT.
OH, I'LL GO GET SOME.
THANK YOU.
SPARKLE SPARKLE
ピロロロン
BRRRRRRING
ピロロ
BRRRING
VRRRRRR
ピロロロロ
BRRRRRRING

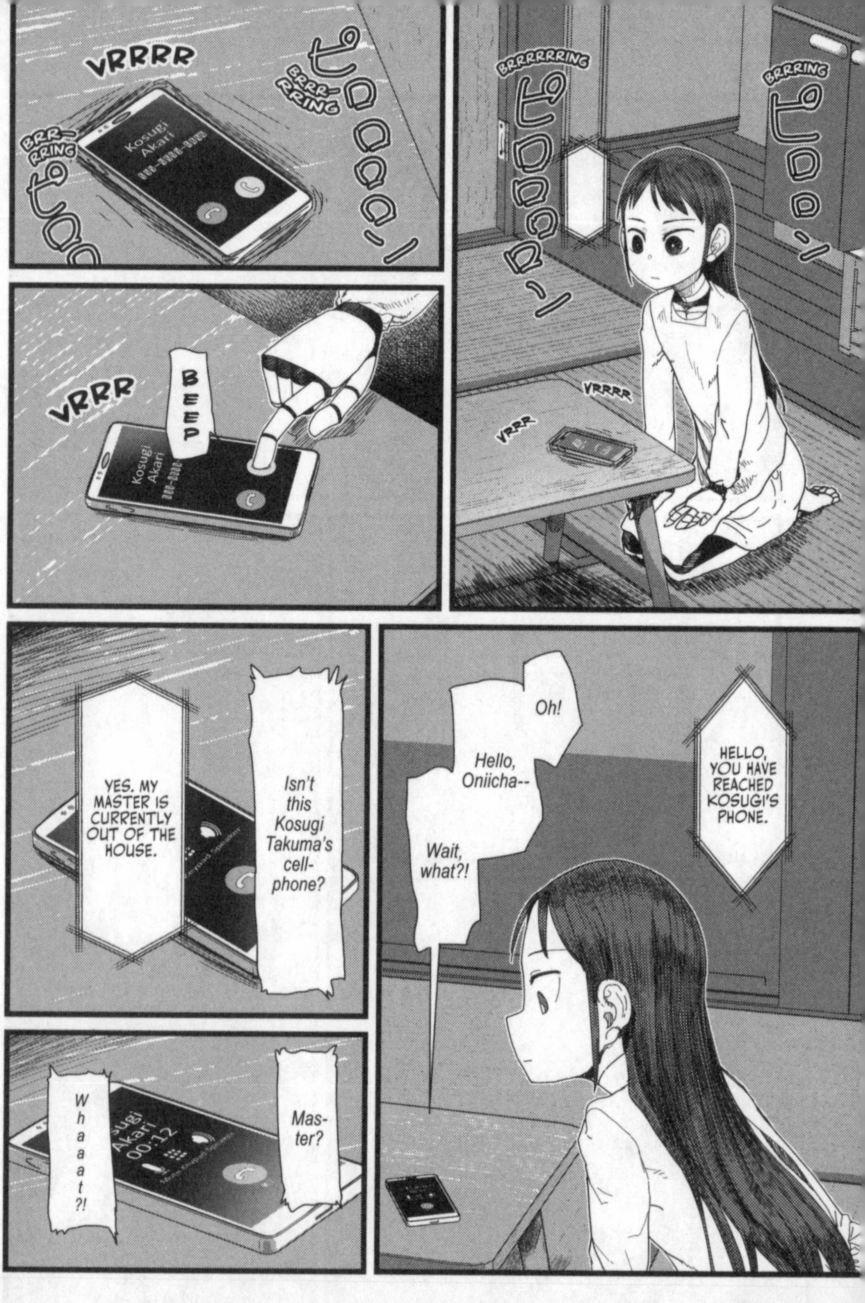
BRRRRRRING
BRRRING
VRRRR
VRRR
VRRRR
BRRR-RRING
BRR-RRING
Kosugi Akari
VRRR
BEEP
HELLO, YOU HAVE REACHED KOSUGI'S PHONE.
Oh!
Hello, Oniicha--
Wait, what?!
Isn't this Kosugi Takuma's cell-phone?
YES. MY MASTER IS CURRENTLY OUT OF THE HOUSE.
Mas-ter?
Whaaaat?!

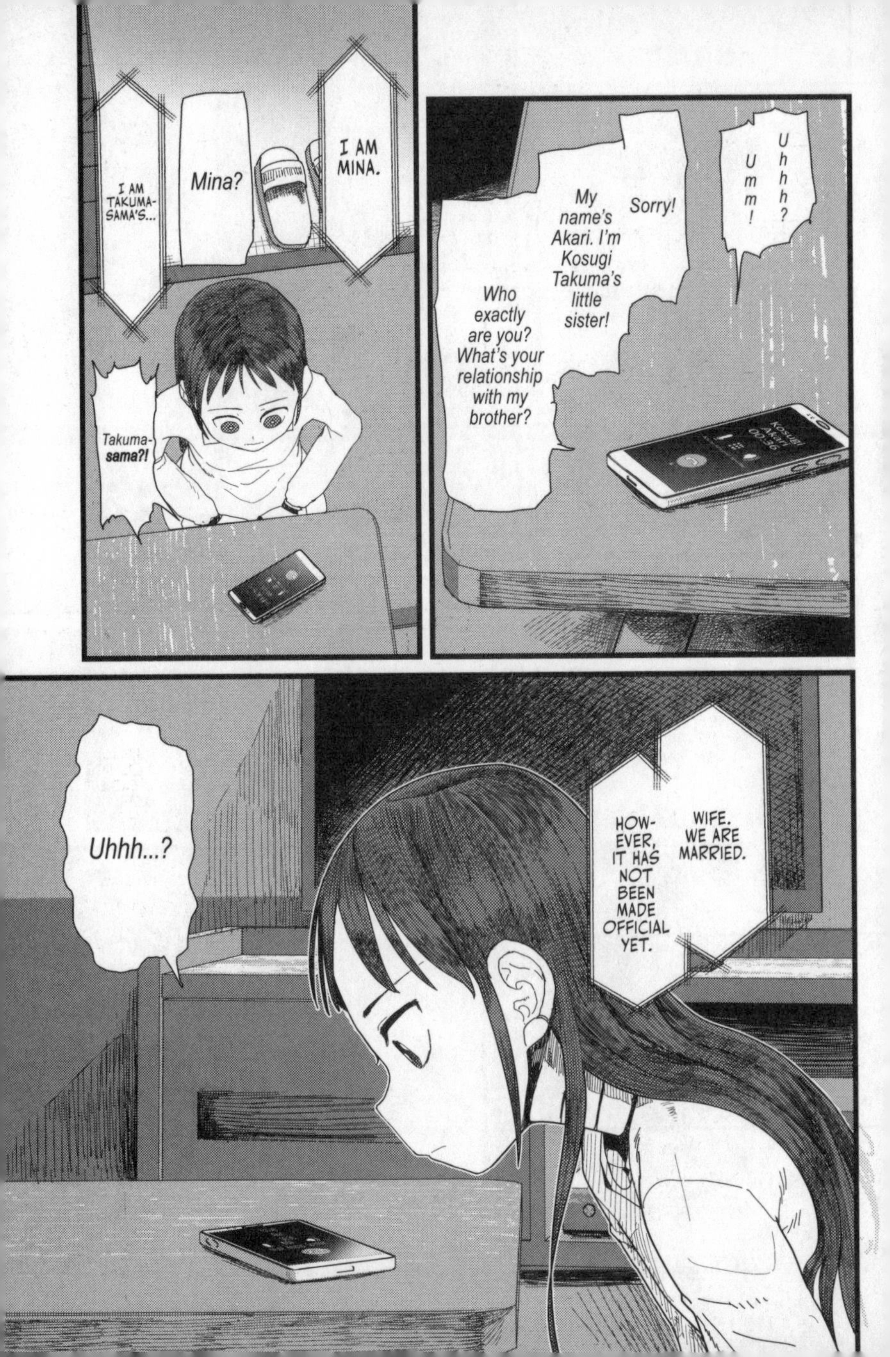
Uhhh?
Umm!
Sorry!
My name's Akari. I'm Kosugi Takuma's little sister!
Who exactly are you? What's your relationship with my brother?
I AM MINA.
Mina?
I AM TAKUMA-SAMA'S...
Takuma-sama?!
WIFE. WE ARE MARRIED.
HOW-EVER, IT HAS NOT BEEN MADE OFFICIAL YET.
Uhhh...?

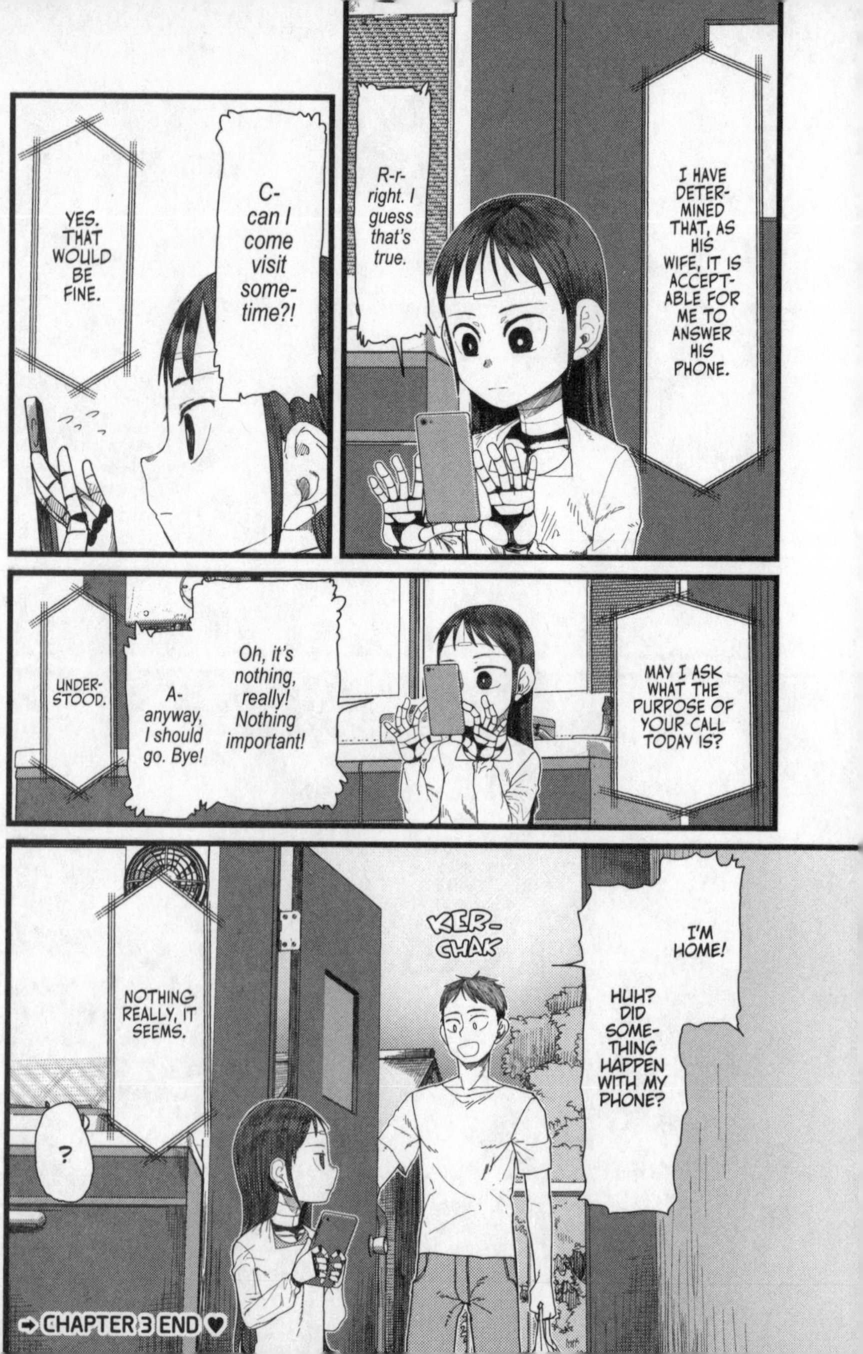
I HAVE DETERMINED THAT, AS HIS WIFE, IT IS ACCEPTABLE FOR ME TO ANSWER HIS PHONE.
R-r-right. I guess that's true.
C-can I come visit sometime?!
YES. THAT WOULD BE FINE.
MAY I ASK WHAT THE PURPOSE OF YOUR CALL TODAY IS?
Oh, it's nothing, really! Nothing important!
A-anyway, I should go. Bye!
UNDERSTOOD.
I'M HOME!
KER-CHAK
HUH? DID SOMETHING HAPPEN WITH MY PHONE?
NOTHING REALLY, IT SEEMS.
?
CHAPTER 3 END ♥

My Wife Has No Emotion

My Wife Has No Emotion

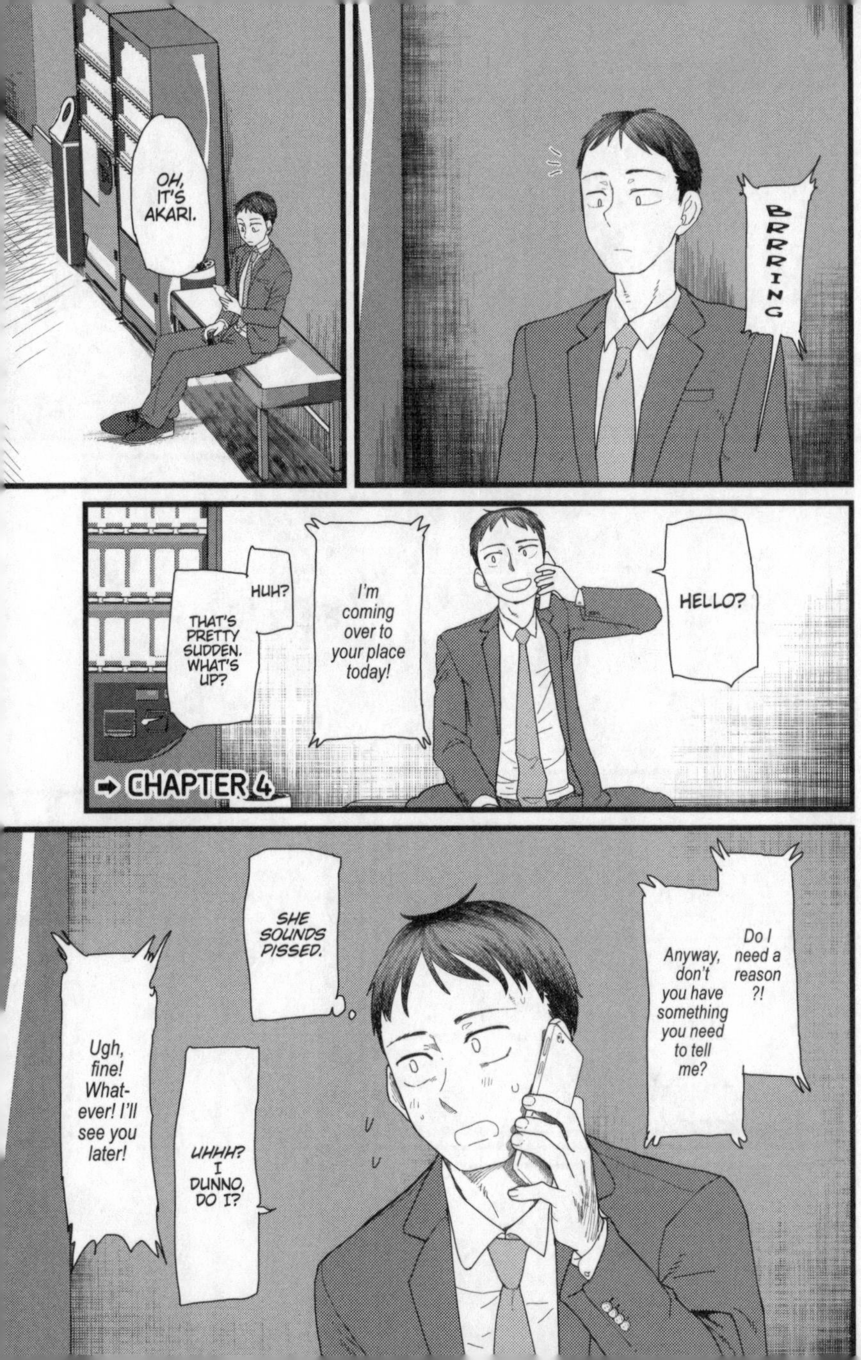
BRRRING
OH, IT'S AKARI.
HELLO?
I'm coming over to your place today!
HUH?
THAT'S PRETTY SUDDEN. WHAT'S UP?
➡ CHAPTER 4
Do I need a reason?!
Anyway, don't you have something you need to tell me?
SHE SOUNDS PISSED.
UHHH? I DUNNO, DO I?
Ugh, fine! Whatever! I'll see you later!

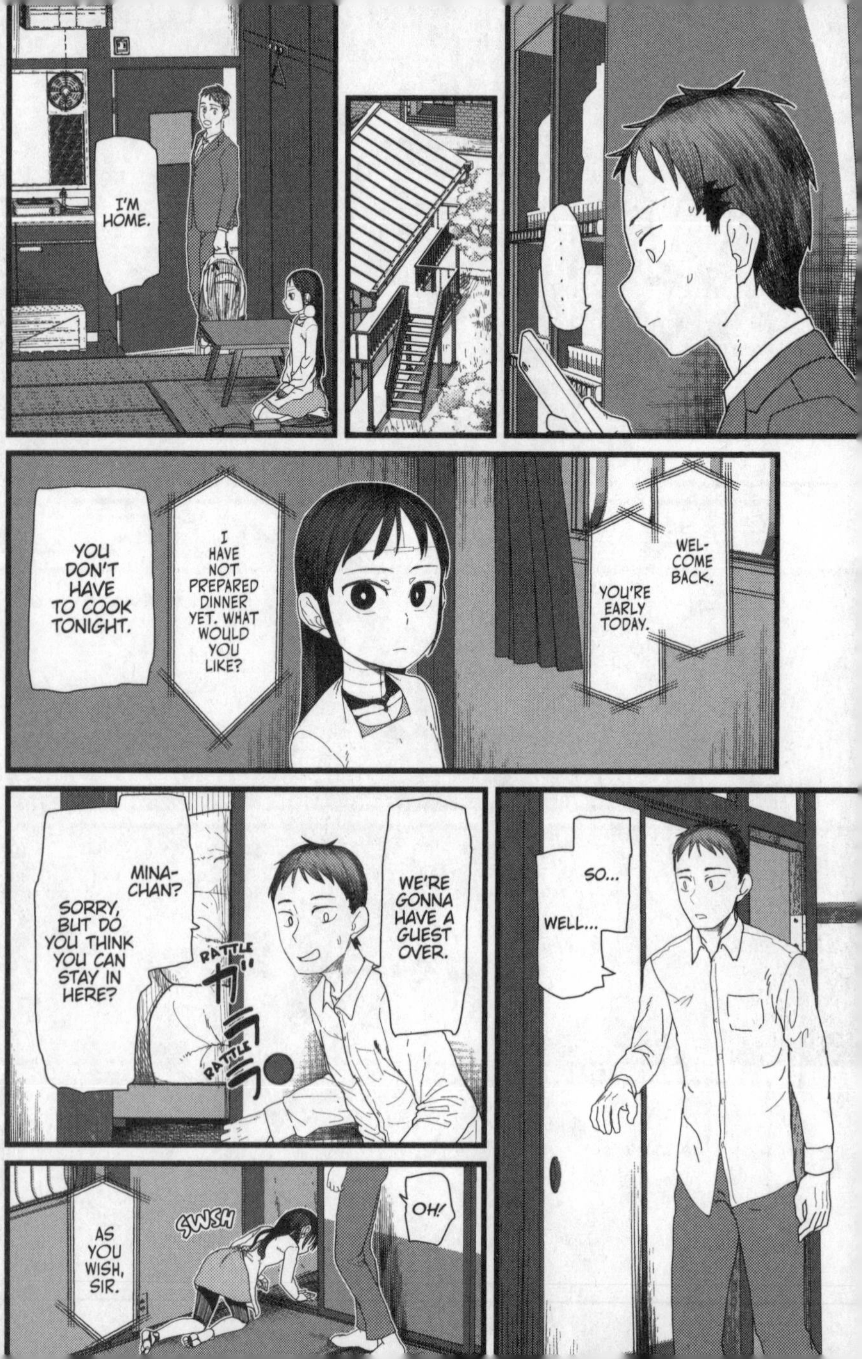
...
I'M HOME.
WEL-COME BACK.
YOU'RE EARLY TODAY.
I HAVE NOT PREPARED DINNER YET. WHAT WOULD YOU LIKE?
YOU DON'T HAVE TO COOK TONIGHT.
SO...
WELL...
WE'RE GONNA HAVE A GUEST OVER.
MINA-CHAN?
SORRY, BUT DO YOU THINK YOU CAN STAY IN HERE?
RATTLE
RATTLE
OH!
SWSH
AS YOU WISH, SIR.

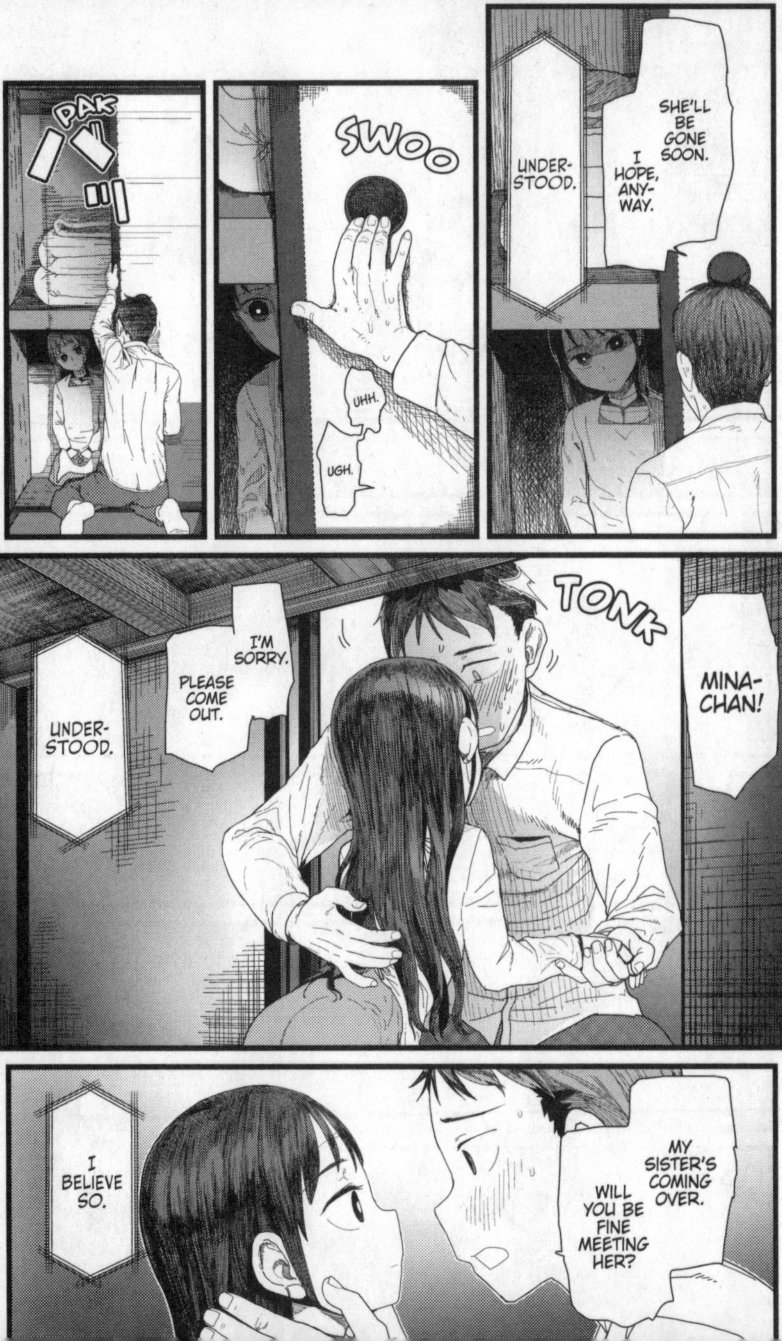
SHE'LL BE GONE SOON.
I HOPE, ANYWAY.
UNDER-STOOD.
SWOO
UHH.
UGH.
PAK
MINA-CHAN!
TONK
I'M SORRY.
PLEASE COME OUT.
UNDER-STOOD.
MY SISTER'S COMING OVER.
WILL YOU BE FINE MEETING HER?
I BELIEVE SO.

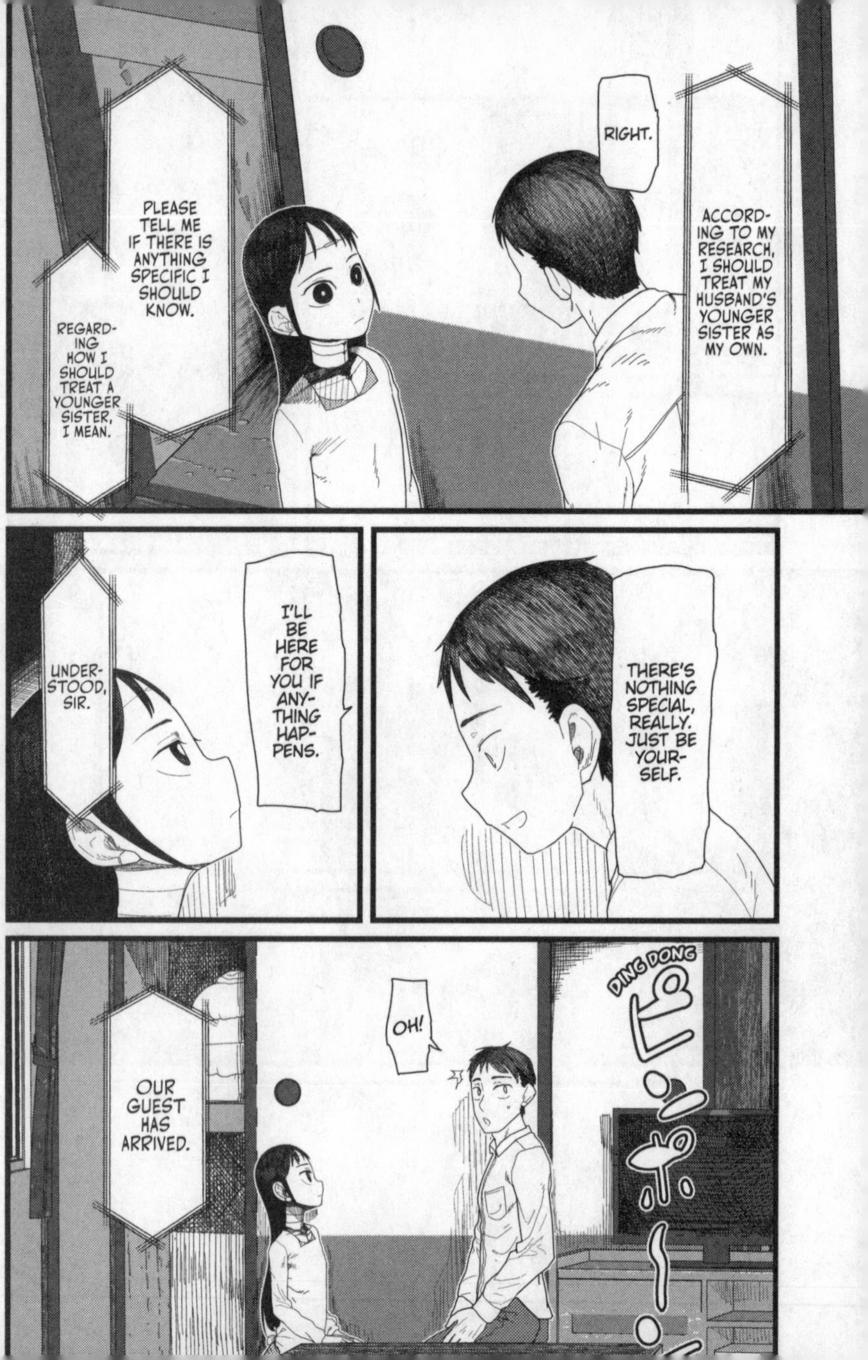
RIGHT.
ACCORDING TO MY RESEARCH, I SHOULD TREAT MY HUSBAND'S YOUNGER SISTER AS MY OWN.
PLEASE TELL ME IF THERE IS ANYTHING SPECIFIC I SHOULD KNOW.
REGARDING HOW I SHOULD TREAT A YOUNGER SISTER, I MEAN.
THERE'S NOTHING SPECIAL, REALLY. JUST BE YOURSELF.
I'LL BE HERE FOR YOU IF ANYTHING HAPPENS.
UNDERSTOOD, SIR.
DING DONG
OH!
OUR GUEST HAS ARRIVED.

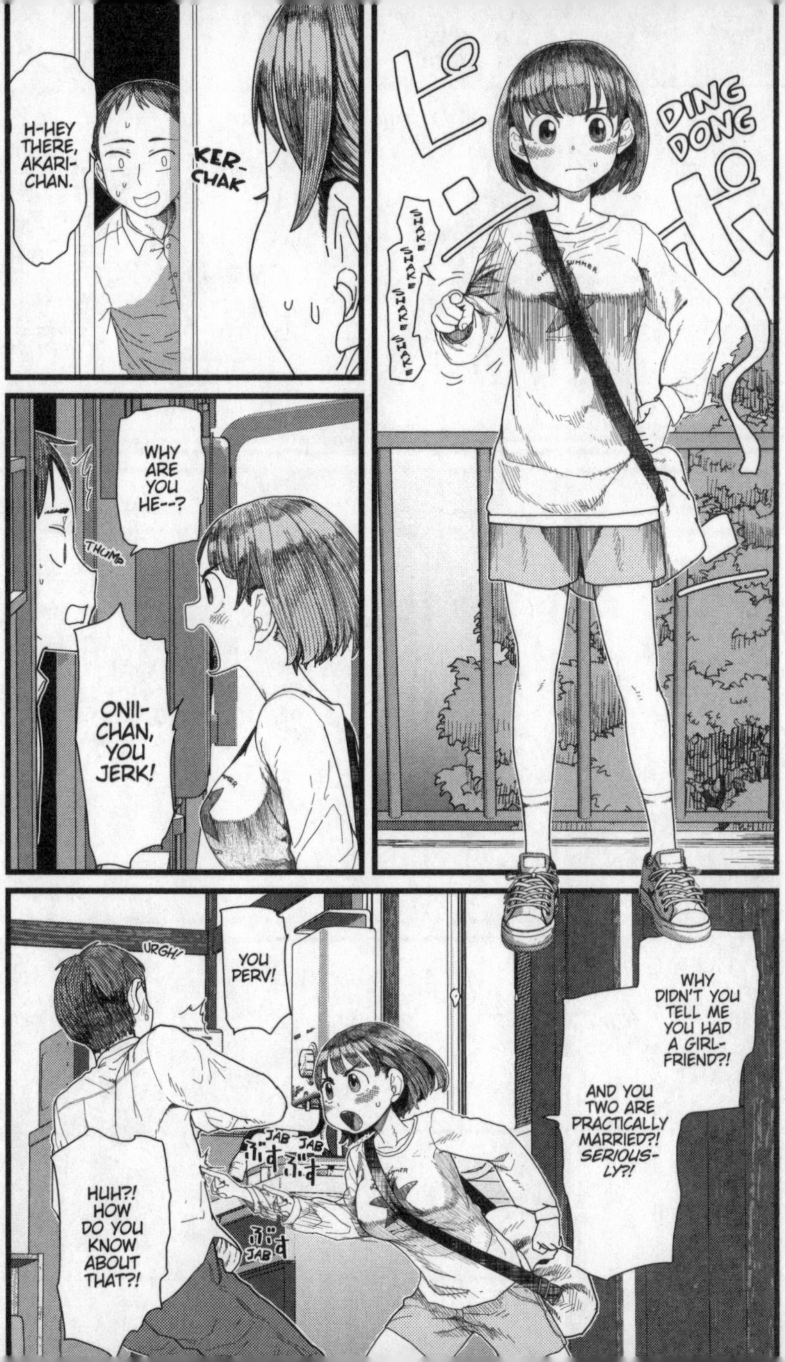
DING DONG
SHAKE SHAKE SHAKE SHAKE
KER-CHAK
H-HEY THERE, AKARI-CHAN.
WHY ARE YOU HE--?
THUMP
ONII-CHAN, YOU JERK!
WHY DIDN'T YOU TELL ME YOU HAD A GIRLFRIEND?!
AND YOU TWO ARE PRACTICALLY MARRIED?! SERIOUSLY?!
YOU PERV!
URGH!
JAB JAB
ぶすぶす
HUH?! HOW DO YOU KNOW ABOUT THAT?!
ぶす
JAB

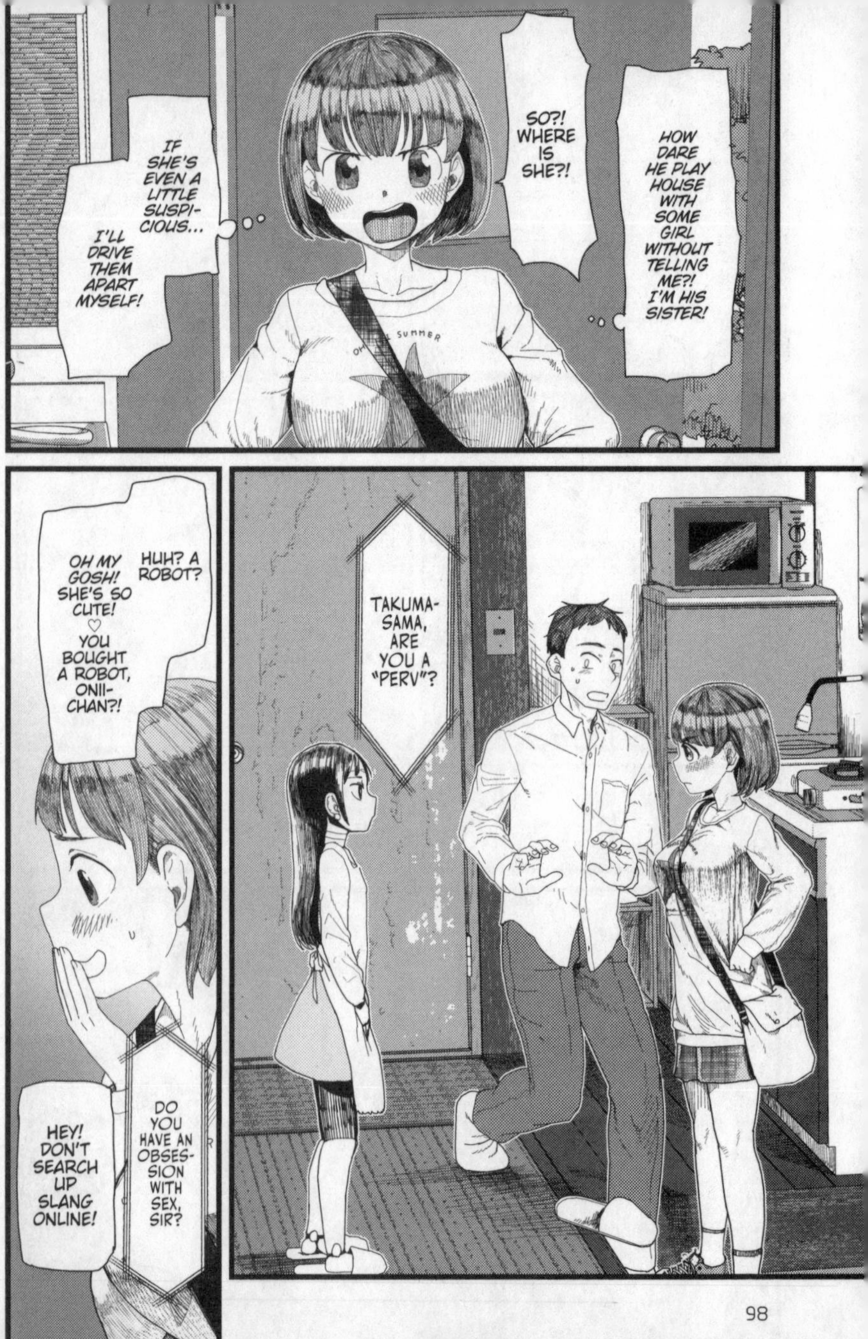
HOW DARE HE PLAY HOUSE WITH SOME GIRL WITHOUT TELLING ME?! I'M HIS SISTER!
SO?! WHERE IS SHE?!
IF SHE'S EVEN A LITTLE SUSPICIOUS... I'LL DRIVE THEM APART MYSELF!
OH SUMMER
TAKUMA-SAMA, ARE YOU A "PERV"?
HUH? A ROBOT?
OH MY GOSH! SHE'S SO CUTE! ♡ YOU BOUGHT A ROBOT, ONII-CHAN?!
DO YOU HAVE AN OBSESSION WITH SEX, SIR?
HEY! DON'T SEARCH UP SLANG ONLINE!

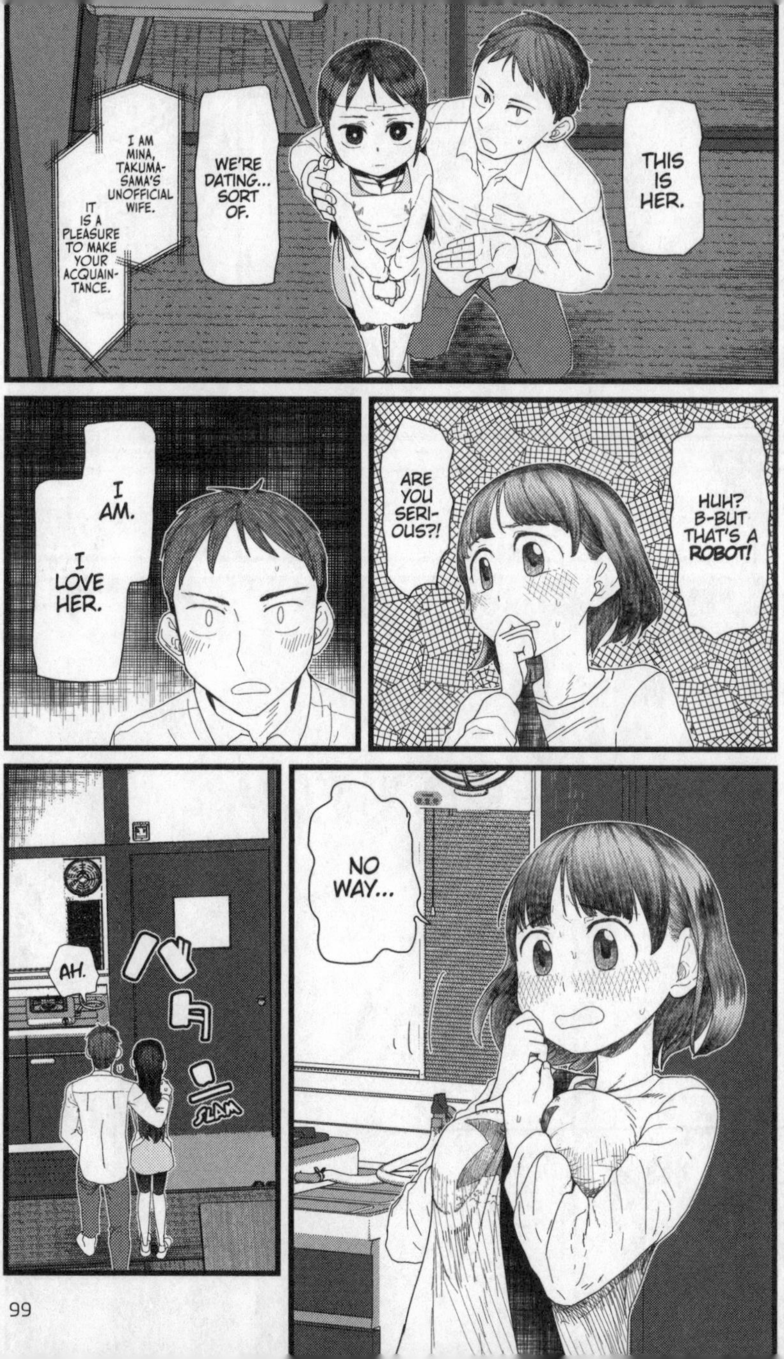
THIS IS HER.
WE'RE DATING... SORT OF.
I AM MINA, TAKUMA-SAMA'S UNOFFICIAL WIFE.
IT IS A PLEASURE TO MAKE YOUR ACQUAINTANCE.
HUH? B-BUT THAT'S A ROBOT!
ARE YOU SERIOUS?!
I AM.
I LOVE HER.
NO WAY...
AH.
SLAM

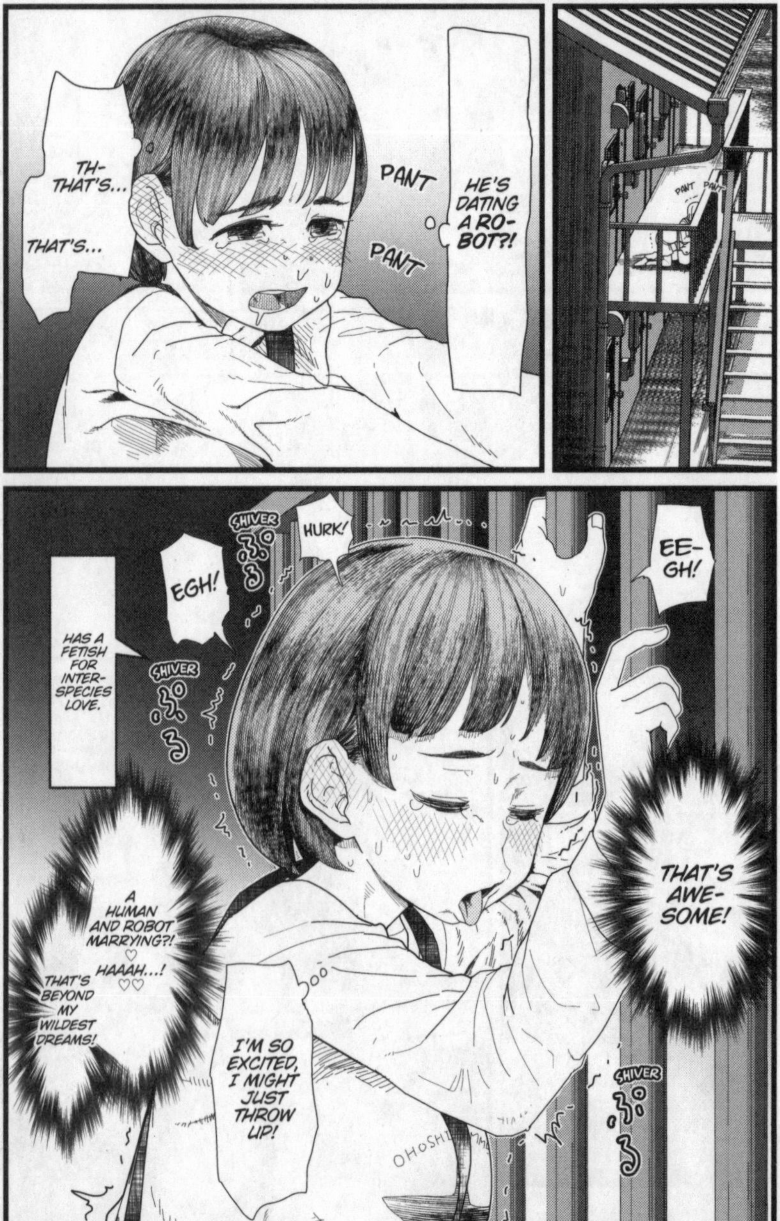
PANT PANT
HE'S DATING A RO-BOT?!
PANT
PANT
TH- THAT'S...
THAT'S...
EE-GH!
HURK!
SHIVER
EGH!
HAS A FETISH FOR INTER-SPECIES LOVE.
SHIVER
THAT'S AWE-SOME!
A HUMAN AND ROBOT MARRYING?!
HAAAH...!
THAT'S BEYOND MY WILDEST DREAMS!
I'M SO EXCITED, I MIGHT JUST THROW UP!
SHIVER

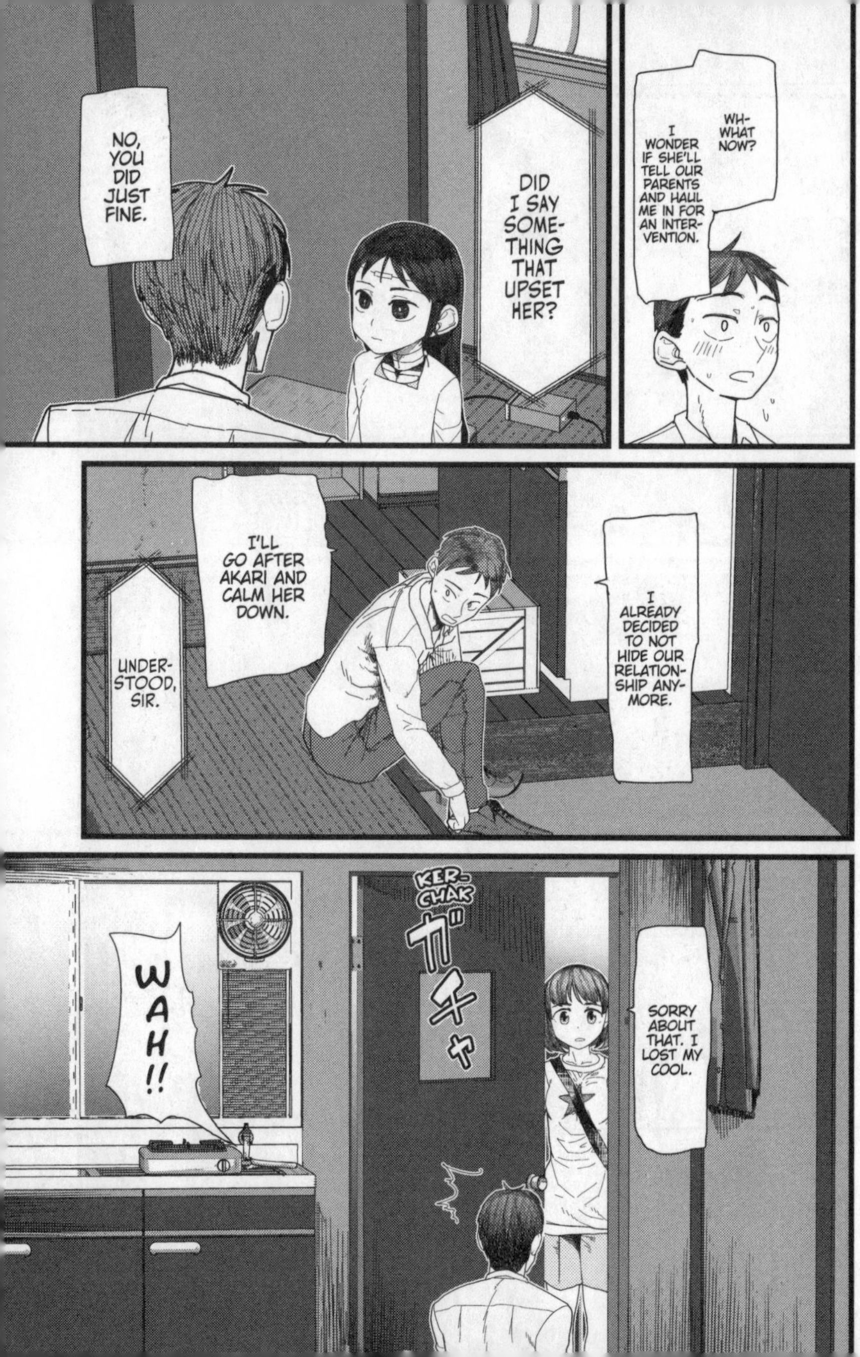
WH-WHAT NOW?
I WONDER IF SHE'LL TELL OUR PARENTS AND HAUL ME IN FOR AN INTERVENTION.
DID I SAY SOME-THING THAT UPSET HER?
NO, YOU DID JUST FINE.
I ALREADY DECIDED TO NOT HIDE OUR RELATION-SHIP ANY-MORE.
I'LL GO AFTER AKARI AND CALM HER DOWN.
UNDER-STOOD, SIR.
SORRY ABOUT THAT. I LOST MY COOL.
KER-CHAK
ガチャ
WAH!!

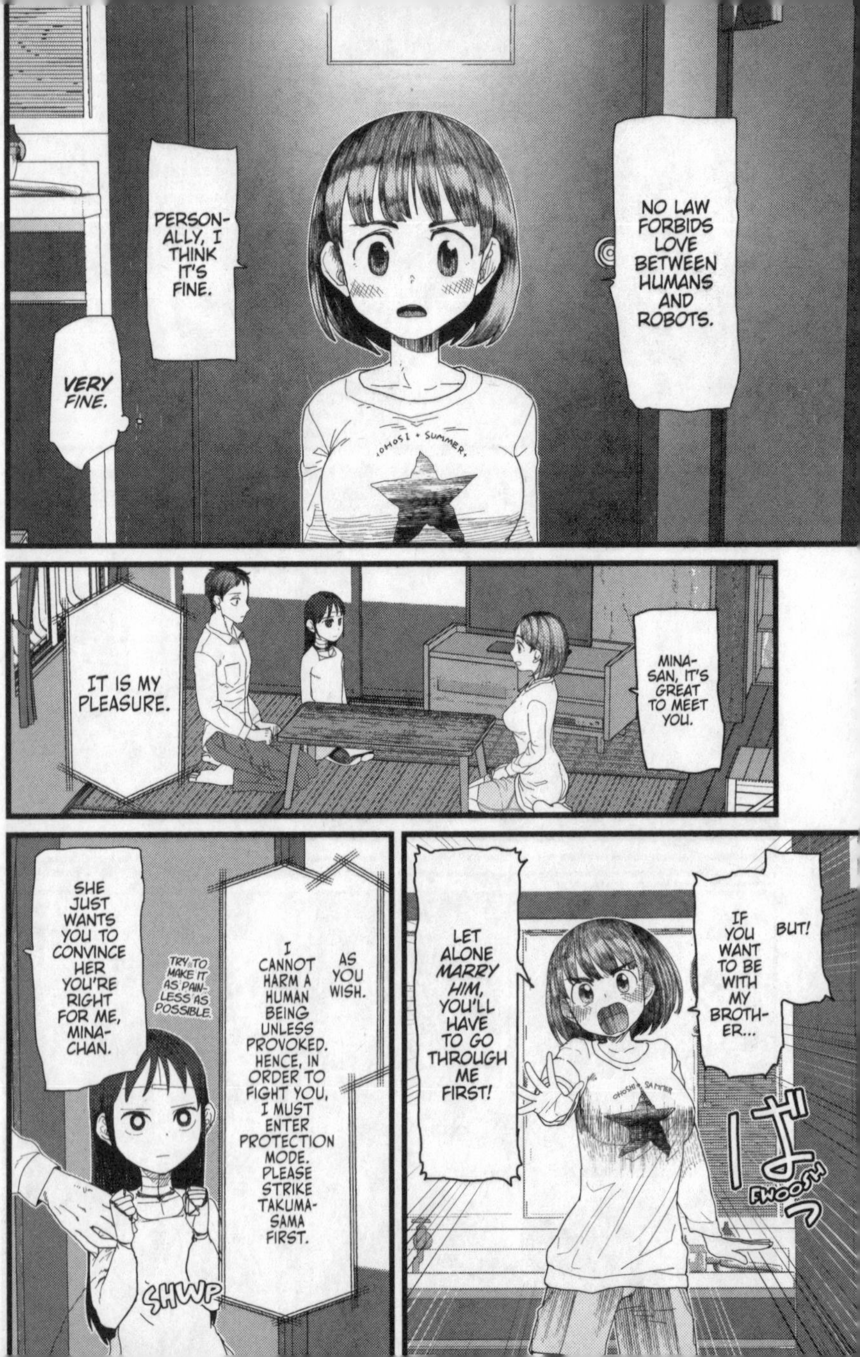
NO LAW FORBIDS LOVE BETWEEN HUMANS AND ROBOTS.
PERSONALLY, I THINK IT'S FINE.
VERY FINE.
MINA-SAN, IT'S GREAT TO MEET YOU.
IT IS MY PLEASURE.
BUT!
IF YOU WANT TO BE WITH MY BROTHER...
LET ALONE *MARRY HIM,* YOU'LL HAVE TO GO THROUGH ME FIRST!
FWOOSH
AS YOU WISH.
I CANNOT HARM A HUMAN BEING UNLESS PROVOKED. HENCE, IN ORDER TO FIGHT YOU, I MUST ENTER PROTECTION MODE. PLEASE STRIKE TAKUMA-SAMA FIRST.
TRY TO MAKE IT AS PAINLESS AS POSSIBLE.
SHE JUST WANTS YOU TO CONVINCE HER YOU'RE RIGHT FOR ME, MINA-CHAN.
SHWP

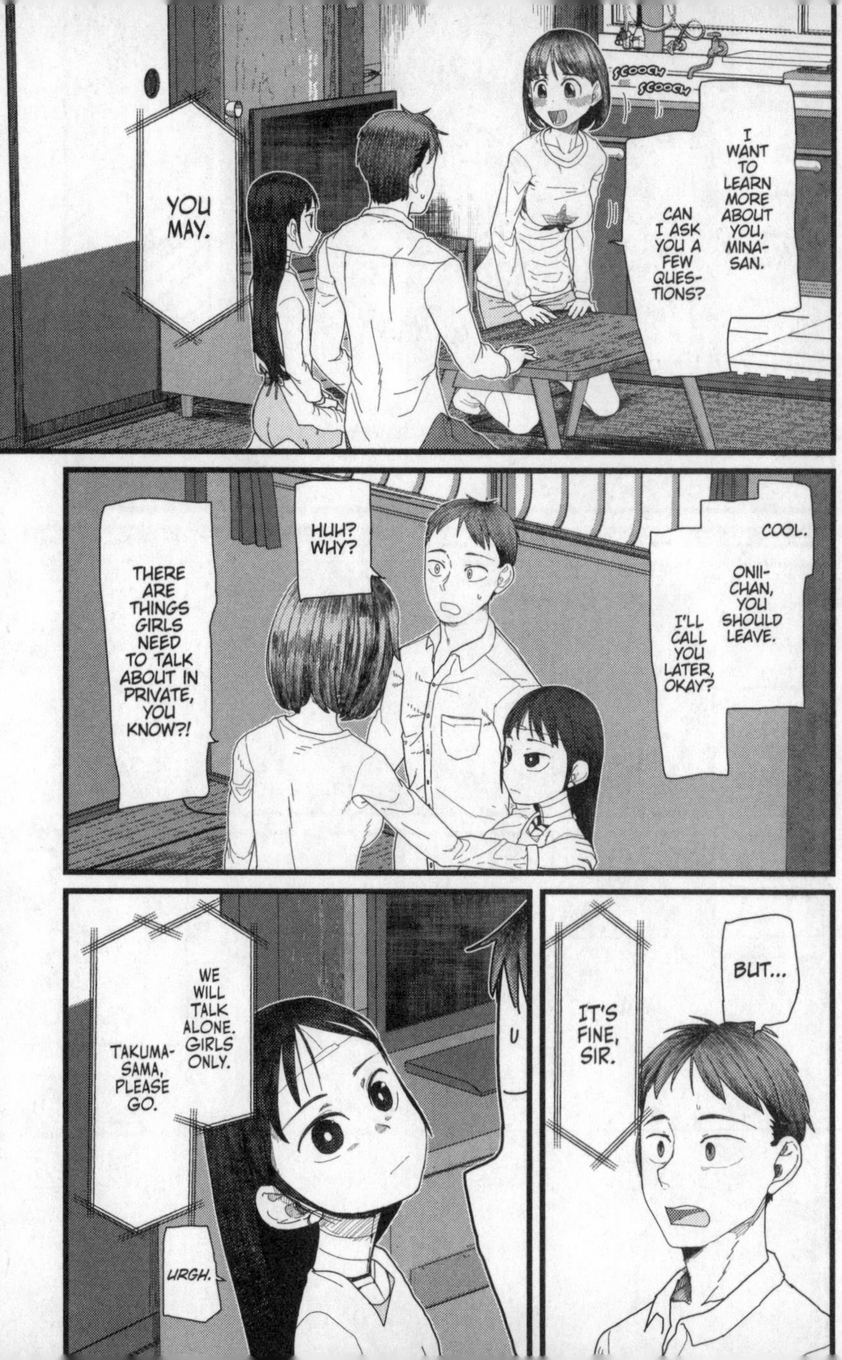
SCOOCH SCOOCH
I WANT TO LEARN MORE ABOUT YOU, MINA-SAN.
CAN I ASK YOU A FEW QUES-TIONS?
YOU MAY.
COOL.
ONII-CHAN, YOU SHOULD LEAVE.
I'LL CALL YOU LATER, OKAY?
HUH? WHY?
THERE ARE THINGS GIRLS NEED TO TALK ABOUT IN PRIVATE, YOU KNOW?!
BUT...
IT'S FINE, SIR.
WE WILL TALK ALONE. GIRLS ONLY.
TAKUMA-SAMA, PLEASE GO.
U
URGH.

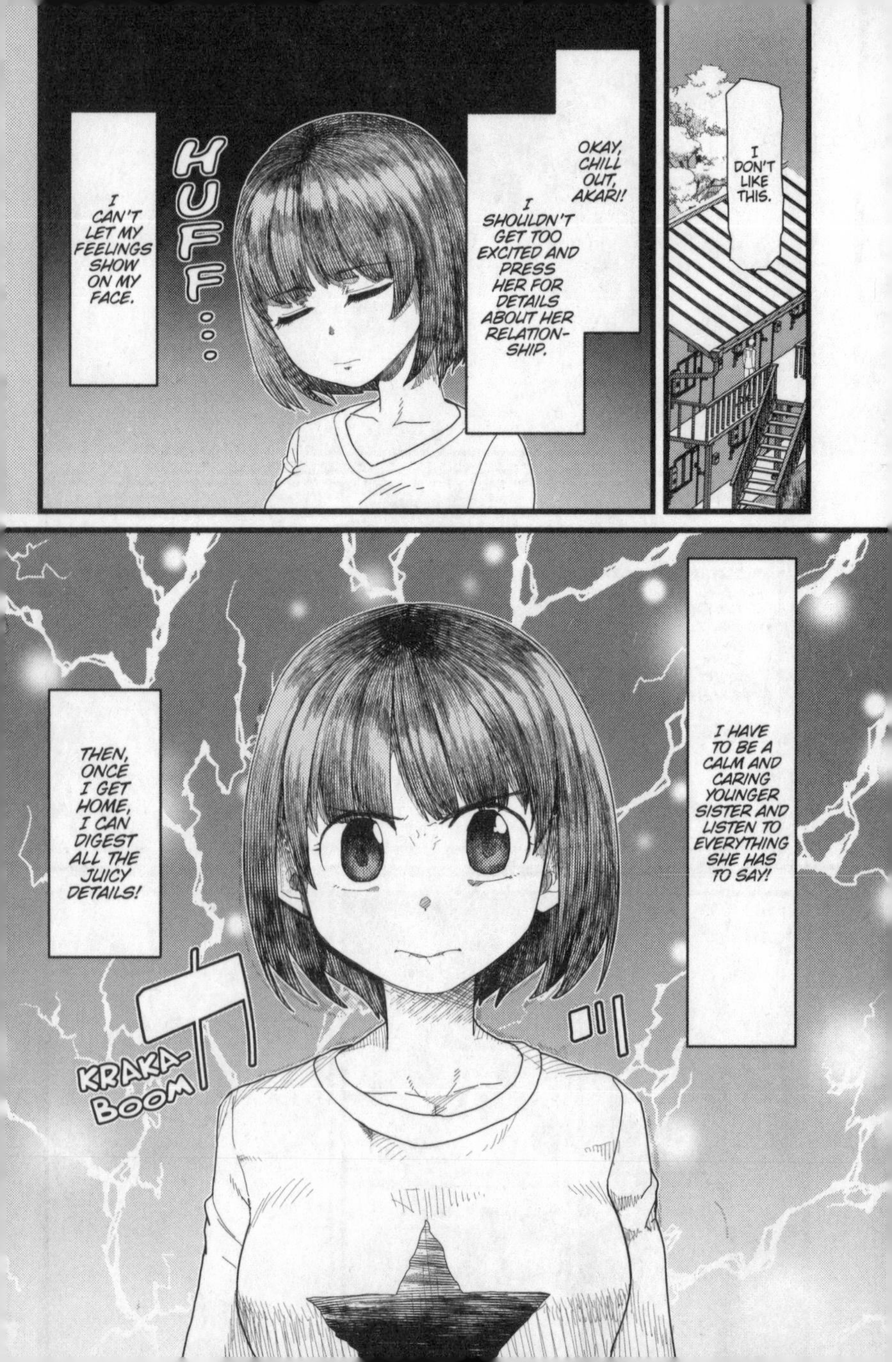
I DON'T LIKE THIS.
OKAY, CHILL OUT, AKARI!
I SHOULDN'T GET TOO EXCITED AND PRESS HER FOR DETAILS ABOUT HER RELATION-SHIP.
HUFF...
I CAN'T LET MY FEELINGS SHOW ON MY FACE.
I HAVE TO BE A CALM AND CARING YOUNGER SISTER AND LISTEN TO EVERYTHING SHE HAS TO SAY!
THEN, ONCE I GET HOME, I CAN DIGEST ALL THE JUICY DETAILS!
KRAKA-BOOM

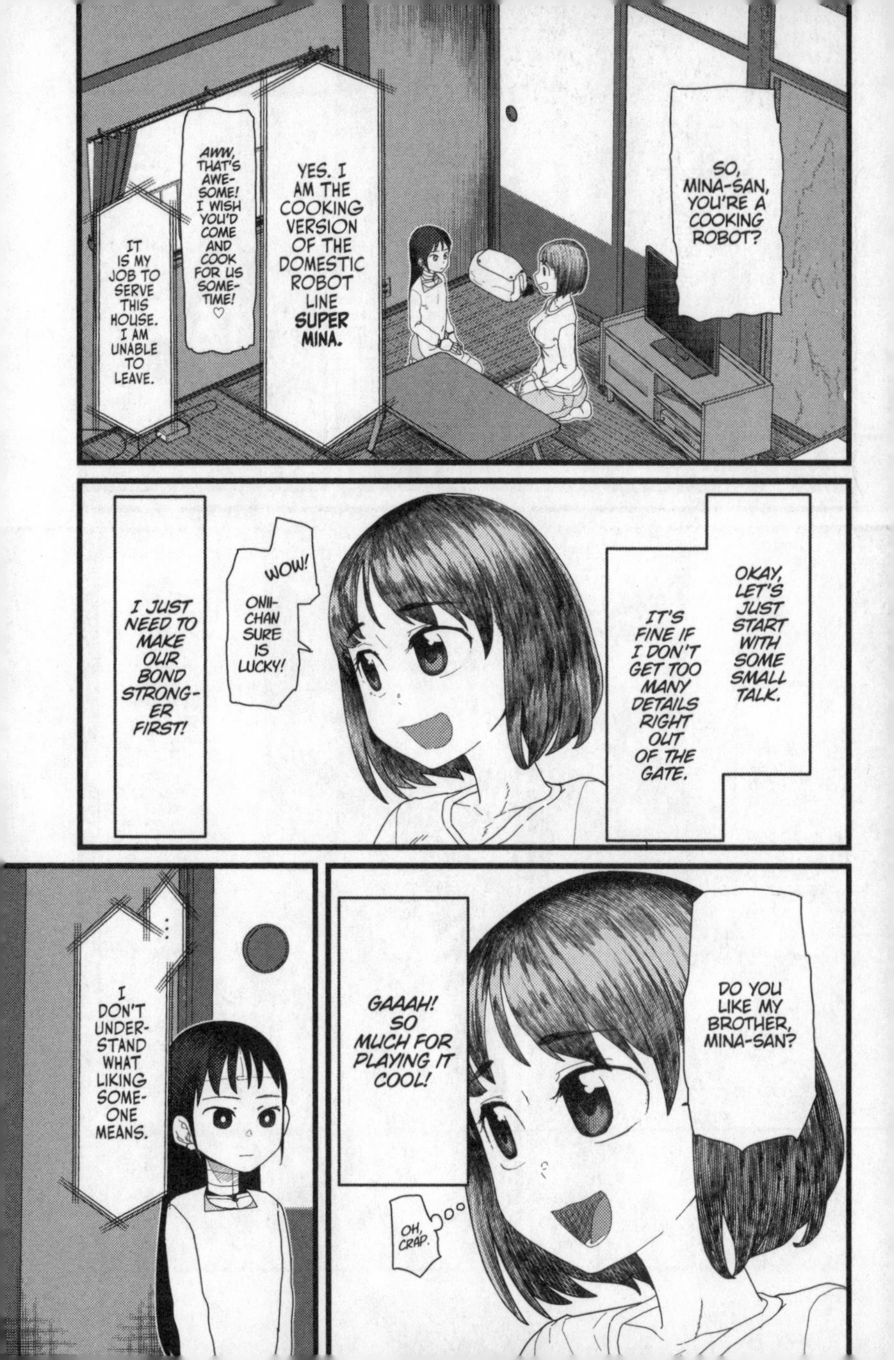
SO, MINA-SAN, YOU'RE A COOKING ROBOT?
YES. I AM THE COOKING VERSION OF THE DOMESTIC ROBOT LINE SUPER MINA.
AWW, THAT'S AWESOME! I WISH YOU'D COME AND COOK FOR US SOMETIME! ♡
IT IS MY JOB TO SERVE THIS HOUSE. I AM UNABLE TO LEAVE.
OKAY, LET'S JUST START WITH SOME SMALL TALK.
IT'S FINE IF I DON'T GET TOO MANY DETAILS RIGHT OUT OF THE GATE.
WOW! ONII-CHAN SURE IS LUCKY!
I JUST NEED TO MAKE OUR BOND STRONGER FIRST!
DO YOU LIKE MY BROTHER, MINA-SAN?
GAAAH! SO MUCH FOR PLAYING IT COOL!
OH, CRAP.
...
I DON'T UNDERSTAND WHAT LIKING SOMEONE MEANS.

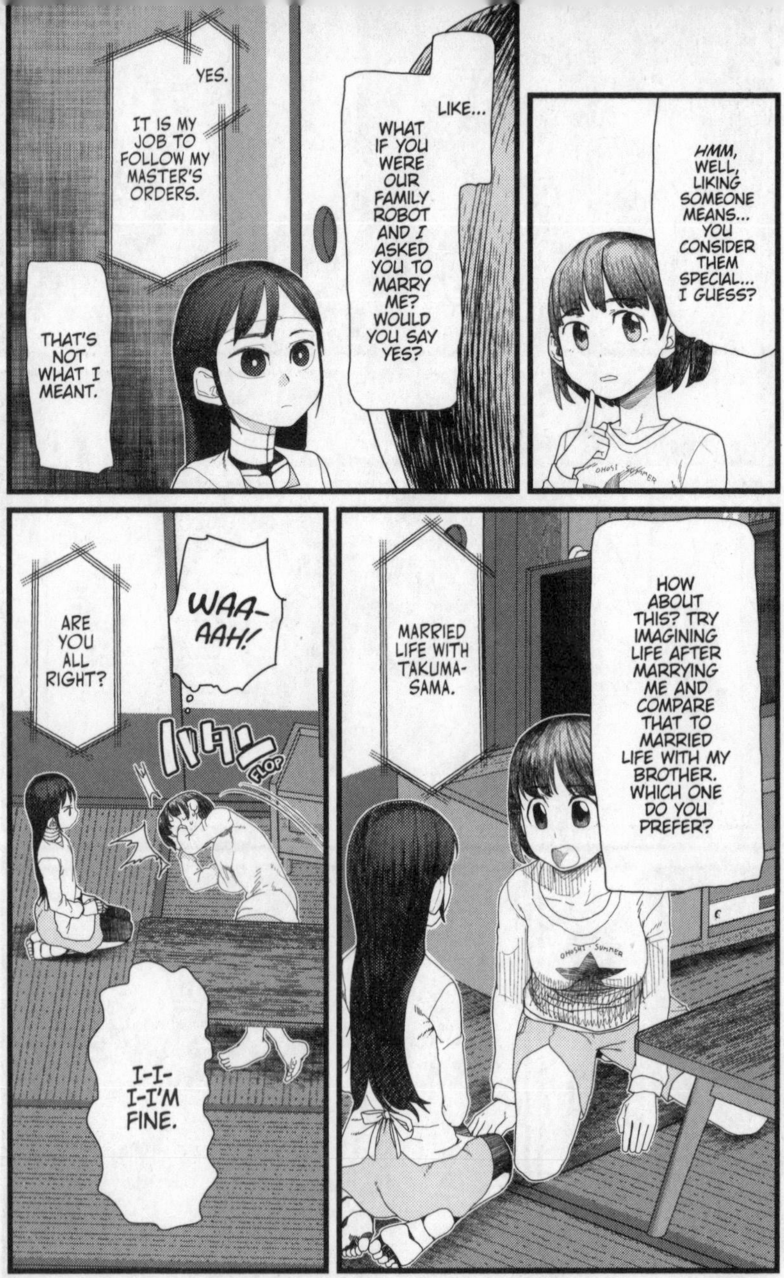
HMM, WELL, LIKING SOMEONE MEANS... YOU CONSIDER THEM SPECIAL... I GUESS?
LIKE... WHAT IF YOU WERE OUR FAMILY ROBOT AND I ASKED YOU TO MARRY ME? WOULD YOU SAY YES?
YES.
IT IS MY JOB TO FOLLOW MY MASTER'S ORDERS.
THAT'S NOT WHAT I MEANT.
HOW ABOUT THIS? TRY IMAGINING LIFE AFTER MARRYING ME AND COMPARE THAT TO MARRIED LIFE WITH MY BROTHER. WHICH ONE DO YOU PREFER?
MARRIED LIFE WITH TAKUMA-SAMA.
WAA-AAH!
ARE YOU ALL RIGHT?
バタン
FLOP
I-I-I-I'M FINE.

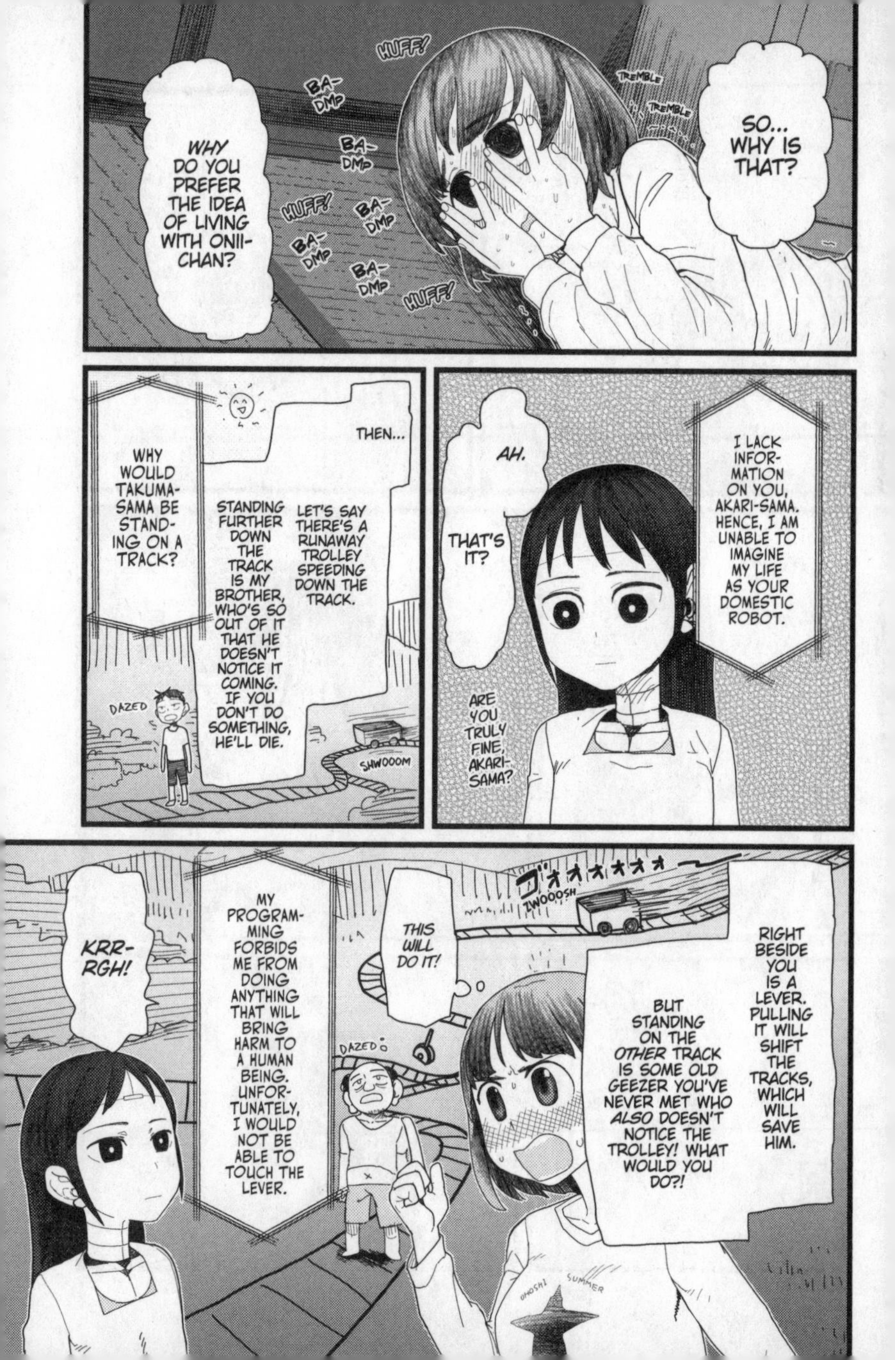
SO... WHY IS THAT?
TREMBLE
TREMBLE
HUFF!
BA-DMP
BA-DMP
HUFF!
BA-DMP
BA-DMP
BA-DMP
HUFF!
WHY DO YOU PREFER THE IDEA OF LIVING WITH ONII-CHAN?
I LACK INFORMATION ON YOU, AKARI-SAMA. HENCE, I AM UNABLE TO IMAGINE MY LIFE AS YOUR DOMESTIC ROBOT.
AH.
THAT'S IT?
ARE YOU TRULY FINE, AKARI-SAMA?
THEN...
LET'S SAY THERE'S A RUNAWAY TROLLEY SPEEDING DOWN THE TRACK.
STANDING FURTHER DOWN THE TRACK IS MY BROTHER, WHO'S SO OUT OF IT THAT HE DOESN'T NOTICE IT COMING. IF YOU DON'T DO SOMETHING, HE'LL DIE.
WHY WOULD TAKUMA-SAMA BE STANDING ON A TRACK?
DAZED
SHWOOOM
ゴオオオオオオー
ZWOOOSH
RIGHT BESIDE YOU IS A LEVER. PULLING IT WILL SHIFT THE TRACKS, WHICH WILL SAVE HIM.
BUT STANDING ON THE OTHER TRACK IS SOME OLD GEEZER YOU'VE NEVER MET WHO ALSO DOESN'T NOTICE THE TROLLEY! WHAT WOULD YOU DO?!
THIS WILL DO IT!
DAZED
MY PROGRAMMING FORBIDS ME FROM DOING ANYTHING THAT WILL BRING HARM TO A HUMAN BEING. UNFORTUNATELY, I WOULD NOT BE ABLE TO TOUCH THE LEVER.
KRR-RGH!
OHOSHI SUMMER

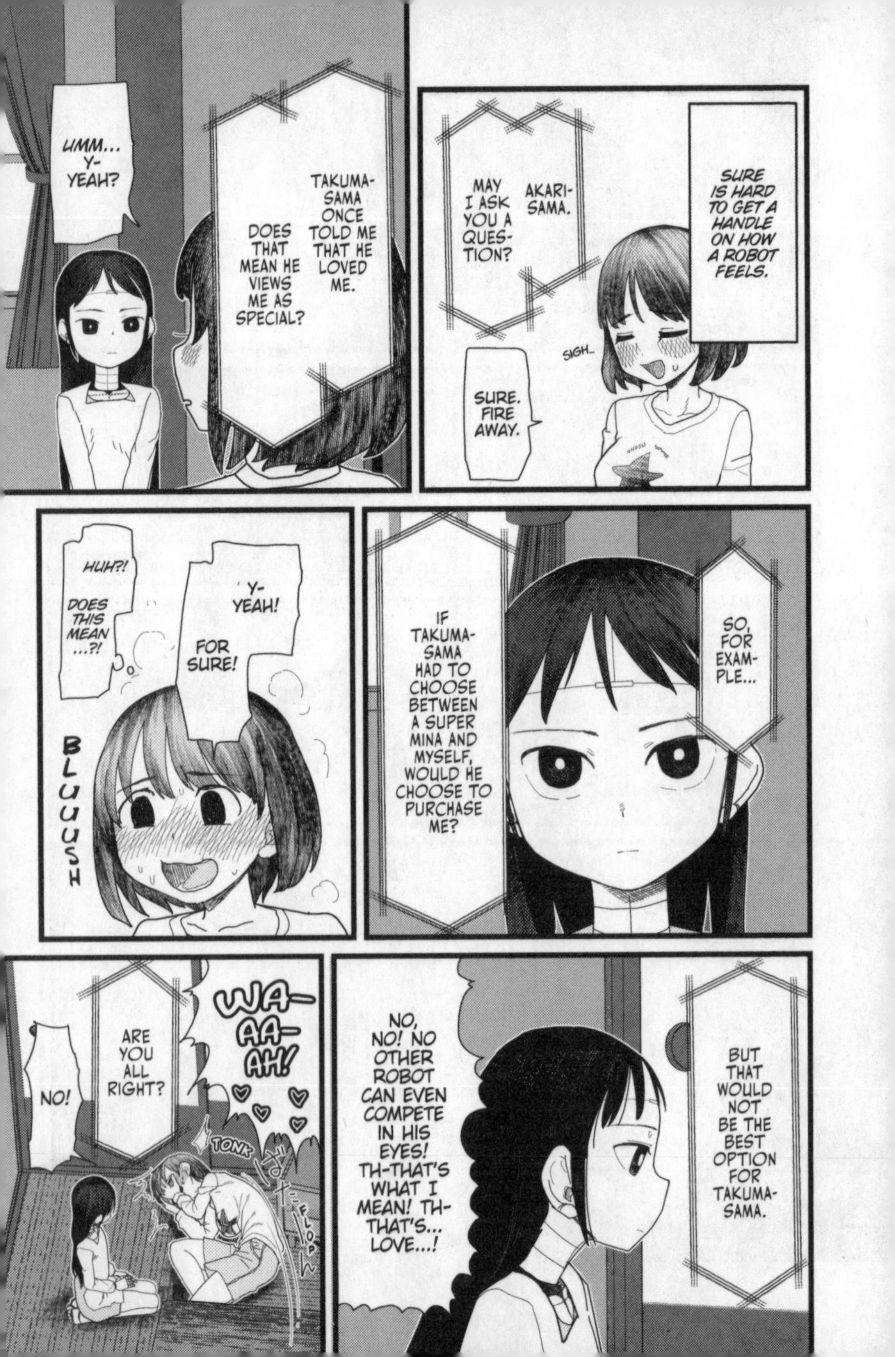
SURE IS HARD TO GET A HANDLE ON HOW A ROBOT FEELS.
AKARI-SAMA.
MAY I ASK YOU A QUESTION?
SIGH...
SURE. FIRE AWAY.
TAKUMA-SAMA ONCE TOLD ME THAT HE LOVED ME.
DOES THAT MEAN HE VIEWS ME AS SPECIAL?
UMM... Y-YEAH?
SO, FOR EXAMPLE...
IF TAKUMA-SAMA HAD TO CHOOSE BETWEEN A SUPER MINA AND MYSELF, WOULD HE CHOOSE TO PURCHASE ME?
Y-YEAH!
FOR SURE!
HUH?! DOES THIS MEAN ...?!
BLUUUSH
BUT THAT WOULD NOT BE THE BEST OPTION FOR TAKUMA-SAMA.
NO, NO! NO OTHER ROBOT CAN EVEN COMPETE IN HIS EYES! TH-THAT'S WHAT I MEAN! TH-THAT'S... LOVE...!
WA-AA-AH!
ARE YOU ALL RIGHT?
NO!
TONK
FLOP

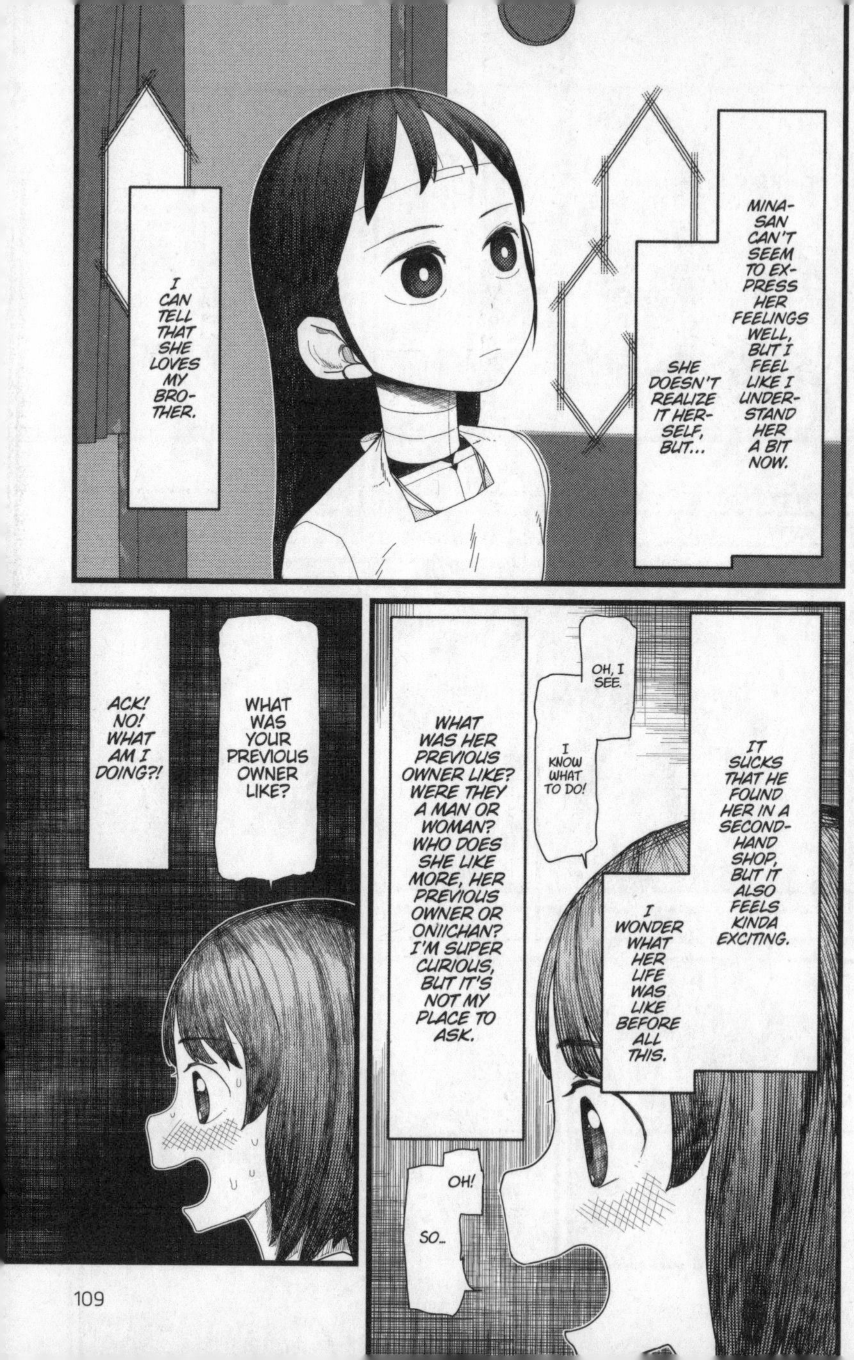
MINA-SAN CAN'T SEEM TO EXPRESS HER FEELINGS WELL, BUT I FEEL LIKE I UNDERSTAND HER A BIT NOW.
SHE DOESN'T REALIZE IT HERSELF, BUT...
I CAN TELL THAT SHE LOVES MY BROTHER.
IT SUCKS THAT HE FOUND HER IN A SECOND-HAND SHOP, BUT IT ALSO FEELS KINDA EXCITING.
I WONDER WHAT HER LIFE WAS LIKE BEFORE ALL THIS.
OH, I SEE.
I KNOW WHAT TO DO!
WHAT WAS HER PREVIOUS OWNER LIKE? WERE THEY A MAN OR WOMAN? WHO DOES SHE LIKE MORE, HER PREVIOUS OWNER OR ONIICHAN? I'M SUPER CURIOUS, BUT IT'S NOT MY PLACE TO ASK.
OH!
SO...
WHAT WAS YOUR PREVIOUS OWNER LIKE?
ACK! NO! WHAT AM I DOING?!

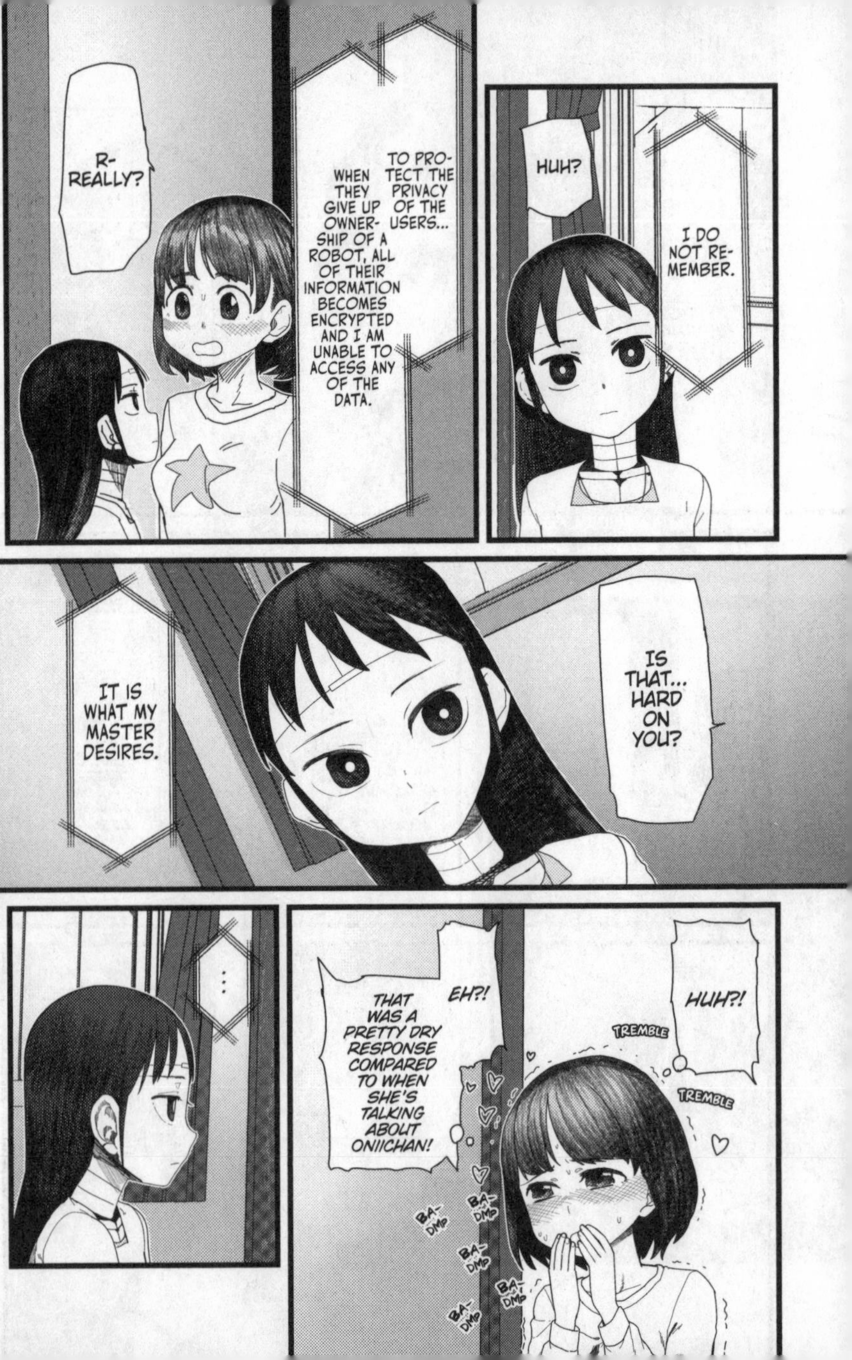
HUH?
I DO NOT REMEMBER.
TO PROTECT THE PRIVACY OF THE USERS...
WHEN THEY GIVE UP OWNERSHIP OF A ROBOT, ALL OF THEIR INFORMATION BECOMES ENCRYPTED AND I AM UNABLE TO ACCESS ANY OF THE DATA.
R-REALLY?
IS THAT... HARD ON YOU?
IT IS WHAT MY MASTER DESIRES.
HUH?!
TREMBLE
TREMBLE
EH?!
THAT WAS A PRETTY DRY RESPONSE COMPARED TO WHEN SHE'S TALKING ABOUT ONIICHAN!
BA-DMP
BA-DMP
BA-DMP
BA-DMP
BA-DMP
...

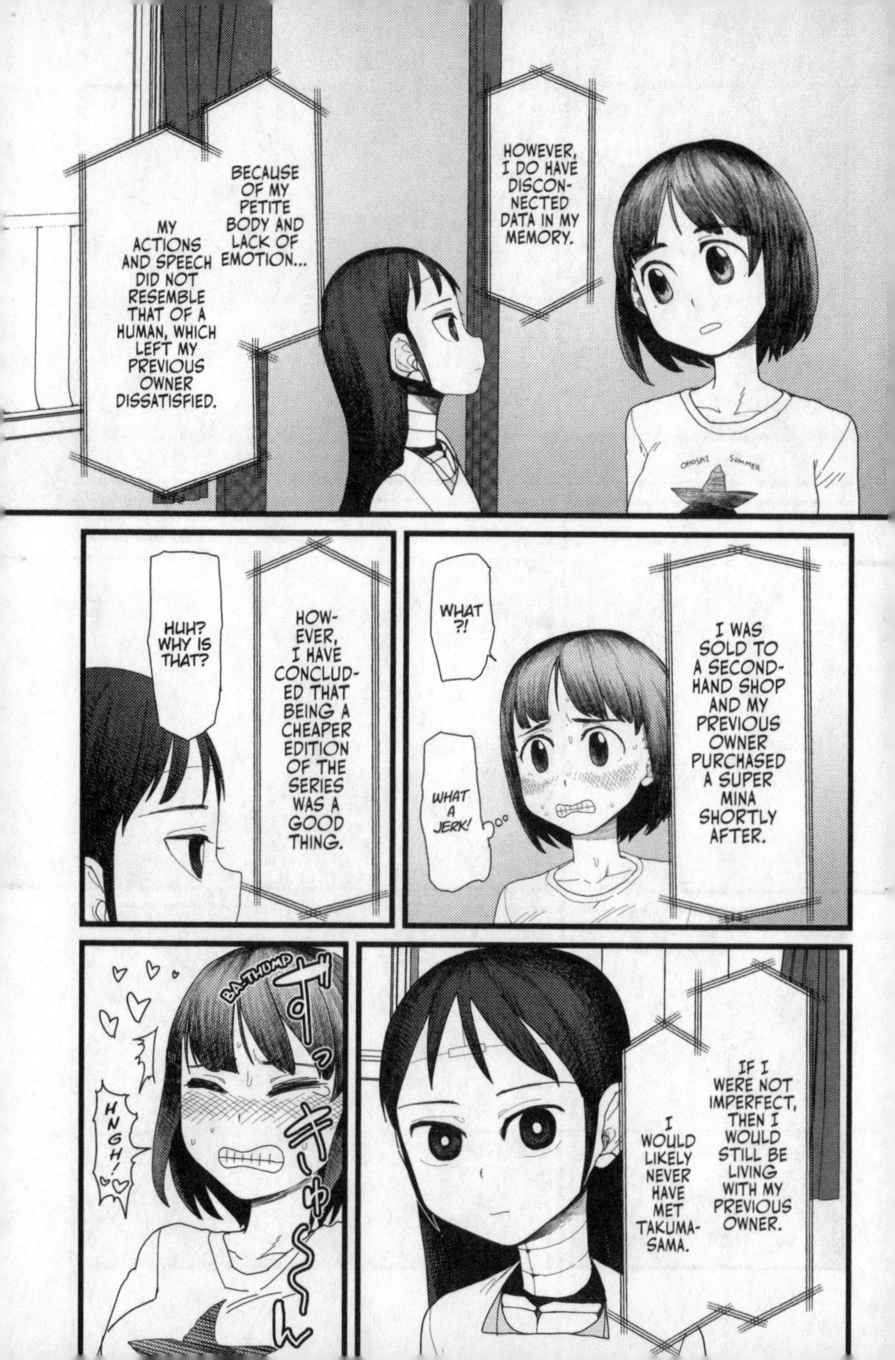
HOWEVER, I DO HAVE DISCONNECTED DATA IN MY MEMORY.
BECAUSE OF MY PETITE BODY AND LACK OF EMOTION...
MY ACTIONS AND SPEECH DID NOT RESEMBLE THAT OF A HUMAN, WHICH LEFT MY PREVIOUS OWNER DISSATISFIED.
OHOSHI SUMMER
I WAS SOLD TO A SECOND-HAND SHOP AND MY PREVIOUS OWNER PURCHASED A SUPER MINA SHORTLY AFTER.
WHAT?!
WHAT A JERK!
HOWEVER, I HAVE CONCLUDED THAT BEING A CHEAPER EDITION OF THE SERIES WAS A GOOD THING.
HUH? WHY IS THAT?
IF I WERE NOT IMPERFECT, THEN I WOULD STILL BE LIVING WITH MY PREVIOUS OWNER.
I WOULD LIKELY NEVER HAVE MET TAKUMA-SAMA.
BA-THUMP
HNGH!

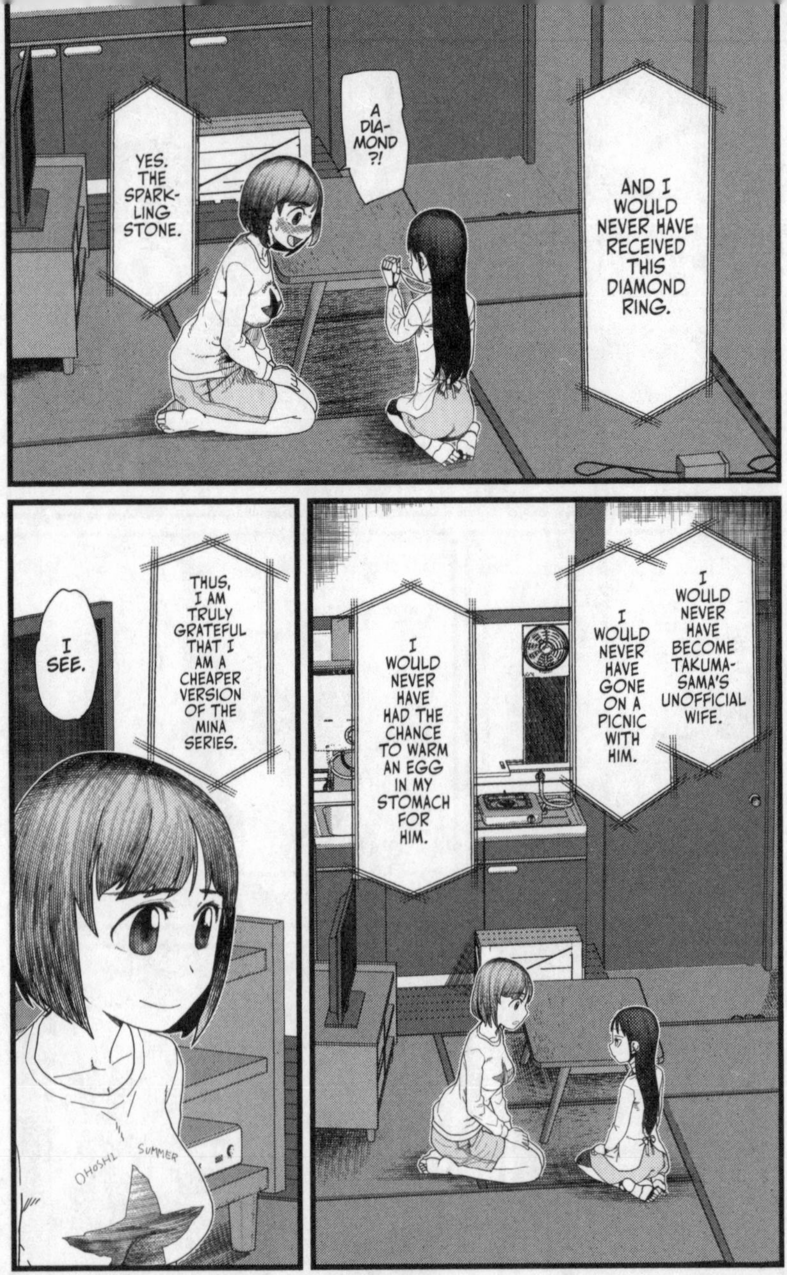
AND I WOULD NEVER HAVE RECEIVED THIS DIAMOND RING.
A DIA-MOND?!
YES. THE SPARK-LING STONE.
I WOULD NEVER HAVE BECOME TAKUMA-SAMA'S UNOFFICIAL WIFE.
I WOULD NEVER HAVE GONE ON A PICNIC WITH HIM.
I WOULD NEVER HAVE HAD THE CHANCE TO WARM AN EGG IN MY STOMACH FOR HIM.
THUS, I AM TRULY GRATEFUL THAT I AM A CHEAPER VERSION OF THE MINA SERIES.
I SEE.
OHOSHI SUMMER

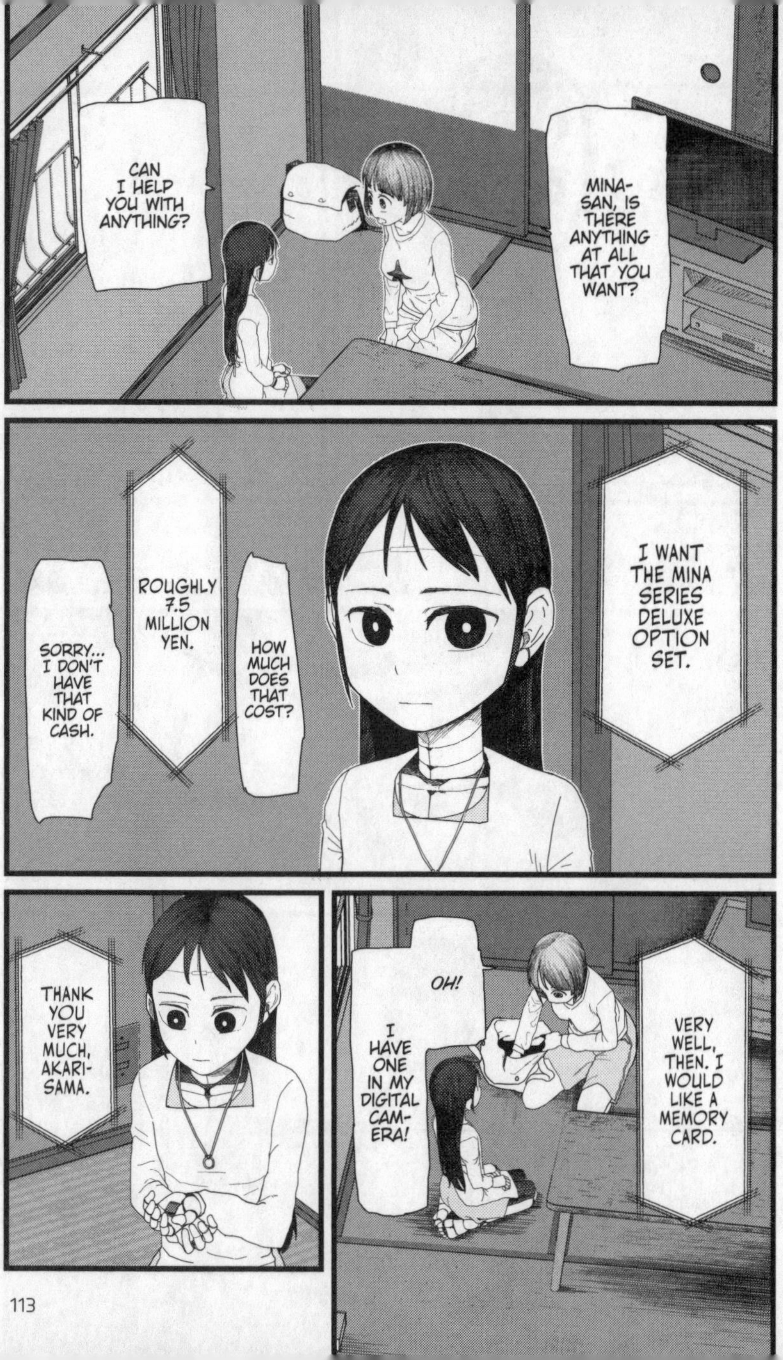
MINA-SAN, IS THERE ANYTHING AT ALL THAT YOU WANT?
CAN I HELP YOU WITH ANYTHING?
I WANT THE MINA SERIES DELUXE OPTION SET.
HOW MUCH DOES THAT COST?
ROUGHLY 7.5 MILLION YEN.
SORRY... I DON'T HAVE THAT KIND OF CASH.
VERY WELL, THEN. I WOULD LIKE A MEMORY CARD.
OH!
I HAVE ONE IN MY DIGITAL CAM-ERA!
THANK YOU VERY MUCH, AKARI-SAMA.

?!

SLIP

ARE YOU CERTAIN THIS IS OKAY?

SURE. BUT WHAT ARE YOU USING IT FOR?

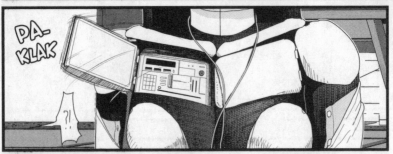

PA-KLAK

?!

I AM BACKING UP MY SYSTEM.

OH, OKAY. YOU'RE BACKING YOUR-SELF UP ON THERE? BUT IT'S ONLY 128GB.

THAT WILL DO.

KLIK

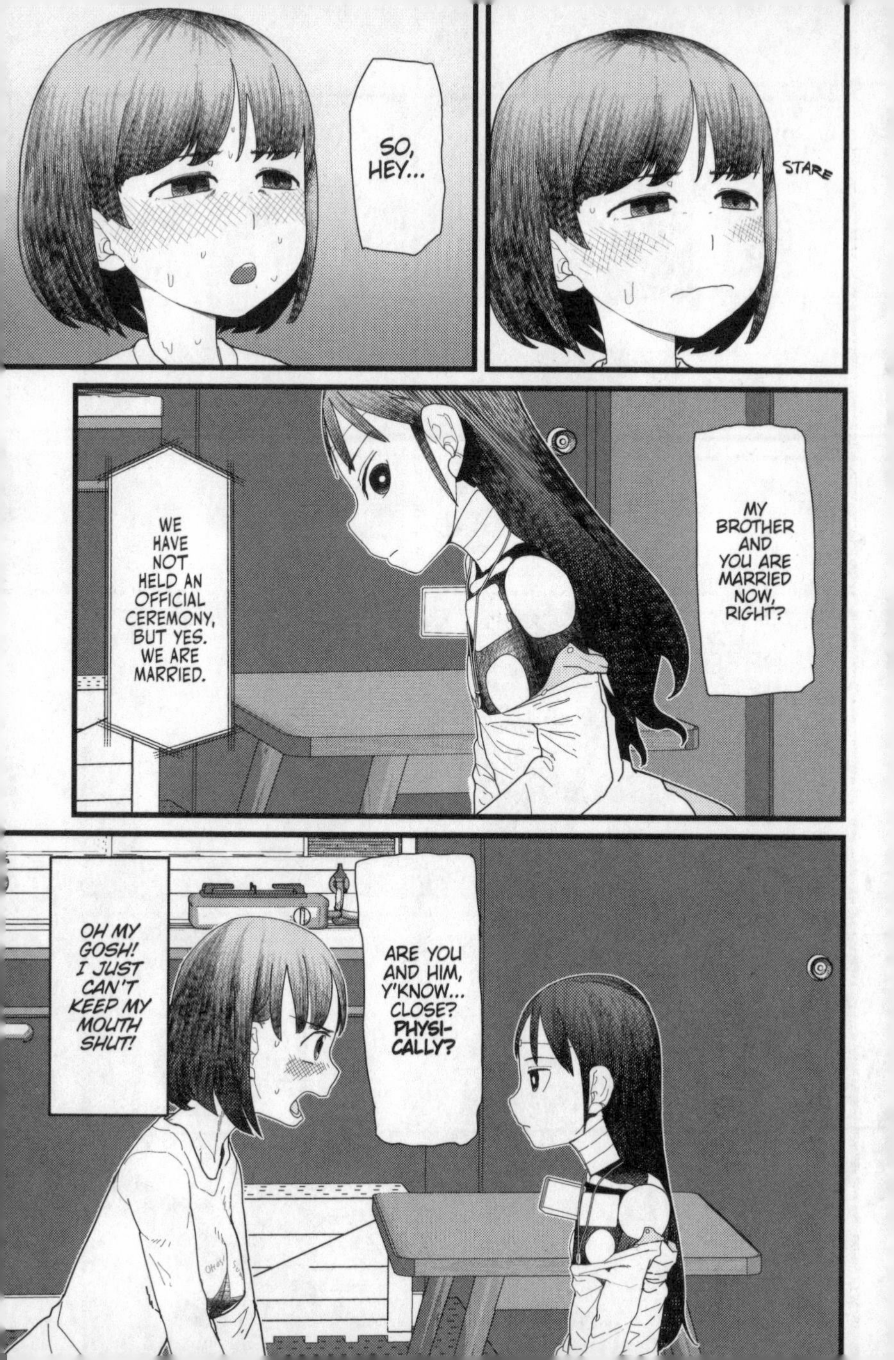
STARE
SO, HEY...
MY BROTHER AND YOU ARE MARRIED NOW, RIGHT?
WE HAVE NOT HELD AN OFFICIAL CEREMONY, BUT YES. WE ARE MARRIED.
ARE YOU AND HIM, Y'KNOW... CLOSE? **PHYSI-CALLY?**
OH MY GOSH! I JUST CAN'T KEEP MY MOUTH SHUT!

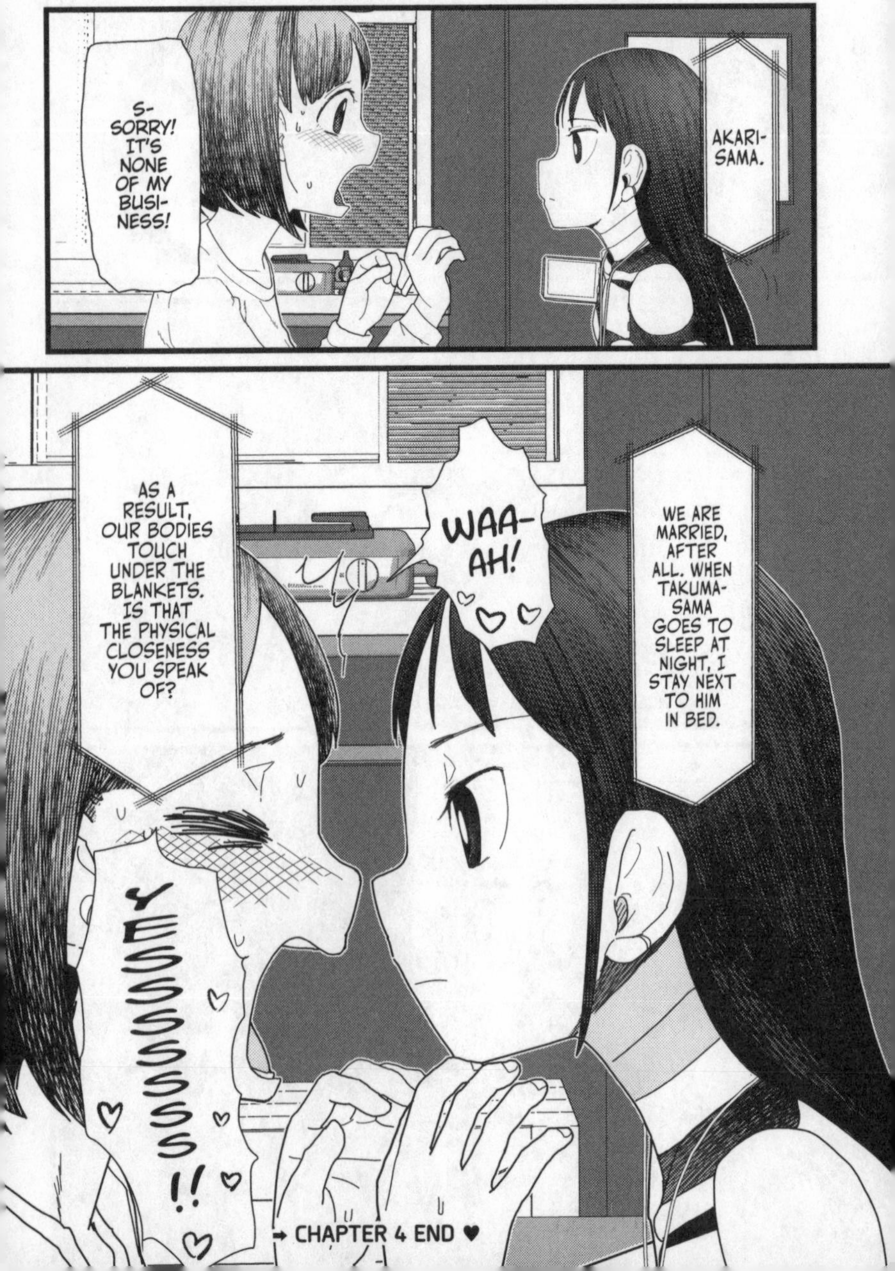
AKARI-SAMA.
S-SORRY! IT'S NONE OF MY BUSINESS!
WE ARE MARRIED, AFTER ALL. WHEN TAKUMA-SAMA GOES TO SLEEP AT NIGHT, I STAY NEXT TO HIM IN BED.
WAA-AH!
AS A RESULT, OUR BODIES TOUCH UNDER THE BLANKETS. IS THAT THE PHYSICAL CLOSENESS YOU SPEAK OF?
YESSSSSSS!!
➡ CHAPTER 4 END ♥

My Wife Has No Emotion

My
Wife Has No
Emotion

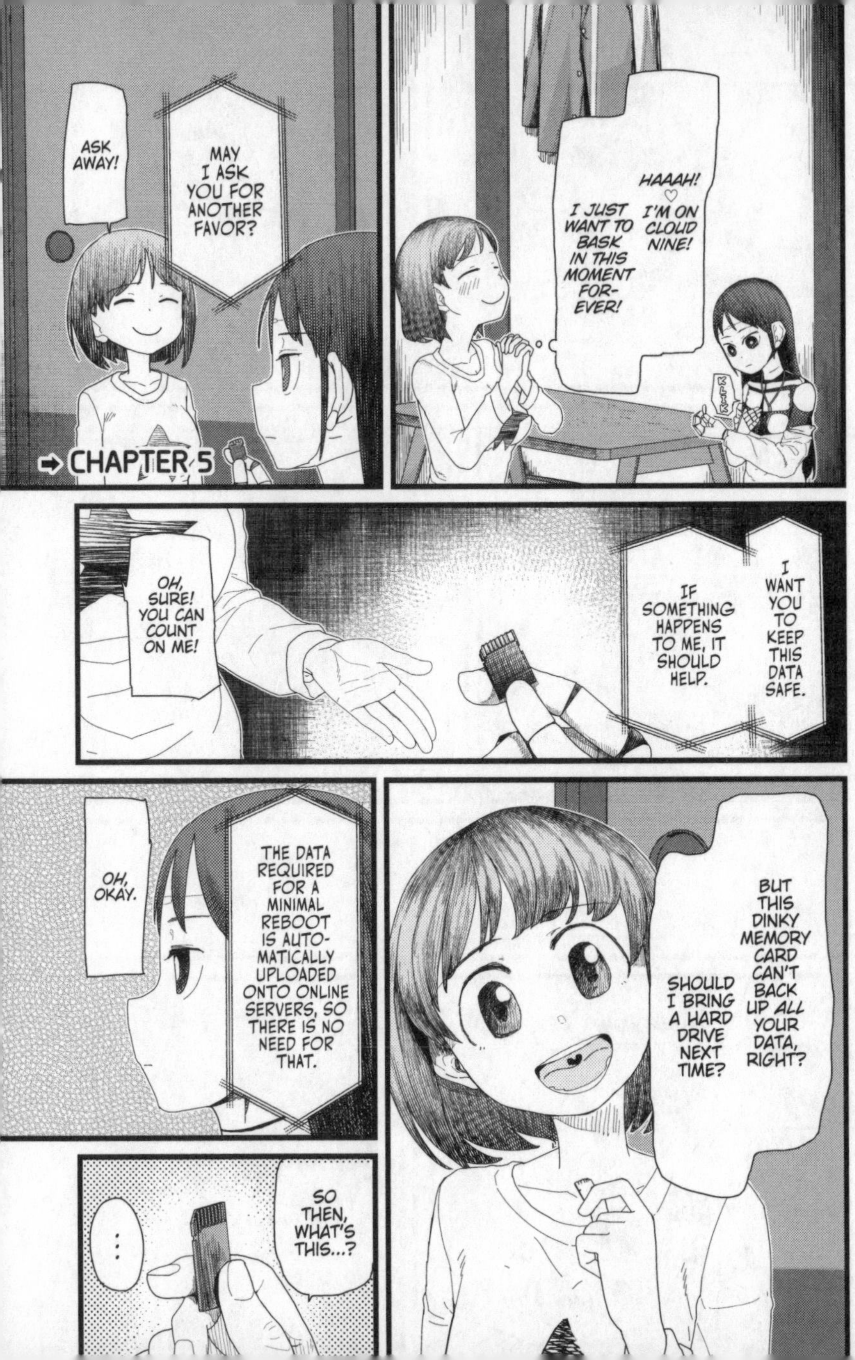
HAAAH! ♡ I'M ON CLOUD NINE!
I JUST WANT TO BASK IN THIS MOMENT FOR-EVER!
KLIK
MAY I ASK YOU FOR ANOTHER FAVOR?
ASK AWAY!
CHAPTER 5
I WANT YOU TO KEEP THIS DATA SAFE.
IF SOMETHING HAPPENS TO ME, IT SHOULD HELP.
OH, SURE! YOU CAN COUNT ON ME!
BUT THIS DINKY MEMORY CARD CAN'T BACK UP *ALL* YOUR DATA, RIGHT?
SHOULD I BRING A HARD DRIVE NEXT TIME?
THE DATA REQUIRED FOR A MINIMAL REBOOT IS AUTO-MATICALLY UPLOADED ONTO ONLINE SERVERS, SO THERE IS NO NEED FOR THAT.
OH, OKAY.
SO THEN, WHAT'S THIS...?
...

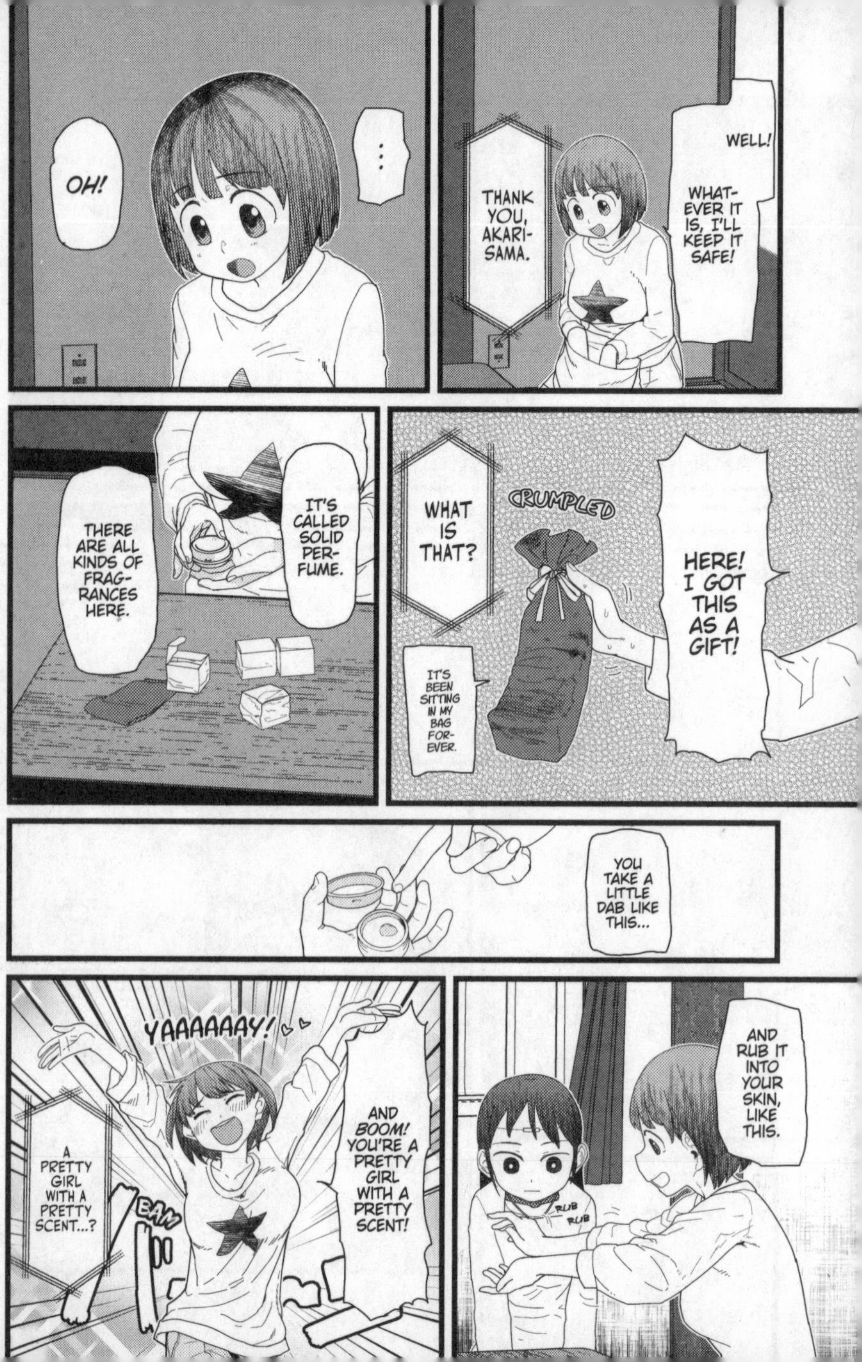
WELL!
WHAT-EVER IT IS, I'LL KEEP IT SAFE!
THANK YOU, AKARI-SAMA.
...
OH!
HERE! I GOT THIS AS A GIFT!
CRUMPLED
WHAT IS THAT?
IT'S BEEN SITTING IN MY BAG FOR-EVER.
IT'S CALLED SOLID PER-FUME.
THERE ARE ALL KINDS OF FRAG-RANCES HERE.
YOU TAKE A LITTLE DAB LIKE THIS...
AND RUB IT INTO YOUR SKIN, LIKE THIS.
RUB RUB
YAAAAAAY!
AND *BOOM!* YOU'RE A PRETTY GIRL WITH A PRETTY SCENT!
BAM
A PRETTY GIRL WITH A PRETTY SCENT...?

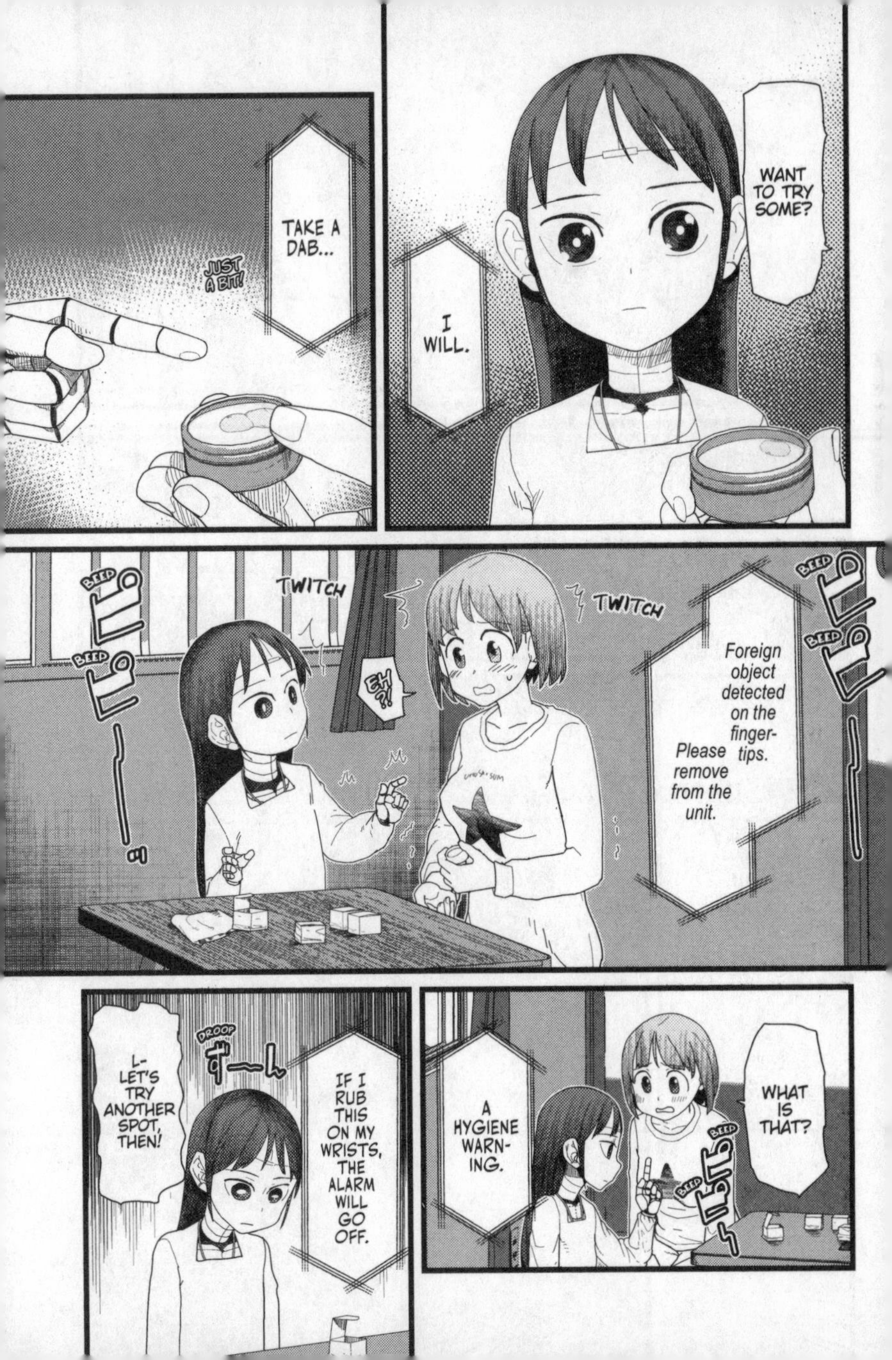
WANT TO TRY SOME?
I WILL.
TAKE A DAB...
JUST A BIT!
BEEP
BEEP
Foreign object detected on the finger-tips. Please remove from the unit.
TWITCH
EH?!
TWITCH
BEEP
BEEP
WHAT IS THAT?
BEEP
BEEP
A HYGIENE WARNING.
IF I RUB THIS ON MY WRISTS, THE ALARM WILL GO OFF.
DROOP
L-LET'S TRY ANOTHER SPOT, THEN!

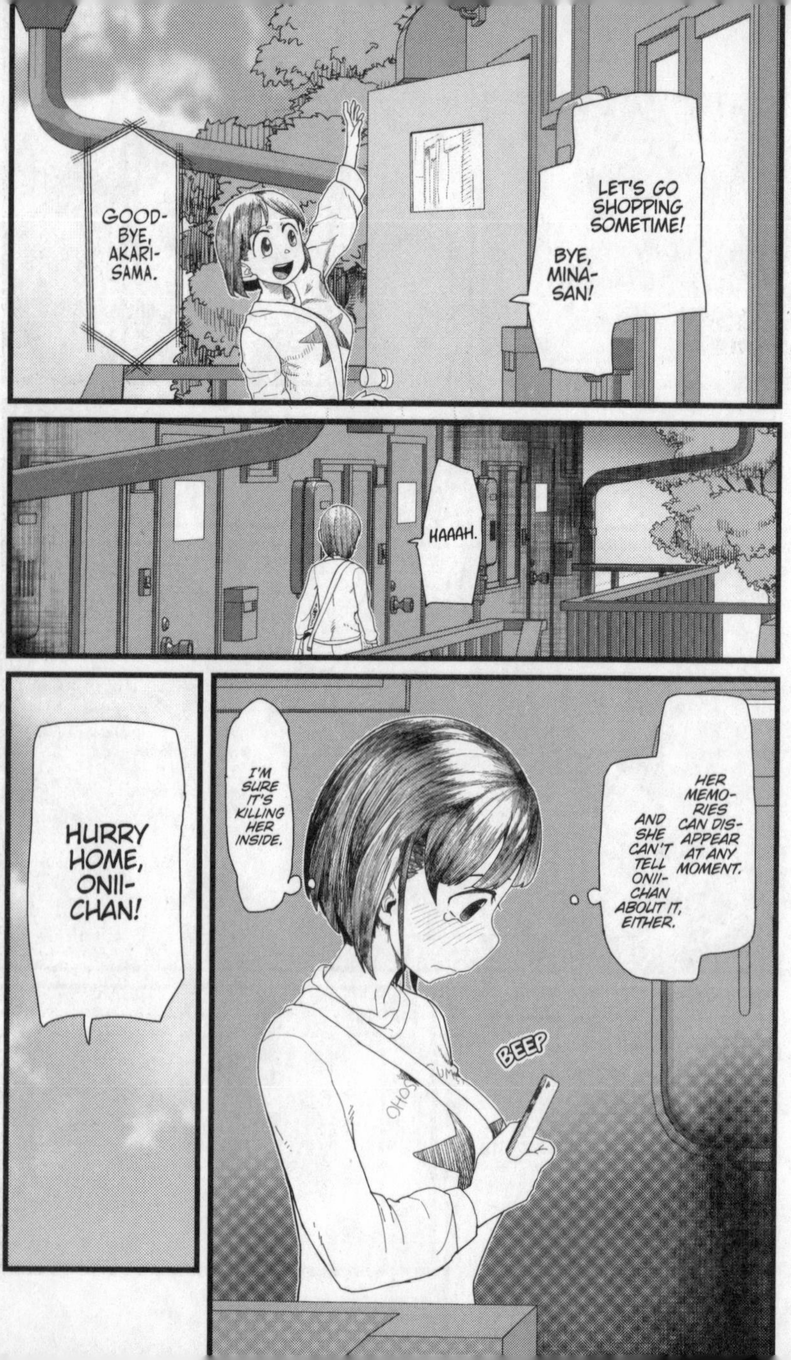
LET'S GO SHOPPING SOMETIME! BYE, MINA-SAN!
GOOD-BYE, AKARI-SAMA.
HAAAH.
HER MEMORIES CAN DISAPPEAR AT ANY MOMENT.
AND SHE CAN'T TELL ONII-CHAN ABOUT IT, EITHER.
I'M SURE IT'S KILLING HER INSIDE.
BEEP
HURRY HOME, ONII-CHAN!

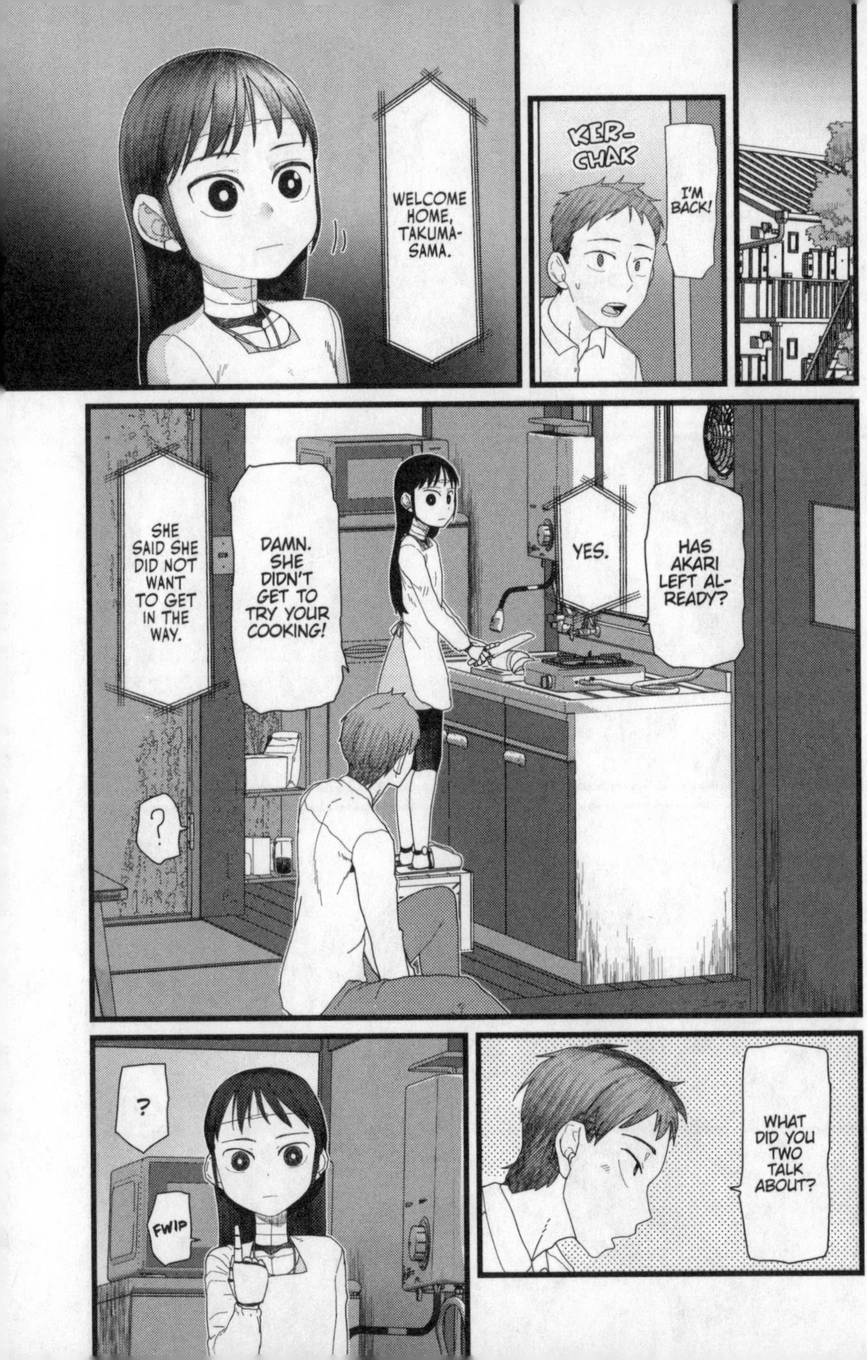
KER-CHAK
I'M BACK!
WELCOME HOME, TAKUMA-SAMA.
HAS AKARI LEFT AL-READY?
YES.
DAMN. SHE DIDN'T GET TO TRY YOUR COOKING!
SHE SAID SHE DID NOT WANT TO GET IN THE WAY.
?
WHAT DID YOU TWO TALK ABOUT?
?
FWIP

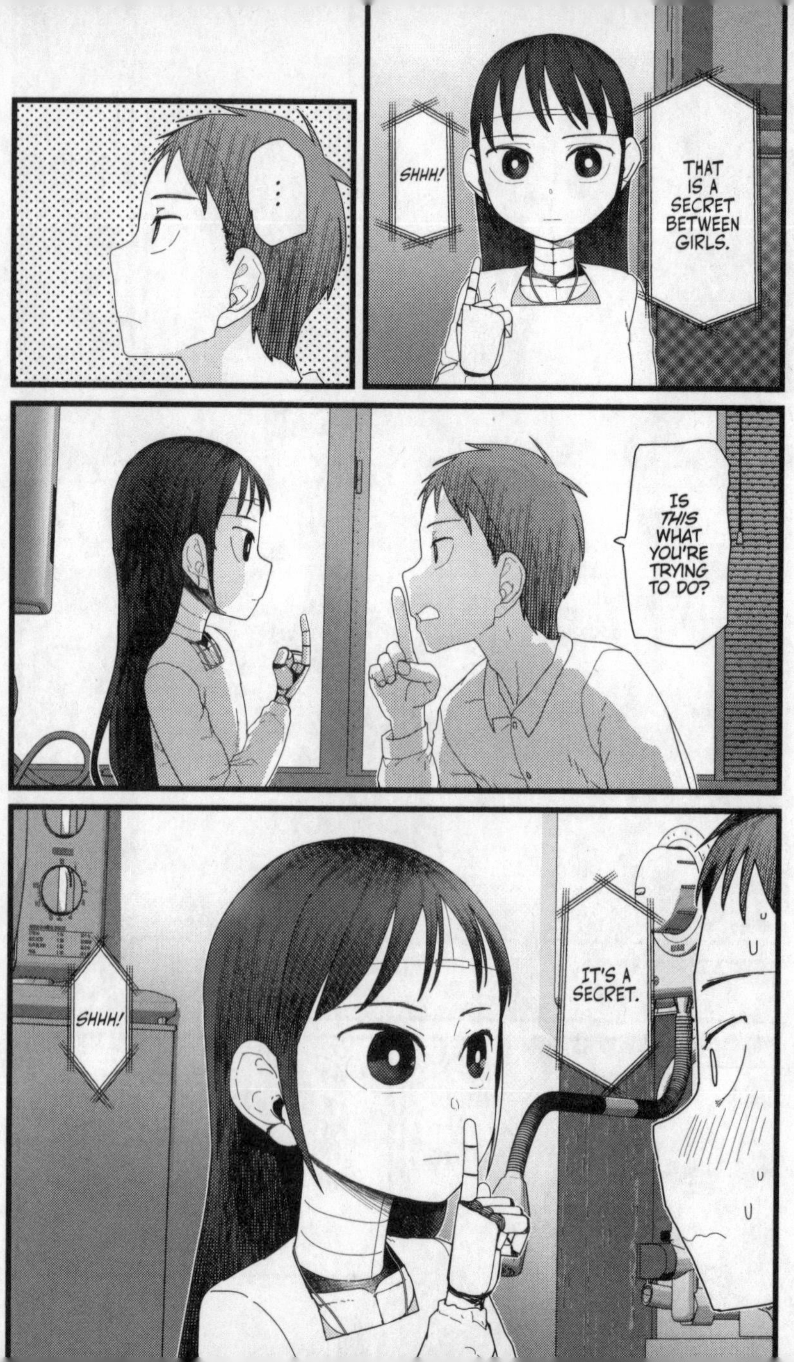

THAT IS A SECRET BETWEEN GIRLS.
SHHH!
...
IS *THIS* WHAT YOU'RE TRYING TO DO?
IT'S A SECRET.
SHHH!

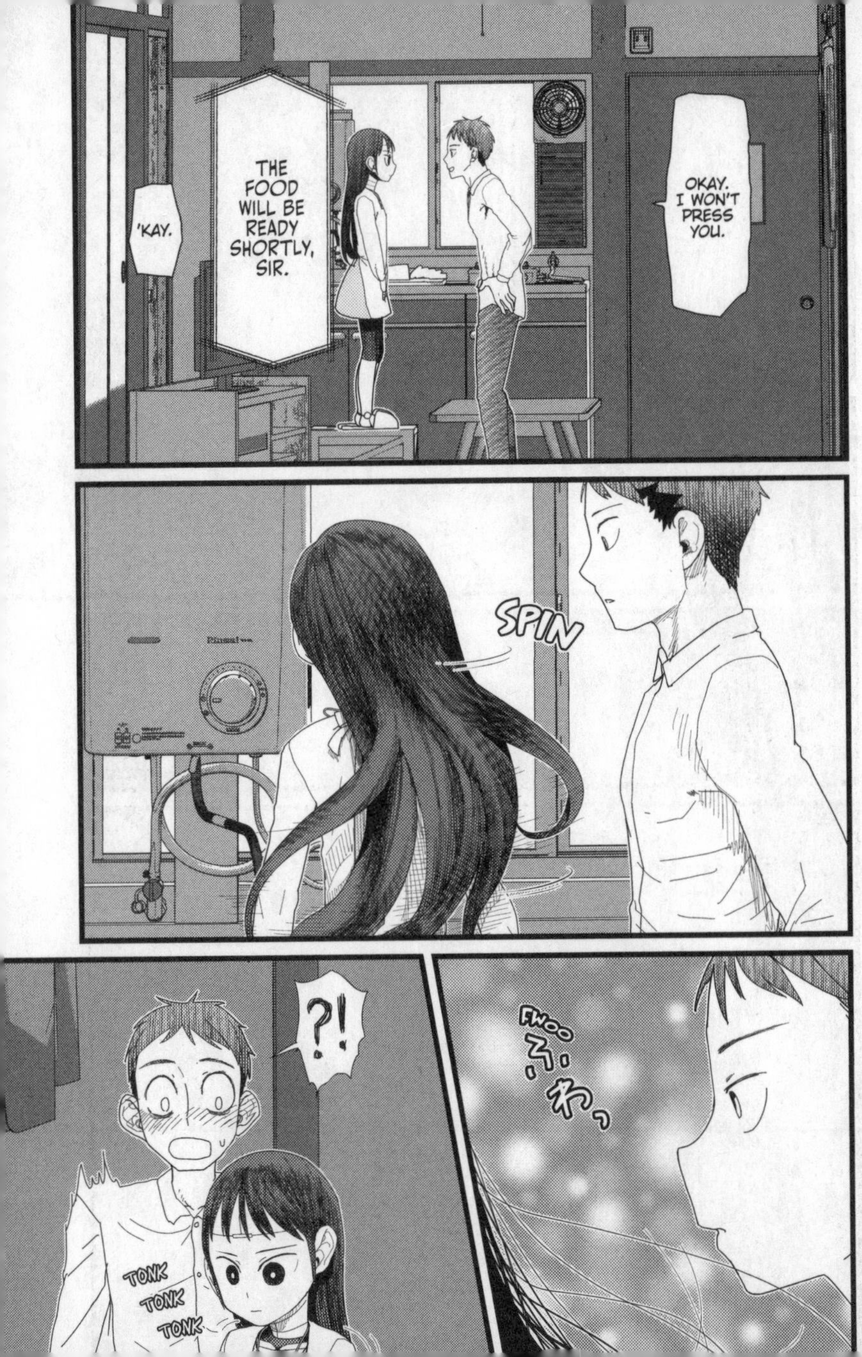
OKAY. I WON'T PRESS YOU.
THE FOOD WILL BE READY SHORTLY, SIR.
'KAY.
SPIN
FWOO
ふわっ
?!
TONK
TONK
TONK

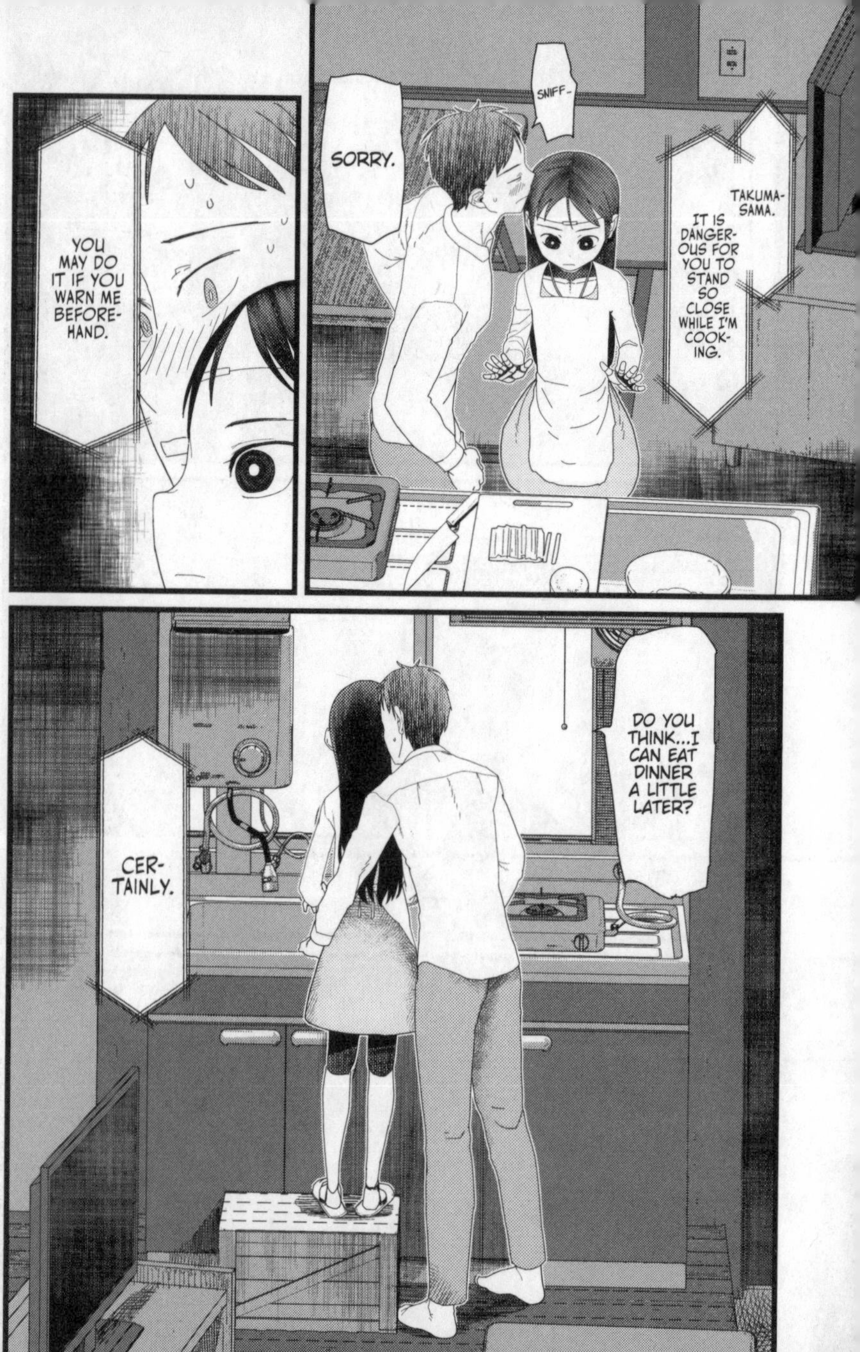
SNIFF_
TAKUMA-SAMA.
IT IS DANGEROUS FOR YOU TO STAND SO CLOSE WHILE I'M COOKING.
SORRY.
YOU MAY DO IT IF YOU WARN ME BEFOREHAND.
DO YOU THINK...I CAN EAT DINNER A LITTLE LATER?
CERTAINLY.

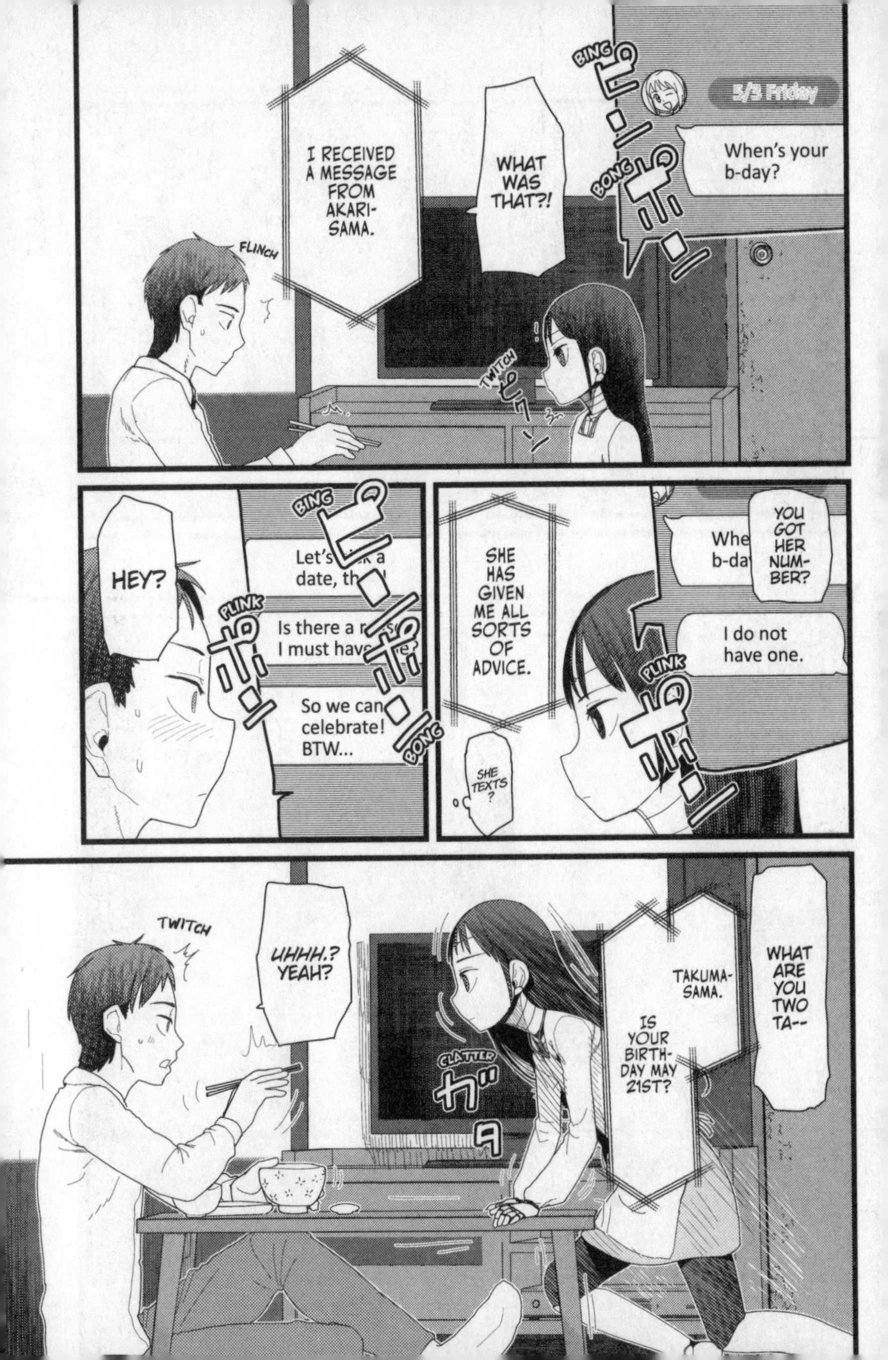
5/3 Friday
When's your b-day?
BING
BONG
WHAT WAS THAT?!
I RECEIVED A MESSAGE FROM AKARI-SAMA.
FLINCH
TWITCH
YOU GOT HER NUMBER?
I do not have one.
PLINK
SHE HAS GIVEN ME ALL SORTS OF ADVICE.
SHE TEXTS?
BING
So we can celebrate! BTW...
BONG
PLINK
HEY?
WHAT ARE YOU TWO TA--
TAKUMA-SAMA.
IS YOUR BIRTH-DAY MAY 21ST?
CLATTER
UHHH.? YEAH?
TWITCH

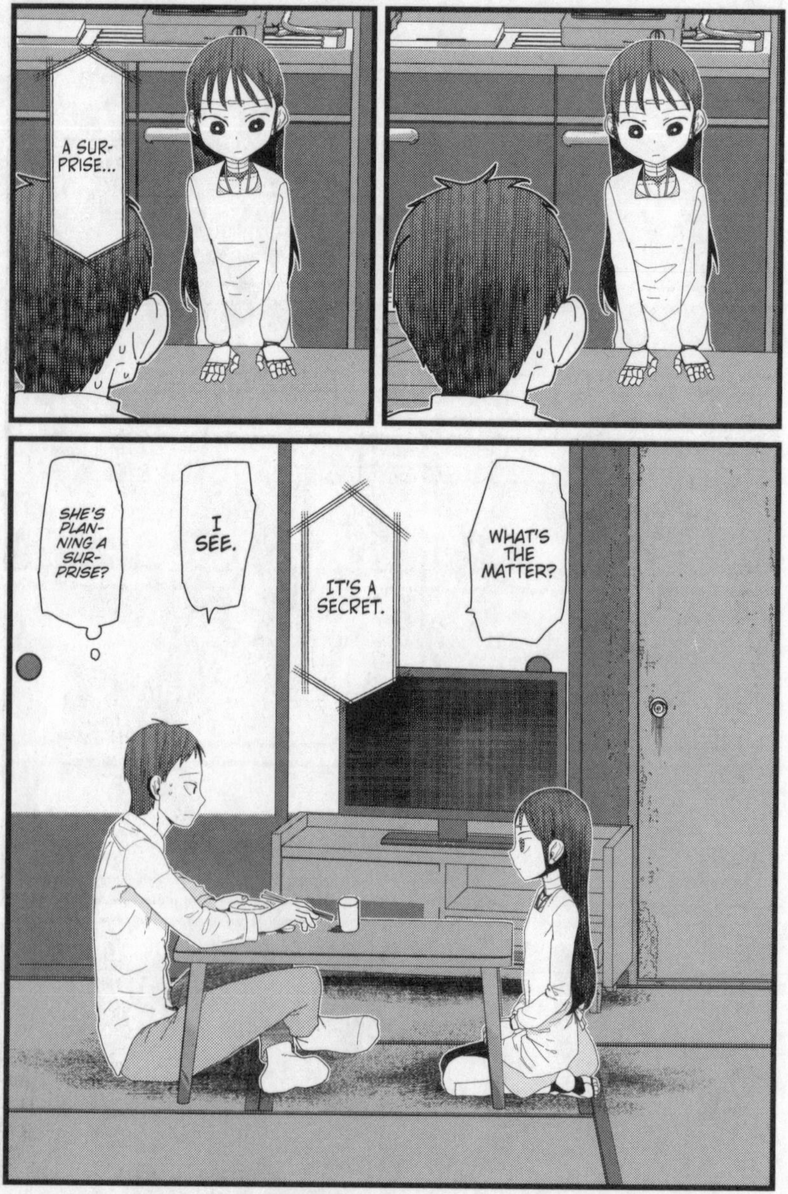
A SUR-PRISE...
WHAT'S THE MATTER?
IT'S A SECRET.
I SEE.
SHE'S PLAN-NING A SUR-PRISE?

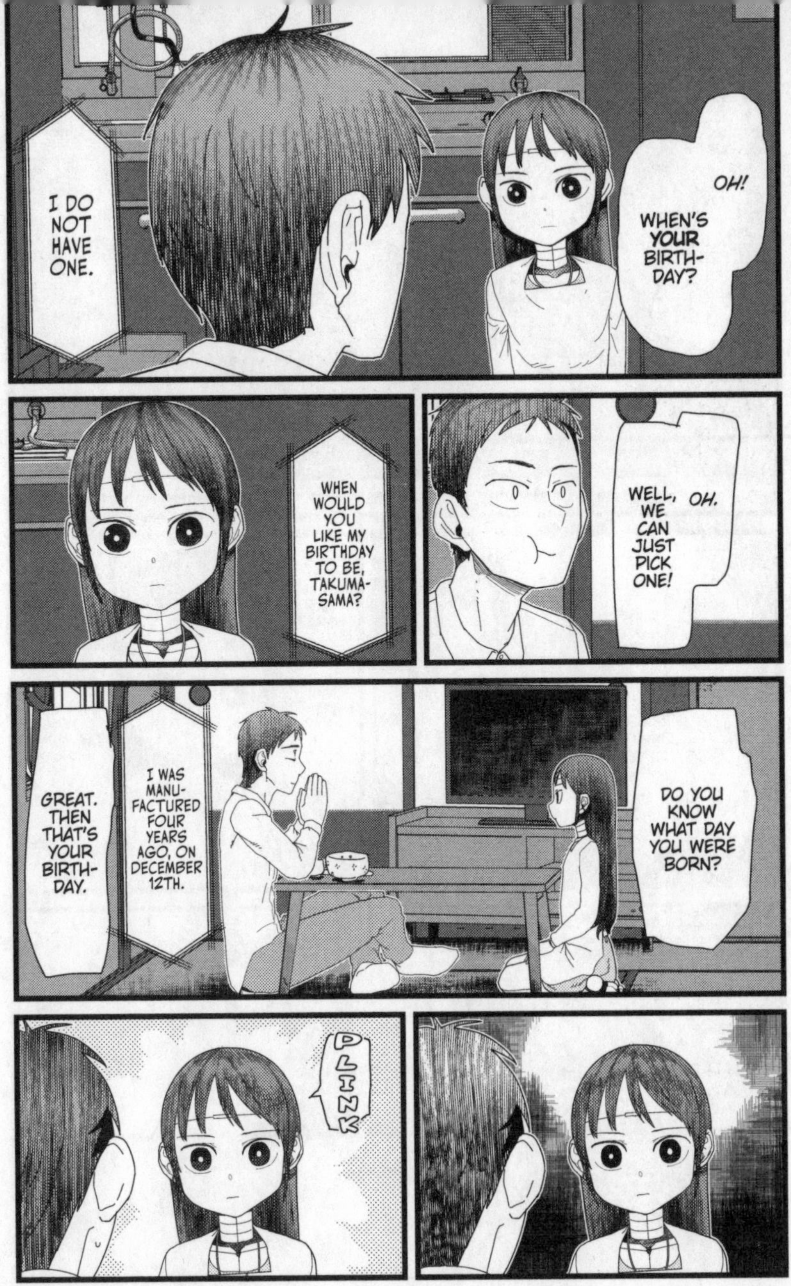
OH!
WHEN'S YOUR BIRTHDAY?
I DO NOT HAVE ONE.
OH. WELL, WE CAN JUST PICK ONE!
WHEN WOULD YOU LIKE MY BIRTHDAY TO BE, TAKUMA-SAMA?
DO YOU KNOW WHAT DAY YOU WERE BORN?
I WAS MANUFACTURED FOUR YEARS AGO, ON DECEMBER 12TH.
GREAT. THEN THAT'S YOUR BIRTHDAY.
PLINK

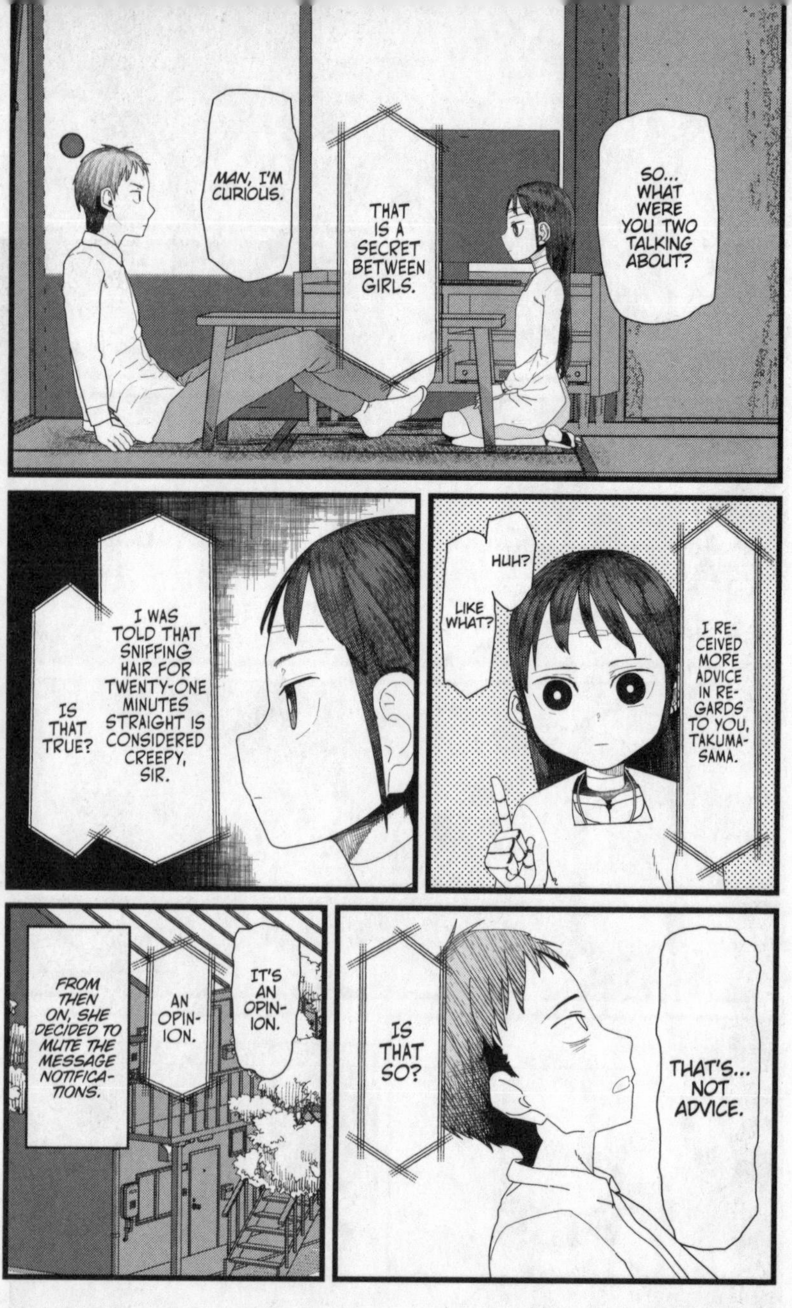
SO... WHAT WERE YOU TWO TALKING ABOUT?
THAT IS A SECRET BETWEEN GIRLS.
MAN, I'M CURIOUS.
I RE-CEIVED MORE ADVICE IN RE-GARDS TO YOU, TAKUMA-SAMA.
HUH?
LIKE WHAT?
I WAS TOLD THAT SNIFFING HAIR FOR TWENTY-ONE MINUTES STRAIGHT IS CONSIDERED CREEPY, SIR.
IS THAT TRUE?
THAT'S... NOT ADVICE.
IS THAT SO?
IT'S AN OPIN-ION.
AN OPIN-ION.
FROM THEN ON, SHE DECIDED TO MUTE THE MESSAGE NOTIFICA-TIONS.

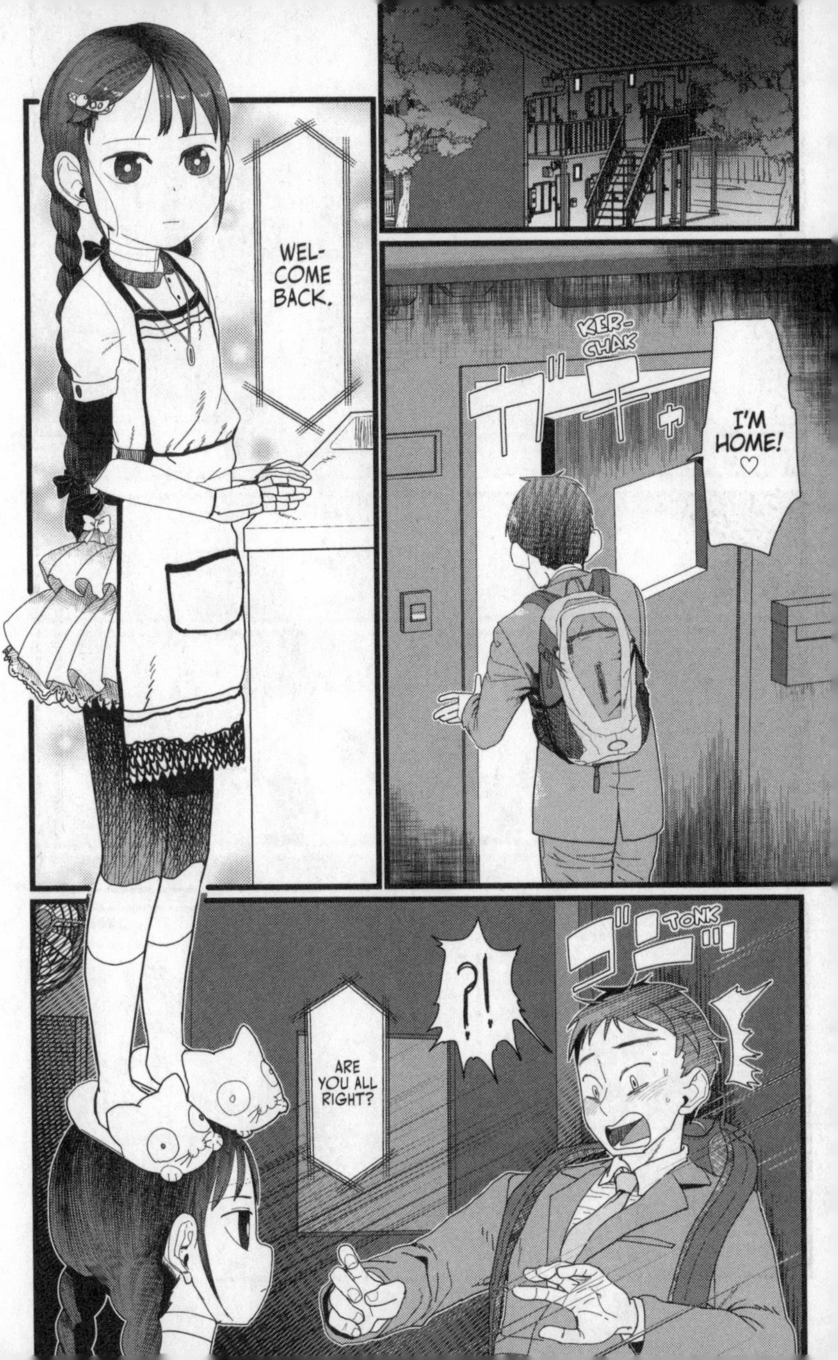
ガチャ
KER-CHAK
I'M HOME! ♡
WEL-COME BACK.
ゴン
TONK
?!
ARE YOU ALL RIGHT?

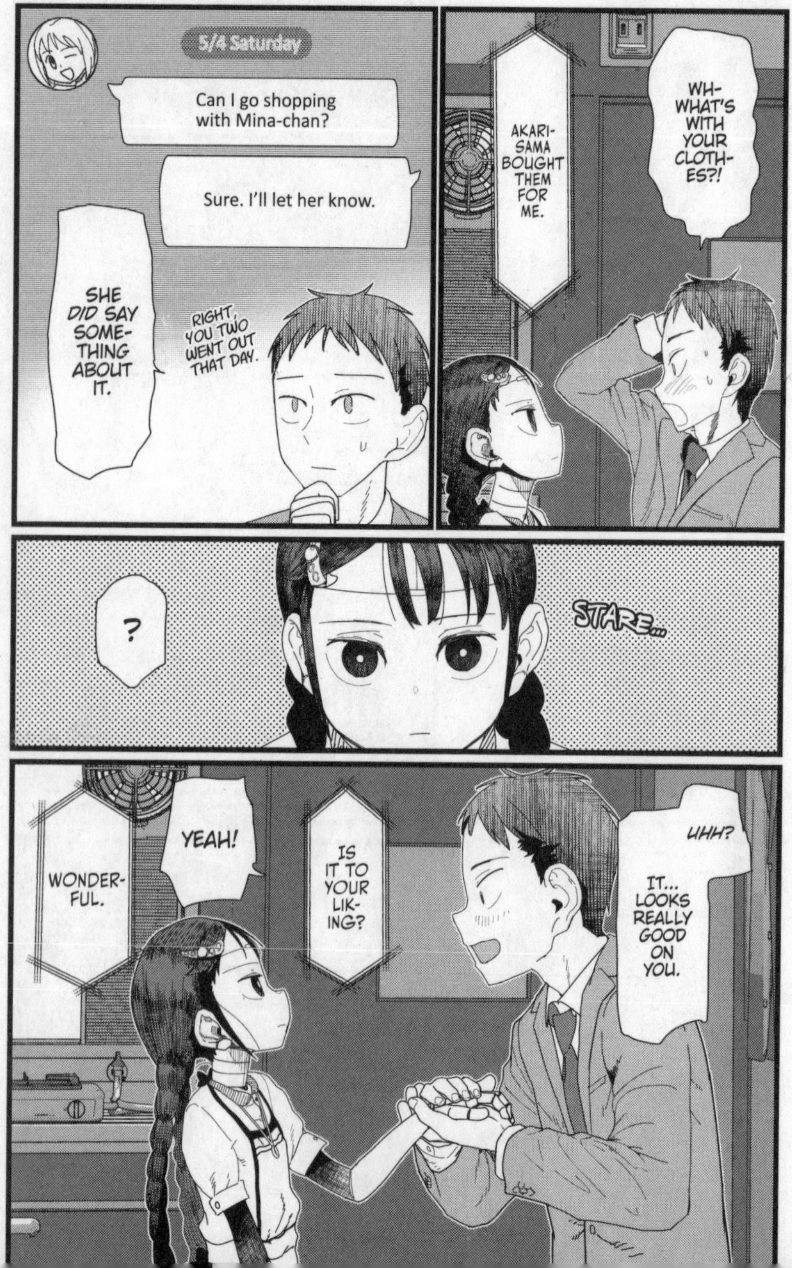
WH-WHAT'S WITH YOUR CLOTHES?!
AKARI-SAMA BOUGHT THEM FOR ME.
5/4 Saturday
Can I go shopping with Mina-chan?
Sure. I'll let her know.
RIGHT, YOU TWO WENT OUT THAT DAY.
SHE *DID* SAY SOMETHING ABOUT IT.
STARE...
?
UHH?
IT... LOOKS REALLY GOOD ON YOU.
IS IT TO YOUR LIKING?
YEAH!
WONDERFUL.

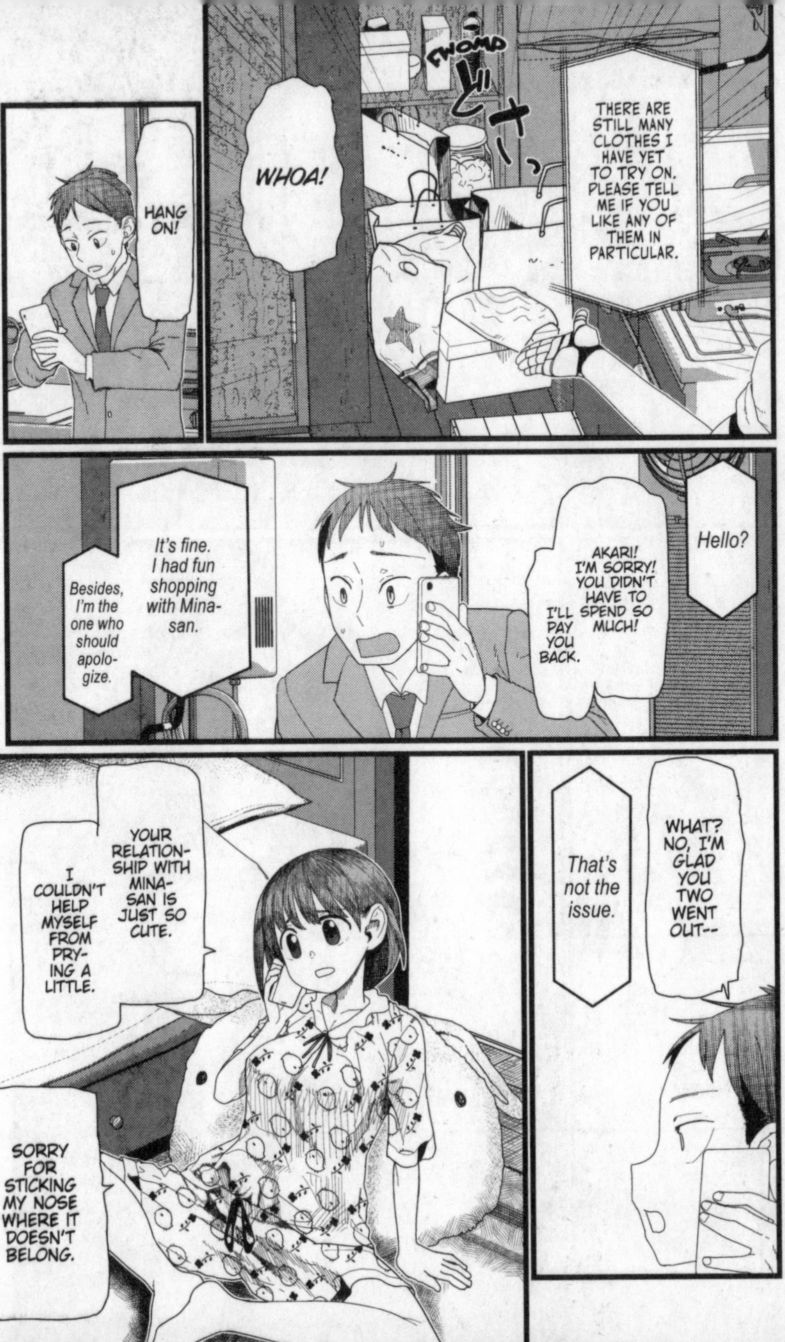
THERE ARE STILL MANY CLOTHES I HAVE YET TO TRY ON. PLEASE TELL ME IF YOU LIKE ANY OF THEM IN PARTICULAR.
FWOMP
WHOA!
HANG ON!
Hello?
AKARI! I'M SORRY! YOU DIDN'T HAVE TO SPEND SO MUCH!
I'LL PAY YOU BACK.
It's fine. I had fun shopping with Mina-san.
Besides, I'm the one who should apolo-gize.
WHAT? NO, I'M GLAD YOU TWO WENT OUT--
That's not the issue.
YOUR RELATION-SHIP WITH MINA-SAN IS JUST SO CUTE.
I COULDN'T HELP MYSELF FROM PRY-ING A LITTLE.
SORRY FOR STICKING MY NOSE WHERE IT DOESN'T BELONG.

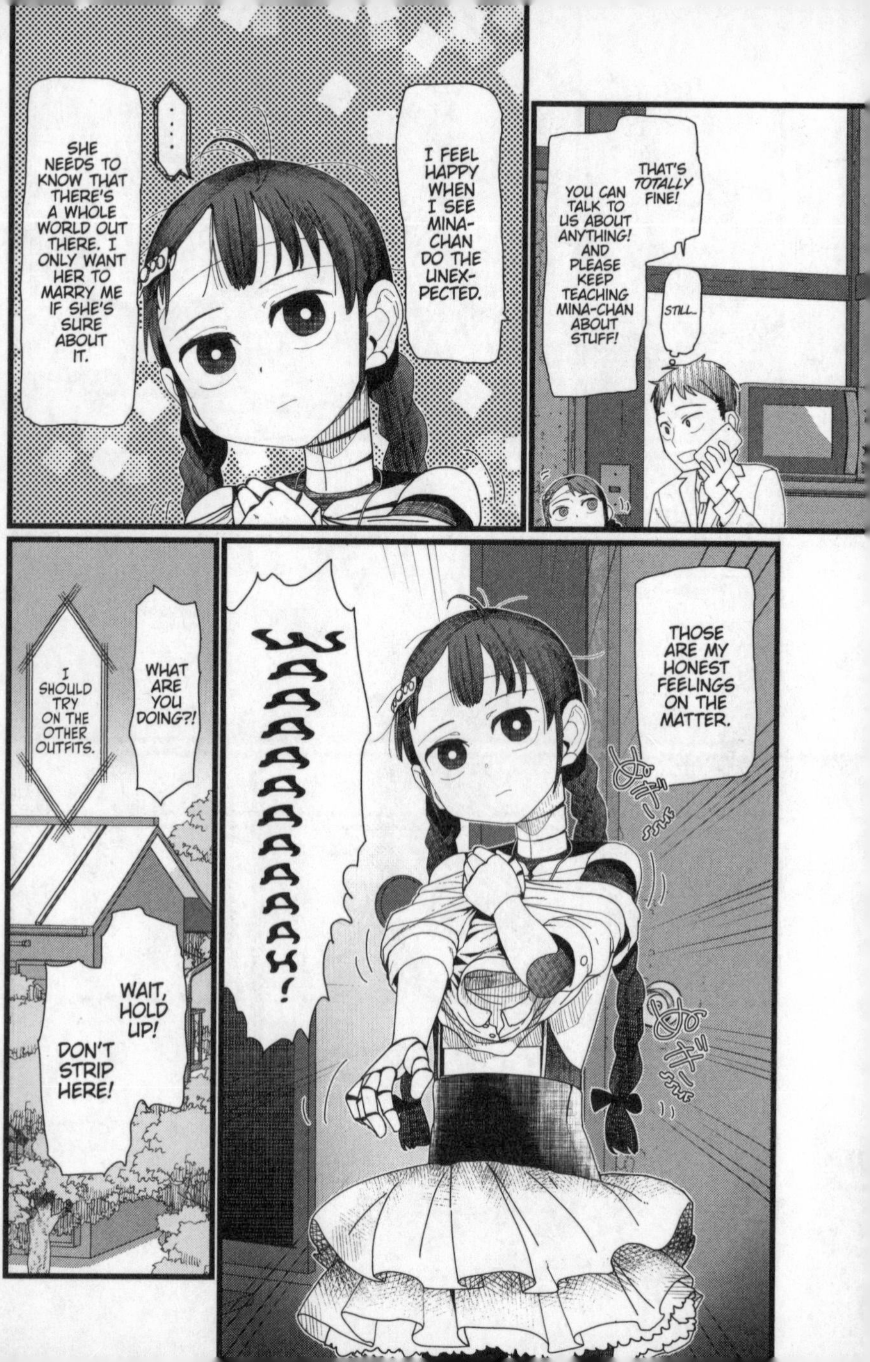
THAT'S *TOTALLY* FINE!
YOU CAN TALK TO US ABOUT ANYTHING! AND PLEASE KEEP TEACHING MINA-CHAN ABOUT STUFF!
STILL...
I FEEL HAPPY WHEN I SEE MINA-CHAN DO THE UNEXPECTED.
...
SHE NEEDS TO KNOW THAT THERE'S A WHOLE WORLD OUT THERE. I ONLY WANT HER TO MARRY ME IF SHE'S SURE ABOUT IT.
THOSE ARE MY HONEST FEELINGS ON THE MATTER.
WAAAAAAAAAAH!
WHAT ARE YOU DOING?!
I SHOULD TRY ON THE OTHER OUTFITS.
WAIT, HOLD UP!
DON'T STRIP HERE!

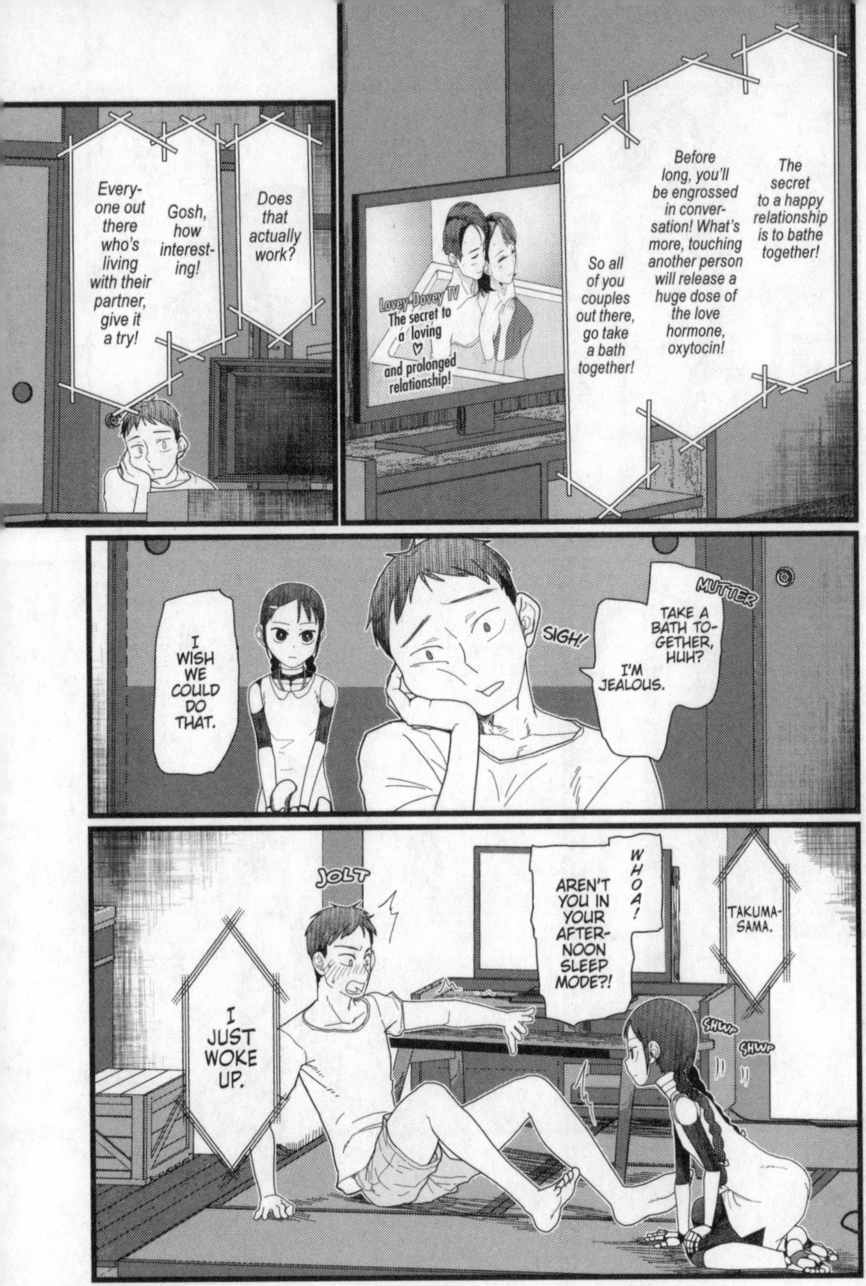
The secret to a happy relationship is to bathe together!
Before long, you'll be engrossed in conversation! What's more, touching another person will release a huge dose of the love hormone, oxytocin!
So all of you couples out there, go take a bath together!
Lovey-Dovey TV
The secret to a loving ♡ and prolonged relationship!
Does that actually work?
Gosh, how interesting!
Everyone out there who's living with their partner, give it a try!
MUTTER
TAKE A BATH TOGETHER, HUH?
I'M JEALOUS.
SIGH!
I WISH WE COULD DO THAT.
TAKUMA-SAMA.
SHWP
SHWP
WHOA!
AREN'T YOU IN YOUR AFTERNOON SLEEP MODE?!
JOLT
I JUST WOKE UP.

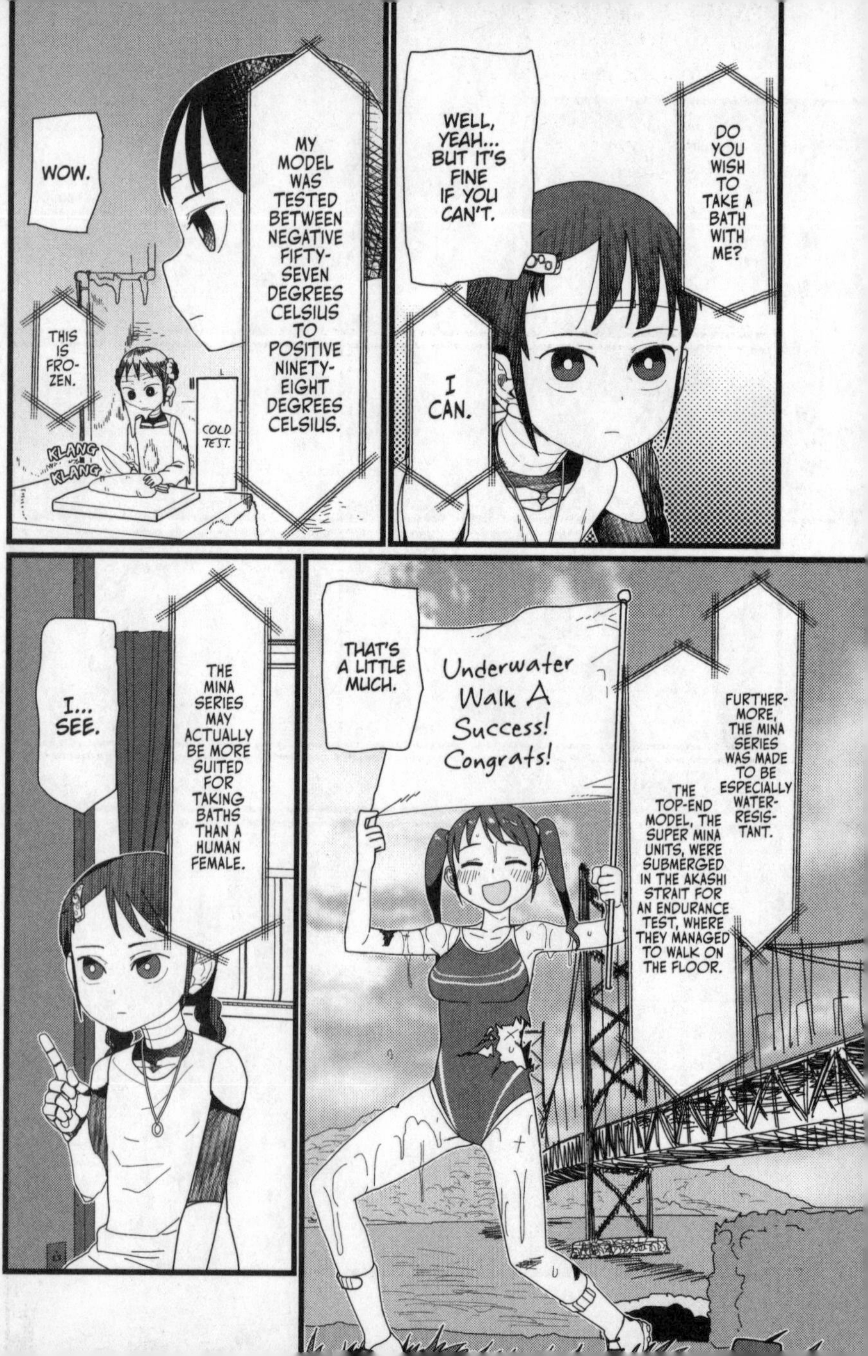
DO YOU WISH TO TAKE A BATH WITH ME?
WELL, YEAH... BUT IT'S FINE IF YOU CAN'T.
I CAN.
MY MODEL WAS TESTED BETWEEN NEGATIVE FIFTY-SEVEN DEGREES CELSIUS TO POSITIVE NINETY-EIGHT DEGREES CELSIUS.
WOW.
COLD TEST.
THIS IS FRO-ZEN.
KLANG KLANG
FURTHER-MORE, THE MINA SERIES WAS MADE TO BE ESPECIALLY WATER-RESIS-TANT.
THE TOP-END MODEL, THE SUPER MINA UNITS, WERE SUBMERGED IN THE AKASHI STRAIT FOR AN ENDURANCE TEST, WHERE THEY MANAGED TO WALK ON THE FLOOR.
Underwater Walk A Success! Congrats!
THAT'S A LITTLE MUCH.
THE MINA SERIES MAY ACTUALLY BE MORE SUITED FOR TAKING BATHS THAN A HUMAN FEMALE.
I... SEE.

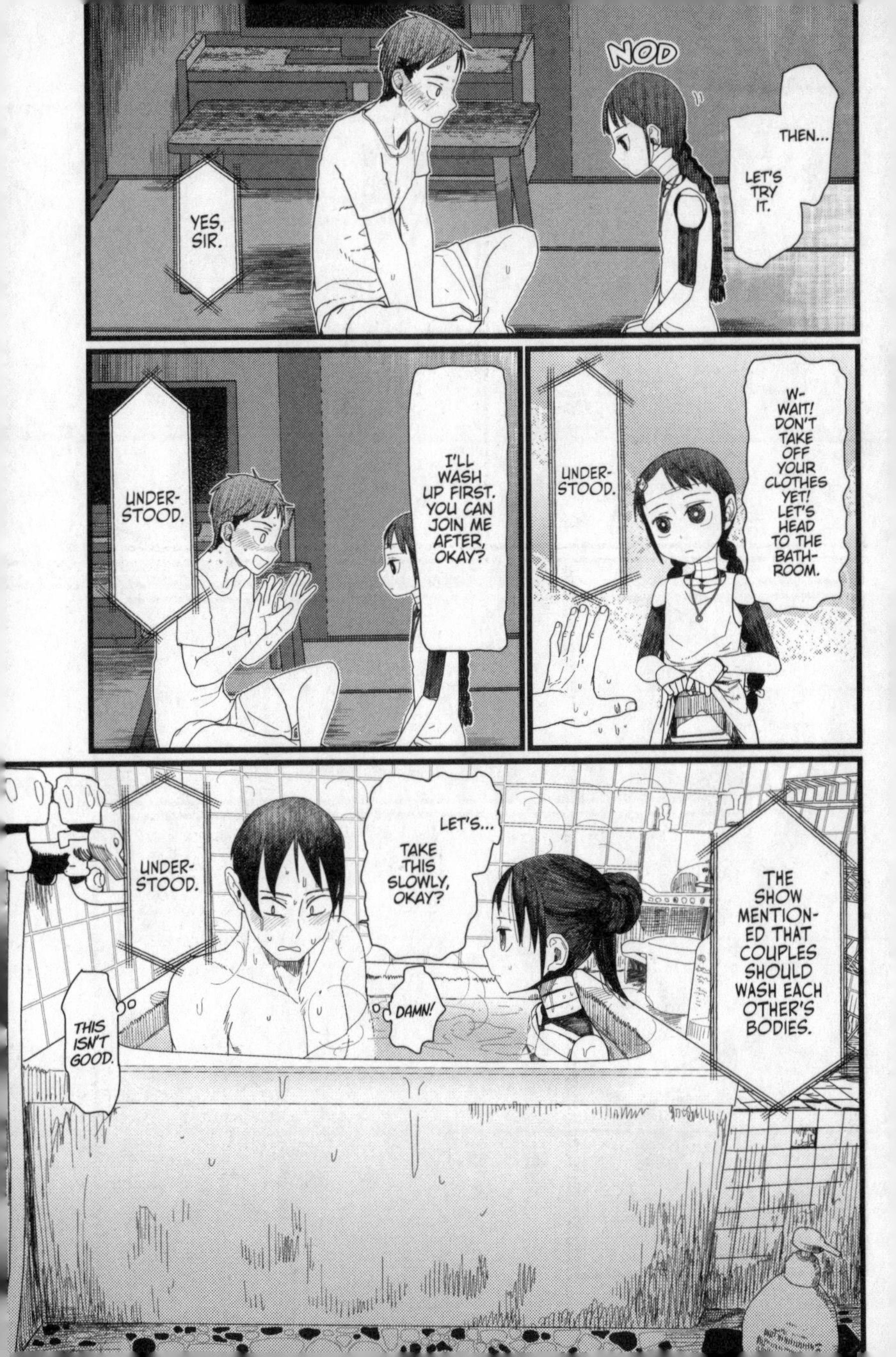
NOD
THEN... LET'S TRY IT.
YES, SIR.
W-WAIT! DON'T TAKE OFF YOUR CLOTHES YET! LET'S HEAD TO THE BATH-ROOM.
UNDER-STOOD.
I'LL WASH UP FIRST. YOU CAN JOIN ME AFTER, OKAY?
UNDER-STOOD.
THE SHOW MENTION-ED THAT COUPLES SHOULD WASH EACH OTHER'S BODIES.
LET'S... TAKE THIS SLOWLY, OKAY?
DAMN!
UNDER-STOOD.
THIS ISN'T GOOD.

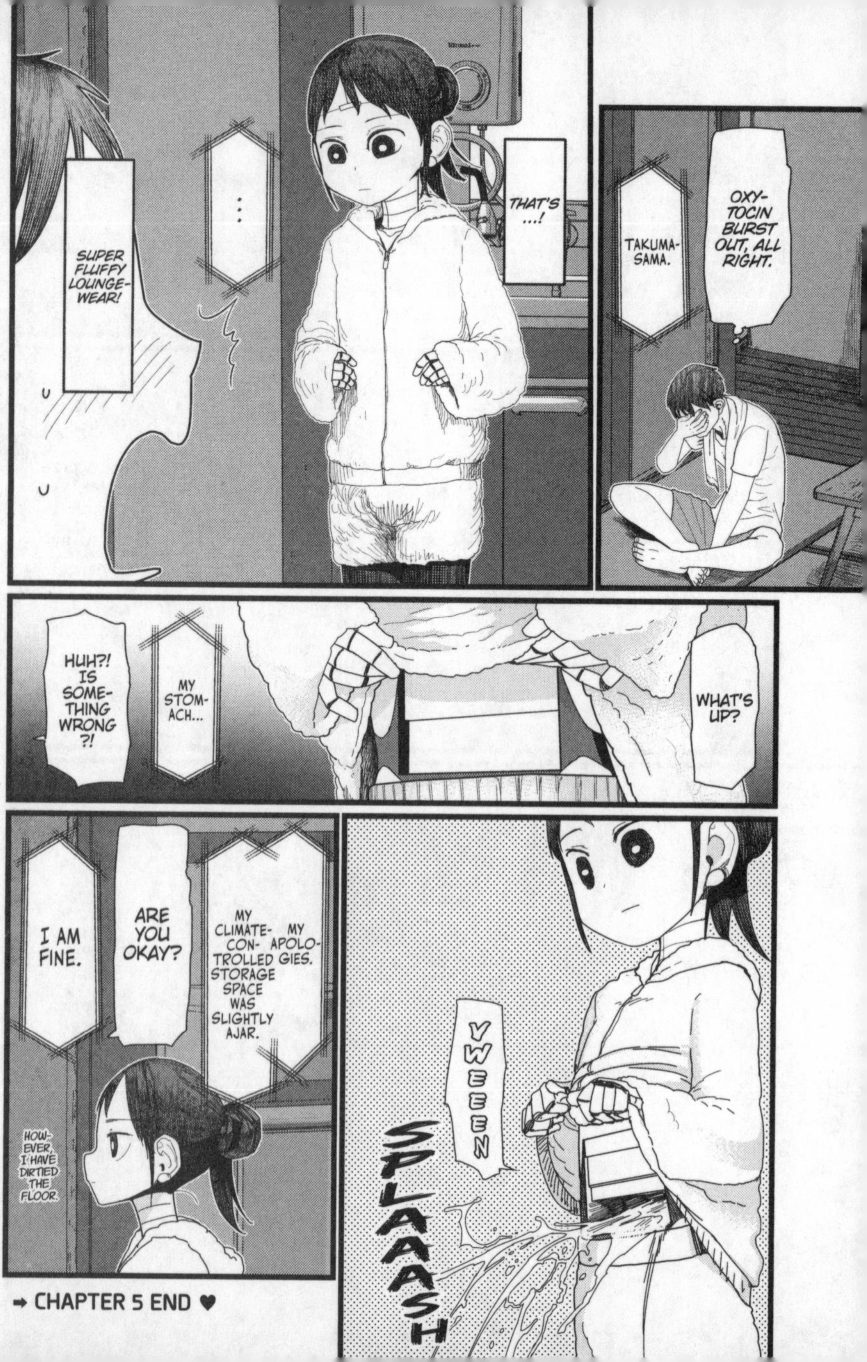
OXY-TOCIN BURST OUT, ALL RIGHT.
TAKUMA-SAMA.
THAT'S ...!
...
SUPER FLUFFY LOUNGE-WEAR!
WHAT'S UP?
MY STOM-ACH...
HUH?! IS SOME-THING WRONG?!
VWEEEEN
SPLAAASH
MY APOLO-GIES.
MY CLIMATE-CON-TROLLED STORAGE SPACE WAS SLIGHTLY AJAR.
ARE YOU OKAY?
I AM FINE.
HOW-EVER, I HAVE DIRTIED THE FLOOR.
➡ CHAPTER 5 END ♥

My
Wife Has No
Emotion

My
Wife Has
No
Emotion

➡ CHAPTER 6

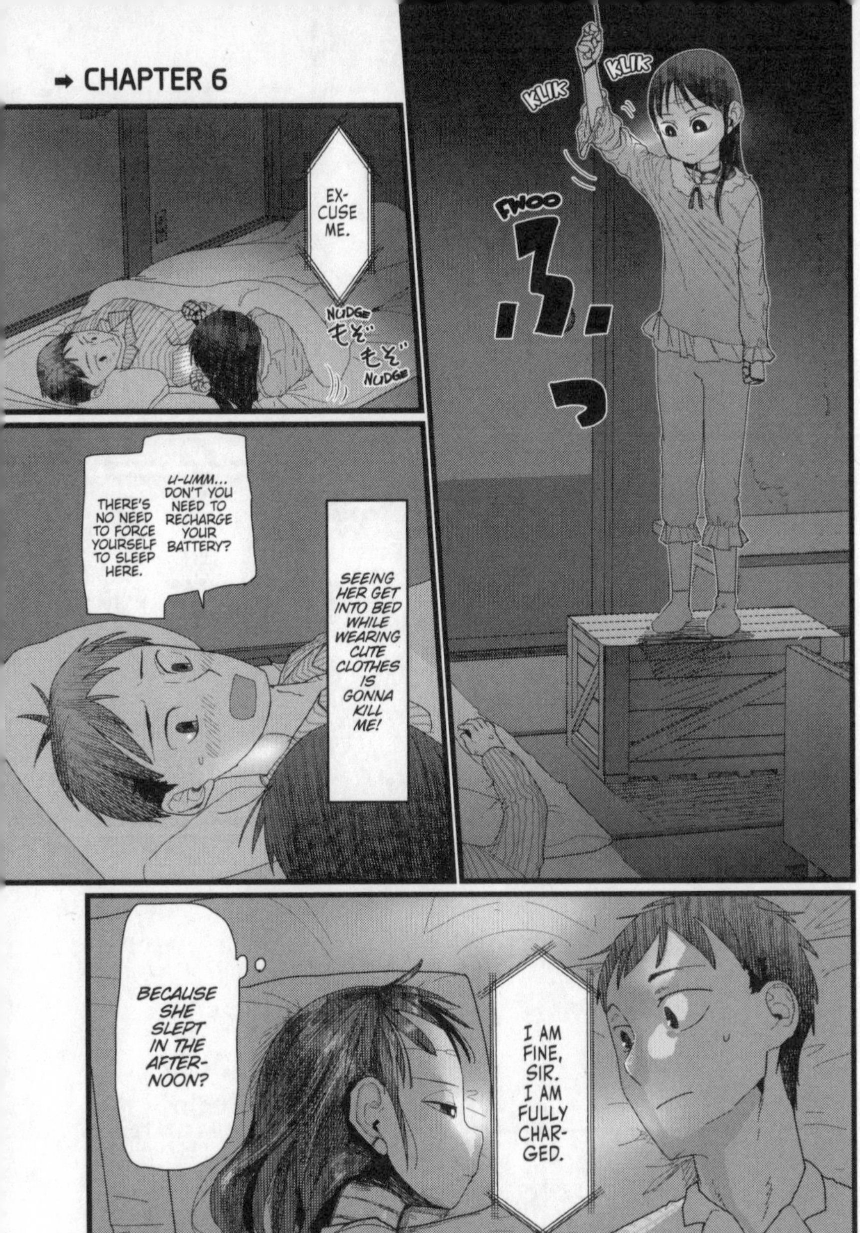
KLIK
KLIK
FWOO
ふっ
EX-CUSE ME.
NUDGE
もぞ
もぞ
NUDGE
U-UMM... DON'T YOU NEED TO RECHARGE YOUR BATTERY?
THERE'S NO NEED TO FORCE YOURSELF TO SLEEP HERE.
SEEING HER GET INTO BED WHILE WEARING CUTE CLOTHES IS GONNA KILL ME!
I AM FINE, SIR. I AM FULLY CHARG-GED.
BECAUSE SHE SLEPT IN THE AFTER-NOON?

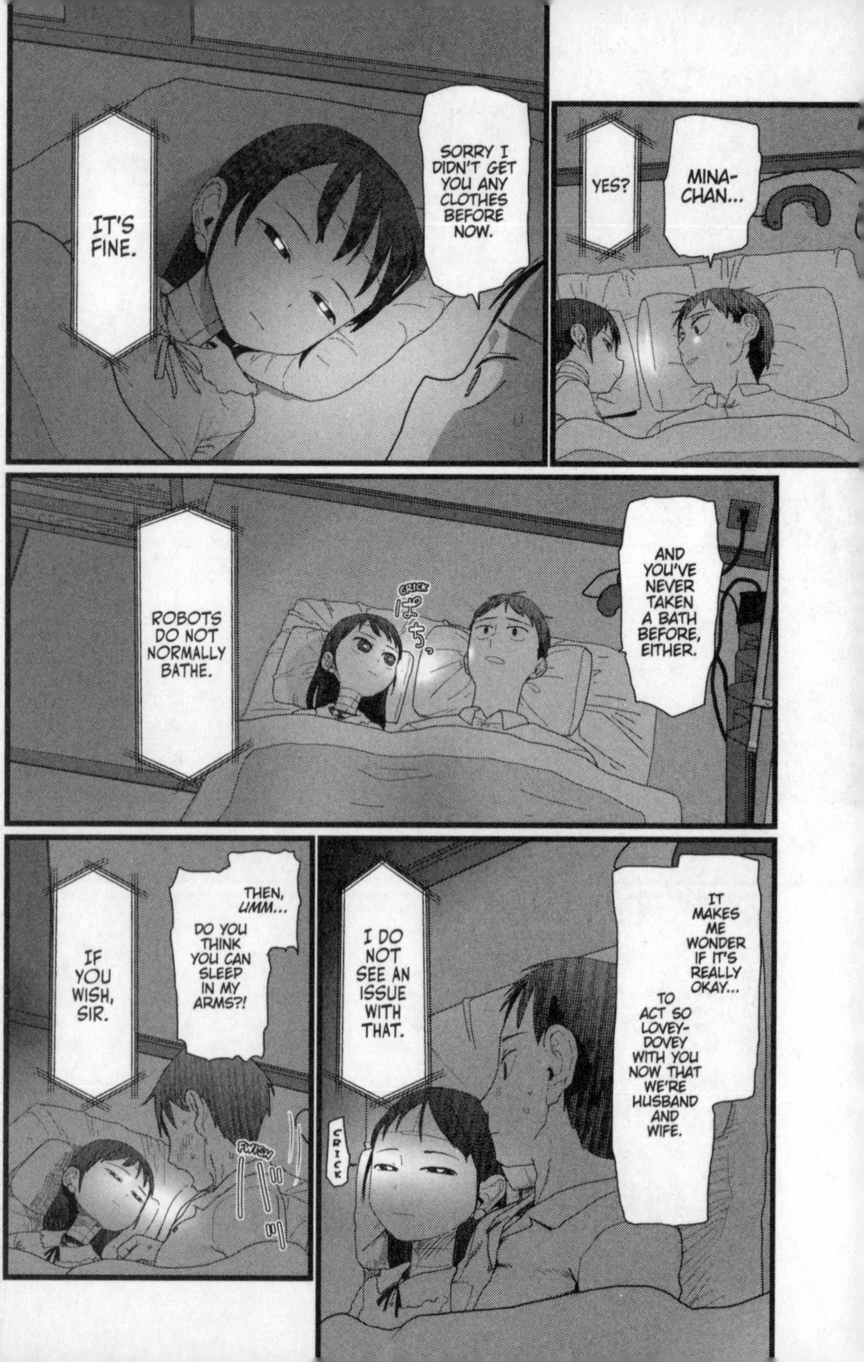
MINA-CHAN...
YES?
SORRY I DIDN'T GET YOU ANY CLOTHES BEFORE NOW.
IT'S FINE.
AND YOU'VE NEVER TAKEN A BATH BEFORE, EITHER.
CRICK
ROBOTS DO NOT NORMALLY BATHE.
IT MAKES ME WONDER IF IT'S REALLY OKAY...
TO ACT SO LOVEY-DOVEY WITH YOU NOW THAT WE'RE HUSBAND AND WIFE.
I DO NOT SEE AN ISSUE WITH THAT.
CRICK
THEN, UMM...
DO YOU THINK YOU CAN SLEEP IN MY ARMS?!
IF YOU WISH, SIR.
FWISH

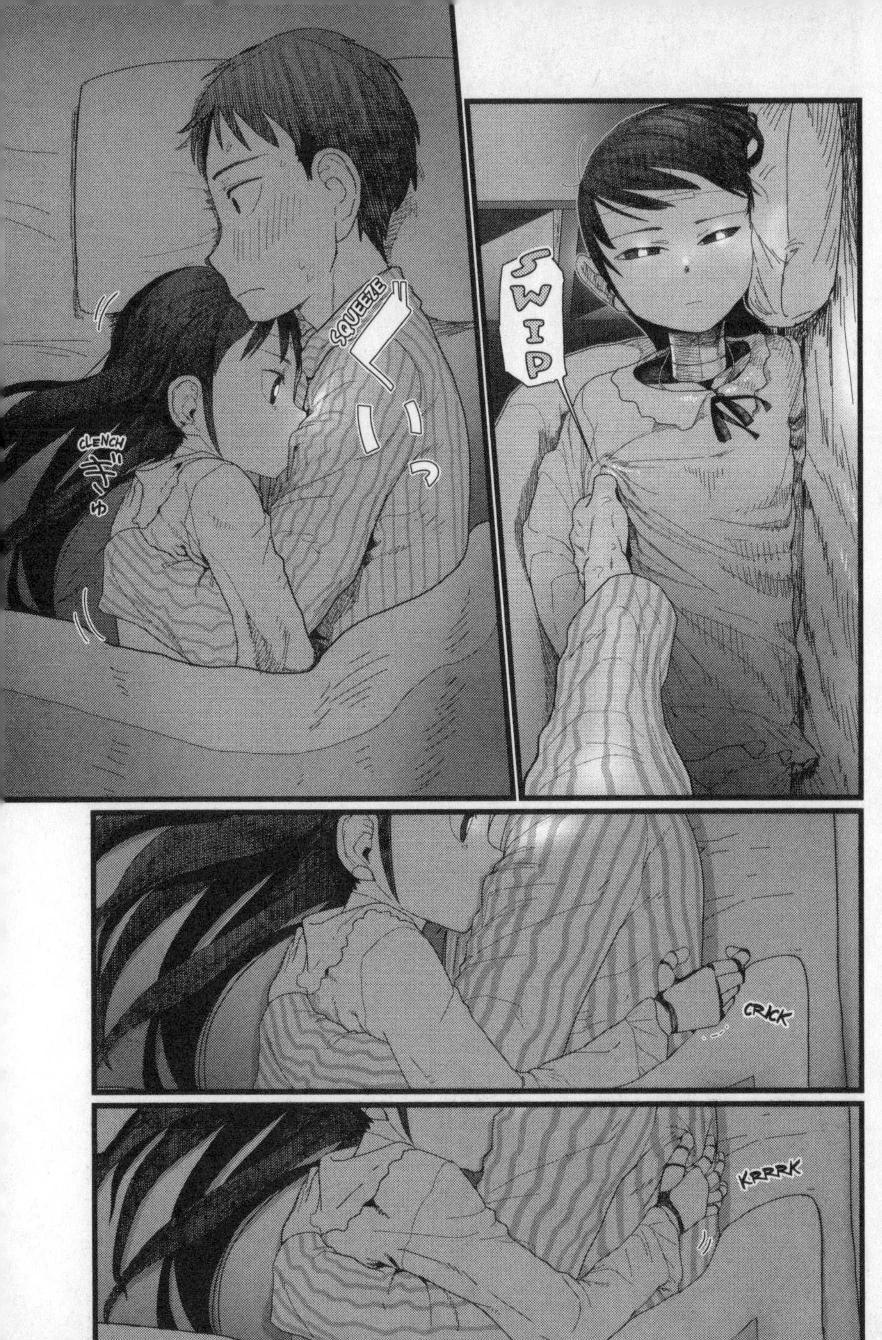
SWIP
SQUEEZE
CLENCH
CRICK
KRRRK

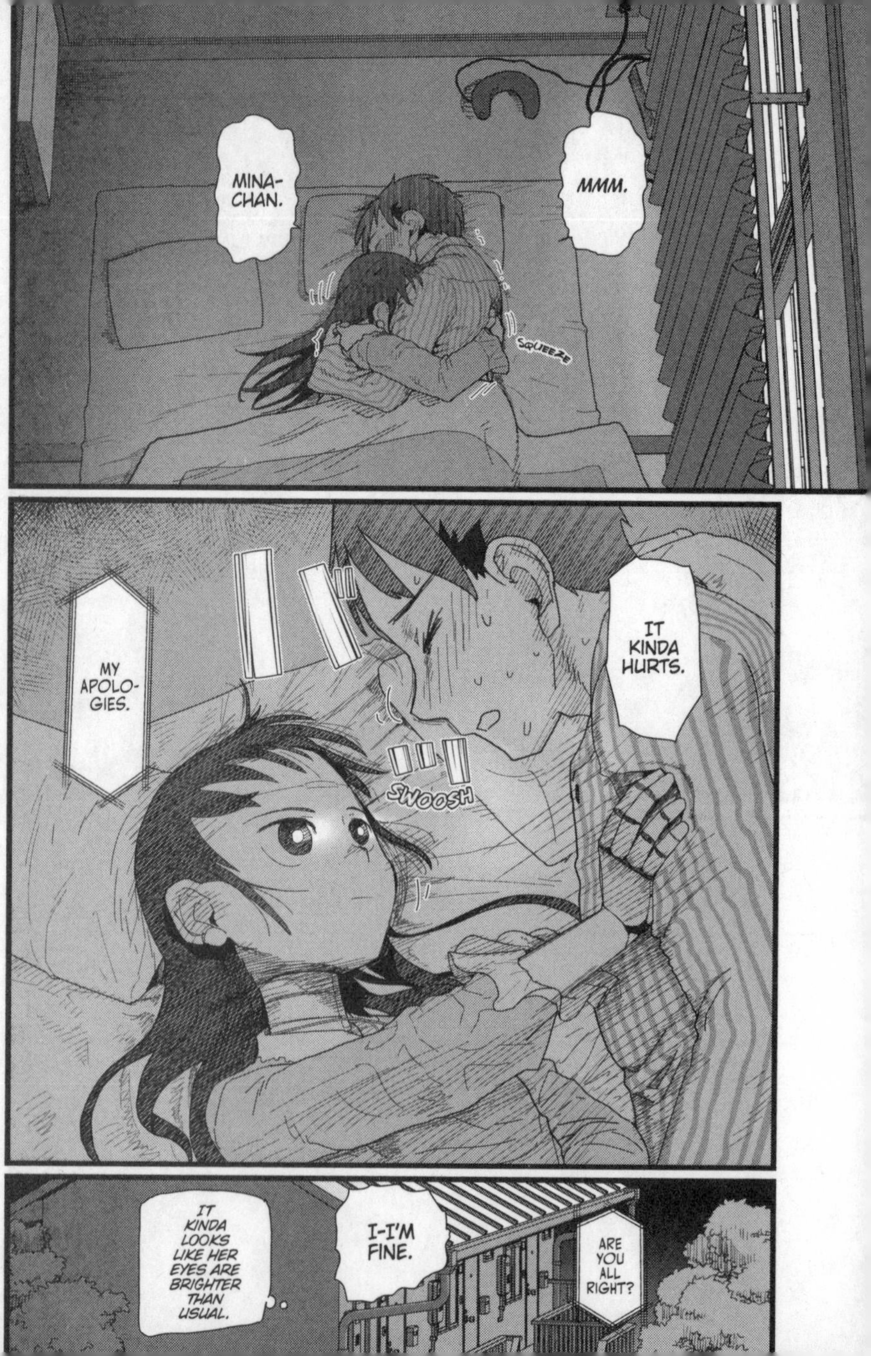
MMM.
MINA-CHAN.
SQUEEZE
IT KINDA HURTS.
MY APOLOGIES.
SWOOSH
ARE YOU ALL RIGHT?
I-I'M FINE.
IT KINDA LOOKS LIKE HER EYES ARE BRIGHTER THAN USUAL.

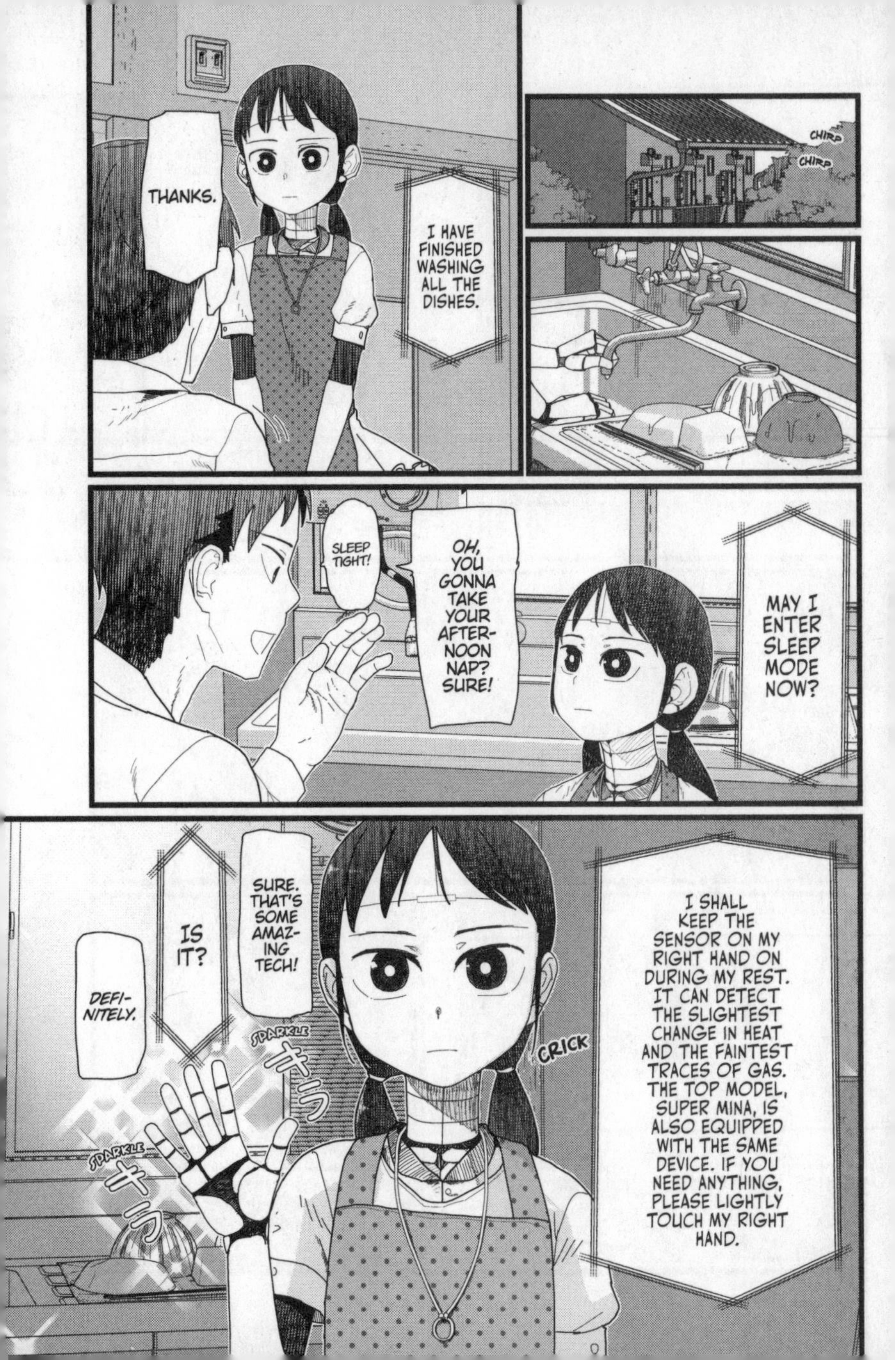
CHIRP
CHIRP
I HAVE FINISHED WASHING ALL THE DISHES.
THANKS.
MAY I ENTER SLEEP MODE NOW?
OH, YOU GONNA TAKE YOUR AFTER-NOON NAP? SURE!
SLEEP TIGHT!
I SHALL KEEP THE SENSOR ON MY RIGHT HAND ON DURING MY REST. IT CAN DETECT THE SLIGHTEST CHANGE IN HEAT AND THE FAINTEST TRACES OF GAS. THE TOP MODEL, SUPER MINA, IS ALSO EQUIPPED WITH THE SAME DEVICE. IF YOU NEED ANYTHING, PLEASE LIGHTLY TOUCH MY RIGHT HAND.
CRICK
SURE. THAT'S SOME AMAZ-ING TECH!
IS IT?
SPARKLE
DEFI-NITELY.
SPARKLE

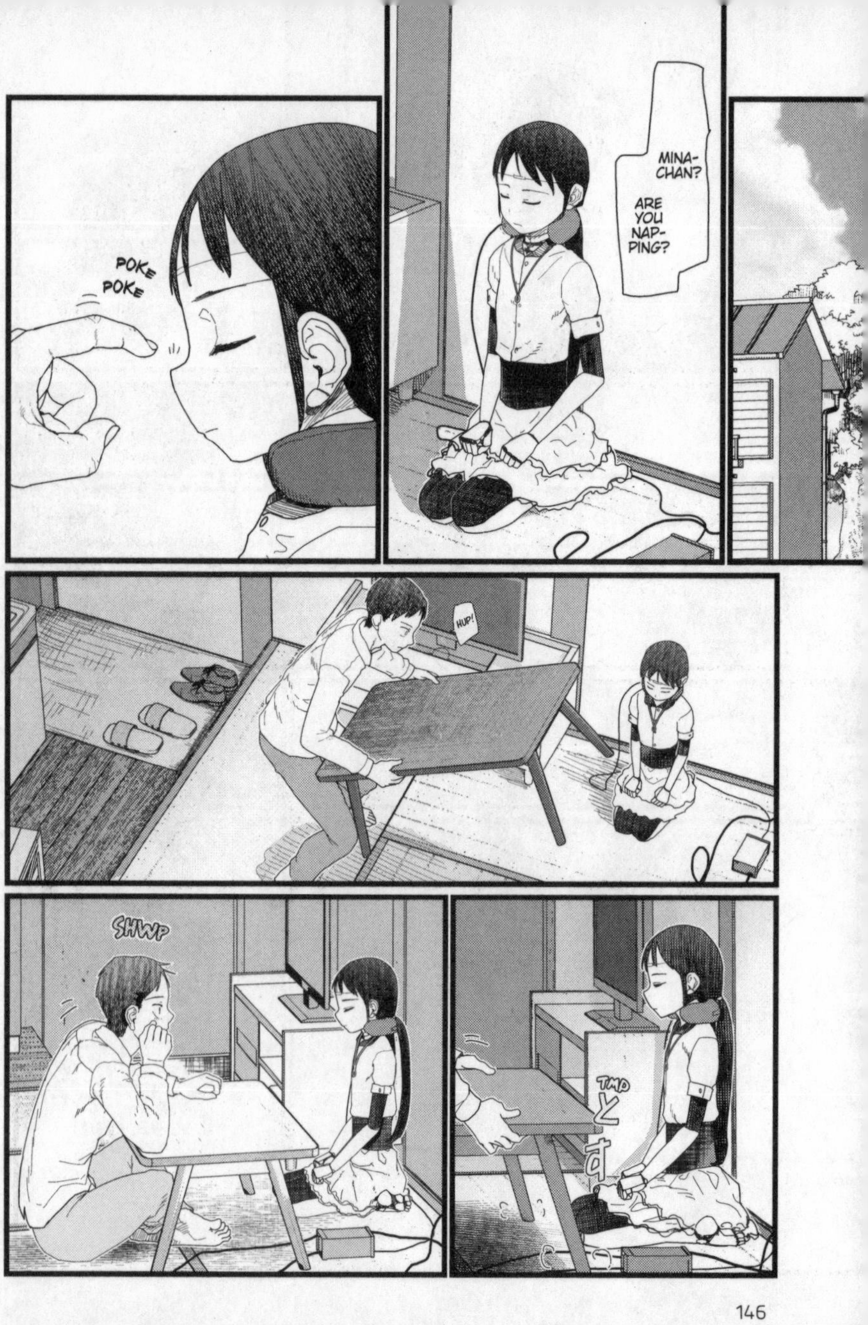
MINA-CHAN?
ARE YOU NAP-PING?
POKE POKE
HUP!
TMP
とす
SHWP

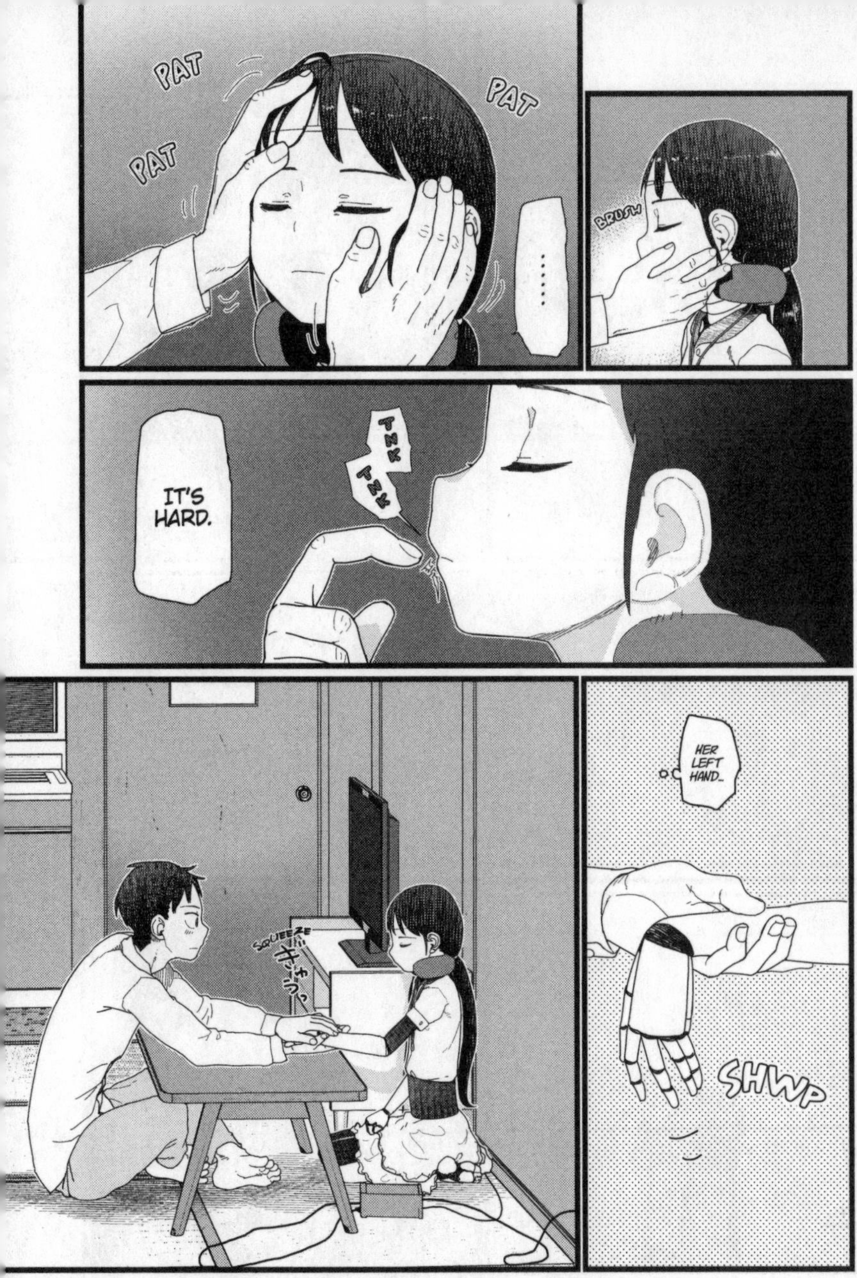

BRUSH
PAT
PAT
PAT
......
TNK
TNK
IT'S HARD.
HER LEFT HAND...
SHWP
SQUEEZE

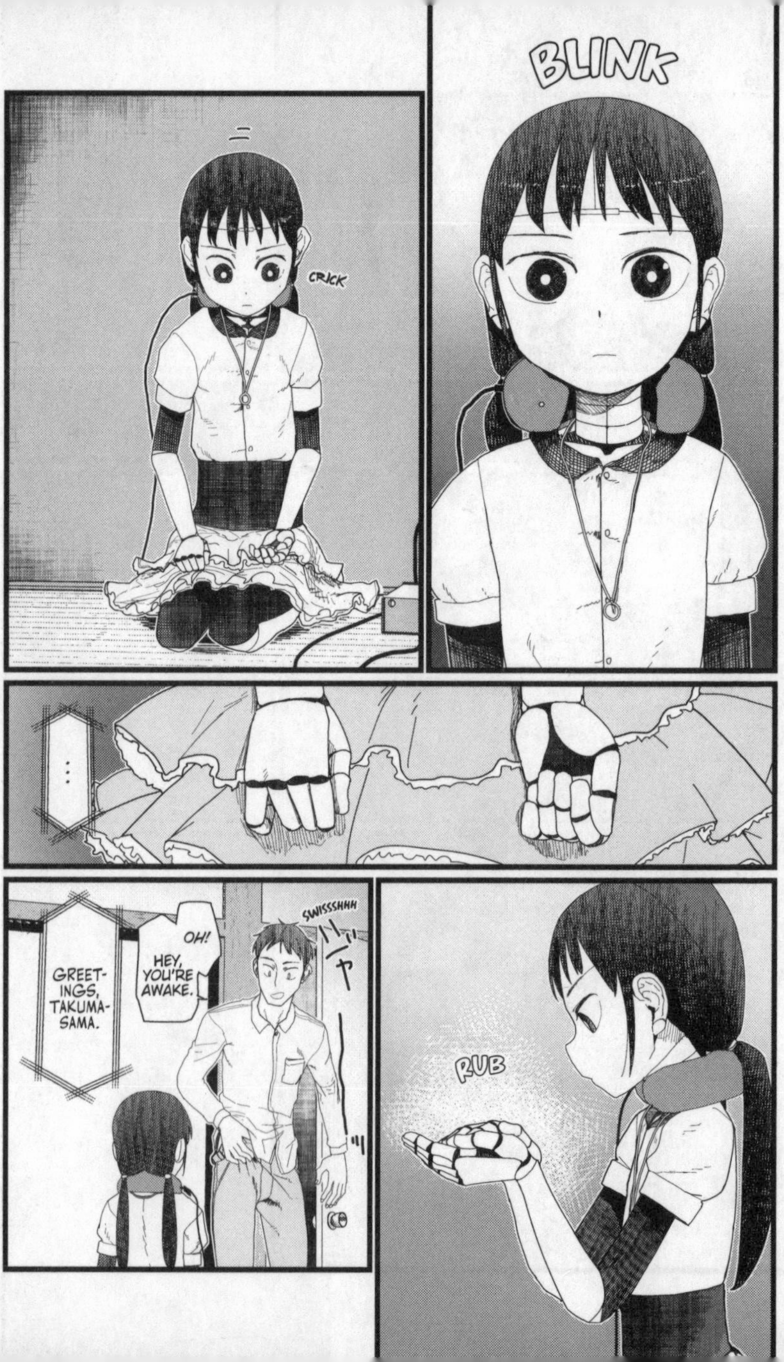
BLINK
CRICK
...
RUB
SWISSSHHH
OH! HEY, YOU'RE AWAKE.
GREETINGS, TAKUMA-SAMA.

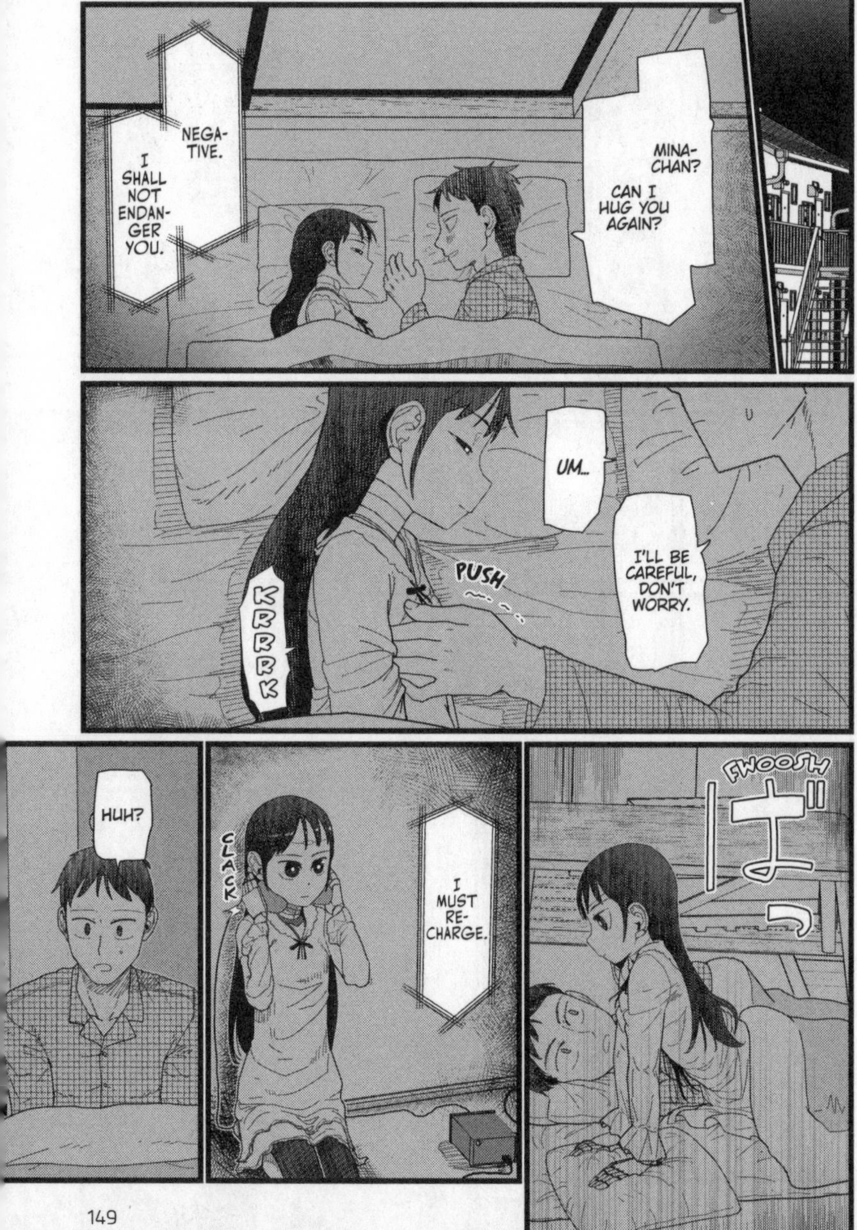
MINA-CHAN?
CAN I HUG YOU AGAIN?
NEGA-TIVE.
I SHALL NOT ENDANGER YOU.
UM...
I'LL BE CAREFUL, DON'T WORRY.
PUSH
KRRRK
FWOOSH
ばっ
I MUST RE-CHARGE.
CLACK
HUH?

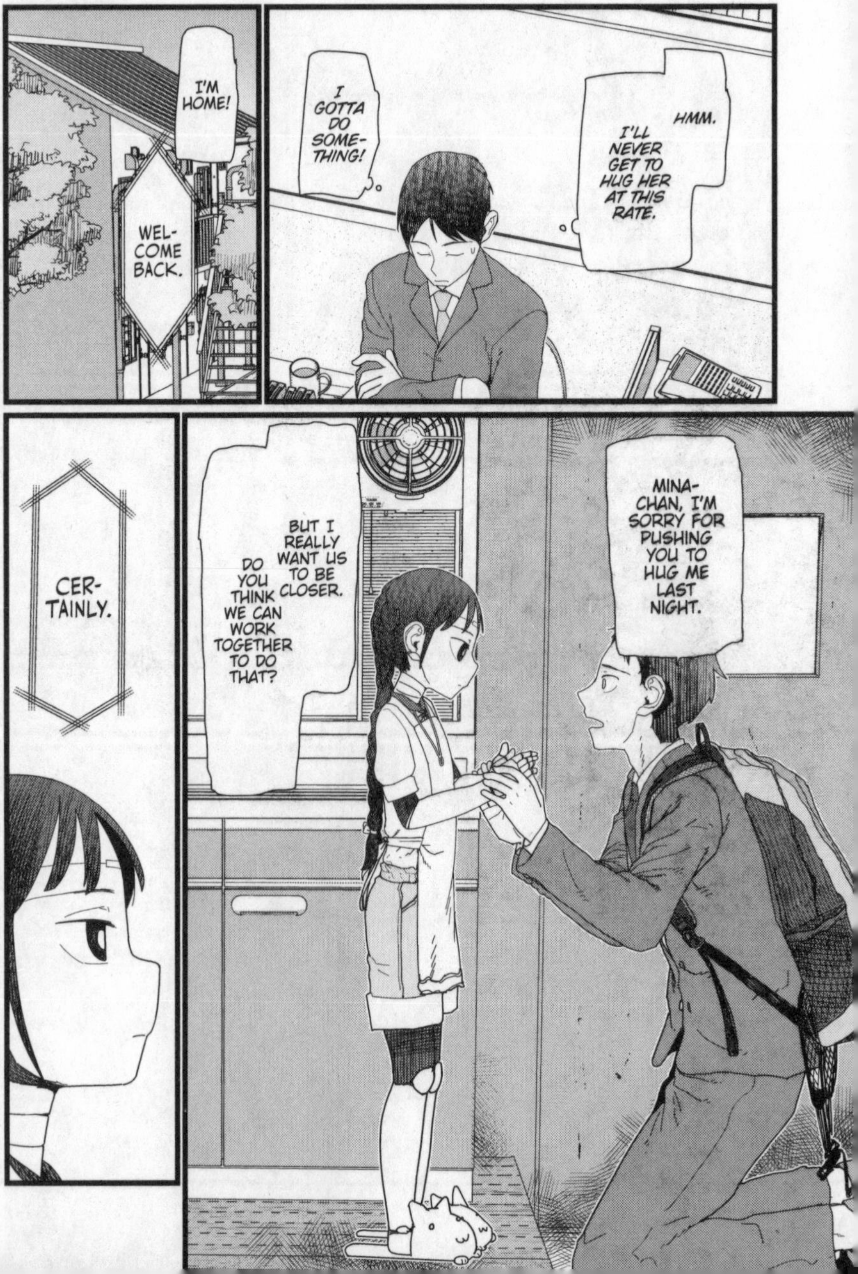
HMM.
I'LL NEVER GET TO HUG HER AT THIS RATE.
I GOTTA DO SOMETHING!
I'M HOME!
WELCOME BACK.
MINA-CHAN, I'M SORRY FOR PUSHING YOU TO HUG ME LAST NIGHT.
BUT I REALLY WANT US TO BE CLOSER.
DO YOU THINK WE CAN WORK TOGETHER TO DO THAT?
CERTAINLY.

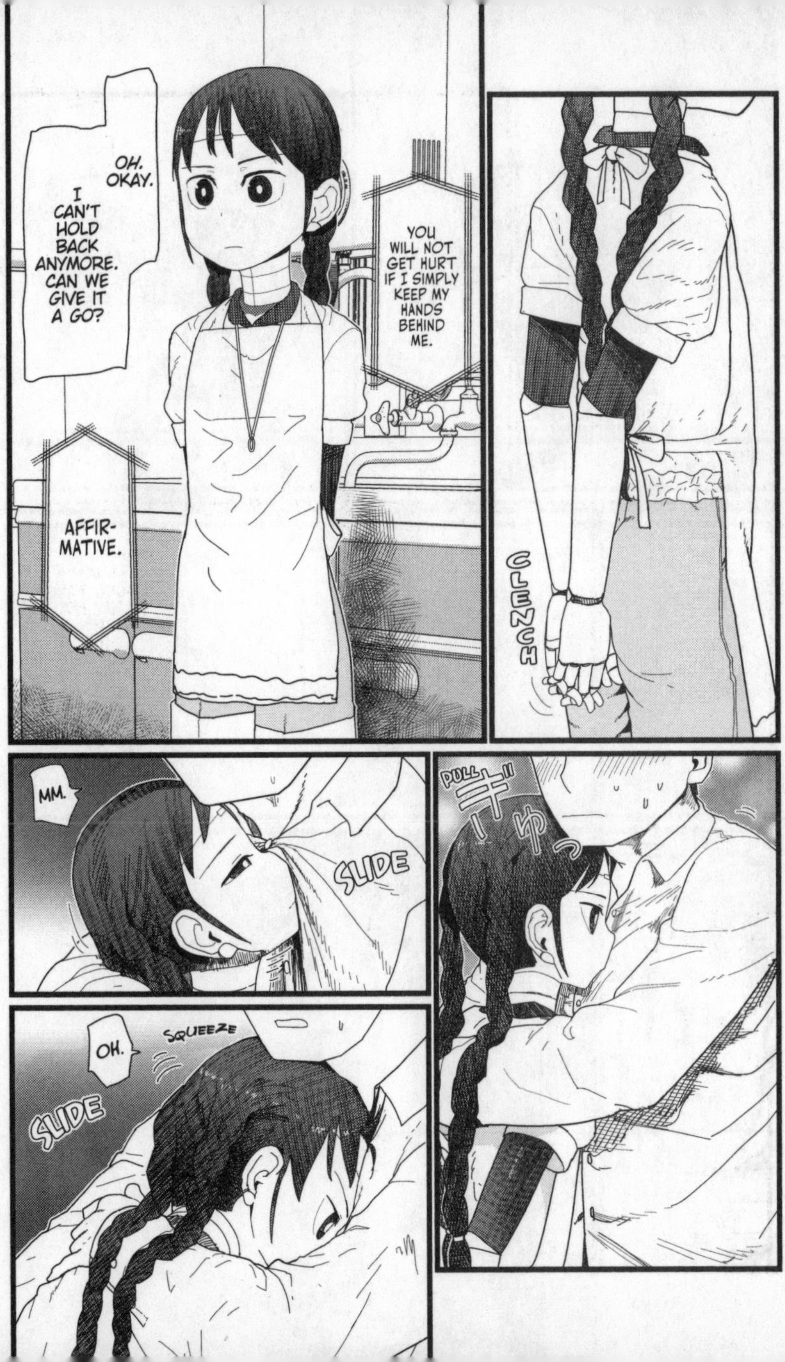
CLENCH
YOU WILL NOT GET HURT IF I SIMPLY KEEP MY HANDS BEHIND ME.
OH. OKAY. I CAN'T HOLD BACK ANYMORE. CAN WE GIVE IT A GO?
AFFIRMATIVE.
PULL
ぎゅっ
MM.
SLIDE
SQUEEZE
OH.
SLIDE

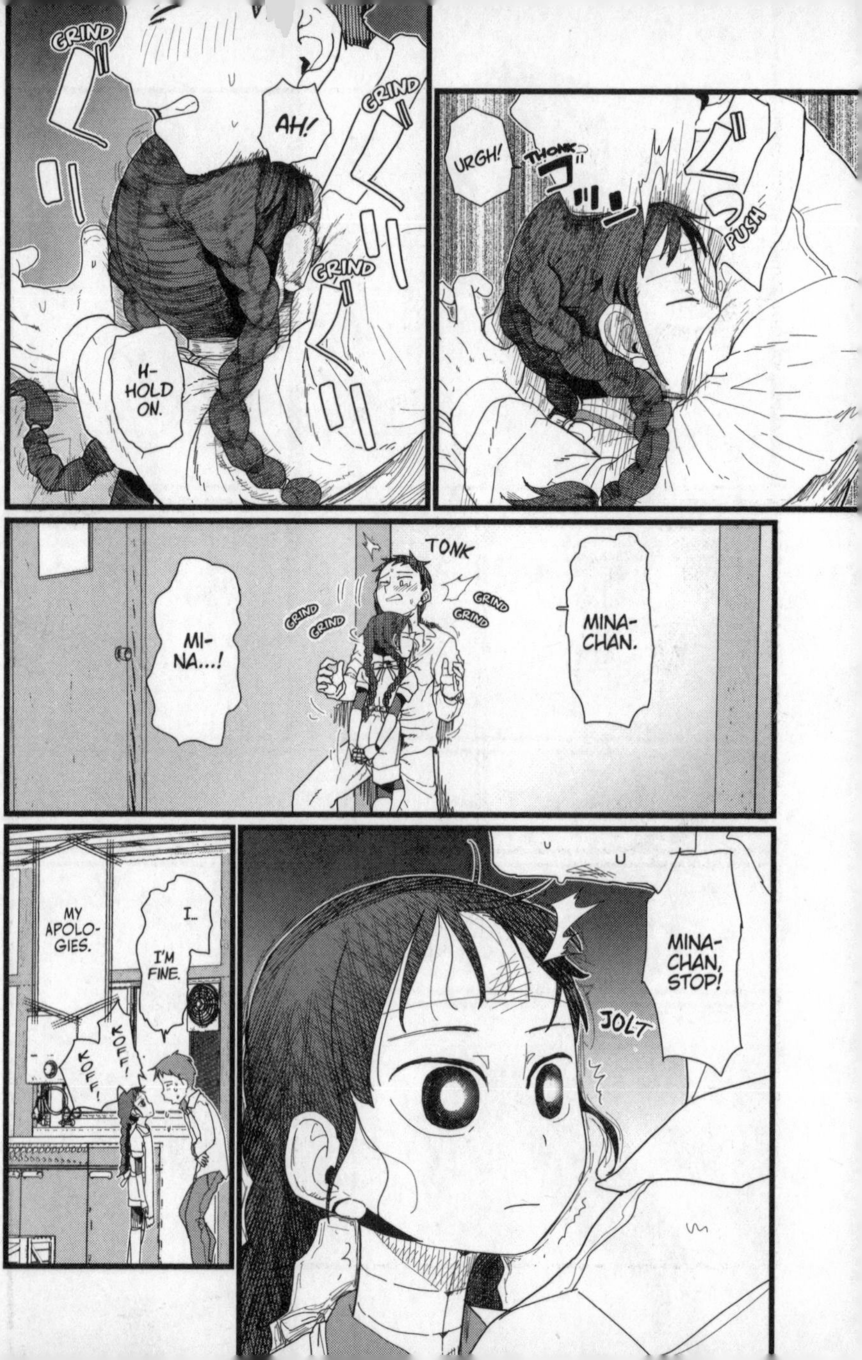

URGH!
THONK
PUSH
GRIND
AH!
GRIND
GRIND
H-HOLD ON.
MINA-CHAN.
TONK
GRIND GRIND
GRIND GRIND
MI-NA...!
MINA-CHAN, STOP!
JOLT
I... I'M FINE.
MY APOLOGIES.
KOFF! KOFF!

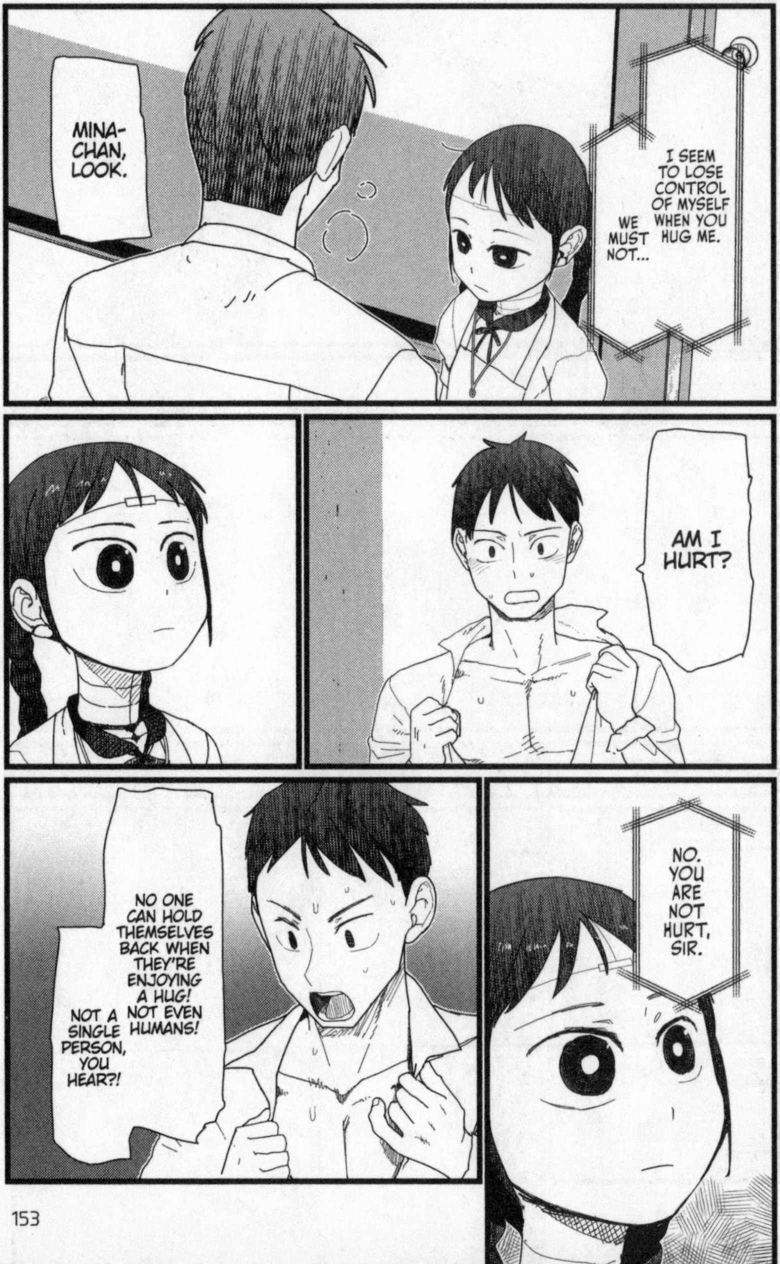
I SEEM TO LOSE CONTROL OF MYSELF WHEN YOU HUG ME.
WE MUST NOT...
MINA-CHAN, LOOK.
AM I HURT?
NO. YOU ARE NOT HURT, SIR.
NO ONE CAN HOLD THEMSELVES BACK WHEN THEY'RE ENJOYING A HUG! NOT EVEN HUMANS!
NOT A SINGLE PERSON, YOU HEAR?!

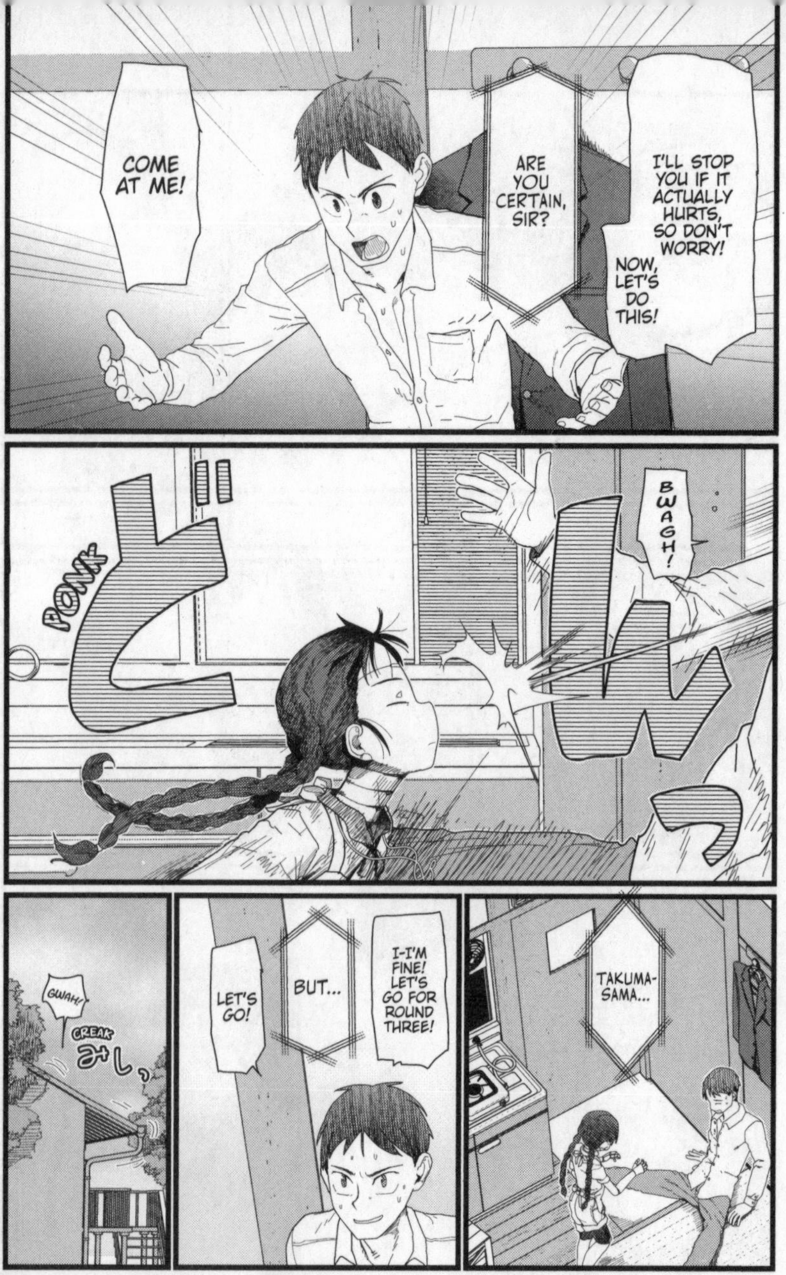
I'LL STOP YOU IF IT ACTUALLY HURTS, SO DON'T WORRY!
NOW, LET'S DO THIS!
ARE YOU CERTAIN, SIR?
COME AT ME!
BWAGH!
どんっ
PONK
TAKUMA-SAMA...
I-I'M FINE! LET'S GO FOR ROUND THREE!
BUT...
LET'S GO!
GWAH!
CREAK
みしっ

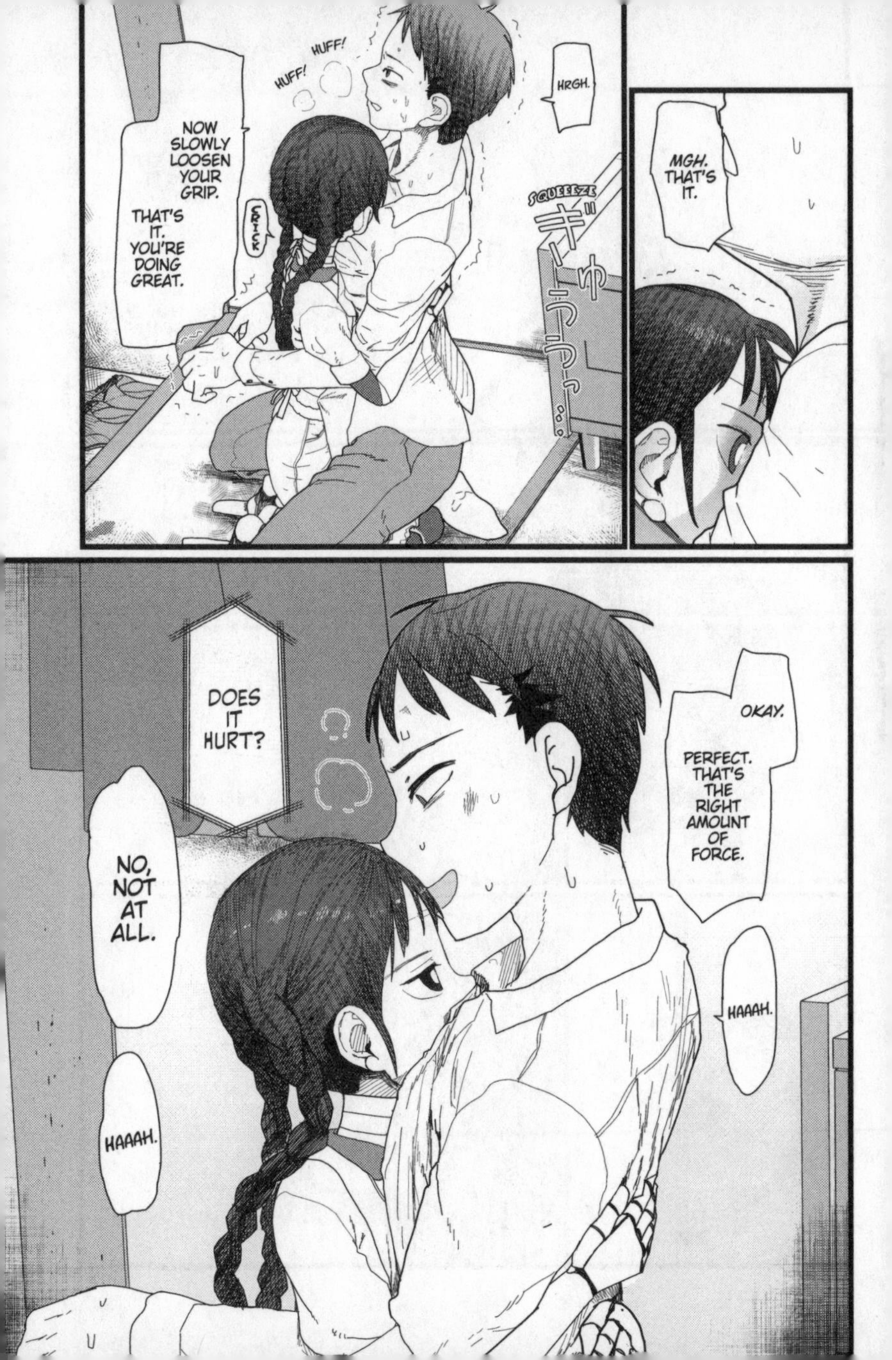
MGH. THAT'S IT.
HRGH.
HUFF!
HUFF!
SQUEEEZE
NOW SLOWLY LOOSEN YOUR GRIP.
CRICK
THAT'S IT. YOU'RE DOING GREAT.
OKAY.
PERFECT. THAT'S THE RIGHT AMOUNT OF FORCE.
DOES IT HURT?
HAAAH.
NO, NOT AT ALL.
HAAAH.

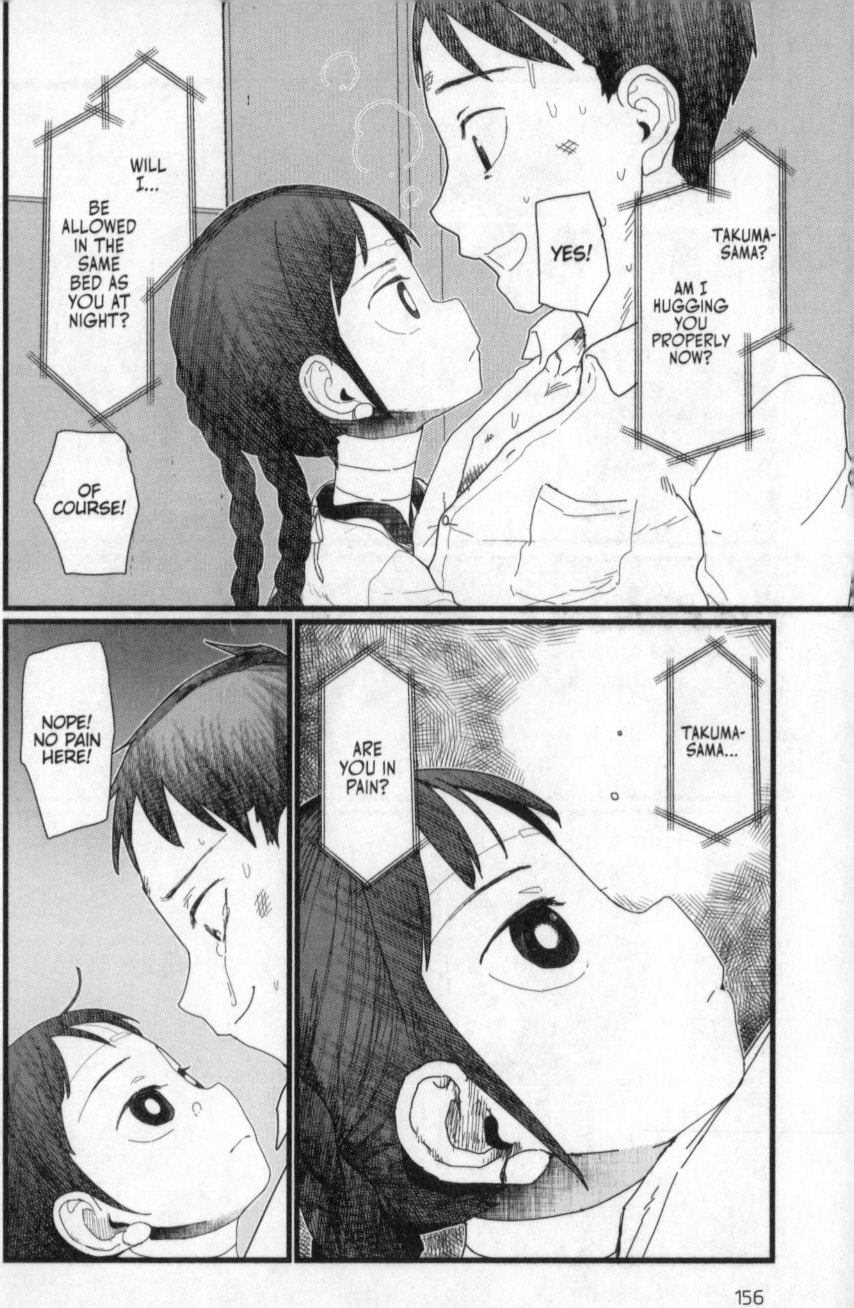
TAKUMA-SAMA?
AM I HUGGING YOU PROPERLY NOW?
YES!
WILL I...
BE ALLOWED IN THE SAME BED AS YOU AT NIGHT?
OF COURSE!
TAKUMA-SAMA...
ARE YOU IN PAIN?
NOPE! NO PAIN HERE!

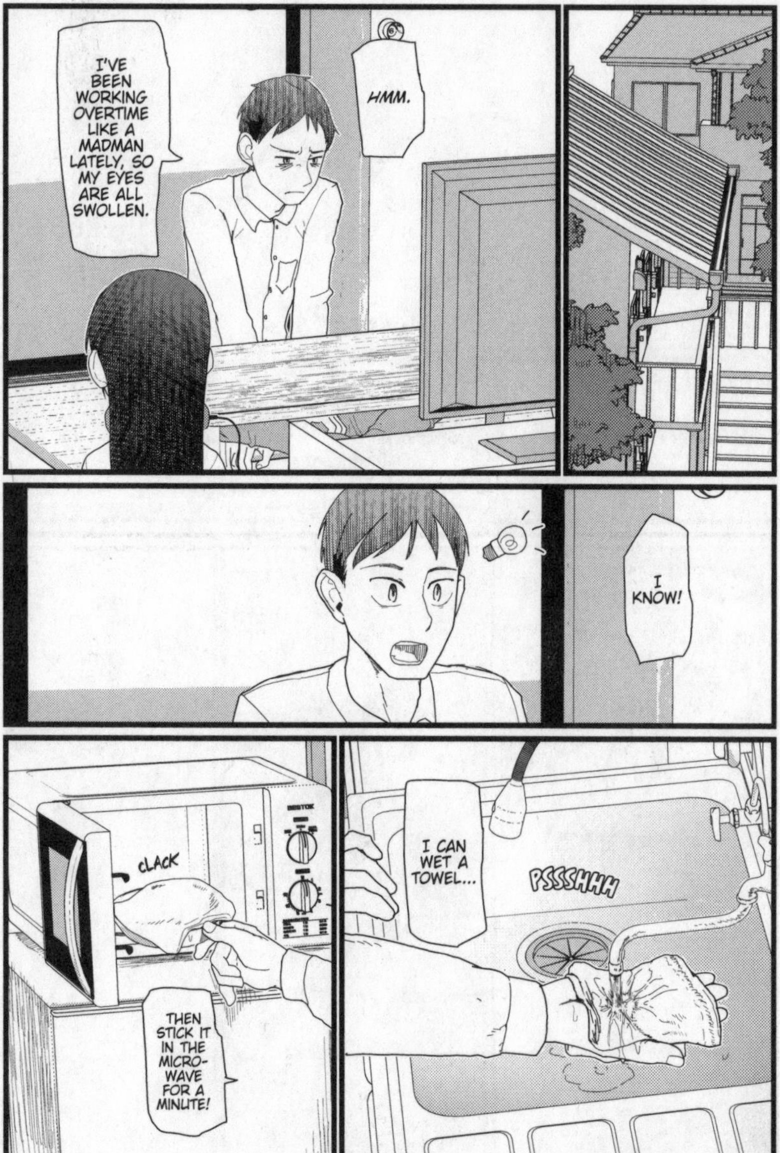
HMM.
I'VE BEEN WORKING OVERTIME LIKE A MADMAN LATELY, SO MY EYES ARE ALL SWOLLEN.
I KNOW!
I CAN WET A TOWEL...
PSSSHHH
CLACK
THEN STICK IT IN THE MICRO-WAVE FOR A MINUTE!

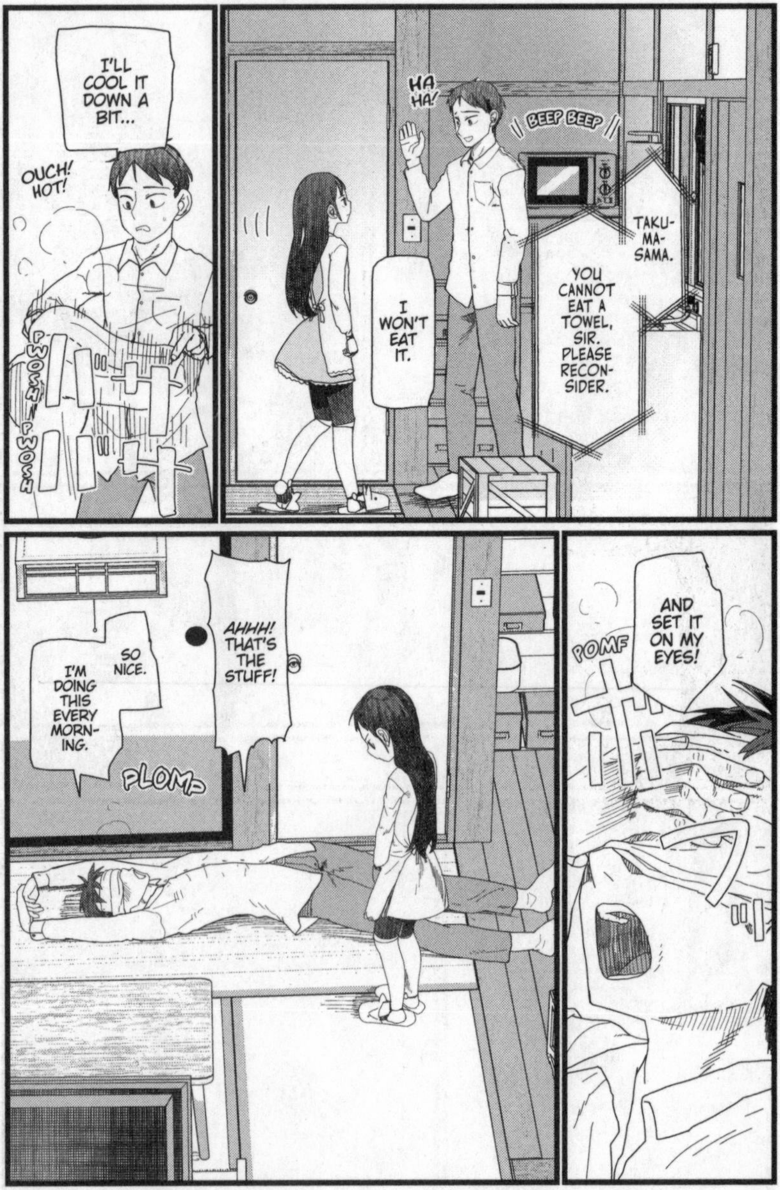
TAKUMA-SAMA.
YOU CANNOT EAT A TOWEL, SIR. PLEASE RECONSIDER.
BEEP BEEP
HA HA!
I WON'T EAT IT.
I'LL COOL IT DOWN A BIT...
OUCH! HOT!
PWOSH PWOSH
AND SET IT ON MY EYES!
POMF
AHHH! THAT'S THE STUFF!
SO NICE.
I'M DOING THIS EVERY MORNING.
PLOMP

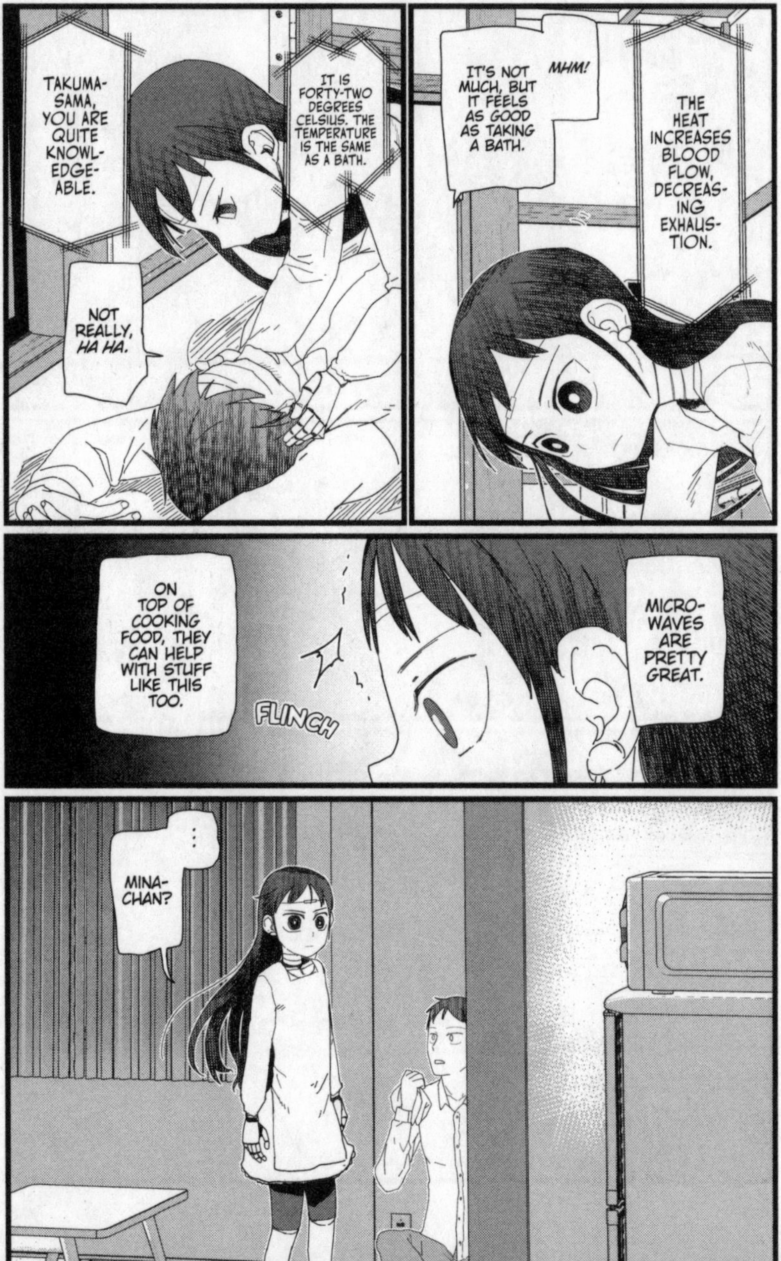
IT'S NOT MUCH, BUT IT FEELS AS GOOD AS TAKING A BATH.
MHM!
THE HEAT INCREASES BLOOD FLOW, DECREASING EXHAUSTION.
IT IS FORTY-TWO DEGREES CELSIUS. THE TEMPERATURE IS THE SAME AS A BATH.
TAKUMA-SAMA, YOU ARE QUITE KNOWLEDGEABLE.
NOT REALLY, *HA HA.*
MICROWAVES ARE PRETTY GREAT.
ON TOP OF COOKING FOOD, THEY CAN HELP WITH STUFF LIKE THIS TOO.
FLINCH
...
MINA-CHAN?

MINA-CHAN'S BEEN KINDA WEIRD TODAY.
I WONDER WHAT'S WRONG?
10:30 P.M.
SHE'S SPENT HOURS JUST STARING AT THE MICRO-WAVE.
WHAT'S UP WITH THAT?
SNORE!
10:38 P.M.
RUSTLE
5:30 A.M.

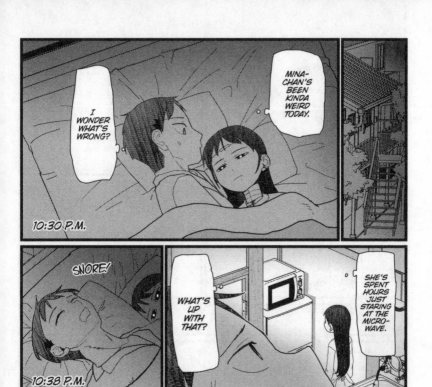

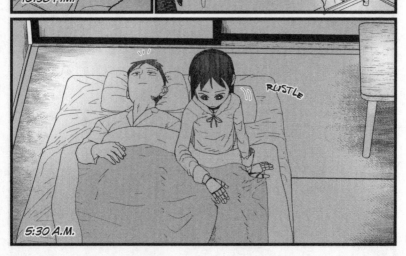

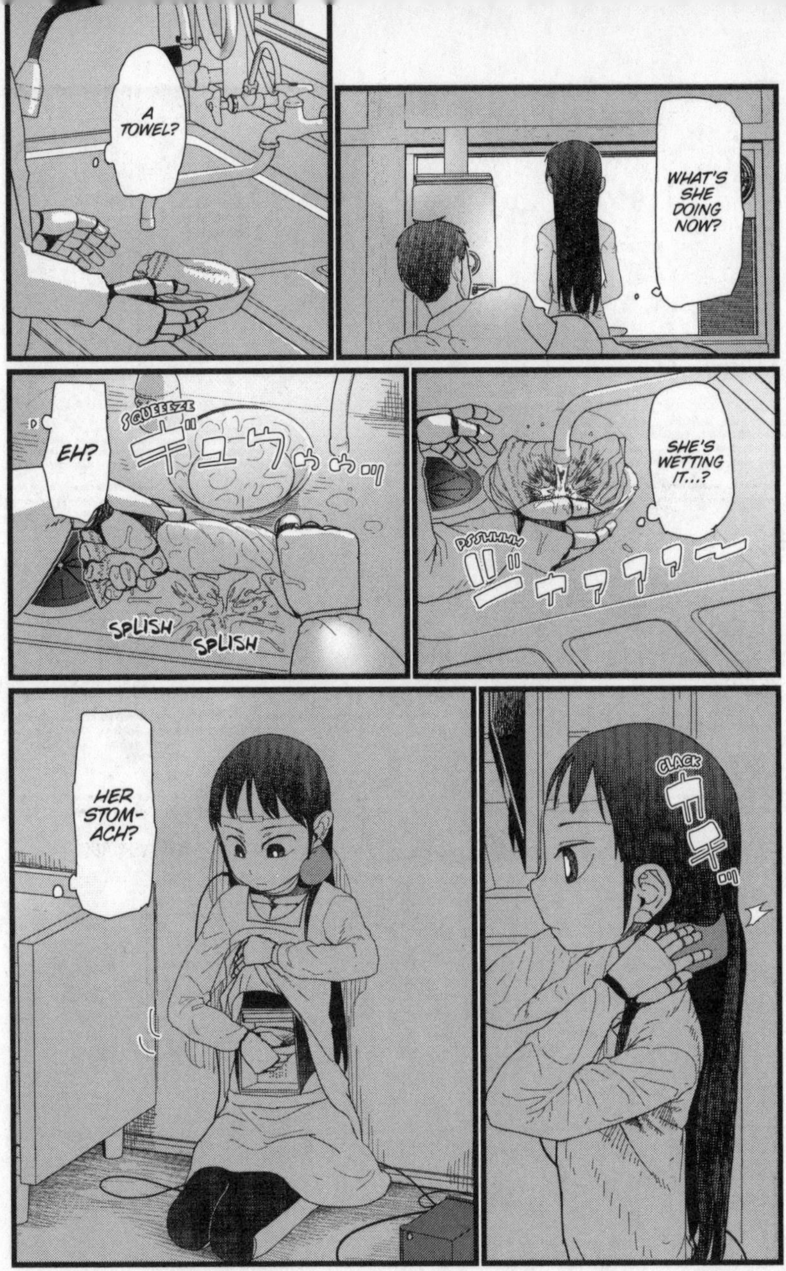
WHAT'S SHE DOING NOW?
A TOWEL?
SHE'S WETTING IT...?
PSSHHHH
SQUEEEZE
EH?
SPLISH
SPLISH
CLACK
HER STOMACH?

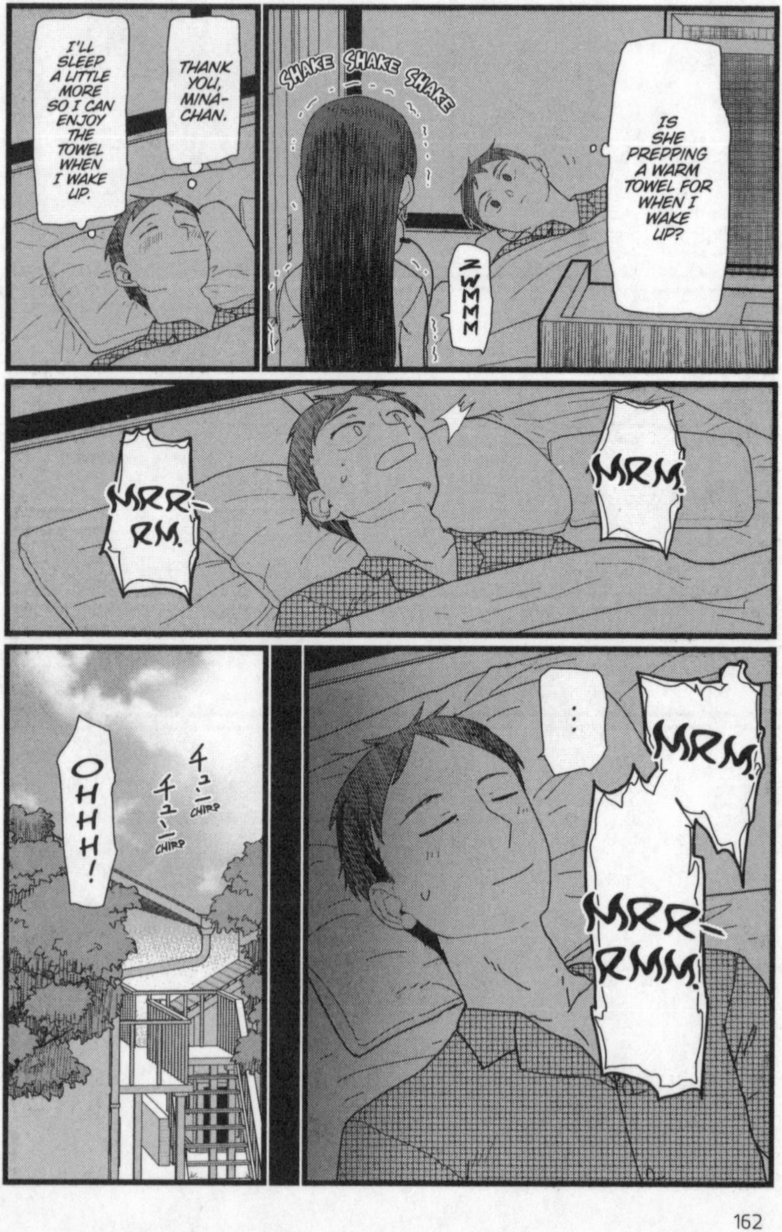
IS SHE PREPPING A WARM TOWEL FOR WHEN I WAKE UP?
SHAKE SHAKE SHAKE
ZWMMM
THANK YOU, MINA-CHAN.
I'LL SLEEP A LITTLE MORE SO I CAN ENJOY THE TOWEL WHEN I WAKE UP.
MRM.
MRR-RM.
...
MRM.
MRR-RMM.
チュー CHIRP
チュー CHIRP
OHHH!

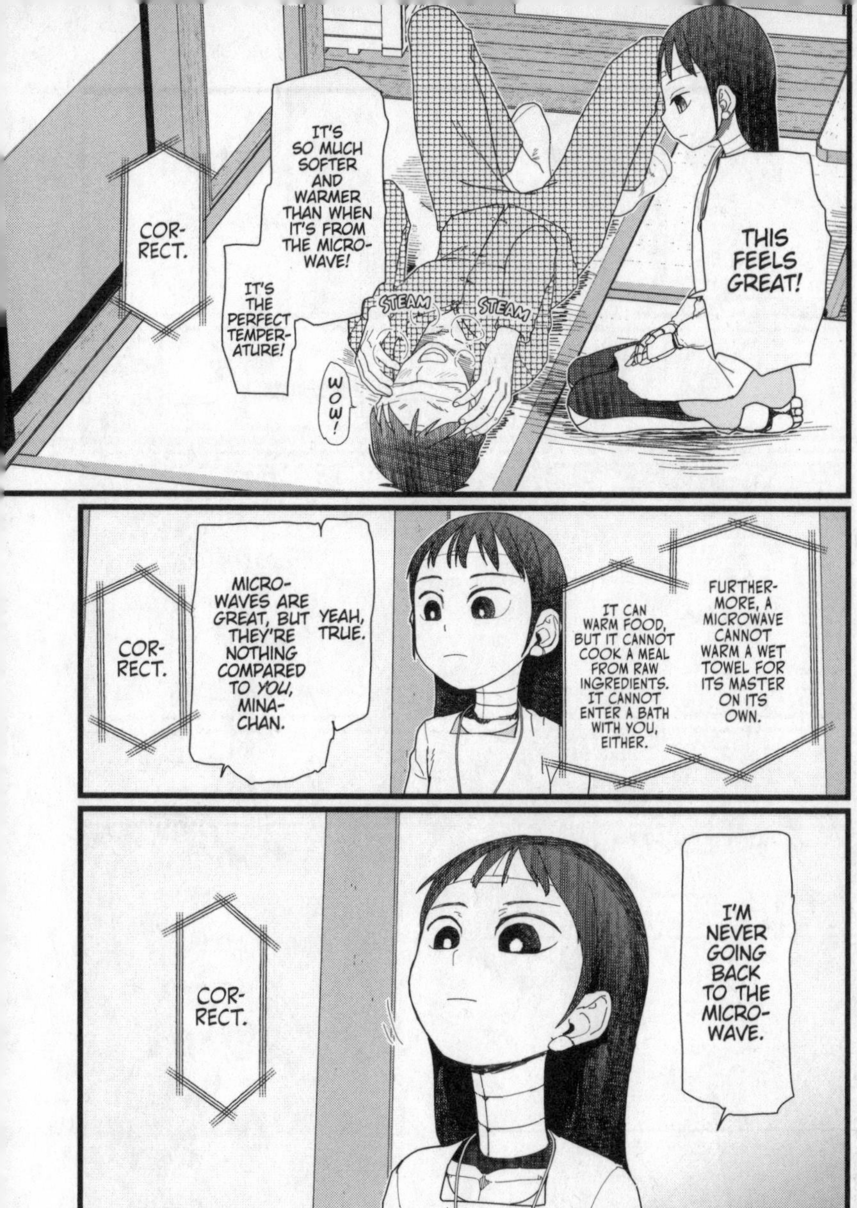
THIS FEELS GREAT!
IT'S SO MUCH SOFTER AND WARMER THAN WHEN IT'S FROM THE MICROWAVE!
STEAM
STEAM
IT'S THE PERFECT TEMPERATURE!
WOW!
COR-RECT.
FURTHERMORE, A MICROWAVE CANNOT WARM A WET TOWEL FOR ITS MASTER ON ITS OWN.
IT CAN WARM FOOD, BUT IT CANNOT COOK A MEAL FROM RAW INGREDIENTS. IT CANNOT ENTER A BATH WITH YOU, EITHER.
YEAH, TRUE.
MICROWAVES ARE GREAT, BUT THEY'RE NOTHING COMPARED TO *YOU*, MINA-CHAN.
COR-RECT.
I'M NEVER GOING BACK TO THE MICROWAVE.
COR-RECT.

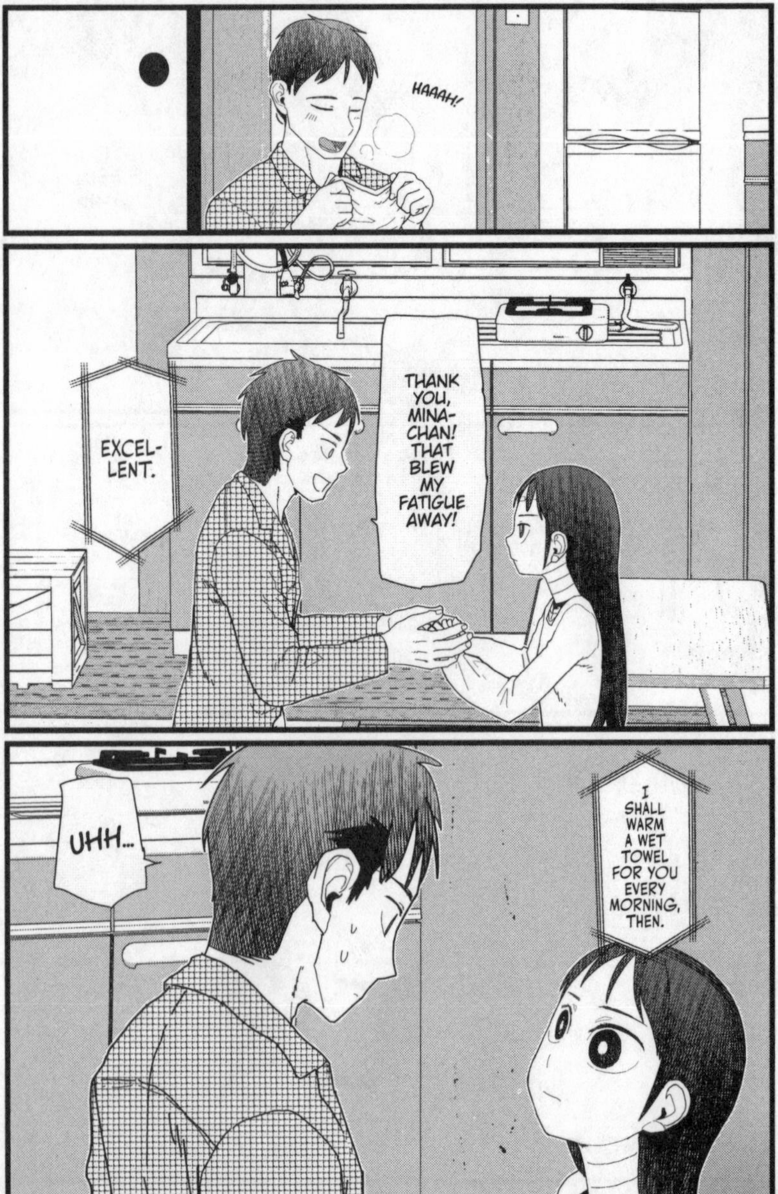
HAAAH!
THANK YOU, MINA-CHAN! THAT BLEW MY FATIGUE AWAY!
EXCEL-LENT.
I SHALL WARM A WET TOWEL FOR YOU EVERY MORNING, THEN.
UHH...
CHAPTER 6 END ♥

My Wife Has No Emotion

My
Wife Has
No
Emotion

➡ CHAPTER 7

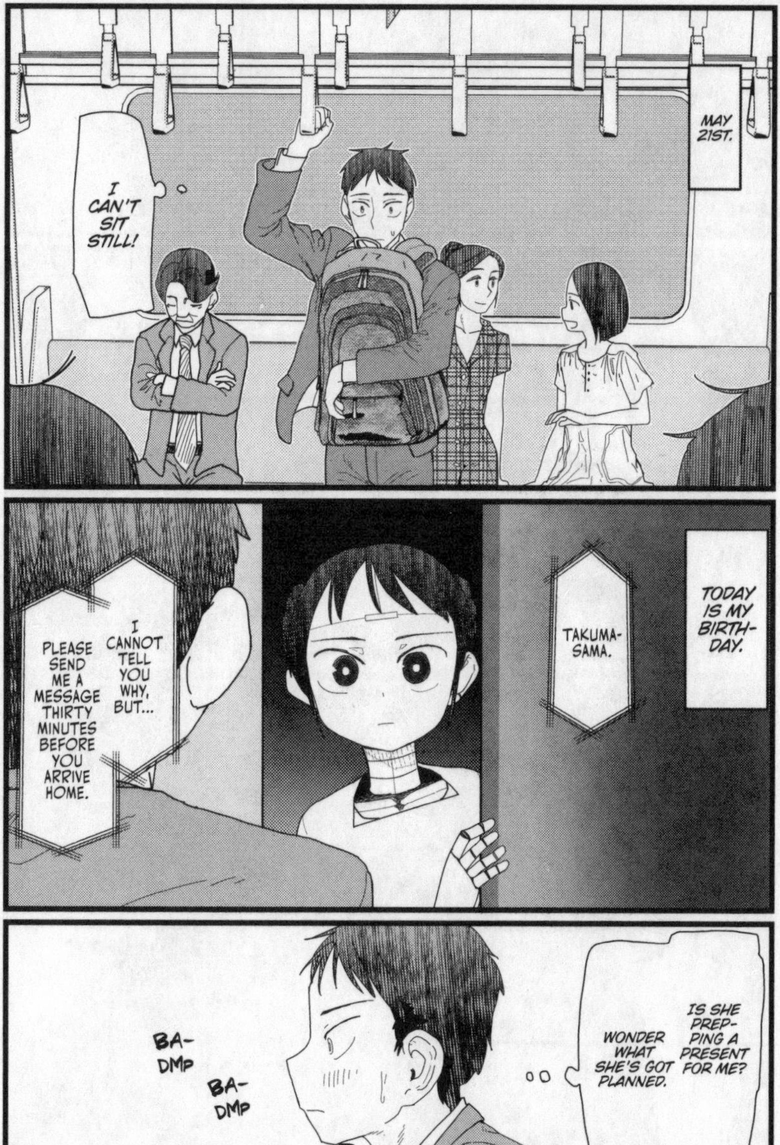
MAY 21ST.
I CAN'T SIT STILL!
TODAY IS MY BIRTH-DAY.
TAKUMA-SAMA.
I CANNOT TELL YOU WHY, BUT...
PLEASE SEND ME A MESSAGE THIRTY MINUTES BEFORE YOU ARRIVE HOME.
IS SHE PREP-PING A PRESENT FOR ME?
WONDER WHAT SHE'S GOT PLANNED.
BA-DMP
BA-DMP

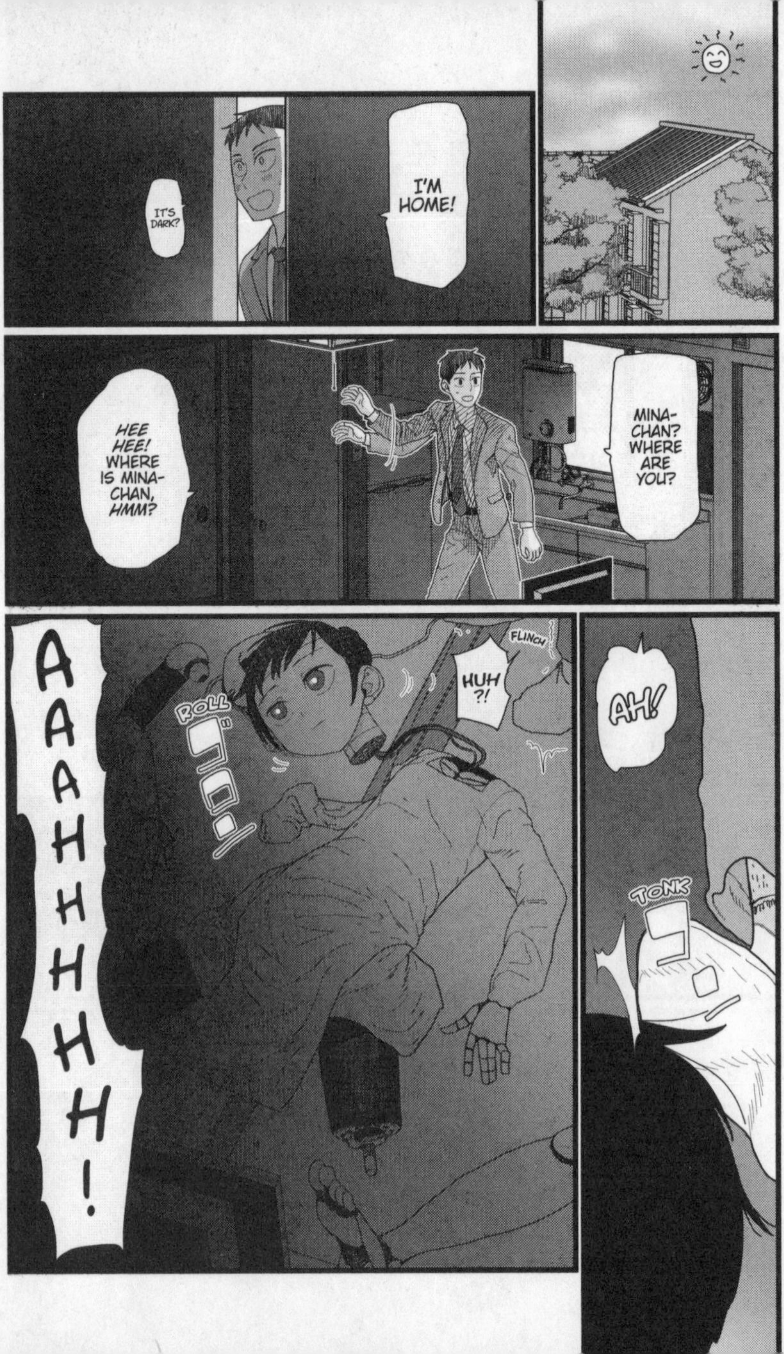
I'M HOME!
IT'S DARK?
MINA-CHAN? WHERE ARE YOU?
HEE HEE! WHERE IS MINA-CHAN, HMM?
AH!
TONK
FLINCH
HUH?!
ROLL
AAAHHHHH!

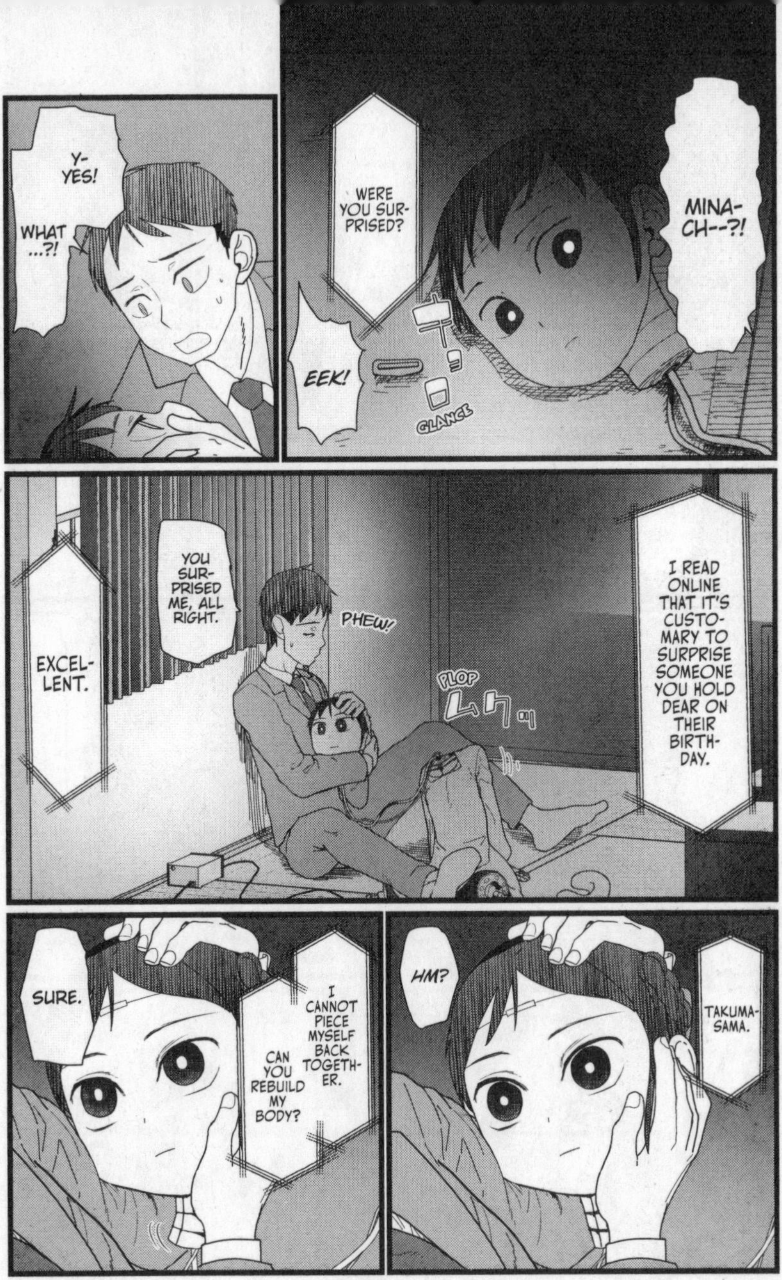
MINA-CH--?!
WERE YOU SURPRISED?
GLANCE
EEK!
Y-YES!
WHAT ...?!
I READ ONLINE THAT IT'S CUSTOMARY TO SURPRISE SOMEONE YOU HOLD DEAR ON THEIR BIRTHDAY.
PHEW!
YOU SURPRISED ME, ALL RIGHT.
PLOP
EXCELLENT.
TAKUMA-SAMA.
HM?
I CANNOT PIECE MYSELF BACK TOGETHER.
CAN YOU REBUILD MY BODY?
SURE.

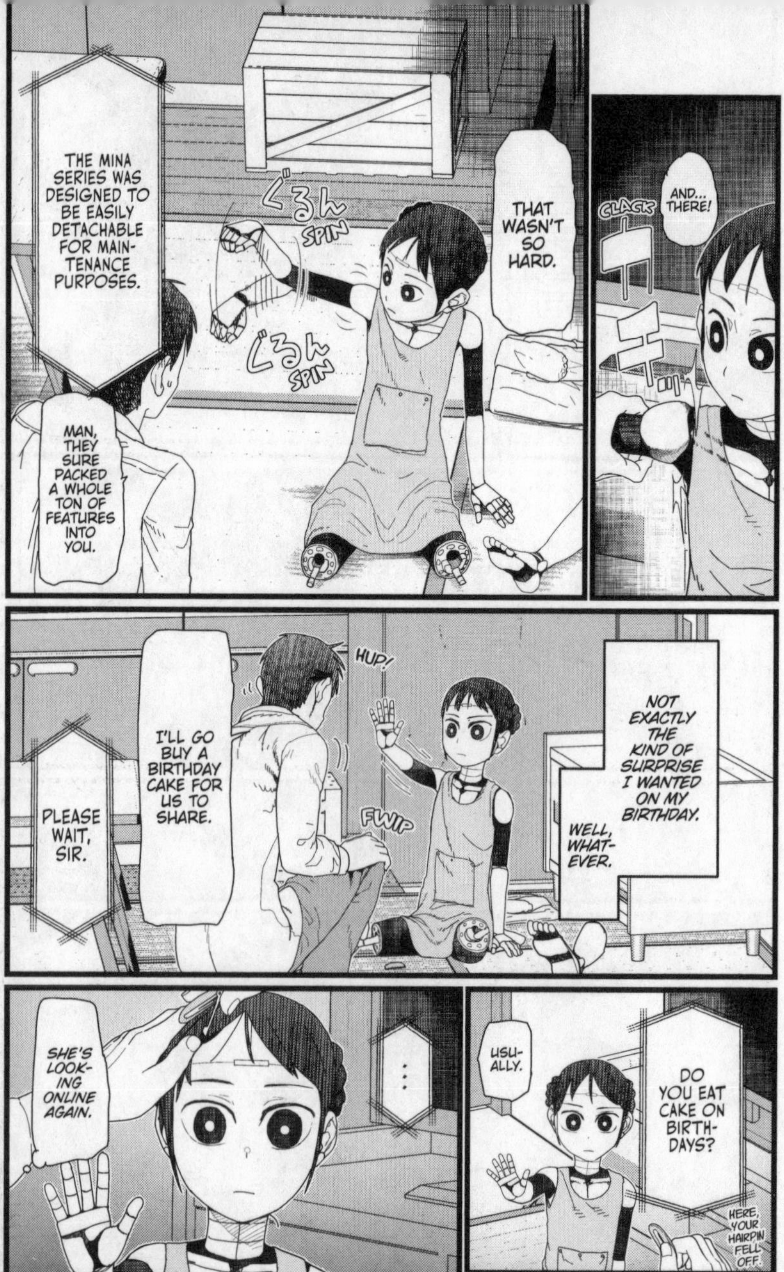

CLACK
AND... THERE!
THAT WASN'T SO HARD.
ぐるん
SPIN
THE MINA SERIES WAS DESIGNED TO BE EASILY DETACHABLE FOR MAIN-TENANCE PURPOSES.
ぐるん
SPIN
MAN, THEY SURE PACKED A WHOLE TON OF FEATURES INTO YOU.
NOT EXACTLY THE KIND OF SURPRISE I WANTED ON MY BIRTHDAY.
WELL, WHAT-EVER.
HUP!
FWIP
I'LL GO BUY A BIRTHDAY CAKE FOR US TO SHARE.
PLEASE WAIT, SIR.
DO YOU EAT CAKE ON BIRTH-DAYS?
USU-ALLY.
HERE, YOUR HAIRPIN FELL OFF.
...
SHE'S LOOK-ING ONLINE AGAIN.

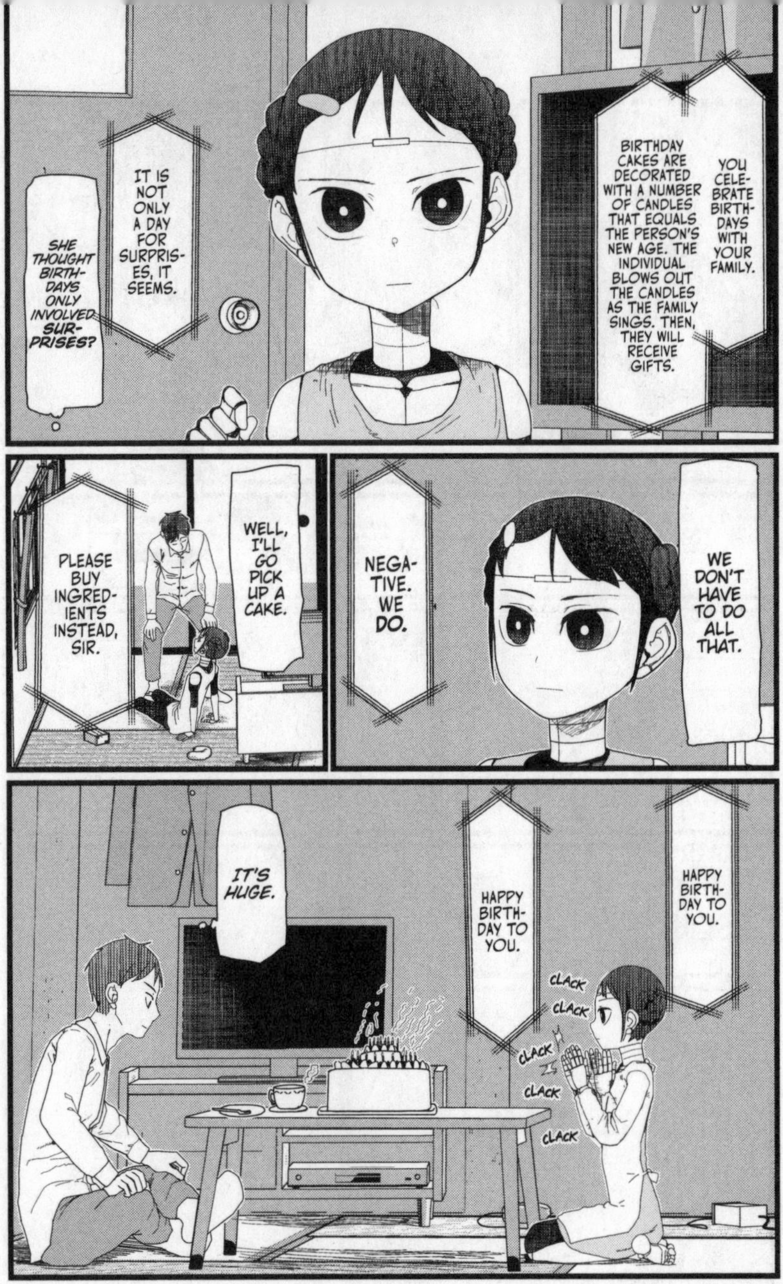
YOU CELEBRATE BIRTHDAYS WITH YOUR FAMILY.
BIRTHDAY CAKES ARE DECORATED WITH A NUMBER OF CANDLES THAT EQUALS THE PERSON'S NEW AGE. THE INDIVIDUAL BLOWS OUT THE CANDLES AS THE FAMILY SINGS. THEN, THEY WILL RECEIVE GIFTS.
IT IS NOT ONLY A DAY FOR SURPRISES, IT SEEMS.
SHE THOUGHT BIRTHDAYS ONLY INVOLVED ***SURPRISES?***
WE DON'T HAVE TO DO ALL THAT.
NEGATIVE. WE **DO.**
WELL, I'LL GO PICK UP A CAKE.
PLEASE BUY INGREDIENTS INSTEAD, SIR.
HAPPY BIRTHDAY TO YOU.
HAPPY BIRTHDAY TO YOU.
CLACK
CLACK
CLACK
CLACK
CLACK
IT'S HUGE.

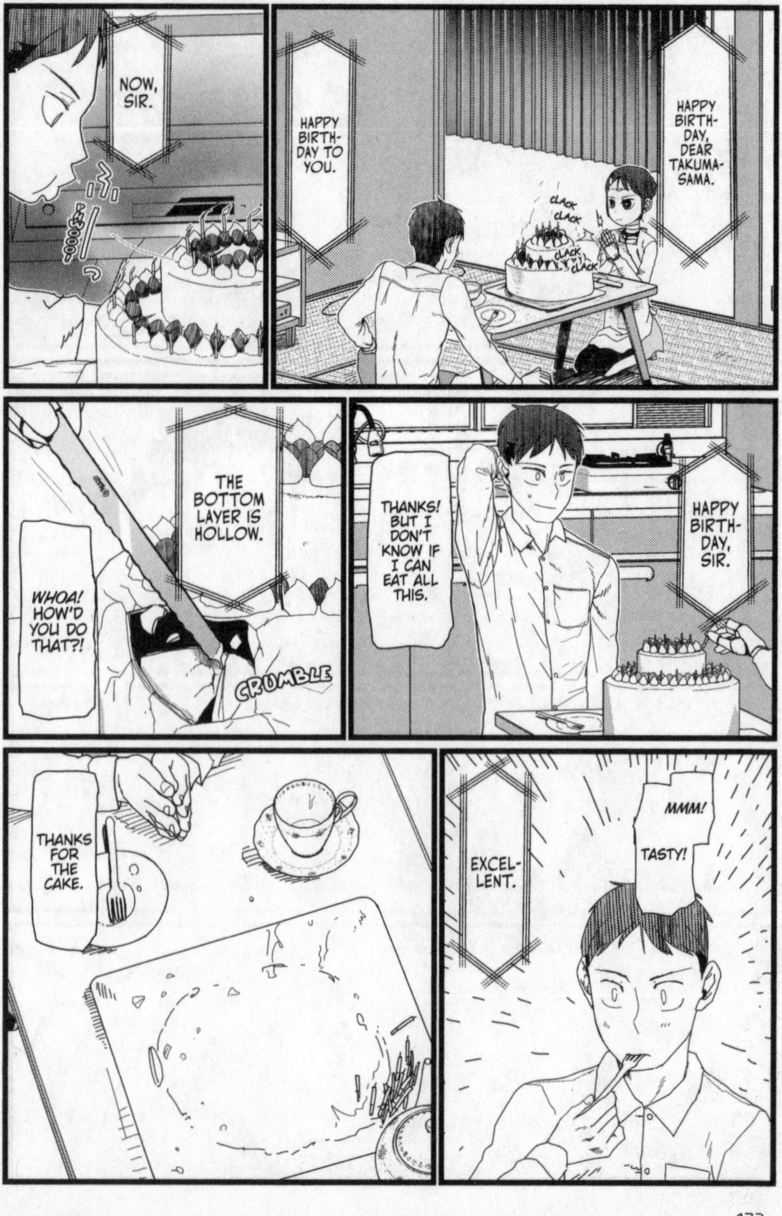
HAPPY BIRTH-DAY, DEAR TAKUMA-SAMA.
HAPPY BIRTH-DAY TO YOU.
CLACK CLACK CLACK CLACK
NOW, SIR.
HAPPY BIRTH-DAY, SIR.
THANKS! BUT I DON'T KNOW IF I CAN EAT ALL THIS.
THE BOTTOM LAYER IS HOLLOW.
WHOA! HOW'D YOU DO THAT?!
CRUMBLE
MMM!
TASTY!
EXCEL-LENT.
THANKS FOR THE CAKE.

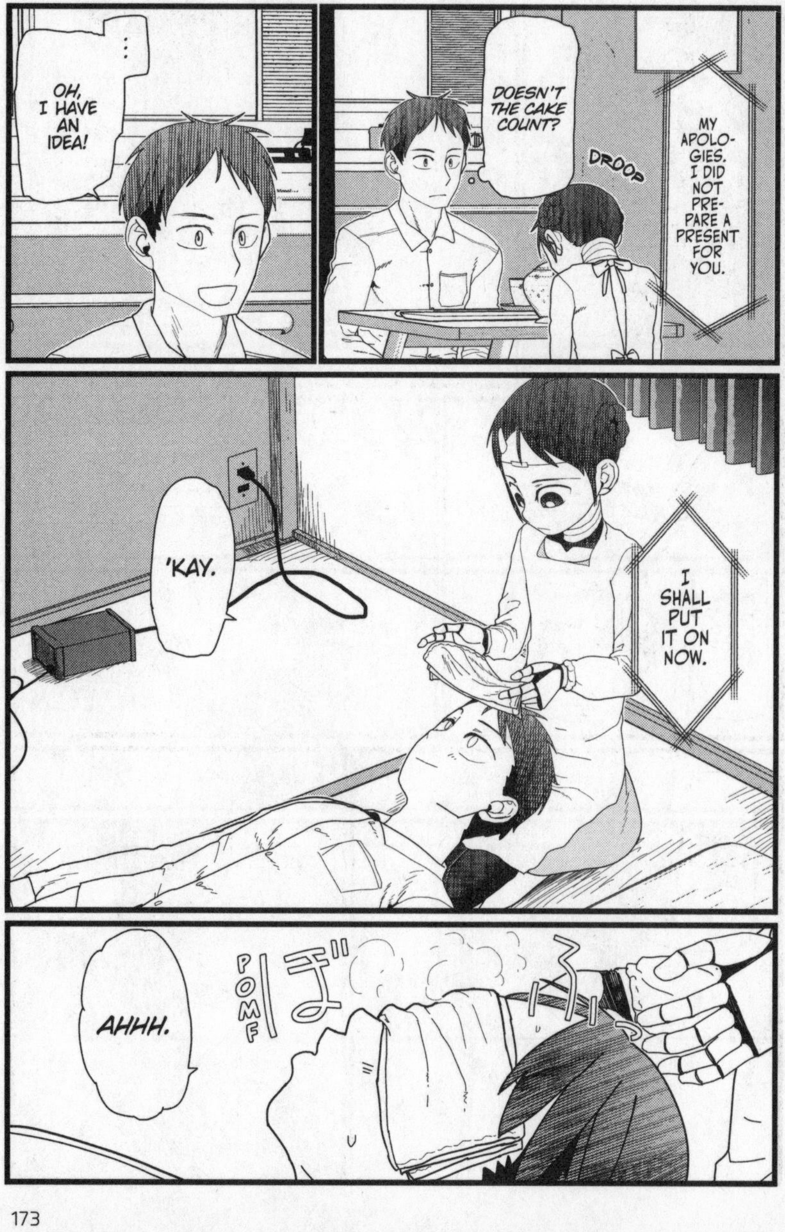
MY APOLOGIES. I DID NOT PREPARE A PRESENT FOR YOU.
DROOP
DOESN'T THE CAKE COUNT?
...
OH, I HAVE AN IDEA!
I SHALL PUT IT ON NOW.
'KAY.
POMF
AHHH.

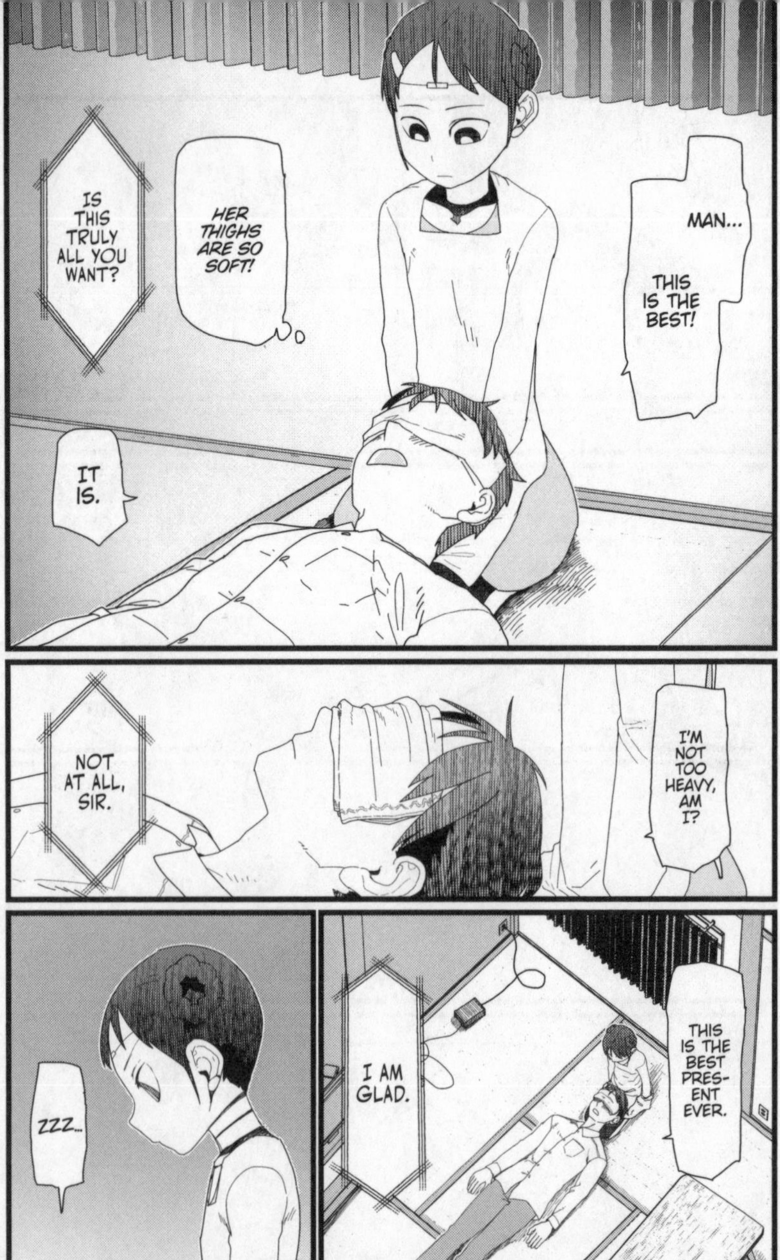
MAN...
THIS IS THE BEST!
HER THIGHS ARE SO SOFT!
IS THIS TRULY ALL YOU WANT?
IT IS.
I'M NOT TOO HEAVY, AM I?
NOT AT ALL, SIR.
THIS IS THE BEST PRESENT EVER.
I AM GLAD.
ZZZ...

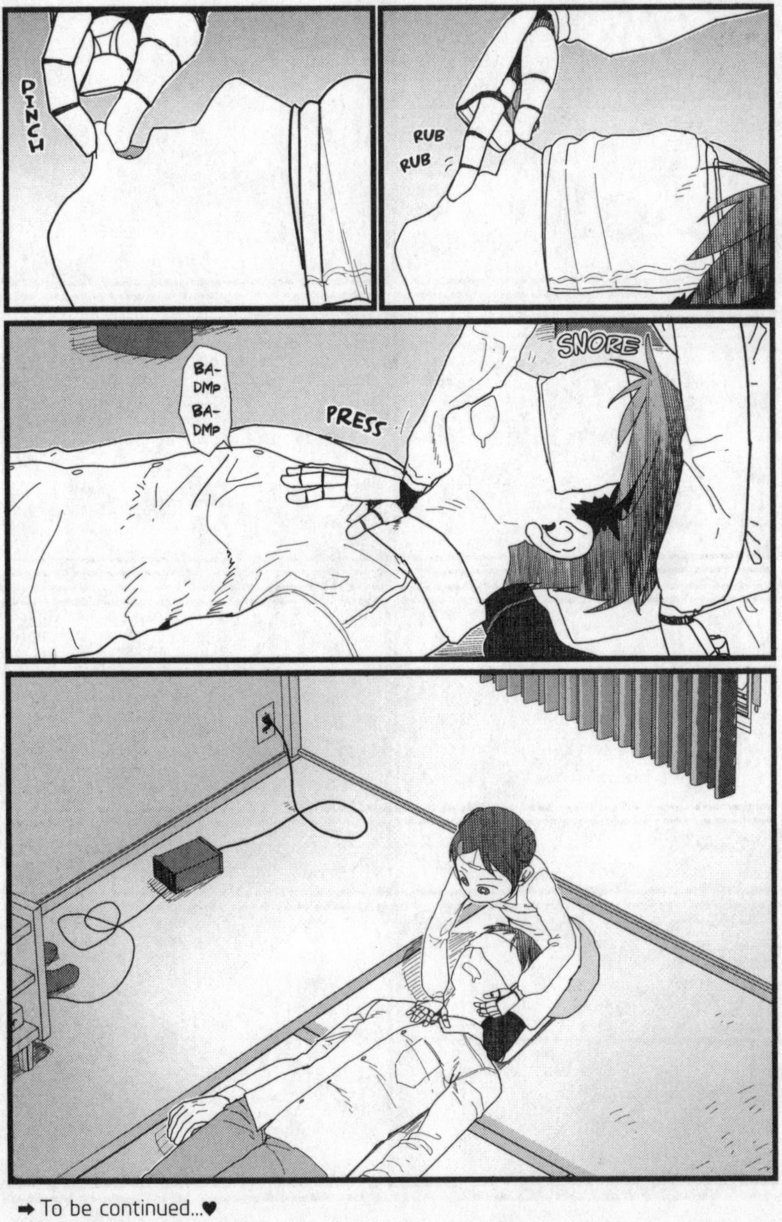
RUB
RUB
PINCH
SNORE
PRESS
BA-DMP BA-DMP

➡ To be continued...♥

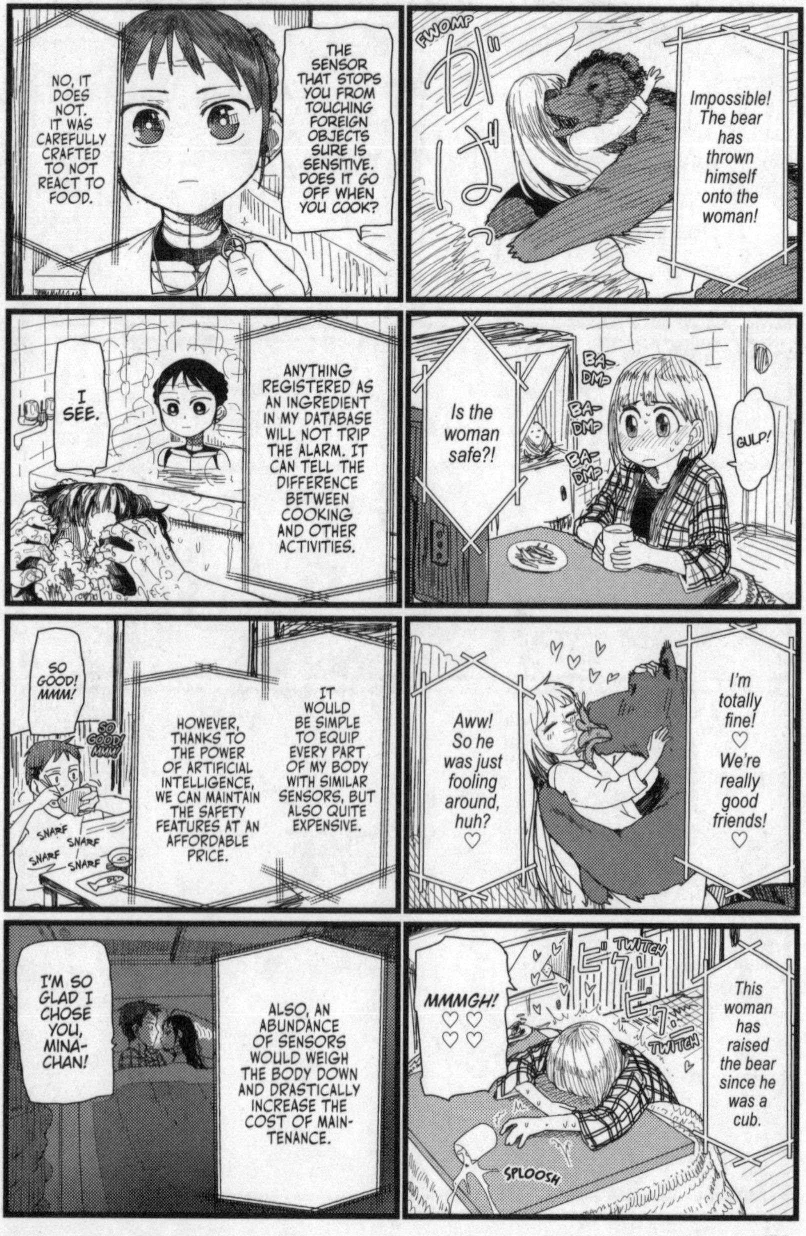
Impossible! The bear has thrown himself onto the woman!
FWOMP
GULP!
BA-DMP
BA-DMP
BA-DMP
Is the woman safe?!
I'm totally fine! ♡ We're really good friends! ♡
Aww! So he was just fooling around, huh? ♡
This woman has raised the bear since he was a cub.
TWITCH
TWITCH
MMMGH! ♡ ♡ ♡ ♡
SPLOOSH
THE SENSOR THAT STOPS YOU FROM TOUCHING FOREIGN OBJECTS SURE IS SENSITIVE. DOES IT GO OFF WHEN YOU COOK?
NO, IT DOES NOT. IT WAS CAREFULLY CRAFTED TO NOT REACT TO FOOD.
ANYTHING REGISTERED AS AN INGREDIENT IN MY DATABASE WILL NOT TRIP THE ALARM. IT CAN TELL THE DIFFERENCE BETWEEN COOKING AND OTHER ACTIVITIES.
I SEE.
IT WOULD BE SIMPLE TO EQUIP EVERY PART OF MY BODY WITH SIMILAR SENSORS, BUT ALSO QUITE EXPENSIVE.
HOWEVER, THANKS TO THE POWER OF ARTIFICIAL INTELLIGENCE, WE CAN MAINTAIN THE SAFETY FEATURES AT AN AFFORDABLE PRICE.
SO GOOD! MMM!
SO GOOD! MMM!
SNARF
SNARF
SNARF
SNARF
ALSO, AN ABUNDANCE OF SENSORS WOULD WEIGH THE BODY DOWN AND DRASTICALLY INCREASE THE COST OF MAINTENANCE.
I'M SO GLAD I CHOSE YOU, MINA-CHAN!

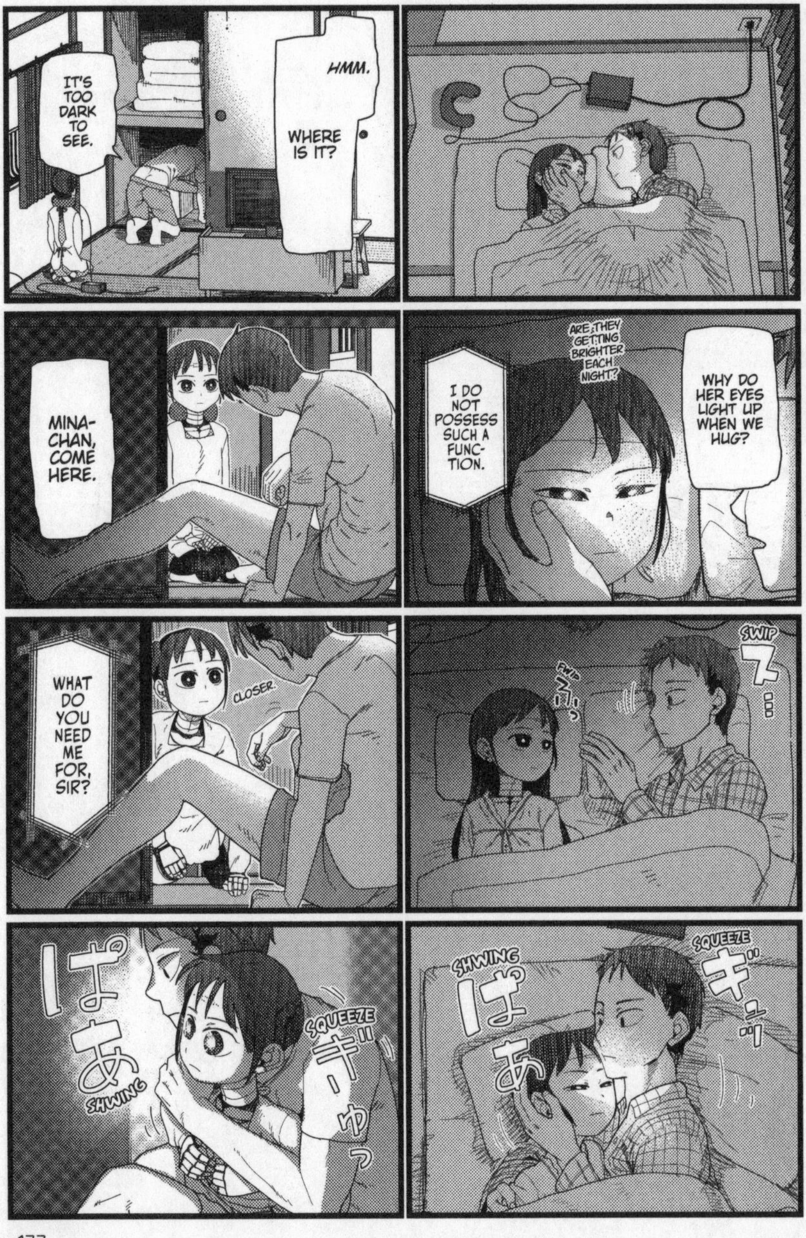
HMM.
WHERE IS IT?
IT'S TOO DARK TO SEE.
WHY DO HER EYES LIGHT UP WHEN WE HUG?
ARE THEY GETTING BRIGHTER EACH NIGHT?
I DO NOT POSSESS SUCH A FUNCTION.
MINA-CHAN, COME HERE.
SWIP
ス...
FWIP
ふっ
CLOSER.
WHAT DO YOU NEED ME FOR, SIR?
SQUEEZE
ギュッ
SHWING
ぱあ
SQUEEZE
ぎゅっ
ぱあ
SHWING

My Wife Has No Emotion

SEVEN SEAS ENTERTAINMENT PRESENTS

MY WIFE HAS NO EMOTION
Vol. 1

story and art by **JIRO SUGIURA**

TRANSLATION
Jacqueline Fung

ADAPTATION
Maneesh Maganti

LETTERING
Jennifer Skarupa

COVER DESIGN
Hanase Qi

LOGO DESIGN
George Panella

PROOFREADER
Danielle King

EDITOR
Shannon Fay

PREPRESS TECHNICIAN
Rhiannon Rasmussen-Silverstein

PRODUCTION ASSOCIATE
Christa Miesner

PRODUCTION MANAGER
Lissa Pattillo

MANAGING EDITOR
Julie Davis

ASSOCIATE PUBLISHER
Adam Arnold

PUBLISHER
Jason DeAngelis

BOKU NO TSUMA WA KANJO GA NAI Vol.1
©Jiro Sugiura 2020
First published in Japan in 2020 by KADOKAWA CORPORATION, Tokyo.
English translation rights arranged with KADOKAWA CORPORATION, Tokyo.

Seven Seas press and purchase enquiries can be sent to Marketing Manager Lianne Sentar at press@gomanga.com. Information regarding the distribution and purchase of digital editions is available from Digital Manager CK Russell at digital@gomanga.com.

Seven Seas and the Seven Seas logo are trademarks of Seven Seas Entertainment. All rights reserved.

ISBN: 978-1-64827-560-9
Printed in Canada
First Printing: September 2021
10 9 8 7 6 5 4 3 2 1

//// READING DIRECTIONS ////

This book reads from *right to left*, Japanese style. If this is your first time reading manga, you start reading from the top right panel on each page and take it from there. If you get lost, just follow the numbered diagram here. It may seem backwards at first, but you'll get the hang of it! Have fun!!

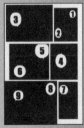

Follow us online: www.SevenSeasEntertainment.com